The IPO Decision

To my parents

The IPO Decision

Why and How Companies Go Public

Jason Draho

Edward Elgar
Cheltenham, UK • Northampton, MA, USA

Published by
Edward Elgar Publishing Limited
Glensanda House
Montpellier Parade
Cheltenham
Glos GL50 1UA
UK

Edward Elgar Publishing, Inc.
William Pratt House
9 Dewey Court
Northampton
Massachusetts 01060
USA

Paperback edition 2005

A catalogue record for this book
is available from the British Library

Library of Congress Cataloguing in Publication Data
Draho, Jason, 1971–
   The IPO decision : why and how companies go public / Jason Draho.
     p. cm.
   Includes bibliographical references and index.
   1. Going public (Securities) I. Title: Initial public offering decision. II. Title.

   HG4028.S7D7 2004
   658.15'224–dc22   2004041562

ISBN: 1 84376 613 2 (cased)
       978 1 84542 638 5 (paperback)

Printed by Biddles Ltd, King's Lynn, Norfolk

Contents

List of figures and tables   *vi*
Preface   *vii*

1. Introduction   1
2. IPO timing and information   10
3. Financing options and costs   36
4. Strategic behavior   64
5. Control, monitoring and governance   80
6. The external market: an international comparison   110
7. Corporate restructuring   136
8. Valuation   158
9. Preparing for the IPO   182
10. IPO mechanisms: allocations and pricing   215
11. The IPO aftermarket   251
12. Post-IPO financing   283
13. Long-run performance   306
14. Final thoughts   338

References   344
Index   376

List of figures and tables

FIGURES

2.1	US monthly IPO volume	11
2.2	Biotechnology industry valuation and monthly IPO volume	15
2.3	US monthly IPO volume and average initial returns	25
9.1	Timeline of events for the firm commitment IPO process	183
10.1	The distribution of allocation fill rates for Isreali IPOs	237
11.1	Distribution of IPO returns over the first month	262
13.1	Five-year annual return for IPOs and non-issuers	308
13.2	Contemporaneous correlation of IPO returns	317

TABLES

1.1	International IPO volume and initial returns	4
3.1	Advisory and listing fees	38
3.2	US private equity funding by type of investor	46
3.3	Venture capital disbursements by stage of investment	48
5.1	Contractual provisions pertaining to VC control rights	93
5.2	Anti-takeover charter provisions	105
6.1	Investor rights	119
6.2	Largest privatization IPOs	125
6.3	Largest privatized SOEs	131
9.1	Minimum listing standards for the NYSE and NASDAQ	185
9.2	Underwriter rankings based on 2002 US IPOs	188
9.3	IPO costs as a percentage of the gross proceeds	191
10.1	IPO mechanism use across countries	220
13.1	Corporate finance post-event abnormal returns	333

Preface

Initial public offerings (IPOs) garnered unprecedented public notoriety during the bubble years of the late 1990s for their spectacular returns and key role in the creation of new companies. Revelations during the bubble's aftermath of corrupt practices by investment banks have left IPOs with a more infamous reputation. As both a financing event and an action by a company, IPOs remain rather mysterious to most observers. Relying on incomplete information and a lack of understanding of the entire process, the general public is left to draw inaccurate and false conclusions about why companies go public and how IPOs work.

IPOs have been the subject of intense academic inquiry since the mid-1970s and that has only increased since the bubble. Individual studies have clarified our understanding of specific aspects of IPOs and the going-public decision. *The IPO Decision* collects and synthesizes in one comprehensive whole the entire body of research pertaining in some way to the IPO process. The systematic organization of all the relevant theories and empirical evidence into a logical framework leaves the reader with a much deeper understanding of why and how companies go public than if the individual pieces were examined separately.

The IPO process is reviewed in chronological order, beginning with the questions of when and why a private firm goes public and ending with the long-run performance of newly public companies. Most survey articles on IPOs emphasize the major puzzles related to IPOs: hot markets, underpricing and long-run underperformance. The only similar book-length treatment of IPOs is Jenkinson and Ljungqvist (2001), who provide a very thorough review of the three puzzles. However, their book does not cover many of the topics included in this one, such as the financial and strategic benefits to being public, the external market, corporate restructuring, valuation and post-IPO financing. In addition, this book examines the specific IPO puzzles within the larger context of the going-public process and therefore provides a broader perspective on these issues.

The IPO Decision is scholarly in nature, focused on distilling down the ideas and results from a vast number of theoretical and empirical studies into a single manageable source. The material is presented in a non-technical yet rigorous manner, emphasizing the intuition for a particular idea or fact. It assumes a basic understanding of economics and finance, and some knowledge of how actual financial markets work. The book describes, where applicable, institutional structure, such as the operation of stock markets and the filing requirements for an IPO. These details, along with most of the empirical evidence presented, does have a strong US-bias, although the book is international in scope.

Readers from a wide range of backgrounds and positions will find the book to be a useful reference for IPOs. Researchers in finance, economics, accounting and law have access to a detailed review of the academic literature on all topics related to the IPO process. Practitioners in investment banking, venture capital, accounting, consulting, law and market regulation along with entrepreneurs and business people gain the insight of this research in a straight forward manner that is otherwise unavailable from a single source.

This book would not be possible without the considerable help and support from a number of people. I thank all those who provided invaluable comments and suggestions on the early drafts: Roger Ibbotson, Stefano Athanasoulis, Ricky Lam, Ross Barrett, John Bernstein, Eugene Choo, Michael Vaney, Pilar Murray and two anonymous referees. I thank those who graciously provided some of the figures and tables that appear in the book: Yakov Amihud, Alon Brav, Robert Keischnick, Josh Lerner, Jay Ritter and Ann Sherman. The book is an outgrowth of my dissertation, which benefited enormously from the advice and guidance of my advisors: Dirk Bergemann, Ben Polak and Arturo Bris. The staff at Edward Elgar was unyielding in their belief in this project. Karen McCarthy, Alan Sturmer and Tara Gorvine guided me through the process and were always happy to answer my many questions. I reserve my biggest thank you for my family – my parents, Lisa, Josh and Ruby – who provided unwavering support and encouragement throughout the process of writing the book. Many sacrifices had to be made to see it through completion and they helped make that a little easier.

1 Introduction

Few events in the life of a company are as great in magnitude and consequence as an initial public offering (IPO). An IPO is the first time that shares in a company are sold to public investors and subsequently traded on the stock market. A public listing fundamentally alters the firm's legal and economic structure. Management is now responsible to a new group of dispersed shareholders, unlike the concentrated ownership of a private company. Information regarding the firm's financial health and operations that had been kept private must now be publicly divulged. The competitive environment may ratchet up as rivals treat the firm as a more serious threat. Given these and other factors, the key decision-makers of a private company must answer two questions in order to enhance the firm's long-term viability and to make a smooth transition to public ownership. Why should the firm be taken public? And if it is, how should the IPO be completed?

Industry professionals offer many reasons why private firms want to go public. The IPO can be used to raise capital for expansion of operations, increase liquidity for the shareholders, improve the company's reputation and to create a valuable currency – the stock – that can be used to make acquisitions and compensate employees. An investor who got burned on an Internet IPO may volunteer a much more cynical response; companies go public so that the insiders can cash in their valuable stock options when the shares are overvalued. Uninformed conjectures such as these can become accepted fact if repeated often enough.

How IPOs are conducted is an even more contentious issue. The tension arises from the conflicting interests of the three main participants to the IPO process: the issuing firm, the investment bank underwriting the offering and investors. The bubble period of the late 1990s exhibited extreme IPO pricing patterns, often to the detriment of the issuing firm and many investors. Revelations during the bubble post-mortem of unscrupulous, and in some cases illegal, share allocation and recommendation practices by investment banks have been used to explain the pricing excesses and led to calls for reform. As with the motives for going public, an incomplete understanding of how IPOs really work leads to flawed inferences about the problems with the current system and what should be changed.

The principal objective of this book is to provide a detailed factual account of why and when firms benefit from going public and the specific steps of the IPO process. This approach satisfies two goals. First, it separates fact from fiction by disabusing any false notions the public may have about the going-public process. Second, the analytically thorough review of the entire process fosters a much deeper understanding of the relevant issues. For example, it is insufficient to simply state that companies go public to raise cheap capital without trying to quantify where and why the cost savings arise.

Public awareness of IPOs reached unprecedented heights during the Internet bubble that climaxed in 1999 and 2000. Even the most casual observer is familiar with the staggering payoffs these offerings rewarded investors lucky enough to receive an IPO allocation. What these same observers might be surprised to learn is that the experience was not all that unique. Certainly there are no prior periods in which IPO share prices routinely doubled or tripled at the start of aftermarket trading. But the general pattern of a cluster of IPOs by similar firms characterized by large first-day price 'pops' is a frequent phenomenon – notable other examples being the natural resource sector in 1980 and computer software in 1983. The remainder of the book therefore focuses on developing a general framework for analyzing all past, present and future IPO activity, instead of only trying to explain the Internet bubble.

1.1 WHY GO PUBLIC?

Why do private companies decide to go public? A few beneficial reasons for an IPO are already mentioned above. Of course, all benefits must be weighed against the costs associated with a public listing. The issuing firm – henceforth referred to as the issuer – is burdened with the direct costs of an IPO and the distraction it imposes on management, both of which continue to some extent after the offering. The issuer must disclose proprietary information that may weaken it competitively. Conflicts could arise between the entrenched owner/manager and the new shareholders. In the spirit of conducting a cost-benefit analysis, the owners of a private company should ask themselves 'Why should we go public?'

Evaluating the merits of an IPO must go beyond simply listing all the costs and benefits to actually probing for the source of each. The example of going public to raise cheap capital provides a useful illustration of this point. A public equity offering involves higher fixed direct costs – filing and registration fees, and investment bank, auditor and lawyer compensation – compared to private equity. The expected return demanded by investors is a function of the risk, liquidity and marketability of the shares. While it is lower for public relative to private equity, the reduction is minimal if the stock is thinly traded. Thus, plausible circumstances do exist, especially for smaller firms, in which public equity is the more expensive option, contradicting the blanket statement that an IPO provides cheap capital. This level of detailed analysis is warranted for all factors pertinent to the IPO decision.

The preceding discussion offers a pedantic motivation for studying why firms go public. For the reader who believes that most firms would attempt an IPO if given the chance, this analysis may seem too academic and unnecessary. A quick perusal of the IPO data, however, provides ample evidence to refute this presumption. The sheer volume of IPOs in the US over the past few decades – approximately 15,000 since 1960 – does appear to leave little room for debate about the relative merits of private versus public ownership. There are exceptions to the hegemony of public corporations; Cargill, Bechtel and the formerly private UPS are all dominant companies in their respective industries and the anomalies become more frequent among small and mid-sized companies. The more compelling evidence is the diversity in the number of IPOs and types of issuers across countries.

The data in Table 1.1 presents the findings from dozens of studies, which Loughran, Ritter and Rydqvist (1994) originally summarized and have since updated. The table lists 38 countries and the number of IPOs occurring in each over the specified time period. Direct comparisons across countries must account for the non-overlapping sample periods and the different size of the economies. Nonetheless, some back-of-the-envelope calculations reveal just how unique the US experience has been. Almost 10,000 IPOs occurred from 1980 to 1999, with 5,100 in the 1990s alone.[1] The only country that had a comparable size-adjusted number is the UK.

The most striking counter-points to the US experience are the three largest continental European economies: Germany, France and Italy. To illustrate, consider that over the 1987–99 period Germany had 407 IPOs, whereas there were 10,115 in the US. Even a quarter of the US total, which roughly adjusts for the size difference, is still six times the German total. All three European countries are major advanced economies, yet there is something fundamentally distinct about them that clearly impacts the going-public decision. While one could reasonably claim that most American companies would choose to go public if given the option, this appears to be the exception to the norm in continental Europe.

Table 1.1 International IPO volume and initial returns[2]

Country	No. of IPOs	Time Period	Initial Return (%)
Australia	382	1976 – 95	12.1
Austria	76	1984 – 99	6.5
Belgium	86	1984 – 99	14.6
Brazil	62	1979 – 90	78.5
Canada	500	1971 – 99	6.3
Chile	52	1982 – 97	8.8
China	432	1990 – 2000	256.9
Denmark	117	1984 – 99	5.4
Finland	99	1984 – 97	10.1
France	448	1983 – 98	9.5
Germany	407	1987 – 99	27.7
Greece	129	1987 – 94	51.7
Hong Kong	334	1980 – 96	15.9
India	98	1992 – 93	35.3
Indonesia	106	1989 – 94	15.1
Israel	285	1990 – 94	12.1
Italy	164	1985 – 2000	23.9
Japan	1,542	1970 – 2000	26.4
Korea	477	1980 – 96	74.3
Malaysia	401	1980 – 98	104.1
Mexico	37	1987 – 90	33.0
Netherlands	143	1982 – 99	10.2
New Zealand	201	1979 – 99	23.0
Nigeria	63	1989 – 93	19.1
Norway	68	1984 – 96	12.5
Philippines	104	1987 – 97	22.7
Poland	149	1991 – 98	35.6
Portugal	21	1992 – 98	10.6
Singapore	128	1973 – 92	31.4
South Africa	118	1980 – 91	32.7
Spain	99	1986 – 98	10.7
Sweden	251	1980 – 94	34.1
Switzerland	42	1983 – 89	35.8
Taiwan	293	1986 – 98	31.1
Thailand	292	1987 – 97	46.7
Turkey	138	1990 – 96	13.6
United Kingdom	3,042	1959 – 2000	17.5
United States	14,760	1960 – 2000	18.4

Source: Loughran, Ritter and Rydqvist (1994) and updates on Jay Ritter's web site: http://bear.cba.ufl.edu/ritter/ipodata.htm. The article and the update list the references for the country-specific data.

Differences between the types of US and European issuers further highlights the need to examine the IPO decision. Loughran and Ritter (2002b) reported that the median company age at the IPO for US issuers has stayed remarkably constant at roughly seven years during the 1980s and 1990s. The median masks the considerable variation between very recent start-ups in new industries and mature companies in traditional sectors. Nevertheless, the typical issuer went public during the early growth phase in its life cycle, likely to raise capital. In contrast, the average issuer age in many European countries was around 40 years up to the mid-1990s, although it fell to about 10 years during the Internet boom (Rydqvist and Hogholm 1995; Giudici and Roosenboom 2003). These mature issuers were usually not raising capital for investment purposes and instead went public for other reasons.

The cross-country differences in the volume and age of issuers suggest that external factors affect the IPO decision. Since public companies need a stock market to list on, countries with poorly developed markets are likely to experience fewer IPOs. Public ownership creates a new class of dispersed shareholders who may be in a minority position relative to the old shareholders. The legal and political environment determines how well minority shareholders are protected, consequently influencing their initial decision to invest in the IPO. The attractiveness of being a public company hinges on these factors beyond a firm's control. Therefore, a complete understanding of why companies go public requires a review of the general economic environment within a country.

1.2 HOW TO GO PUBLIC

The essence of an IPO is nothing more than a sale of shares by the issuing firm to investors. This simple characterization, however, belies the complexity of conducting an IPO. Uncertainty is pervasive throughout the process, stemming in large part from the poor quality of public information. Investors usually know very little about the issuer prior to the offering. The issuer in turn knows neither the investors who may be interested nor their level of interest. Investment banks function as intermediaries between issuers and investors, and ameliorate some but not all of these information problems. The critical question that issuers, investment banks and market regulators all must ask is 'how should the IPO sale occur, given the reality of the new issues market?'

The optimal selling mechanism depends on the specific group. For example, investment banks – interchangeably referred to as underwriters throughout the book – are interested in profit maximization, resulting in preferences that regulators are not likely to share. Nonetheless, a reasonable starting point for evaluating IPO mechanisms is to assume that the primary goal is to maximize the expected proceeds for the issuer. This facilitates a direct comparison of the efficiency of different types of mechanisms. All mechanisms are defined by the rules that determine how the shares are priced and allocated to investors. These rules are set by regulators – the Securities and Exchange Commission (SEC) in the US – and typically limit issuers to only a couple of selling options. Given that the total IPO proceeds raised in any given year can well exceed ten billion dollars, designing an efficient mechanism is not a trivial matter.

To determine the best mechanism it is first necessary to understand the operation of actual IPOs. Specifically, this involves examining how and why shares are priced and allocated. The most striking aspect of the IPO data is the positive initial or first-day returns, measured as the percentage increase in the share price from the offer to the first trading day close. Table 1.1 lists the average initial return for each country. The 18.4 percent average return in the US from 1960 to 2000 has been fairly constant across time, with temporary 'hot markets' reminiscent of the Internet bubble exhibiting much larger returns. The positive return is not a US phenomenon; all countries have experienced positive average returns and 33 of the 38 countries averaged returns in excess of 10 percent.

The consistency of positive initial returns across time and countries is, at first glance, puzzling. Issuers appear to routinely and voluntarily leave 'money on the table' equal to the nominal price increase on the first-day times the number of shares issued. The amount left is quite staggering; Loughran and Ritter (2002a) estimated a total of $63 billion in the US in 1999 and 2000 alone. The initial return is commonly referred to as underpricing because issuers and their underwriters must be intentionally lowering the offer price below the market clearing level. Trying to explain why underpricing is an accepted practice has been a fertile area of research since Ibbotson (1975). A number of proposed theories rationally justify underpricing as a means to maximize expected proceeds or satisfy some other issuer objective, although none of them rule out irrational behavior affecting the price setting process.

The choice of offer price, over which the underwriter has considerable influence, is usually intertwined with the share allocation decision. The underwriter has almost complete discretion on who will receive an allocation, with the exception of shares reserved for 'friends and family,' which it can exploit for its own benefit. After the stock market and IPO bubble started to burst in 2000, reports of illegal methods used by investment banks to allocate shares began to surface. In some cases investors had to agree to pay an exorbitantly high commission when the shares were sold or to buy more shares in the aftermarket at a higher price in order to receive an allocation. It was also common for banks to allocate shares to chief executive officers (CEOs) in the hope of winning new investment banking business. These practices gave the underwriter a strong incentive to increase underpricing, to the detriment of the issuer.

The most notorious scandal related to these IPOs was not allocation-related, but rather analysts' recommendations. Certain research analysts issued favorable ratings for issuers as an implicit payoff for the underwriting business, even when the analyst privately held a negative opinion about the firm.

The revelation of these investment banking practices led to fines and a global settlement between the market regulators and the major banks that outlined new rules for analyst participation in the IPO and placed some limits on the share allocation. Debate continues about what should be done to further reform the IPO process to prevent future abuse of the system and to ensure a healthy market for new issues. In order to constructively discuss any proposed changes, one must thoroughly understand the economics of the IPO market. Chapters later in the book delve into this topic extensively and provide a foundation for evaluating all possible mechanisms.

A final puzzle regarding IPOs that has been the subject of a heated academic debate is their long-run stock performance. Some researchers argue that IPOs have generated abnormally poor returns over three- to five-year time horizons, starting from the closing price on the first trading day, when compared to risk-adjusted expected returns. Others counter that the apparent anomaly is a consequence of models that are statistically and economically mis-specified, and the underperformance is eliminated when proper adjustments are made. Irrespective of the arguments made by both sides of the debate, IPOs have produced low absolute returns.

1.3 A PREVIEW

The remainder of the book consists of roughly two equal parts. The first, covering Chapters 2 through 7, focuses on why companies go public. Factors internal or specific to a firm that could motivate an IPO are reviewed, as is the influence of the external environment. Chapter 2 sets the scene by presenting data on the time series patterns of IPOs. In addition to providing a general characterization of the new issues market for the past 40 years, the timing evidence highlights the influence of market conditions and information on the IPO decision.

The frequently cited financial and strategic motives for going public are discussed in Chapters 3 and 4, respectively. A purported benefit to an

IPO is that it gives the issuer access to a large pool of cheap capital. The conditions for why and when this is true are analyzed indepth. The nature of competition and the industrial composition dictates the circumstances in which an IPO provides a firm with a strategic advantage.

A firm's ownership structure is explicitly linked to the IPO decision. Chapter 5 reviews the theoretical benefits to public and private ownership and the actual governance structures adopted by firms at their IPO. Ownership decisions also depend on the external environment. Chapter 6 examines the affect of the stock market and the legal and political environment on the ownership structure, providing a basis for an international comparison of the IPO decision. The restructuring of corporate ownership of assets and its implication for the divestiture of subsidiaries through public offerings are examined in Chapter 7.

The second part of the book, Chapters 8 through to 13, concentrates specifically on the sequential steps in the IPO process. These chapters present the findings of a vast body of empirical research and describe in some detail the institutional structure of the new issues market. Valuing the issuer is the first step, covered in Chapter 8. Valuation methods applicable to IPOs, the information that goes into forming a value estimate and the success of these methods are all explored.

The actual IPO process is broken up into three stages, examined in Chapters 9 to 11 sequentially. The first stage reviews the IPO preparations, principally the selection of the underwriter, auditor and legal counsel. The selection criteria for the underwriter, its compensation and the contractual relationship are investigated thoroughly. Stage two is the IPO mechanism for pricing and allocating shares. The basic properties of the main mechanisms, their theoretical efficiency and how they work in practice are analyzed. The last stage begins with the start of aftermarket trading. Price stabilization activities by the underwriter and trading patterns are reviewed first. An inquiry into the research coverage by analysts sheds light on the potential conflicts of interest. Lastly, the effect of lockup expirations is explored.

The performance and actions of newly public companies provides further insight into the IPO decision. Chapter 12 tracks the post-IPO financing decisions of issuers to draw further inferences about the financial and control motives for going public. Long-run stock returns and the underperformance anomaly are the focus of Chapter 13. The statistical and economic challenges in testing for abnormal returns are discussed. Explanations for why underperformance might exist are scrutinized.

Chapter 14 concludes the book by offering some final summary thoughts and assessments. Suggestions are offered to policy-makers about reforms to the IPO process. The bulk of the empirical evidence presented throughout the book, and almost all of the institutional detail, are specific to the US market. These biases reflect the disproportionate amount of all IPO activity occurring in the US, which has attracted the most attention from researchers. However, the international data implies that IPO behavior is fairly consistent across countries. Thus, the conclusions drawn and theories developed for evaluating the entire IPO process have universal applicability.

NOTES

1.   The IPO totals in the US exclude Regulation A offerings (small issues, raising less than $1.5 million during the 1980s), real-estate investment trusts (REITs) and closed-end funds. IPO totals from 1988 to 2000 exclude best efforts offerings.
2.   Reprinted from *Pacific-Basin Finance Journal,* Vol 2, Loughran, T., J. Ritter and K. Rydqvist, "Initial Public Offerings: International Insights," pp. 169-99, Copyright (1994), with permission from Elsevier.

2 IPO timing and information

For some private companies it is not a question of why go public, but rather when. In those cases, what is of interest is isolating the factors that determine the timing of the IPOs. By doing so, it also provides additional insight into why companies go public. There are two distinct ways the question of when do firms go public can be approached. The first is to emphasize the stage in a company's development at its IPO. The second perspective, which is pursued in this chapter, considers IPO timing relative to market conditions and other IPOs. The time series of IPO volume should reflect companies going public when conditions are most favorable. The question then is which factors are most important for creating a favorable environment and thus are best able to explain IPO timing patterns.

The theme unifying all IPO timing theories is the emphasis on information. Theories on the supply of IPOs can be grouped into three categories. The first group focuses on informational externalities at the market-wide level. Investors extrapolate market valuations to potential issuers, creating an incentive for more firms to go public when valuations are high. Issuers effectively try to time the market during a temporary 'window of opportunity'. The second group builds on information asymmetries between firm insiders and investors. Going public when the asymmetry is severe can be costly to issuers, who instead wait for periods in which the information differential is low. The third category is based on information spillovers within the IPO market. Potential issuers observe the success of preceding IPOs and condition their decision on the outcome. Finally, a fourth group of theories concentrates on the information effects that impacts investor demand for IPOs.

2.1 TIME SERIES DATA

Analysis of the timing decision begins with an examination of the IPO time series data. Figure 2.1 plots the US aggregate monthly volume of IPOs from January 1960 to February 2002. The data from the 1960s and the early 1970s was collected by Roger Ibbotson and has been continually updated by Jay Ritter from the University of Florida.[1]

10

Figure 2.1 US monthly IPO volume: January 1960 – December 2002

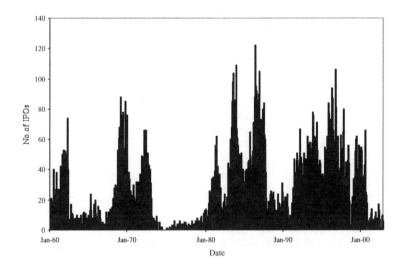

Source: Jay Ritter's web page http://bear.cba.ufl.edu/ritter/ipodata.htm.

A few immediate observations jump out from Figure 2.1. First, IPO volume exhibits extreme volatility, with either heavy volume or little activity. The all-or-nothing pattern to the volume is consistent with IPOs occurring only when a temporary window is open. The volume volatility exceeds the volatility of the stock market in general, suggesting a high sensitivity of IPO activity to market conditions.

The second observation is the oscillation between hot and cold IPO markets. While there is no clear cyclical pattern to the volume, the extreme fluctuations mean that hot and cold markets tend to alternate and last for varying lengths of time. Heavy volume periods in the early 1960s, the late 1960s and early 1970s, for most of the 1980s and the bulk of the 1990s were followed by cold markets that lasted for at least a few years.

The final observation is the persistence of current volume. When volume is heavy it tends to remain high for a while, with the same being true for low volume. Ritter (2003) estimated a one-month lagged correlation of 0.88, implying that if there were 10 more IPOs in the current month then the following month would have an additional nine IPOs. Consistent with this fact, Lowry (2003) found no evidence to suggest that IPO volume had a tendency to revert to a 'normal' level.

2.1.1 Preliminary Explanations

Digging deeper into the data produces a few preliminary explanations for the IPO volume patterns. At least three contributing factors are apparent.

Macroeconomy: The macro-level trends in IPO volume follow fairly closely with the economic cycle. The hot IPO markets of the 1980s and 1990s correspond to periods of strong economic growth and increasing stock market valuations. The cold markets of the 1970s, the early 1990s and the early 21st century occurred during recessions and periods of weak economic growth.

Greater volume during the growth periods reflects both demand and supply factors. Investors are more willing to provide capital to fund risky and unproven businesses when economic prospects are good. Firms go public after stock market valuations increase because the cost of equity is lower and dilution is minimized. Lastly, a growing economy is associated with an increase in the number of valuable investment opportunities, enticing more firms to go public to raise capital. Tests conducted by Lowry (2003) showed that measures of capital demand were economically and statistically significant in explaining IPO volume.

Exogenous fluctuations: IPO activity fluctuates between hot and cold markets in time horizons as short as a few months. Seasonal factors explain some of the short-term volatility. Issuing activity tends to diminish in January and in the summer, following the vacation periods of investment bankers and investors. Active marketing of an IPO takes place a few weeks prior to the actual offer date and simple logistics keep the market from gearing up again until the end of January and September. Sudden shocks to the market can also cause a temporary suspension of IPO activity. The Russian financial crisis caused issuing activity to all but cease in September and October 1998 before returning to heavy volume.

Industries: High aggregate volume is often a consequence of industry-specific hot markets. IPOs by similar firms tend to cluster together in time, with one or a few industries accounting for a disproportionately large fraction of the total volume. The Internet sector in the late 1990s is the most recent and prominent example of this phenomenon. Prior industry hot markets include the natural resource sector in 1980, biotechnology at different times in the 1980s and early 1990s, and even riverboat gambling firms in the early 1990s.[2] Industry-specific hot markets rarely occur when the overall market is not itself hot and Helwege and Liang (2004) found that they tend to occur simultaneously with other industry hot markets.

The collective evidence on the timing and volume of IPOs clearly suggests that factors external to a firm affect when it will go public. If potential issuers make their decision in isolation, then the aggregate volume should be more uniformly distributed across time. Instead, firms go public when their competitors do and when market conditions are most favorable. Both factors suggest that information plays a big part in the timing decision. Informational externalities – information relevant to a firm that is generated by or related to other companies and external events – allow a potential issuer to gauge the likely investor reception for its offering and to forecast its market valuation.

Competitive interaction can also give rise to industry-specific hot markets. A firm may have no choice but to go public and raise the capital necessary to compete with rivals that have already gone public. A pure informational externality affects the timing decision for non-competitive reasons. Information produced by and about similar companies can lower the cost of public equity for a private firm, potentially leading to an IPO.

2.2 MARKET TIMING

The market timing theory argues that firms successfully conduct their IPO during a temporary 'window of opportunity', usually characterized by industry or market-wide share overvaluation that results in a lower cost of equity. All firms wait for the window to open before going public, which leads to clustering. The assumption of temporarily overvalued shares rests on the belief that the market is driven by investor sentiment. Investor attitudes toward equities ebb and flow over time. A period of high sentiment – defined by investors interpreting information pertaining to stock valuations positively – could result in share prices above their true intrinsic value. Successful market timing requires that investors extrapolate the high valuations of public companies to IPOs as well. Market prices that fluctuate because of changing sentiment impact the timing decision because issuers wait until sentiment is high.

Market timing does not require overvaluation, only that share prices fluctuate up and down over time as sentiment changes. Overvaluation, if it does occur, must ultimately be caused by some form of investor irrationality. The exact nature of the irrationality or why the degree of irrationality fluctuates does not have to be specified. As an explanation for IPO volume, market timing is more powerful if investors do collectively suffer from temporary episodes of irrationality.

Asymmetric information between an issuer and investors does not alter the potential for market timing. Both groups could have the same information set, yet irrational investors may interpret it in such a manner as to lead to overvaluation. However, an issuer that possesses private information need not be able to exploit rational investors. The IPO would signal overvaluation to the investors, who immediately lower the share price, reducing the benefit to market timing.

The manifestation of market timing behavior should be evident in the data. A direct test of the theory requires a link between timing and investor sentiment. Unfortunately, sentiment is an intangible attitude that defies easy quantification. Indirect evidence based on IPO timing relative to market valuations and IPO long-run performance provides an indication whether issuers successfully exploit temporary overvaluation.

2.2.1 Industry and Market Valuations

A large body of compelling evidence supports the conjecture that IPOs are timed to take advantage of share overvaluation. A major piece of the evidence is industry valuations surrounding the IPO date. Firms in the same industry have a common component to their value, which provides a useful starting point for investors to price an IPO. This and other factors supporting the market timing theory are presented below.

Industry valuations: IPOs normally occur following abnormally good industry stock returns and sometimes prior to a downturn in the valuation. Lerner (1994) documented that from 1979 to 1993, biotechnology IPOs occurred after an average 9 percent return to a biotech industry index in the three months prior to the offer date. The average index return in the first two months after the IPOs was approximately -4 percent. Figure 2.2, reprinted from Lerner, demonstrates quite clearly that the IPOs clustered near the valuation peaks, strongly indicative of market timing.

Industry market-to-book (M/B) equity ratios are positively related to the occurrence of IPOs. Pagano, Panetta and Zingales (1998) reported that in a sample of Italian IPOs the most significant factor in explaining why the firms went public was the industry M/B ratio. A one standard deviation increase in the ratio increased the probability of an IPO by 25 percent. Rajan and Servaes (1995) showed that the average industry M/B ratio at the time of US IPOs was 8 percent higher than the average over the surrounding five years and 18 percent higher than the average for all public firms. Helwege and Liang (2004) found that the industry M/B ratios were higher in heavy relative to low volume markets.[3] Aggregate market measures for M/B were also economically and statistically significant in explaining IPO volume in Lowry (2003).

Figure 2.2 Biotechnology industry valuation and monthly IPO volume[4]

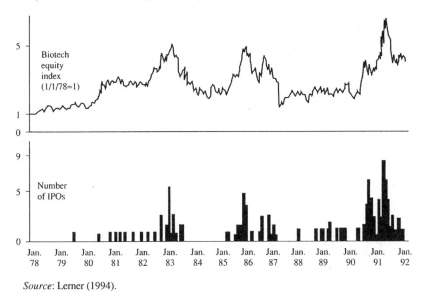

Source: Lerner (1994).

IPO valuations: The best expectation for the potential market value of an issuer is the valuations of other recent IPOs from the industry. Investment bank analysts issue forecasts for the future earnings of recent IPOs, which form the basis of these valuations. Higher growth rates in projected earnings could proxy for higher investor sentiment. Rajan and Servaes (1997) showed that the number of IPOs from an industry in a given quarter was positively related to the long-term earnings growth projections for recent similar IPOs. The relationship could be picking up on the fact that firms with more growth opportunities go public to raise the capital needed to finance the projects. However, Rajan and Servaes found the number of IPOs to be positively correlated with the difference between the forecasted and actual earnings. Thus it is most likely that issuers were taking advantage of investor optimism to time the market.

Closed-end fund discount: A pricing anomaly that has long puzzled economists is the closed-end fund discount. In theory, a fund's share price should equal the value-weighted average of the individual, publicly observable, security prices. The puzzle is that the shares routinely trade at a 10 to 20 percent discount relative to the value of their component securities, providing an arbitrage opportunity. The discount fluctuates over time and Lee, Shleifer and Thaler (1991) argued that it provides a good proxy for

15

investor sentiment. Higher sentiment would lead to a smaller discount. Lee, Shleifer and Thaler subsequently showed that the yearly IPO volume was negatively correlated with the discount, further implying that most IPOs occurred when sentiment was high.

SEO overvaluation: Public firms interested in completing a seasoned equity offering (SEO) also have an incentive to time the market. These firms offer the advantage of an observable market price that enables a more direct test of the market timing theory. A measure of overvaluation requires a comparison between the actual stock price and an estimated fair value. Jindra (2000) estimated that SEO issuers were overvalued by a significant 15 to 28 percent relative to matched non-SEO firms, with the overvaluation peaking in the year of issuance. After controlling for firm-specific factors, the probability of an SEO increased in the misvaluation.

Demand for funds: Market timing is more apt to apply to firms that have flexilibity in deciding when to go public. IPOs that consist primarily of secondary shares sold by the existing shareholders are not motivated by a demand for capital. Such issuers are likely to wait for the most opportune time. Lowry (2002) concluded that the timing of IPOs consisting of a majority of secondary shares was highly related to investor sentiment. Jindra (2000) found that undervalued SEO issuers were older, larger and significantly more levered than overvalued issuers. Financial constraints would have prevented these firms from waiting until they were overvalued.

2.2.2 Long-Run Performance

Going public when the shares are overvalued implies that the issuer will have poor post-IPO stock returns as investors adjust the price to the appropriate level. There is ample evidence that IPOs generate poor raw long-run stock returns (Ritter and Welch 1995). More controversial is whether these returns are abnormally poor.[5] Loughran and Ritter (1995) estimated that the average annual return over a five-year time horizon starting from the first-day closing were 5 percent less than a comparable risk-adjusted benchmark. Evidence of underperformance is further support for issuers successfully timing the market when sentiment is too high.

In order for IPOs to generate abnormally poor returns investors must be even more optimistic about issuers than the industry as a whole. Evidence cited in the preceding section showed that industry values declined post-IPO and that alone would lead to poor returns. Rajan and Servaes (1997) estimated that analysts' earnings forecasts at the time of an IPO for other industry firms were too optimistic by about 5 percent. However, the forecasts for issuers were an incremental 2 to 3 percent too high. Lowry (2003) found that current IPO volume was inversely related to the subsequent raw returns of contemporaneous issuers and the entire market, meaning that more firms went public when the market was overvalued.

Time-varying underperformance further supports the notion that investor sentiment affects IPO timing. Firms that went public during a period of heavy IPO volume generated the worst long-run abnormal returns, whereas IPOs that occurred in cold markets showed no sign of underperforming (Loughran and Ritter 1995; 2000; Helwege and Liang 2004).[6] Positive sentiment could result in overvaluation, inducing more firms to go public. Poor long-run returns would result as the market corrects the initial pricing error. Fewer firms would find it attractive to go public when valuations are in line with fundamentals. Those that do are properly priced and produce normal returns.

2.2.3 Rational Timing

An alternative explanation, proposed by Draho (2000), exists for the time series pattern of IPOs. The theory posits that the timing decision is made by firms optimally exercising their option to go public. It is based on a few assumptions that must hold for the market timing theory to be correct. First, a private firm has the option to go public at any time. Second, investors use the market prices of industry firms to value an IPO. Third, stock prices evolve according to a random process. The shares do not have to be priced correctly all the time, but the future prices cannot be perfectly forecast.

The combination of these three assumptions means that the IPO timing decision can be modeled as a real option problem. The manager of a private firm can decide at any time to take the firm public, but doing so costs the issuer the option of waiting longer. The stochastic price path makes the future value of an IPO unknown, which actually increases the timing option value. There is always the possibility that prices will suddenly increase in the near future. If the price does not increase, or even falls, the firm simply waits longer before going public.[7]

Optimally exercising the timing option produces clear predictions for the profile of IPO volume. Firms wait for an increase in the industry valuation before going public and never go public after a market downturn. Limiting the set of possible pre-IPO industry returns to be positive introduces a bias that shows up as abnormally positive returns. The post-issue returns should display a normal rate of return. The pre- and post-IPO returns that result could produce an unintended clustering of IPOs near valuation peaks.[8] The theory can account for many of the stylized facts of

17

IPO timing without requiring irrational investor mis-pricing, asymmetric information or issuers exploiting IPO investors.

2.2.4 Insider Exploitation

A commonly held belief, especially pertaining to Internet IPOs, is that firms are taken public to allow the insiders to sell their overvalued shares. The conjecture goes that the entrepreneur and other insiders exploit their private information to sell their shares to gullible and possibly irrational investors. It is impossible know with certainty if this was a motive for going public because the insiders do not disclose their true intentions. But if their words do not give them away, their actions are more revealing.

Examining insider sales in and after the IPO provides some indication of whether they were motivated by a desire to sell overvalued shares. The insiders of overvalued issuers should anticipate the future share price decline as the true value is learned by investors. Therefore, if issuers are exploiting investors, there should be a negative correlation between the amount of insider sales and subsequent stock performance.

Chadha (2003) conducted an interesting test of the exploitation hypothesis by comparing the sales of insiders – the CEO, executive officers and directors, VCs and other large shareholders – in firms that delisted within three years of their IPO to those of matched issuers that remained active. The delisting was due to performance related reasons, meaning that the insiders should have predicted the inevitable share price decline before the market did, providing an opportunity to dump overpriced shares.

The evidence does not support the exploitation hypothesis. Chadha found that the equity stakes held by pre-IPO shareholders before and after the IPO were similar for the delisted and active issuers. There was no relation between the trading activities of insiders and the probability of delisting shortly after the IPO. In fact, in the year prior to delisting insiders sold significantly less and on the net purchased more shares than insiders of active IPOs. Schultz and Zaman (2001) specifically examined Internet IPOs and concluded that insider selling was not a major factor in the going-public decision. Insiders of Internet and non-Internet issuers retained 45.6 and 39.7 percent of the shares, respectively, at the IPO. The Internet IPOs also consisted of a smaller percentage of insider shares.

Two plausible theories can explain why the insiders hung on to their shares when it appeared that the firm was going to fail, both of which argue against the insider exploitation hypothesis. First, managers that are overconfident in their ability and the firm's prospects are victims of their own hubris. These managers see no reason to sell because they believe that the share price will eventually rise. Second, entrepreneurs have a great deal of pride in their business and are reluctant to let go when the firm appears to be failing. The mindset of an individual who would start a business in the face of adverse odds seems to be incompatible with the idea of going public to dump the shares. The timing of IPOs is consistent with an honest attempt by issuers to raise capital when it is relatively cheap, coinciding with periods in which investors are overly optimistic.

2.3 ASYMMETRIC INFORMATION

The second channel through which information affects the timing decision is an asymmetry between firm insiders and investors. Insiders have an informational advantage over outside investors in their ability to value the company. The asymmetry raises the specter of the 'lemons problem' of Akerlof (1970) and Myers and Majluf (1984), in which all companies willing to sell equity are perceived by investors to be overvalued.

Investors cannot perfectly distinguish between good and bad firms, resulting in a share price that equals the expected value. Consequently, good firms tend to be undervalued and bad ones overvalued. High value firms forego a public offering because the value of the existing shareholders stock will be diluted by the sale of underpriced equity. Investors rationally interpret the decision to sell equity as a signal that the issuer is overvalued and respond by lowering the share price. The new issues market can break down entirely if the remaining high value firms sequentially decide to pass on an IPO because of undervaluation. The inability to sell equity on the public market represents the maximum cost of asymmetric information.

A necessary condition for asymmetric information to affect IPO timing is that the cost it imposes on the issuer is time-varying. This is equivalent to assuming that the extent of the asymmetry is constantly fluctuating. Hot IPO markets should then be characterized by a low degree of asymmetry and its resulting cost. An estimate of the asymmetry cost and its time series profile is required to test whether this is a factor in IPO timing.

2.3.1 Cost of Asymmetry

A direct estimate of the asymmetry cost for potential issuers is not possible because of the absence of an observable pre-IPO valuation. Seasoned equity offerings provide an acceptable substitute. IPO and SEO volume have high contemporaneous correlation – about 0.85 based on data in Loughran and Ritter (1995) – implying that the timing decision is similar for both equity offerings. Many SEO issuers are also young and risky like most IPOs. The conventional measure for the asymmetry cost is the change in firm value at the time of the SEO announcement. The signaling theory discussed above argued that investors react negatively to an SEO because only overvalued firms sell equity. The loss in value upon announcement is a proxy for the cost.

The price response to the SEO announcement must be isolated from general price movements. The cumulative abnormal return (CAR) is the difference between the actual return during the two- to three-day window surrounding the announcement and the normal return over a few days. A broad range of studies covering different time periods has consistently found SEO announcements to be associated with CARs that average a significant -3 percent.[9] Asquith and Mullins (1986) estimated that the average loss in shareholder value at announcement represented 30 percent of the value of the equity being issued.[10]

Value-maximizing firms should try to issue equity when the asymmetry cost is low. Firms have some control over the degree of asymmetry by virtue of their ability to release information to investors. Announcing an equity issue shortly after the release of value-relevant information can minimize the cost. Korajczyk, Lucas and McDonald (1991) found that SEO announcements occurred on an average 20 days after a quarterly earnings report. The earnings release preceding the SEO was both unusually informative and conveyed unexpected good news about the firm. Taking advantage of the reduced asymmetry was economically significant. Delaying the announcement of a SEO by one month led to an incremental 0.44 percent price decline on the announcement day.

2.3.2 Time-varying Asymmetric Information

An asymmetric information-based theory for IPO clustering requires that a market-wide component to the asymmetry change over time. Reduced asymmetry at the firm level is not sufficient to explain clustering unless all firms simultaneously take actions to lower the information cost. Two hypotheses have been proposed for why market-wide information asymmetries may be time-varying.

2.3.2.1 Economic expansion

Firm values can be roughly decomposed into the value derived from existing assets-in-place and the intangible value from growth options. Asymmetric information should be more severe over the existing assets. Firm insiders know better if the assets are becoming less productive or need to be replaced. Neither the insiders nor investors will have precise information about the payoff from growth options, minimizing any asymmetries. Accordingly, the negative price reaction to a SEO announcement must be due to the overvaluation of existing assets.[11] Thus, the negative announcement CAR will become larger as the percentage of firm value derived from existing assets increases.

Periods of macroeconomic expansion endow firms with additional positive net present value (NPV) growth options, leading to a reduction in the fraction of the firm value affected by asymmetries. Choe, Masulis and Nanda (1993) argued that this change in the value composition could account for the increased issuing volume in expansions. High quality firms will now find an equity offering more attractive because the asymmetry cost is lower. Since there are more high quality issuers in an expansion, the average overvaluation declines and along with it the negative announcement reaction. Choe, Masulis and Nanda confirmed this prediction, demonstrating that SEO announcement CARs were inversely related – less negative – to measures of economic expansion.

The macro-asymmetry explanation for clustering can be challenged on a number of fronts. First, the increased volume could be due to a greater demand for capital as firms discover more positive NPV projects. Lowry (2003) showed that the demand for capital and investor sentiment motives were far more economically significant than asymmetric information in explaining IPO volume. Second, the smaller announcement CARs during the expansion could reflect investors' beliefs that firm values will increase more, or decrease less, because of greater investment in positive NPV projects. Finally, the macro-asymmetry explanation also predicts that the average issuer quality is higher in the expansion phase. Yet Helwege and Liang (2001) found that industry-adjusted operating performance measures indicated little quality difference between hot and cold market issuers.

2.3.2.2 Hot markets

A detailed examination of SEO volume reveals that macroeconomic cycles are a crude and often incorrect proxy for market conditions. Bayless and Chaplinsky (1996) categorized hot and cold markets using a rolling average of aggregate SEO volume. Based on this classification they found relatively low correlation between volume and the level of macroeconomic expansion.

According to their criterion, Bayless and Chaplinsky found that the SEO announcement CARs in hot and cold markets were significantly different at -2.0 and -3.3 percent, respectively. The estimated difference was actually closer to 2 percent after controlling for firm and offer characteristics, and was not attributable to varying stock market or macroeconomic conditions. They argued that changes in the characteristics of issuers could account for the lower asymmetry cost in a hot market, although it is not clear which characteristics were responsible for this change. Regardless of why the cost varies across time, there were substantial savings to be had from going public in a hot market. The additional two-percentage point price decline in a cold market would have translated into an average incremental loss in equity value of approximately $13 million.

The overall evidence does not offer much support for asymmetry-based explanations for IPO clustering. Further undermining the hypothesis is that it contradicts the market timing theory. The asymmetry hypothesis predicts that the average issuer quality is higher in a hot market and overvaluation is lower, which is captured by the smaller announcement CARs. The market timing theory predicts that firms issue when they are most overvalued. If true, the announcement CARs should be more, not less, negative during heavy volume periods. The strong support for market timing is evidence against the asymmetric information theory.

2.3.3 Pre-Issue Returns

Asymmetric information on a firm-specific level is still useful for understanding the timing of individual IPOs. There is little doubt that managers continually possess superior information about the firm's prospects compared to investors. Current private information is learned by investors at some point in the future and replaced by new inside information.

The dynamic evolution of asymmetric information was used by Lucas and McDonald (1990) to account for the stock returns surrounding equity offerings. They assume that insiders know if the firm is currently undervalued and that the share price will rise as the private information is revealed. Waiting until the mis-pricing is corrected before issuing results in abnormally positive pre-SEO stock returns. The opposite holds when the private information is negative. The overvalued firm sells equity immediately before the stock price drops. The pre-SEO stock returns should be normal, assuming that the need to raise equity is independent of the price history. Combining the two pre-SEO stock price paths results in an abnormally positive average return. The average issuer is also overvalued, justifying negative announcement CARs.

Returns surrounding SEOs are consistent with the predictions of the theory. Lucas and McDonald (1990) estimated raw returns of about 30 to 35 percent in the year preceding the SEO. Loughran and Ritter (1995) found that half of their measured 72 percent pre-SEO return was attributable to the market return and half to firm-specific performance. Optimal market timing could also explain the pre-issue returns. The factor that lends support to the importance of asymmetric information is the post-SEO returns. Loughran and Ritter found that SEO issuers generated an average total five-year return of 26 percent. Non-SEO firms matched to the issuers based on similar pre-SEO returns generated average five-year returns of 98 percent. The divergent returns suggest that the management of issuers knew their firm was overvalued, whereas the non-issuers were not.

2.4 INFORMATIONAL EXTERNALITIES

The third major way in which information influences IPO timing is externalities. The market timing theory implicitly relies on externalities as investors use the share prices of public firms to form a preliminary valuation for a potential issuer. New information that causes market prices to change directly affects the IPO valuation and the decision to go public. This type of informational externality is exogenous to the IPO market.

A defining characteristic of IPO timing is industry clustering. Exogenous informational externalities partly explain this phenomenon. Private firms wait for the industry valuation to rise before pulling the trigger on an IPO. Each firm decides independently when to go public, but collectively they produce a clustering. This clustering explanation is incomplete for three reasons. First, public firms may not offer a good benchmark valuation. IPOs often involve young risky companies that are operationally quite distinct from the mature public firms within the industry. Second, in a nascent industry there are few or no public firms with the share prices to signal when to go public. Third, a firm contemplating an IPO benefits from knowing the likely reception that its offering will receive from investors. Market prices cannot provide that information.

Informational externalities generated endogenously within the new issues market are the most relevant for industry clustering. When a firm goes public it produces useful information that spills over to the remaining private firms, allowing them to learn the extent of investor interest in IPOs from their industry. Specifically, they learn the price they can expect to receive for their offering and whether it is above or below their initial expectation. Endogenous externalities are also important to investors because they learn about the industry's ability to attract other investors.

Endogenous externalities are especially important in nascent industries. Genentech became the first pure biotechnology company to go public with its 1980 IPO. Prior to the IPO, there was considerable skepticism about the biotech industry's viability and whether there was sufficient investor interest. The Genentech IPO was a great success, with an initial return in excess of 100 percent. Investors and other biotech firms learned from the experience, launching a wave of biotech IPO clusterings throughout the 1980s and 1990s.

The primary quantifiable form of endogenous informational externalities is the prices associated with preceding IPOs. Potential issuers can easily observe the market and offer prices, and their relation to the initial expectation. Drawing a link between price information and issuing volume gives some measure of the importance of endogenous externalities.

2.4.1 Price Patterns

Before analyzing the informational externalities generated by IPO prices, a basic understanding of the pricing process is necessary. A firm that files with the SEC to go public in the US must include an initial price range – say $10 to $12 – that is a reasonable expectation for the final offer price. The mid-point of the initial range is typically deemed the preliminary offer price. The underwriter canvasses investors during the marketing phase of the IPO to gauge the price they are willing to pay. The final offer price is chosen immediately prior to the offer date, conditional on investor interest. A revision has occurred if the offer price does not equal the preliminary price. Aftermarket trading begins within hours of the IPO. The percentage difference between the offer and first-day closing prices is the initial return.

The two pieces of pricing information relevant to potential issuers are the price revision and initial return. An offer price set above (below) the preliminary price indicates that unexpected positive (negative) information has been revealed during the course of the IPO. Underwriters generally underprice IPOs below the expected aftermarket price. An initial return larger (smaller) than the expected underpricing suggests that investors had a more (less) favorable impression of the issuer than anticipated.

2.4.1.1 Initial returns

The 18 percent average initial return documented for the US in the post-1960 period masks considerable variation across firms and time. Temporary periods arise in which the average return far exceeds 18 percent, although such returns are usually concentrated within a particular industry. The Internet hot market is the most famous example, when initial returns over 100 percent were the norm not the exception. The intertemporal volatility of initial returns is best seen graphically. Figure 2.3 plots the monthly average initial return – with individual returns equal-weighted – from January 1960 to June 2003.[12] The graph overlays the initial return on the monthly volume to show the relationship between the two.

Figure 2.3 US monthly IPO volume and average initial returns

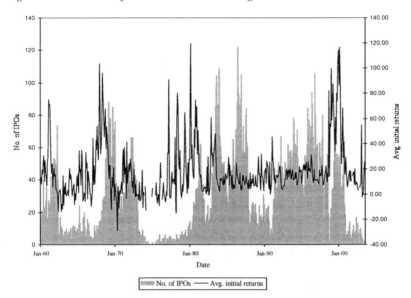

Source: Jay Ritter's web page http://bear.cba.ufl.edu/ritter/ipodata.htm.

Inspection of Figure 2.3 reveals that months of high initial returns are generally followed by months with similarly high returns. The return pattern is consistent with hot markets characterized by high initial returns that persist for short periods. Lowry and Schwert (2002) estimated the one-month and one-year autocorrelations to be 0.60 and 0.11, respectively. High initial returns do not exhibit the same degree of persistence as IPO volume, which had equivalent autocorrelations of 0.88 and 0.44 (Ritter 2003).

Focusing on initial returns instead of the offer price revision does not result in a significant loss of information because a strong positive correlation exists between the two.[13] According to Loughran and Ritter (2002a), approximately half of all IPOs have a final offer price within the initial range, a quarter are priced below the lower bound and a quarter above the range. They reported that the average initial returns for IPOs priced below, within and above the range were significantly different at 4.0, 10.8 and 28.9 percent, respectively.

2.4.1.2 A caveat

Fluctuations in the level of initial returns provide private firms with valuable information about the current IPO market conditions. However, the informativeness of initial returns cannot be taken too far. The initial returns vary as the characteristics of issuers change and are heavily influenced by intentional underpricing. An increased supply of risky, venture capital-backed issuers with small offering sizes will affect the average initial return even if no new information is revealed. Therefore only the abnormal component to initial returns – the difference between the actual return and the expected return conditional on the IPO characteristics – is a valuable informational externality.

2.4.2 Prices and Volume

The effect of endogenous externalities on the IPO decision should manifest as a lead–lag relationship between pricing information and issuing volume. Unexpected positive performance by a few IPOs would induce additional firms to go public. The lag between positive information and increased volume will be months, as it takes time to prepare for and complete an IPO. Close inspection of the initial return and volume data in Figure 2.3 hints at such a relation. In addition, the data in the figure are at the aggregate level. Information spillovers matter most at the industry level where firms have a common component to their value.

2.4.2.1 Aggregate data

The lead–lag relation between average initial returns and aggregate volume observed visually was proven to be statistically significant by Lowry and Schwert (2002). Higher initial returns in the present led to an increase in IPO volume approximately six months later. There is an aspect of this positive correlation that is somewhat puzzling. Issuers presumably want to minimize the costs of going public. The initial return proxies for intentional underpricing, a real and substantial cost. Cost minimization predicts that more firms would go public when initial returns are low, the exact opposite of what occurs.

Two explanations exist for the positive lead–lag relationship. The first stems from the fact that firms ultimately care about maximizing their net IPO proceeds, not minimizing the issuing costs. Unusually large initial returns are an indication of positive price revision, which implies that investors believe the firms are worth more than the issuers had expected. More firms will go public when the cost of equity is cheaper than originally thought. The larger than expected proceeds overwhelm the additional underpricing cost.

The second reason why high initial returns were not a deterrent to going public is that they did not predict future returns. Lowry and Schwert

(2002) found that the average level of initial returns at the time the IPO is filed was unrelated to the issuers' subsequent initial return. Instead, the expected initial return for an issuer was a function of firm-specific characteristics known at the time of filing and unexpected information produced during the marketing phase. Most of the characteristics, such as total assets or industry classification, cannot easily be changed. Consequently, the expected initial return was largely unaffected by the timing of the IPO, regardless of the current level of returns.

Average initial returns levels that are persistent across time appear to be inconsistent with time-invariant expected returns, although two factors account for this phenomenon. First, IPOs by similar firms are clustered together, largely because of informational externalities, and their fixed characteristics produce a correlation in the returns. Second, the registration period – the time between the filing and offer dates – overlaps for many issuers. Unexpected information learned during this period, whether from other IPOs or general market developments, affects the level of underpricing for all similar firms.

2.4.2.2 Industry spillovers

The effect of information spillovers within well-defined industries on the going-public decision was studied by Benveniste et al. (2003). An ideal test for the spillover effect would examine whether unexpected positive information induces more firms to go public and if negative information deters additional IPOs. Since private firms cannot be observed deciding against an IPO, Benveniste et al. instead looked at the relationship between spillovers and the withdrawal rates and price revisions of firms that have already filed. The spillover variables were the price revision, initial return and filing and withdrawal rates of same industry IPOs occurring contemporaneously with the registration period of an issuer. Three main findings all confirm the influence of endogenous informational externalities on IPO timing.

Price revision: The price revision for an issuer was positively related to the price revisions and initial returns for contemporaneous IPOs. The revision also increased with the industry returns during the registration period. Revisions were greater for firms that were more speculative in nature, measured by the percentage of their value derived from growth options and intangible assets, highlighting the importance of investor feedback.

Withdrawal: Market conditions during the registration period of issuers who completed their IPO were significantly better than the conditions occurring for issuers that withdrew their offering. The average proceeds revision among all contemporaneous offerings was 4.6 percent if the issuer completed the IPO, but only 0.8 percent when the offer was withdrawn.[14] Among the firms in registration at the time an issuer filed to go public, 43 percent subsequently withdrew their offering if the issuer also withdrew, but only 9 percent eventually withdrew if the issuer completed the IPO. There was also greater variation in proceeds revision and initial returns during the registration period for withdrawn IPOs, implying a riskier issuing environment.

Learning: Uncertainty about the best offer price is most severe for the first IPO in a cluster. Neither the pioneering firm nor investors have spillover information that can be used to improve the accuracy of the preliminary offer price. Such spillovers enable later issuers to select a more precise offer price and increase the probability of a successful offering. The typical pioneering issuer revised its gross proceeds upward 5.5 percentage points more than follower firms. The difference is large, given that the average proceeds revision was -0.7 percent. Pioneer firms were also 14.6 percent less likely to complete their IPO compared to later followers.

2.4.3 Clustering Explanations

Endogenous informational externalities create clusters in both obvious and subtle ways. High valuations or withdrawn offerings provide clear signals to potential issuers about the market conditions. The extraordinarily high market prices for Internet IPOs were impossible to ignore and undoubtedly lead to more firms going public. The Internet sector is, however, the exception rather than the norm for IPO pricing. Industry clusters are far more likely to be associated with initial returns ranging from 10 to 30 percent. Such pricing signals are not nearly as unambiguous to potential issuers, which makes the IPO decision less clear-cut. There are other, less obvious channels through which informational externalities work to generate clusters.

2.4.3.1 Information production

Every IPO involves a learning process for the participants. The issuer and underwriter learn the price investors are willing to pay, while investors face an even bigger hurdle in trying to learn about the company. There is rarely any publicly disseminated information about the issuer prior to the IPO, except for the offering prospectus (Rao 1993). Investors must expend costly time and effort to learn about and evaluate the company before deciding

28

whether to participate in the offering. Some form of compensation must be offered to persuade investors to incur the learning cost and truthfully reveal their assessment to the underwriter. The standard assumption, for reasons discussed fully in Chapter 10, is that investors are compensated with intentional underpricing. Therefore the issuer ultimately bears any information costs in the form of a lower offer price.

The cost of information production depends on the complexity of the issuer and on the prior information investors possess that speeds up the learning process. Investors require information about a company – such as the operating efficiency, managerial quality and governance structures – and its industry and competitive environment to properly value the firm. Company-specific information can only be learned once the issuer files to go public. In contrast, general market information can be acquired through the analysis of similar firms. Information generated by one IPO lowers the required information production for subsequent issuers from the same industry. The result is a declining marginal information cost with each additional offering.

Lower information costs reduce the required underpricing, equivalent to a fall in the cost of public equity, which could result in a cluster. The evidence cited in the previous section substantiates the claim of a declining information cost. The offer price revision for the pioneering issuer was significantly larger than that for later issuers. Since price revisions are positively related to the initial return, the pioneer likely incurred a larger information cost compared to followers. The information produced by the early IPOs does not have to be abnormally positive to cause a cluster. The only requirement is that information useful to valuing subsequent issuers from the industry be produced.

2.4.3.2 First-mover disadvantage

There are advantages and disadvantages to being the first IPO in an industry cluster. The pioneering firm can gain a competitive advantage over rivals by getting a jump on financing new investment opportunities. By the same token the pioneer is the guinea pig that tests the market to learn the investor interest. The pioneer also bears the largest information production cost. The latter two aspects create a strong incentive to delay the IPO and let another firm go public first. The incentive to wait increases when there are significant economies of scale in the information cost. A first-mover problem can arise in which no company wants to take on the burden of being first in the industry to go public. Firms acting in their own self-interest can prevent or delay a cluster from arising, which can be socially harmful if the firms are better off public.

29

The first-mover problem can be overcome if similar IPOs are bundled together by investment banks. Benveniste, Busaba and Wilhelm (2002) suggested that an underwriter could use its monopsony power to spread the information/underpricing cost across a sequence of IPOs, thereby eliminating the disincentive to be the first issuer.[15] The more IPOs there are from an industry, the larger the base over which to spread the underpricing. The theory predicts a negative correlation between average initial returns and total contemporaneous industry IPO volume.

Evidence produced by Benveniste et al. (2003) is moderately consistent with the bundling theory. An increase in the number of firms from the same industry filing to go public within 180 days of the pioneer filing resulted in lower average initial returns. The industry data was aggregated across all underwriters, weakening the bundling argument because the banks need not coordinate on spreading the costs across issuers. However, the general result still held for individual banks, albeit with weaker statistical support because of the smaller sample sizes.

2.4.3.3 Information cascades

An information cascade is an extreme consequence of informational externalities. Each potential issuer starts with an expectation for the payoff from an IPO, conditional on its private information. Information spillovers allow issuers to update their respective expectations and re-evaluate the IPO decision. An information cascade is said to arise if the spillover information dominates the private information in the IPO decision. This occurs if, after observing a few successful IPOs, all potential issuers believe that an IPO produces positive value and go public themselves, irrespective of their initial expectation. Once an information cascade starts no new learning occurs in the market because all subsequent issuers blindly follow the herd.

A herding theory for IPO clustering is built on four assumptions. First, issuers have a binary action choice, either go public or stay private. Second, there is a series of potential issuers, all of whom have the same action choice. Third, issuers possess private information regarding the expected payoff from the action. Finally, issuers can observe the actions but not the private information of preceding potential issuers and update their payoff expectation conditional on the action sequence.

The IPO setting fosters many plausible scenarios that could be associated with information cascades and herding. One example, based on Scharfstein and Stein (1990), is an industry characterized by rapidly changing technology. Firms might have to choose between the old reliable technology and the new risky technology. Each firm has an expectation, either positive or negative, for the incremental payoff from the new technology, which can only be financed with an IPO. If a few firms go public because they have a positive expectation, then the remaining private firms revise upwards their beliefs about the new technology. Firms with an initial negative expectation could now view the new technology favorably. If that happens all private firms go public, creating a cluster.

Information cascades might pertain specifically to the new issues market. Nelson (2002) built a model based on the assumption that market conditions are uncertain from the perspective of potential issuers. An IPO will be successful only if the conditions are favorable, but an issuer cannot know this with certainty until the offering is complete. A few successful IPOs are a positive signal for the conditions, inducing more firms to go public. Market conditions evolve over time. Consequently, spillovers from long-past IPOs become stale. The information cascade eventually breaks down as firms base the IPO decision on their own private information, ensuring only temporary clusters.

2.5 INVESTOR DEMAND

The new issues market is two-sided; issuers supply and investors demand shares in new investments. The examination of IPO timing and clustering thus far has focused on the supply side. Investor demand was exogenous and assumed to absorb the supply of shares. Yet market participants frequently assert that issuers can only go public when the IPO window is open, meaning only when investors have an appetite for new issues. A complete explanation for IPO timing patterns requires an understanding of why aggregate investor demand is time-varying.

A simple story for fluctuating demand begins with investors getting excited by the IPOs from a new industry and investing heavily. When the industry or technology does not pan out, investors get burned and swear off IPOs, if only temporarily. This scenario might be appropriate for a few famous circumstances, but it does not account for the subtleties that characterize the IPO market on a day-to-day basis. A true understanding of why demand oscillates requires a deeper examination of how investors behave in the new issues market.

2.5.1 Rational Demand

The ability of investors to observe and learn from past IPOs affects the level of demand for current offerings. Even if no new investors are drawn to the market, spillovers lower the information production cost borne by issuers, enabling more firms to go public. Informational externalities can rationally increase the demand for IPOs for a number of reasons.

Information production: Investors can incur a cost and become informed about an issuer or remain uninformed at no cost. Informational externalities lower the cost barrier to becoming informed about current IPOs. These spillovers increase aggregate demand for two reasons. First, investors who found the cost of evaluating IPOs too high in the past can now enter the market.[16] The most likely beneficiaries of a lower information cost are retail investors who lack the scale and resources of institutional investors.

The second reason, suggested by Hoffmann-Burchardi (2001), is that spillovers reduce the asymmetry of information among investors. Informed investors have an advantage over the uninformed in determining whether an IPO is fairly priced. The uninformed may be reluctant to invest if they believe that the informed are skimming-off all the underpriced IPOs, leaving the overpriced offerings for them. Spillovers reduce the informational disparity between the two groups and lower the adverse selection risk for the uninformed.

Screening: A negative by-product of spillovers is that investors have less incentive to conduct a thorough evaluation of current issuers. Investors already have a good idea about the industry component to the issuer's value and may not want to exert additional effort to learn about the firm-specific properties. Consequently, investors become less diligent in screening out the bad IPOs from the good, thereby increasing aggregate demand because they are less discriminate (Hoffmann-Burchardi 2001). Investor behavior during the Internet hot market is a perfect example. Any company with a dot-com at the end of its name got a free pass to go public. The problem of poor screening is most severe if investors mistakenly attribute the good performance of the first few IPOs in a cluster to the industry characteristics, as opposed to the specific quality of the issuers.

Strategic bidding: Investors who possess positive information about a group of IPOs have a strong incentive to suppress it. Doing so keeps the offer prices low, making the IPOs even more attractive. In addition, uninformed investors do not learn that the IPOs are a good investment, further restraining total demand. Artificially low aggregate demand and offer prices deter more firms from going public. Alti (2003) argued that spillovers eliminate the information asymmetries among investors, increasing both the demand and prices.

Coordination: The reason many investors want to participate in IPOs is the initial return. Receiving an allocation in an Internet IPO was equivalent to being handed free money. In general, IPOs that attract the strongest investor interest also have the highest initial returns. This is due partly to underwriters intentionally leaving money on the table for hot offerings.

Spillovers from past IPOs can act as a coordinating device that increases demand for the current offering (Draho 2001b). Each investor uses the spillover to form a belief about the beliefs of other investors. When the share prices for past IPOs are high, an investor knows that there are at least some other investors who have a high valuation for the industry. This leads the investor to rationally anticipate that the demand for the current IPO will be high and that it will be significantly underpriced. Positive spillovers coordinate investors into buying the latest IPO for the initial return, even if each privately believes that the value is low. Spillovers perpetuate high demand until it is a public fact that the industry value is low and investors cannot form mistaken beliefs about the beliefs of others.

2.5.2 Noise Traders

Investors are not always perfectly rational. There is ample evidence of pricing anomalies and investor decision-making to support this conjecture. Investors succumb to hype and speculation, and trade for reasons that have little economic justification. The surge in demand for IPO shares in a hot market could easily be a consequence of irrational investors trying to get a piece of the action.

The term 'noise traders' is used by economists to described investors who trade based on changes in expectations or sentiment for a stock that are not fully justified by new fundamental information. During the Internet bubble many observers claimed that standard valuation models were not applicable to these companies, without justifying why that should be the case. An increase in demand due to the acceptance of a new 'popular' valuation model is pure noise. Two scenarios describe how noise trading could increase the number of IPOs.

Sentiment: Sentiment amongst noise traders toward a particular industry continually oscillates and along with it the valuations and demand for new issues. The industry can remain overvalued because, as Shleifer and Summers (1990) argued, there are limits to the ability of rational investors to arbitrage away the mis-pricing caused by noise traders. Arbitrage trading can be costly and it may take years before the mis-pricing is corrected. Even rational investors have short time horizons, especially if they are evaluated on a frequent basis. Furthermore, the mis-pricing only leads to arbitrage opportunities in expectation. An arbitrageur faces the real risk that when he wants to liquidate his position the mis-pricing will be more extreme, not less. Of course, all of this assumes that rational investors can identify expected arbitrage opportunities. In sum, increased noise trader demand can drive up share valuations, which makes an IPO more attractive to potential issuers.

Positive feedback: Noise traders often trade on momentum. De Long et al. (1990) suggested that rational investors may find it optimal to adopt a positive feedback trading strategy. Instead of trying to arbitrage the price down, rational investors buy on a price upswing in an attempt to stimulate further noise trader demand, driving the price further above the fundamental value. Rational investors start selling when the price reaches a peak, eventually driving the price back down.

The logic of the positive feedback trading strategy can be applied to the IPO setting. Noise traders are often small retail investors who do not receive preferential allocations in IPOs. Noise trader demand could be stimulated by price momentum in the IPO. Rational institutional investors can increase their demand for IPO shares and pay a price above the intrinsic value if they expect to resell the shares in the aftermarket to noise traders at a higher price (Ljunqvist, Nanda and Singh 2001).

2.6 SUMMARY

The time series data on IPOs reveals the extreme volatility in the new issues market over the past 40 years and the clustering of IPOs at the industry level. IPO timing is determined in part by general macroeconomic trends and the increased demand for capital in periods of expansion. Information effects exert an enormous influence on the timing decision. The collective evidence strongly supports the conjecture that issuers successfully time the market and go public during a temporary window of opportunity of overvaluation. There is relatively little support for the notion that asymmetric information between firm insiders and investors explains the clustering patterns of IPOs. However, asymmetries likely affect when an individual firm decides to go public.

Informational externalities within the new issues market are the most relevant factor for clustering at the industry level. Price information from past IPOs spills over to current and future offerings, affecting the offer price and the decision to go public. Externalities matter because they lower the information costs for future IPOs and allow issuers to update their expectation for the payoff from going public. Investor demand is also affected by externalities, with positive information attracting additional investors to the market. Greater demand means more firms can go public.

NOTES

1. The IPO data are available at http://bear.cba.ufl.edu/ritter/ipoall/htm. Other sources include Ibbotson and Jaffe (1975), Ritter (1984), Aggarwal and Rivoli (1990) and Ibbotson, Sindelar and Ritter (1994). The data exclude Regulation A offerings (small issues, raising less than $1.5 million during the 1980s), real-estate investment trusts (REITs) and closed-end funds. IPO totals from 1988 to 2002 exclude best efforts offerings.
2. Ritter (1984) documented that 99 natural resource companies, mostly penny stocks, went public in the hot market of 1980, producing an average initial return of 110 percent.
3. Surprisingly, Helwege and Liang (2004) found that the IPO firms' M/B ratios were not different between hot and cold markets. It may be that all firms are priced optimistically in a hot market, not just IPOs. The high M/B ratio for cold market IPOs could reflect a selection bias that only good firms are able to complete an offering.
4. Re-printed from the *Journal of Financial Economics*, Vol. 35, Lerner, J., "Venture Capitalists and the Decision to Go Public," pp. 291-316, Copyright (1994), with permission from Elsevier.
5. Chapter 13 provides an extensive discussion of the long-run performance of IPOs.
6. Lowry (2003) found no significant relation between abnormal IPO returns and volume.
7. Benninga, Helmantel and Sarig (2004) develop a similar timing model for the going-pubic decision. The model incorporates changing private control benefits and cash flows, but does not value the option of waiting.
8. The timing option value increases in the volatility of the industry prices, implying that clustering patterns are likely to be more extreme in high growth industries like biotechnology and technology.
9. See Asquith and Mullins (1986), Masulis and Korwar (1986) and Mikkelson and Partch (1986).
10. Other factors could account for the price decline, including a lower leverage ratio, transaction costs, agency costs from free cash flow and a downward sloping demand curves. None of these factors is likely to be significant.
11. In Myers and Majluf (1984) the information asymmetry over old assets resulted in underinvestment and a negative announcement CAR when overvalued firms issued equity.
12. For the early part of the sample the initial return is calculated as the percentage increase from the offer price to a closing price within the first month of trading.
13. A discussion of why that is the case is left for Chapter 10.
14. The proceeds revision is calculated as the percentage change in the preliminary expected proceeds – the preliminary offer price times the expected number of shares – to the final gross proceeds.
15. The model assumes that there are barriers to entry in underwriting and an investment bank can use its position to enforce a more equitable sharing of information costs.
16. Even with underpricing as compensation, not all investors will find it worthwhile to become informed. Investors differ in their production cost, but the compensation is equal across investors. High cost investors will still find it prohibitive to participate.

3 Financing options and costs

Gaining access to a large pool of cheap capital is the most frequently cited reason why firms go public. There is no denying that public equity markets are a very useful and attractive source of capital. It would be a mistake, however, to presume that public equity is unequivocally superior to alternative financing options. Circumstances do arise in which private equity or bank lending are preferable substitutes for the public market. This chapter focuses on the properties of the primary financing options to determine when and why firms have a financial motive for going public.

The natural alternative to a public offering is private equity. The two options can be evaluated on a cost basis, taking into account the direct selling expenses, the burden placed on management and the expected return demanded by investors. The rates of return for public equity are well documented. Extensive analysis of private equity returns has only recently been conducted, primarily for venture capital and buyout funds. Nonetheless, the estimates enable a comparison between the costs of public and private equity.

Debt is an altogether different financing option. Regular interest payments impose constraints on a firm, but debt does have the virtue of not diluting the ownership position of the controlling shareholders. A firm's characteristics determine whether debt is even a feasible option, which is a very real concern for risky start-ups. A caveat to any conclusions drawn about the use of debt by private companies is that a reliance on bank lending is not independent of the types of firms seeking external capital. Germany, for instance, has relied heavily on universal banks, not capital markets, to finance business activity. Consequently, the industrial make-up of the German economy is biased towards companies that would find bank debt an attractive option.

3.1 COST OF EQUITY CAPITAL

Proponents of public equity tout its virtues as a cheap source of capital. Reality is more complex than this broad conjecture implies. The price of public equity is best defined in relative terms, with private equity being the benchmark alternative. In aggregate, equity is cheaper when it is supplied by public sources, but this does not apply universally to all firms. Breaking down the cost of equity into its component parts reveals when and why public equity is cheaper.

3.1.1 Direct Financing Costs

The sale of both public and private equity results in direct out-of-pocket expenses incurred at the offering and beyond for the issuer. The direct costs take three general forms, discussed below, and increase in the size and complexity of the offering. Table 3.1 lists the costs and their approximate range for an IPO. Based on the numbers in the table a typical $100 million IPO with 10 million shares listed on the NASDAQ would involve total direct costs between $8.4 and $8.8 million. All of the individual costs are either avoided or smaller if equity is sold privately. The savings will be especially great for smaller offer sizes because of the fixed nature of some of the costs.

Advisory counsel: The compensation paid to lawyers, auditors and investment bankers will be higher for an IPO than a private placement. An IPO is more complex; it involves interaction with the SEC and state securities agencies, changing the firm's legal incorporation and applying to a stock market for a listing. Auditors and investment banks are exposed to greater legal liability in a public offering, adding to their cost. A company should be able to save at least a few hundred thousand dollars on legal and accounting fees by selling equity privately. The biggest potential saving comes from avoiding the underwriting spread, $7 million in the example above. An investment bank may be retained to place equity privately, but the percentage fee is considerably smaller. The advisory costs continue to be high after the IPO. Public companies regularly file earnings reports and other disclosures with the SEC, adding to the auditing and legal expenses.

Filing and listing fees: Firms must pay a fee to the SEC, the National Association of Securities Dealers (NASD) and to state regulators to satisfy Blue Sky laws when they go public. All three fees, totaling $50,000 in the example, are avoided with private equity. The same holds true for the listing fee required by the desired stock market, ranging anywhere from a minimum of $150,000 for the NASDAQ to a maximum of $250,000 for the New York Stock Exchange (NYSE). Much of the $200,000 printing cost is avoided with a private placement. Public companies continue to pay annual fees to remain listed on the stock market and to the SEC to fund various regulatory agencies.

Table 3.1 Advisory and listing fees

Cost type	Range
Legal	$600,000 – $800,000
Accounting	$400,000 – $600,000
Underwriting spread	Typically 7%
Printing	$150,000 – $200,000
Blue sky[a]	$10,000
Transfer agent/registrar	$5,000
Miscellaneous	$60,000
SEC filing fee	$278 per $1 million of the aggregate offering amount
NASD fee	$500, plus .01% of the aggregate offering amount. The maximum fee is $30,500.
NASDAQ National Market	$100,000 for < 30 m shares $125,000 for 30+ up to 50 m shares $150,000 for > 50 shares
NYSE	$150,000 minimum, $250,000 maximum, increasing with the number of shares

a. Blue Sky laws are state laws equivalent to the SEC regulations. Issuers must apply to all states in which shares are offered.

Source: PriceWaterhouseCoopers, the NASDAQ and the NYSE.

Corporate resources: Greater corporate resources are devoted to supporting public equity. Preparations for an IPO and the selling process are time consuming and begin several months prior to the offer date. The road show alone occupies senior management for a couple of weeks, time that could be spent managing and growing the company. The additional demands on management continue after the IPO. The CEO must speak regularly with analysts and institutional investors, providing updates and comments on the company's progress. The costs of operating an external investor relations program, pricing and mailing annual reports to shareholders and establishing an independent audit committee, among other costs, are not incurred by private firms.

3.1.2 Market Imperfections

The pure cost of equity capital is the expected return demanded by investors for holding the security. Asset pricing models, such as the capital asset pricing model (CAPM), determine the expected return by pricing the relevant risk factors. The price of equity is the same in public and private markets if there are no imperfections or frictions in the economy. Of course, that condition does not hold in practice. The further a market deviates in one or more directions from the perfect world, the higher the cost of equity. Stronger frictions are generally present in private markets, providing cost savings to public equity.

3.1.2.1 Marketability

The marketability of a stock is defined as the fraction of all investors who are aware of it and know its risk-return properties. Merton (1987) demonstrated using the CAPM model that a stock's expected return is inversely related to its marketability. Inefficient portfolio diversification occurs when only a subset of all investors is aware of each stock. The resulting inefficient risk-sharing drives up the expected return. The marginal benefit to a firm from increasing its informed investor base is highest when there are few current knowledgeable investors.

From a marketing perspective, private firms would get a big boost by going public. The IPO is a major publicized event, which by itself would lower the cost of capital. However, one should not presume that a public listing is a panacea to a private firm's marketability problem. A majority of the approximately 12,000 public companies in the US are not covered by analysts; instead they languish in relative anonymity. The consequence of being part of this 'orphaned' class can be severe. A study conducted by Merrill Lynch examined 1,900 technology sector stocks starting in 1985.[1] Only 3.4 percent of stocks whose price had fallen to single digits rebounded to $15 or higher within the next year, and most never did. The small private firms likely to fall into this class could find the marketability benefit of a public offering more illusory than real.

3.1.2.2 Liquidity

Investors pay a premium for liquidity in the secondary market for assets. Two criteria can be used to measure a stock's liquidity. First, the price of a liquid asset is not very responsive to either buy or sell trades. An investor is able to transact a large position in a liquid market without adversely affecting the price. Second, a liquid market is populated with a large number of investors willing to take the other side of a buy or sell transaction. Investors do not have to wait for the arrival of a trading partner.

Standard asset pricing models assume that investors incur no transaction costs when trading, which is equivalent to assuming perfectly liquid markets. One real cost of trading is the bid–ask spread. Liquidity and the spread should be inversely related as market makers and traders bear less inventory risk in thick markets. Amihud and Mendelson (1986) derived theoretically a positive relationship between the expected return and the spread, and thus a negative relation between liquidity and returns. Empirical analysis has confirmed the predicted spread–return relationship.

There is little doubt that public markets are far more liquid than private ones. Shares in a public company are traded on organized exchanges, with observable and continuously updated prices. Relatively few investors participate in the private equity market and blocks of shares are bought and sold only sporadically. An IPO will lower a firm's cost of equity by increasing the liquidity. The best estimates for the incremental cost of illiquidity in the private equity market range from 7 to 14 percent of firm value (Hertzel and Smith 1993; Bajaj et al. 2003a).[2] This is equivalent to the equity costing roughly 7.5 to 15 percent higher in the private market.

3.1.2.3 Spanning and segmentation

The expected return for a security is a function of the undiversifiable risk factors. While there is an ongoing debate as to what those factors are and how to price them, there is agreement that diversifiable risk should not be priced. Theoretically this is equivalent to the non-systemic risk in a security's payoff being completely 'spanned' by the payoff profile of all other assets. Practically speaking, an investor can form a portfolio of existing securities that has the exact same payoff profile in all possible circumstances as the asset under question. If this condition is violated, then the idiosyncratic risk should be priced into the expected return. Start-up firms engaged in new technologies or products may well have risk-return characteristics that violate the spanning condition.

The combination of incomplete spanning and market segmentation – unequal investor access to different markets – was shown by Mauer and Senbet (1992) to produce higher expected returns for private equity. The private equity market is segmented from the public market since most retail investors cannot access it.[3] Segmentation drives up the expected return because it results in inefficient risk sharing in the private market. This would not matter if the asset's payoff was spanned because private equity investors could shed all idiosyncratic risk. When the spanning condition is violated private investors demand a higher return to compensate for the residual risk.[4] Firms in new industries with no close risk substitutes and shorter operating histories would receive the greatest cost reduction by going public.

3.1.2.4 Portfolio diversification

Private firms tend to have concentrated ownership, often with the founding entrepreneur holding a significant stake. The founder and other early investors are likely to hold a disproportionately large fraction of their investment portfolios in the firm's equity. The lack of diversification increases their portfolio risk and hence the expected return demanded from the assets. The founder can diversify his portfolio by taking the firm public. The firm's cost of equity immediately falls because the founder's required return decreases and he substitutes his costly capital with cheaper market capital. The conclusion does hinge on the presence of market imperfections. The founder must be constrained from effectively diversifying his portfolio while the firm is private.

The best available evidence does not provide much support for a pure portfolio diversification motive for going public. Helwege and Packer (2001) examined private firms that had issued public debt and had produced publicly available financial data prior to the IPO. They found little evidence that the diversification motive was a factor in the IPO decision for family-controlled firms. Pagano, Panetta and Zingales (1998) reported similar evidence for a sample of Italian IPOs. The initial owners divested on average only 6 percent of their pre-IPO stake at the offering and 1.3 percent more over the next three years. The sample was biased towards older – median firm age at the IPO was 26 years – and family-controlled firms, the very issuers that would be expected to benefit most from diversification.

The high cost of private equity could be due to inefficient diversification among the suppliers of capital (Jones and Rhodes-Kropf 2003). Venture capitalists (VCs) specialize in identifying start-up investment opportunities, with diversified limited partners supplying the bulk of the capital. To alleviate the limited partners concerns over the VCs' effort, the VCs' compensation must be tied closely to the performance of the portfolio companies. Venture capitalists only invest in a small number of firms to ensure that they can maximize returns. But doing so exposes them to idiosyncratic risk. As a result, the VCs demand higher returns than do the limited partners. The cost of VC-supplied equity is consequently greater than that for capital supplied directly by the market in an IPO.

3.1.3 Contracting Costs

Imperfections in the capital market extend over to the contracting market, adding to the cost of equity. Investors and firms are never perfectly informed about each other's existence and willingness to transact. Information constraints impact the negotiations over the supply and cost of capital, with differing effects in the public and private markets. Furthermore, the continuation of information problems post-contracting – investors cannot perfectly observe the managerial effort and how the funds are used – are rationally anticipated *ex ante* and affect the contract terms.

3.1.3.1 Information

The price of external equity is determined by bargaining between investors and issuers. Information affects the final price for two reasons. First, gathering the necessary information about the issuer is costly for investors, who will demand compensation in return. Second, bargaining over the price is a zero-sum game; one side benefits at the expense of the other. Consequently, both sides try to exploit their private information to drive the terms in their favor. Three information issues are relevant to the cost of equity. Although no definitive conclusions can be drawn about the optimality of public or private equity from an information perspective, each issuer will have a preference based on their unique situation.

Information production: Readily available public information about private companies is rare. This forces investors to devote time and money to gathering and evaluating information about a firm prior to investing. If the cost of producing this information is ultimately borne by the issuer in the form of a lower offer price, then the choice between an IPO and a private placement is impacted. A private sale to a single large investor would be optimal because the information gathering costs are only incurred once (Chemmanur and Fulghieri 1999). An IPO targeted to many investors, each duplicating the production and collection of information, is more costly.[5]

The relative cost advantage of private equity is conditional on the issuer characteristics. The production cost should decline as a firm ages because more relevant information becomes publicly available over time, increasing the probability of an IPO. The cost should be higher in industries with hard to value products and technology. Information spillovers from previous IPOs also decrease the cost. Industry-specific IPO clusters are partly due to later issuers free-riding on the information produced by early IPOs. The reduced cost makes a public equity offering more attractive.

Information revelation: Informed investors can bargain from a position of strength. They know how much they are willing to pay for the shares, whereas the issuer does not. Investors have every incentive to understate their interest, drive the offer price down and earn an excess return. Issuers want to minimize this form of underpricing as much as possible. Public and private selling mechanisms offer two distinct ways to achieve this objective.

The primary advantage of a public offering is that it restores some of the issuer's bargaining power vis-à-vis investors by pitting them against each other (Maksimovic and Pichler 1999). The key for the issuer is to make an investor's share allocation contingent on the price he is willing to pay. Discriminating against investors who suggest a low price by allocating all the shares to high-price investors induces truthful revelation of investors' private valuations. This strategy enables the issuer to minimize, although not eliminate, the underpricing caused by private information. Private equity is targeted to only a handful of investors, which is insufficient to credibly deny an allocation if the suggested price is low.

Asymmetric information: Managers of private companies possess far superior information about the firm's true value relative to potential investors. Information asymmetries of this sort increase the cost of capital for an issuer because the private information cannot be credibly announced to investors. Investors provide capital at terms based on the expected firm value; undervalued good firms end up paying too high a price, whereas overvalued low quality firms can issue cheap equity. One of two things could happen in response. Good firms could pull out of the equity market entirely, a potentially high cost in itself, which forces the price up for the remaining low quality firms. Alternatively, good firms can incur a cost to convey their information to investors.

A private placement would be optimal if a single large investor could conduct a thorough due diligence review of the issuer to uncover the private information. The issuer would only have to bear the information production cost once. A similar level of due diligence by IPO investors would be prohibitively expensive. In lieu of the due diligence the issuer could try to signal the private information in an IPO through a number of methods. Insiders could retain a large fraction of the shares (Leland and Pyle 1977), hire a reputable investment bank (Booth and Smith 1986) or underprice the offering more than normal (Welch 1989). Any signaling will be costly, but worthwhile if the price of equity falls enough to offset it. It is not obvious whether the asymmetric information cost favors public or private equity.

3.1.3.2 Control and monitoring

The separation between the ownership and the day-to-day control of a company that is a consequence of accessing external equity engenders agency costs. Owner-managers have objectives that need not be perfectly aligned with the value-maximizing priority of investors. Managers may shirk on the costly effort they must put forth, pursue value-decreasing acquisitions in an attempt to build an empire or excessively consume private control benefits. Investors should rationally anticipate such managerial behavior at the initial contracting stage and demand financing terms that recognize this cost.

Designing an organizational structure that efficiently deals with agency conflicts has been a subject of ongoing research. The choice between public and private equity certainly fits within this realm. Public ownership involves a dispersed group of small shareholders. Private firms, in contrast, are dominated by a few concentrated shareholders. These two governance structures offer very distinct ways of minimizing agency costs. A thorough analysis of this topic is taken up in Chapter 5, although no conclusive evidence suggests the superiority of either ownership structure.

3.1.4 Assessment

The frequent claim that public equity is a cheap source of capital has some merit. However, as the review of the equity cost components reveals, the cost savings from public equity can be minimal compared to the private market. A public listing entails far higher direct expenses at the IPO and beyond. Since most of these costs are fixed, they can deter IPOs from smaller firms, negating the pure cost of capital savings emanating from the public market. Even the advantage of shares traded on a liquid public market may be less than it seems. Many issuers remain relatively anonymous after their brief day in the sun at the IPO. Poor liquidity and marketability drive valuations down, making these firms a target for a takeover or subject to price manipulation. Firms that have a reasonable expectation of becoming a solid public company will indeed find that an IPO provides them with cheaper equity. Other firms should think long and hard about whether an IPO confers sufficient other benefits because the cost advantage may not exist.

3.2 PRIVATE EQUITY

Private equity is a broad term that covers multiple types of financing: venture capital, buyout firms, angel investors, and families and friends. These options vary in their importance in the public versus private ownership decision. Venture capital (VC) is synonymous with the going-public process.[6] Close to 50 percent of all operating company IPOs in the late 1990s received some VC backing. However, VC finance is not a substitute for public equity, but rather a complementary stage in the financing of a firm. Buyout firms are similar in structure to VC firms, but differ in purpose because they take public firms private, often with the long-term goal of taking these same firms public again. The remaining sources of private equity are mainly confined to small businesses that do not have the option of going public at the time of financing, although wealthy individuals and families do own or purchase large companies.

The significance of VC and buyout firms on the dynamics of public ownership warrants further attention. In particular, the cost and returns of equity supplied by these two types of firms provide a quantitative measure of the relative advantage of private ownership. To fully appreciate the returns to this form of private equity, a review of the basic structure of the firms and the investments is necessary.

3.2.1 Structure

Actual VC and buyout firms consist of relatively few people; the partners and staff who oversee the investment process and portfolio companies. The typical fund is structured as a partnership with the firm as the general partner (GP) and investors as limited partners (LP). A single firm can have multiple funds, although there is usually a lag of at least a few years between the start of new funds. The GP contributes a small fraction of the fund's capital, about 1 percent, with the rest supplied by the LPs. Table 3.2 lists the largest suppliers of capital to VC and buyout funds, and the percentage of the total capital supplied by each group for the years 1998 to 2002. Buyout funds are larger on average, $263 million under management compared to $50 million for VC funds, as of 2000 (Venture Economics Database). More capital is required to purchase a public firm in its entirety than to make a small investment in a start-up. Most funds possess the following general properties.

Duration: Funds are established with the specific intent of lasting a finite amount of time. The majority of funds have a ten-year horizon before they are closed down, with an option to extend the fund for a few extra years. Limiting the duration of the fund serves two purposes. First, the LPs cannot easily liquidate their contracted position in the fund, nor do they receive a regular stream of income. Capping the fund life at ten years ensures that the investors get some of their investment back within finite time. Second, the finite horizon focuses the GP on generating positive returns on the fund's investment in a short period of time. From the moment an investment is made the GP is looking for an exit event to cash out. Without a fixed deadline the GP may be unwilling to terminate bad investments on the hope they will eventually turn around.

Table 3.2 US private equity funding by type of investor (%)

Investor type	1999	2000	2001	2002
Venture capital funds				
Pension funds	43.5	40.1	41.7	42.2
Endowments and foundations	17.2	21.1	21.8	20.9
Financial and insurance companies	15.5	23.3	24.5	25.5
Private individuals and families	9.6	11.8	9.4	9.1
Corporations (non-employee benefit)	14.2	3.7	2.6	2.3
Buyout funds				
Pension funds	56.5	59.7	60.1	60.6
Endowments and foundations	11.8	13.3	13.5	12.1
Financial and insurance companies	19.4	14.1	15.7	17.6
Private individuals and families	8.0	11.1	9.6	8.8
Corporations (non-employee benefit)	4.3	1.8	1.1	0.9

Source: Thomson Venture Economics/NVCA.

Closed fund: After starting a new fund the GP canvasses investors to determine who would like to be a partner and how much they will invest. The fund is closed to new investors once the target fund size has been reached. The committed capital is not contributed immediately. The GP instead makes periodic capital calls when funds for new investment are needed, gradually drawing down the capital supply. Ljungqvist and Richardson (2003) reported that it took six years to invest 90 percent of the committed capital in the average fund. The proceeds from the sale of portfolio company assets are distributed as they are received.

Compensation: The GP receives an annual fee of 1 to 2 percent of the assets under management. The LPs receive their principal investment back before any of the capital gains are distributed to the partners. The GP usually receives 20 percent of the capital gain, which is called the carried interest, and the rest is split among the LPs. Cash that is received from the sale of assets is distributed to the partners, as is the stock in a portfolio company that goes public. The payoff to the GP fits the profile of a call option, creating an incentive to invest in riskier projects. However, this is partly negated by compensation contracts that involve significant penalties for investment failures.

3.2.2 Investment Strategy

The success of VC and buyout funds is predicated on investing in the right portfolio companies, obtaining favorable financing terms and guiding the companies towards superior performance. An efficient investment strategy is an important part of this process.

Buyout funds purchase public firms, subsidiaries of public firms and private firms in their entirety, often with a significant stake for existing firm management. The general investment philosophy is to purchase firms that are undervalued and have substantial room for operating improvement. The firm is then restructured by selling off assets and concentrating on core activities. The transaction is financed with a high degree of leverage, which helps to focus management on wringing out maximum value. The portfolio companies are taken back public or sold to a third firm so the buyout fund can cash out on the investment.

Venture capital firms have an altogether different method of investing. They identify promising start-ups that have the potential to grow into highly profitable dominant firms within rapidly emerging industries. The disbursement of capital to portfolio companies is designed to nurture their growth, while simultaneously confronting the challenges of investing in risky unproven firms and management. Two properties of VC funding have emerged as optimal responses to the financing challenges.

3.2.2.1 Staging

Capital supplied by VCs to their portfolio companies arrives in stages, which are categorized into four rough groups: seed/start-up, early, expansion and late stage. The stages are frequently labeled Series A, Series B and so on, to correspond with the order of financing rounds. Seed financing provides capital to entrepreneurs exploring an initial concept or idea for a product. Early stage capital allows the company to develop a prototype and begin production. Funding to increase marketing and production is provided in the expansion stage. A successful start-up that is preparing to go public would receive late stage financing to tie it over until the IPO proceeds are received. Table 3.3 lists the percentage of total VC outlays that went to each of the stages for the years 1998 to 2002. Staging is one way for VCs to retain some control over the direction of the company. A deeper examination of why this is true is found in Chapter 5.

Three patterns to staged financing found in a sample examined by Gompers and Lerner (1998) hold generally across most VC investments. First, the typical portfolio company received two to three rounds of

Table 3.3 Venture capital disbursements by stage of investment (%)

Stage	1998	1999	2000	2001	2002
Start-up/Seed	8.6	6.1	2.9	2.0	1.5
Early	25.4	22.1	24.7	22.4	19.3
Expansion	50.3	55.8	57.2	57.2	62.1
Late	15.6	16.0	15.2	18.4	17.1

Source: PriceWaterhouseCoopers/Thomson Venture Economics/National Venture Capital Association MoneyTree™ Survey.

financing and this average increased over time. The number of rounds was higher if the firm eventually went public and lower if it went bankrupt or was acquired. Second, the average duration between financing rounds was about a year. The length of time between the seed and early stages was longer – about a year and a half – and slightly shorter at about nine to ten months between subsequent rounds. Third, the average round raised between $5 and $10 million. The average was highest for firms that eventually went public and for later rounds. Venture capitalists supply more funds once it becomes clear that a company will be successful.

3.2.2.2 Syndication

A common practice among VCs is to syndicate investments. Multiple VC funds provide the capital supplied to the company during each round of financing. There are a number of benefits to syndication. More capital is supplied and each VC takes on a smaller amount of risk. Consensus among a group of VCs that a company is worthy of investment improves decision making by providing reassurances to each individual VC that his or her assessment of the quality is correct (Sah and Stiglitz 1986). Venture capitalists may also demand that the early rounds be syndicated to provide some guarantee that other investors have an incentive to fund later rounds. The value of an investment often depends on the willingness of other investors to jump on the bandwagon.

Syndicating later financing rounds may be necessary to avoid the appearance of opportunistic behavior (Admati and Pfleiderer 1994). Venture capitalists that fund early rounds have superior knowledge about the company's true value after working closely with management. They have an incentive to overstate the value to late round investors to raise cheap capital and not dilute their stake. The VC must retain a constant equity stake and buy into any new financing round to signal this is not the case. Later rounds could also be syndicated in an attempt by VCs to 'window dress' their funds (Lakonishok et al. 1991). The VCs contribute a small amount in a later financing round because they can then claim in their promotional materials that they invested in companies that have gone public and were successful. This gives a false impression of how well their fund performed.

3.2.3 Cost of Capital

The cost of equity for a start-up firm can be interpreted from two different perspectives. To an entrepreneur the cost might be best measured by the fraction of the total equity he must give up to get the necessary capital. The cost and the fraction increase in tandem. The alternative cost of capital measure is the expected or required return demanded by investors. Realized returns can proxy for the expected returns, which are determined by the risk properties of the investment and the necessary GP compensation for providing monitoring and advisory services to the portfolio company.

3.2.3.1 Discount rates

Deciding whether to invest in a start-up company necessitates a comparison between the required return and the expected payoff from the investment. Estimating a required return using standard asset pricing models is difficult because there is no observable share price, the investment is illiquid and early stage firms have a high failure rate. Instead the required returns, or discount rates, used by VCs are often educated guesses. Sahlman (1990) reported that discount rates near 60 to 70 percent are applied at early stages, dropping down to about 25 percent for late stages. Smith and Smith (2000) surveyed a large number of studies and found discount rates in the range of 35 to 50 percent were usually applied.

Caution must be exercised when interpreting what these reported discount rates mean. They are best thought of as the returns desired by LPs and GPs, even if it is known that actual returns will be lower. Buyout firms have it a little easier because many of their investments involve public companies or their subsidiaries, which produce data far more amenable to estimating a required return.

Standard investment theory evaluates projects based on net present value calculations. Expected future cash flows are discounted at the expected rate of return and investment proceeds if the NPV is positive. Private equity investors – VCs in particular – generally do no evaluate investments using NPV. The two most common performance measures used are exit multiples and internal rates of return (IRR). An exit multiple is the ratio of the cash generated by the exit event over the initial capital investment. For example, an investment of $1 million that grows into $3 million in five years produces an exit multiple of three. A GP might set a criteria that a certain exit multiple must be achieved within a specified time horizon before investing.

An IRR can be computed from the exit multiple. The IRR equals the discount rate that, when plugged into the NPV formula, produces a NPV of zero. Using the numbers above, a $1 investment that turns into $3 in five years generates an annual IRR of approximately 25 percent. The IRR is then compared to the required return and investment proceeds if it is higher.

3.2.3.2 Valuations

The terms of investment that implicitly determine the returns received by VCs depend on the pre- and post-money valuations. The pre-money valuation is the firm value estimated prior to the infusion of cash from a new financing round. This value equals the number of outstanding shares before the financing round times the share offer price. The post-money valuation equals the pre-money value plus the financing round. Assuming a fixed amount for the financing round, the cost of equity is inversely related to the pre-money value. As the firm value increases a smaller stake of the total equity must be sold to raise the capital. Similarly, a VC's rate of return on an investment declines with the pre-money value, assuming a fixed exit value.

A private firm that wants to raise a financing round can approach multiple VCs. Each VC estimates a pre-money valuation and the size of the equity stake demanded is specified in the term sheet presented to the entrepreneur. Negotiation between the entrepreneur and VC is possible, but VCs usually have most of the bargaining power. In many situations the offer is take it or leave it. Firms sometimes receive multiple financing offers, in which case they have a choice. Hsu (2003) found that firms frequently selected a VC that did not offer the best financing terms. They instead preferred to be affiliated with a highly reputable VC and were willing to pay for it. Reputable VCs were able to acquire start-up equity at a 10 to 14 percent discount relative to less prestigious VCs.

3.2.3.3 Rates of return

Calculating the returns to private equity is a difficult task. Access to comprehensive and accurate data presents the first serious challenge. Private equity investors are not required to disclose their investments, nor are there continuously observable prices. Two companies, Venture

Economics and VentureOne, compile detailed information on the investments made by private equity funds and their portfolio companies, all of which is voluntarily self-reported. The partnerships report IRRs for their funds on a quarterly and annual basis.

There are a number of drawbacks to relying too heavily on IRR to measure investment performance. Investments in portfolio companies that have not been exited must be valued, either at book value, marked-to-market or assigned a value of zero until exit. The subjectivity involved in estimating the value of outstanding investments means that IRRs reported to Venture Economics only approximate the true returns generated by the fund to that point. Simple IRR calculations do not take into account the time value of money. Funds disburse committed capital gradually over the first few years and start to receive cash inflows long before the fund is closed. Returns should be calculated only over the time when cash is committed to investments, but some IRR estimates fail to make this adjustment. Lastly, IRR can give a misleading impression of how the fund performed. For example, a $100 investment that returns $300 in one year has an IRR of 300 percent. But few investors would choose this option over a $10,000 investment that returns $13,000 over the same period.

A small but growing body of research has tried to estimate the returns to private equity. These studies vary in their access to data and measurement techniques, but collectively provide a fairly thorough picture of private equity returns. The main results from six separate studies are presented below.[7]

Venture capital: Kaplan and Schoar (2003) analyzed 580 VC funds started from 1980 to 1994 using data supplied by Venture Economics. The mean (median) equal-weighted annualized fund IRR was 17 (11) percent and the size-weighted IRRs were 17 (13) percent. A frequently cited performance measure is the public market equivalent (PME) – the ratio of the discounted value of all fund cash inflows to outflows (net of all fees), with the total return to the S&P 500 used as the discount rate. A PME above one means the fund outperformed the S&P 500. The mean (median) equal- and size-weighted fund PMEs were 0.96 (0.66) and 1.21 (0.92), respectively. Individual fund IRRs also exhibited considerable variability. A quarter of all IRRs were below 3 percent and another quarter exceeded 22 percent.

Jones and Rhodes-Kropf (2003) reported similar returns for 866 funds started from 1980 to 1999 using data again supplied by Venture Economics. The mean equal- and size-weighted IRRs were 19.25 and 19.31 percent, respectively. Ljungqvist and Richardson (2003) reported an average IRR of 14 percent based on explicit cash flow data provided by an LP for 19 funds started from 1981 to 1993.

Buyout funds: Kaplan and Schoar (2003) examined 166 buyout funds and reported identical mean (median) equal- and size-weighted IRRs of 18 (13) percent. The respective PMEs were 0.97 (9.80) and 0.93 (0.83). Individual fund IRRs again exhibited considerable volatility, but unlike the VC IRRs the buyout IRRs had low correlation with the market indexes. Jones and Rhodes-Kropf (2003) reported much smaller buyout returns for their 379 funds. The mean equal- and size-weighted IRRs were 9.67 and 4.57 percent. The mean IRR in the Ljungqvist and Richardson (2003) sample of 54 funds was 21.8 percent.

A simple comparison between buyout IRRs and market returns can be misleading. Returns should be compared on a risk-adjusted basis. The risk of a stock increases in the firm's leverage ratio, thereby increasing the expected return. The portfolio companies in a buyout fund typically have leverage ratios around 70 percent, about twice the ratio for the public market as a whole. Ljungqvist and Richardson estimated that the 5.5 percent return premium earned by buyout funds over the S&P 500 would be zero on a risk-adjusted basis if the portfolio companies had had debt–equity ratios of 2:1.[8]

Staging: The returns to early stage investments are higher than late round VC financing. Das, Jagannathan and Sarin (2002) compared three stages: early, expansion and late. The expected annual return to early stage investments was estimated to be about 50 percent, gross of all GP fees, assuming an investment-to-exit period of four years. A three-year investment at the expansion stage was expected to yield an annual return of 26 percent. Finally, the expected return for a one-year late stage investment was 12 percent. The return pattern is consistent with declining risk over the stages. The late stage return is comparable to the S&P 500 return.[9]

Flow of funds: Portfolio company values were positively related to the amount of money flowing into funds, resulting from 'too much money chasing too few deals'. Gompers and Lerner (2000) estimated that a doubling of the amount capital inflows was related to a 7 to 21 percent increase in company valuations. This mechanically lowers the realized returns by about 15 percent, assuming a constant exit value. Ljungqvist and Richardson (2003) similarly found that the more money raised by all funds in a given fund's vintage year – the year of the funds inception – the worse the fund subsequently performed. Kaplan and Schoar (2003) showed that the number of new funds started in a given year adversely affected the returns to new VC funds, but not the existing funds. The number of new funds harmed all buyout funds, regardless of age.

Kaplan and Schoar reported that new funds and partnerships were more likely to be started when the industry had performed well. These new partnerships were less likely to raise a follow-on fund, suggesting that the first fund had done poorly. The increase of capital flowing into private equity during flush markets went to the new partnerships that produced poor returns, not to the established funds. In fact, Kaplan and Schoar found that the decline in industry returns was due primarily to the new funds.

Persistence: Kaplan and Schoar (2003) documented that firms that had a successful fund were more likely to have success with a new fund, and vice versa for partnerships with a poorly performing fund. The persistence in the performance was partly attributable to the successful firms limiting the size of their new funds, allowing them to select only the best possible investments. Another factor was that the more reputable firms had access to the best investment opportunities at favorable financing terms.

The evidence on private equity returns is a bit surprising. The returns are not noticeably greater than public equity returns on a risk-adjusted basis, and may even be smaller. This despite the fact that private equity is much less liquid and marketable.[10] General partners do earn higher returns, but that is partly compensation for their lack of diversification and the services they provide. Given the empirical challenge of measuring private equity returns, more work needs to be done before any definitive conclusions can be drawn about private equity as an asset class.

Also noteworthy is the wide dispersion in fund returns, which are much greater than the variation in mutual fund performance. This would indicate widely divergent skill levels among GPs in their ability to successfully select and monitor investments. Another possibility is that the private equity market is still highly inefficient because of poor information about investment opportunities and potential capital providers. Some VCs may exploit this inefficiency, perhaps to the detriment of others.

3.3 DEBT FINANCING

External financing options fall into either one of two broad groups: equity- or debt-linked securities. Debt contracts provide the borrower with credit in return for regular repayment and seniority in the event of financial distress. The choice of debt over equity is not equivalent to choosing private versus public ownership because equity could be held privately. Nevertheless, the decision to rely heavily on debt is a conscious choice to avoid equity, thereby minimizing the chance of a public listing.

Analyzing the role of debt in the going-public decision must begin by contrasting the economic implications of debt and equity contracts. Whether it is bank lending or bonds, debt possesses unique costs and benefits that make an IPO more and less likely. The relative disadvantages of debt depend on a firm's circumstances. The burden of regular interest payments is too great for high-risk start-ups that generate little positive cash flow. At the other extreme, mature firms with stable profits and few growth opportunities could benefit from more leverage. The debt/equity choices made by a firm are dependent on the type and quality of external financial markets. Economies that rely heavily on large universal banks predispose private firms towards bank financing and away from public equity.

3.3.1 Debt versus Equity

Debt and equity are fundamentally different securities. Shareholders own the firm and have residual cash flow rights, but do not have the contractual right to a regular dividend. The firm – implicitly the shareholders – is obligated to pay debtholders a reoccurring fixed interest installment or else relinquish control in the event of default. The manager of a private firm must decide which contract is best suited for his or her company. Once the decision has been made to issue equity, a comparison between the public and private market can ensue.

A number of factors affect the security choice and those that favor equity are implicit financial motives for going public. High-risk start-ups with meager cash flows are effectively prevented from issuing debt because the threat of default is too great. The rise of venture capital is a market response to the failure of banks to lend sufficiently to firms in unproven industries that require intensive research and development (R&D) efforts. Debt does have the advantage of not diluting the ownership stake of the founder, who can continue to consume private control benefits provided that the debt obligations are met. Debt finance also has a tax advantage over equity in the US and is the cheaper source of capital on an expected return basis. Three additional theories tout the advantages of equity finance for young private firms, providing a rationale for going public.

Debt overhang: A firm's value is the sum of the existing assets-in-place and the option value of future investments. The value of future investment is only realized if the options are exercised. Myers (1977) argued that too much debt creates a disincentive to exercise the options because the debtholders share in the upside. The payoff to equity resembles a call option; shareholders receive nothing until the debt is paid off and then claim every additional dollar in profits. A high debt level means that lenders take a large fraction of any investment payoff, which raises the exercise price for the investment and lowers the option value for shareholders. Consequently, the firm will forego valuable investment opportunities when it has too much debt. The cost of debt overhang will be especially large for high-growth firms with multiple investment options. Equity finance not only allows the firm to grow, it also maximizes the firm value.

Diversity of opinion: Investors frequently disagree about the profit potential of firms in new industries. Some investors are optimistic, while others are pessimistic. Allen and Gale (1999) argued that equity markets are superior to banks at financing investment when the diversity of opinion about the payoff is high. Equity investors decide individually whether to purchase shares. The pool of shareholders is biased towards the most optimistic investors willing to pay the highest price. This lowers the cost of capital for the firm. Banks pool investor funds and make investment decisions on their behalf. The bank will lend only if it is optimistic, but will also take into account that some of its investors have divergent beliefs. This leads the bank to act more conservatively and demand better terms from the firm. When there is substantial diversity of opinion among investors, equity may be cheaper.

Bargaining power: Once a venture has been started both the entrepreneur and investors can hold up further development. The entrepreneur can walk away from the business unless he receives better terms and the investor can withhold capital. The party that needs the most protection in this relationship depends on the entrepreneur's outside opportunities. Landier (2002) argued that the exit options are contingent on the social acceptance of failure. If there is no stigma attached to entrepreneurial failure, then the options are good. Venture capital is the superior financing vehicle in this case because it is protected through the intensive monitoring and staging of finance. Bank lending is better for the entrepreneur when the exit options are poor because it involves less invasive monitoring and committed finance. Entrepreneurs are more willing to pursue high-risk projects when the stigma of failure is low. Thus risky ventures start off with venture capital and eventually graduate to public equity.

3.3.2 Bank Debt

Bank lending is the most prevalent source of credit for private firms for three reasons. First, the cost of issuing bonds, especially on the public market, is prohibitively expensive for small firms looking to borrow a few million dollars. Second, bank-based economies like Germany do not have well-developed debt markets that can effectively compete with bank loans for small issuers. Third and perhaps most important, bank debt offers superior contracting terms and conditions for small and risky borrowers.

The primary type of bank lending is a line of credit, which is a type of loan commitment.[11] Lines of credit are generally pure revolving credit agreements ('revolvers') in which the firm pays a fee to be able to borrow as much of the line as desired at any time over the length of the agreement, provided predetermined financial benchmarks are met. Revolver options are very flexible and convenient for fast-growing borrowers because they offer quick access to finance without having to arrange a bond issue and provide insurance against credit rationing.

The flexibility of revolvers does come at a cost. Commercial bank loans are generally convenant-rich compared to bonds and the covenants are far more restrictive. The covenants are intended to give the bank more control and prevent the borrower from engaging in risk-shifting behavior. The advantage of covenants for borrowers is that they can make funding available for riskier firms at reasonably low cost. The covenants are not as restrictive as they first appear because the borrower and bank can relatively easily renegotiate the terms of the agreement.

3.3.2.1 Benefits

The attractiveness of bank loans over bonds for small firms stems from two differences in the borrowing environment. First, a single bank or a syndicate of banks provides the loan. Bond issues can involve hundreds of participating investors. Second, firms can interact with the same bankers repeatedly over time, but have little contact with bondholders when the bonds are actively traded in the secondary market. A number of benefits flow to bank debt because of these two characteristics.

Screening and monitoring: Banks conduct a much more thorough due diligence review of borrowers than do bondholders before lending capital because they are able to exploit the economies of scale in information production. A single bank lender has more financial incentive to gather information than individual bondholders with small positions. Banks are consequently more efficient than 'arm's length' debt at screening out bad prospective clients, reducing adverse selection risk. They are likewise more effective monitors, diminishing potential agency costs (Diamond 1984; Fama 1985). Thus, banks have the ability to provide cheap 'informed' capital as opposed to costly 'uninformed' arm's length debt (James 1987).

Relationship lending: The intimate and continuous relationship between a borrower and its bankers affords the bank ample opportunity to gather privileged information through the provision of financial services. The accumulation of a repayment history, periodic submissions of financial statements, renegotiations and visits with management collectively inform the bankers about the firm quality (Petersen and Rajan 1994; Berger and Udell 1995). Relationship lending has a number of benefits; a lower borrowing cost, protection against credit crunches and the provision of implicit interest rate or credit risk insurance.

Efficient renegotiation: Bank debt is better suited than bonds to finance risky and unknown borrowers because it is easier to renegotiate in the event of financial distress, resulting in more efficient liquidation decisions (Chemmanur and Fulghieri 1994b; Berlin and Loeys 1988). Bank debt only has to be renegotiated with a single or a few lenders, whereas there are many dispersed bondholders.[12] Coordinating the renegotiation of the bond terms to obtain unanimous agreement is difficult and costly, which could induce bondholders to favor liquidation even when this decision is not optimal (Gertner and Scharfstein 1991). There is some evidence that banks tend to be more lenient towards firms in financial distress than public bondholders (Gilson, John and Lang 1990). The bank's close relationship with the borrower has the effect of giving it an implicit equity stake, creating an incentive to see the firm through the financial distress.

Certification: Bank debt enables the borrower to build a good reputation that can eventually be used to access alternative and less restrictive forms of finance (Diamond 1991; Rajan and Winton 1995). The enhanced reputation of bank borrowers has a material affect on the cost of equity finance. Studies have found that announcements of bank loan commitments and similar credit facilities yield positive average abnormal stock returns for the borrowing firm (Mikkelson and Partch 1986; James 1987). Carter, Stover and Howe (1997) reported that companies that had a bank relationship prior to going public were less underpriced – a benefit shared with pre-IPO public debt – confirming the certification benefit for the issuer.

3.3.2.2 Monopoly

There is a downside to relying on a single bank to finance investment. The bank acquires proprietary information about a borrower during the course of their close relationship that is not verifiable by outside parties, nor is it transferable to other lenders. When the borrower goes back to the bank for additional capital or to renegotiate financing terms the bank's information monopoly enables it to extract out excess concessions (Rajan 1992). This is achieved by demanding interest payments above the competitive level for a borrower of that risk level.

The borrower has little recourse but to accept the high financing costs as the terms offered by other banks are not likely to be any better. Any new lender starts out with little information and would have to spend considerable time and effort to evaluate the company. The extra effort requires compensation in the form of higher lending rates. Furthermore, switching lenders sends a negative signal about the firm because it did not refinance with the original bank. Other banks cannot be sure if the firm voluntarily made the switch or if it was denied additional capital because of a poor credit history.

The market power acquired by a bank has real consequences for the actions and costs of borrowers. Managerial incentives are distorted by the monopoly power because the marginal cash flows accruing from any new project are shared with the bank, thereby leading to less investment and effort. Houston and James (1996) found that large publicly listed firms took into account that their monitoring lender may obtain an information monopoly when setting their mix of private and public debt. The firms had multiple banking relationships in order to obtain additional needed funding that might otherwise be withheld by a monopolist bank. Multiple relationships come at a high cost, including additional transaction costs, duplicated effort and free-rider problems.

The information monopoly could alternatively have a beneficial impact on the financing terms. The high initial lending rates that stem from information problems could fall over time as the lender learns the borrower's quality (Peterson and Rajan 1995). The opposite lending rate pattern could emerge if the banks correctly anticipate the rent extraction due to the market power. Competition among banks drives the rates down in the short term on the expectation that they will be made up with higher rates in the long term (Sharpe 1990).

The overall evidence, while mixed, seems to support the conjecture that banks earn positive rents from their monopoly power and this might be a factor in the going-public decision. Peterson and Rajan (1994) found that bank relationships reduced the interest rate on bank loans to small firms by less than the true decline in the cost when borrower quality improved. Examining a sample of Italian IPOs, Pagano, Panetta and Zingales (1998) found a drop in the cost of bank credit in the IPO year that was sustained for the next three years. They estimated a rate reduction of between 40 and 70 basis points. Moreover, the issuers borrowed from more banks and reduced the concentration of their borrowing after the IPO.

Three possible factors discussed by Pagano, Panetta and Zingales could contribute to the rate reduction. First, the decline in leverage following the IPO made the issuer less risky. However, they documented improved lending terms even after controlling for the economic benefit of increased equity on the balance sheet. Second, the stock market listing meant there was more public information available about the issuer – public companies must adhere to strict disclosure requirements and have external monitoring performed by analysts and shareholders – reducing the amount of time banks would have to spend collecting information about creditworthiness. Third, the outside equity option increases the bargaining power of the issuer vis-à-vis potential lenders. The last two factors demonstrate a direct financial benefit to going public.

3.4 ACCESS TO CAPITAL

Positive cash flow is the lifeblood of any company, especially those looking to invest in new projects and grow. Cash can be generated internally from operations or supplied by external sources. Many start-ups and other new ventures do not generate adequate revenue internally to fund all their capital needs and are dependent on external suppliers. A firm becomes financially constrained when all of its existing sources of capital are unable or unwilling to supply the desired amount of funds. An IPO is attractive because it enables the issuer to access a much larger pool of capital, even if it is not necessarily cheaper. Indeed, surveys of issuers reveal that raising capital to grow the firm ranks among the top reasons cited for going public.[13]

3.4.1 Financing Constraints

Capital constraints are a fact of life for many companies, public or private. Small and risky firms are particularly hard hit by scarce capital during a credit crunch. The existence and impact of financing constraints is a topic of on-going research, specifically focused on the sensitivity of investment to cash flows.[14] There is as yet no definitive conclusion on whether the sensitivity is greater for more or less constrained firms. There is little doubt, however, that companies which lack sufficient capital will seek it out.

Start-up firms in high-tech industries are ripe candidates to go public to alleviate financing constraints. Investors face informational problems trying to evaluate an unproven technology and may be apprehensive about supplying capital to such risky firms. Banks are even more hesitant than equity investors are because there are few collateralizable assets. Guiso

(1998) found some support for this hypothesis by showing that high-tech manufacturers in Italy were more financially constrained than comparable low-tech firms. He did not, however, find this to be related to the decision to go public.

Two other studies did report evidence consistent with financial constraints being a factor in the IPO decision. Bottazzi and Da Rin (2002) reported that companies listing on the new European stock markets were highly levered and unable to expand their bank credit pre-IPO.[15] Both debt and expenditures in fixed assets and R&D increased sharply post-IPO. Companies that raised a large amount of capital in the IPO increased sales, assets and employment faster than companies raising less, again consistent with capital constraints limiting the firm.

Boehmer and Ljungqvist (2001) examined German companies that had announced their intention to go public. Firms that intended to sell primary shares to raise capital for investment or to pay off debt were more likely to complete the IPO than issuers that would not receive funds from the sale of secondary shares by firm insiders. The chances of completing the IPO was also substantially lower when a bank was among the firm's shareholders, which could provide an alternative source of capital if the firm was constrained. Companies that were capital constrained made faster choices between public and private equity, demonstrating a high cost to waiting.

3.4.2 Financing Options

One of the many benefits to a public listing is the increase in the set of financing options available to a firm. Various equity-linked securities are a possibility now that the firm has publicly traded shares; convertible debt and warrants being two prominent examples. Other debt and derivative products become realistic options now that investors have better information about the public company.

The ability to issue straight debt and equity is also enhanced by an IPO. The capital infusion strengthens the equity base and lowers the leverage ratio. A firm's ability to raise additional debt is immediately improved simply because there is a larger cash position. Agency costs stemming from high leverage, including the underinvestment in good projects arising from debt overhang, are mitigated and raise the willingness of investors to supply additional equity capital. Of course, these capital structure benefits could be obtained through a sale of private equity and are not unique to an IPO.

Another important reason why an IPO is helpful in obtaining additional finance is that the publicly observable share price acts as a signal for the company's value. The stock price is a cost-effective way to aggregate information from multiple sources. Many investors can inform the price in a manner that an individual banker could not. The information barrier that deters investors from buying the firm's securities is lowered considerably by the stock price. An active market in the stock also assuages investor concerns about the liquidity of other securities. Knowledge that thousands or millions of investors know and trade the stock provides some assurance that active markets for other securities are likely. This type of logic was cited by T. Boone Pickens in his autobiography when discussing the benefits of public stock:

> But . . . [the acquisition by a stock swap of a small, hopelessly uncompetitive company in an unrelated line of business, whose only attraction was the fact that it has 2,200 stockholders] . . . did provide us with enough stockholders to create a market for Mesa stock. By 1966 we were ready to raise debt capital, and that would have been impossible without an active market for our stock. (Pickens 1987, p. 70)[16]

3.4.3 Financing Terms

The positive externality that an IPO has on the set of financing options extends to the cost of capital. With more feasible options, the firm is able to bargain from a position of strength. The evidence cited earlier of a reduced cost of bank credit following the IPO supports this conjecture. Further anecdotal evidence confirms the beneficial effect of an IPO on bank financing. The financial director at an Italian company that had recently gone public stated:

> What really changed since we went public is the number of offers we receive from banks and other financial institutions: almost everyday somebody comes over or calls me and offers me this form of financing or that . . . In the end we get a much better pick, something that would not happen if we were not listed. (Marchisio and Ravasi 2001, p. 6)

This manager's experience is not unique. Ransley (1984) reported that 52 percent of CEOs responding to a survey felt that their company's enhanced status from being public enabled them to negotiate bank facilities at better rates.

The cost of private capital is influenced by the availability of alternative options, indirectly affecting the IPO decision. Lerner, Shane and Tsai (2003) examined the terms of research alliances between private biotechnology start-ups and major corporate partners. The start-ups lacked capital and received R&D funding from their partner. The funding terms were determined by the start-ups' bargaining power, which was proxied by the frequency of IPOs from the industry. Lerner, Shane and Tsai found that start-ups relied increasingly on external equity finance when more biotech firms issued equity in the previous year and less on strategic alliances, although the economic effect was low.[17] Increased bargaining power gave the start-up greater flexibility, which manifested in the relinquishing of fewer control rights to the alliance partner.

3.5 SUMMARY

Firms have a strong financial incentive to go public and gain access to a large pool of cheap capital. However, public equity does not uniformly dominate the private market as a cheap source. The direct expenses are considerably higher for an IPO, with a large fixed component that can be onerous for small firms. The pure cost of equity is cheaper in the public market because there are fewer frictions, although this benefit is minimal if the stock is thinly traded. Information and monitoring costs offer no clear advantage to either private or public equity. For many small firms public equity does not provide sufficient cost savings alone to justify an IPO.

The best estimates for the returns to private equity show that they have not been significantly better than public equity returns, and perhaps even lower. While this could be interpreted as evidence that private equity is not significantly more expensive than public equity, the terms demanded by investors at the time of financing are probably still less favorable in private markets.

Bank lending is the most viable alternative to equity finance, but it has limited use for risky start-up firms. It is, however, superior to bonds for these firms because it involves a close relationship with the bank, is cheaper because of better screening and monitoring, is more efficiently renegotiated and certifies the firm quality. Going public improves the bank rates by expanding the options open to a firm. The increased bargaining power and public information made possible by a public listing expands the set of financing options, allowing the firm to overcome financing constraints.

NOTES

1. Joe Bartlett originally made this point in a commentary for VC Experts.
2. These estimates were based on the price of a company's shares that were publicly traded and those that were privately placed with restrictions on their resale.
3. Individuals provide private capital to small business started by family or friends. Their access to firms receiving venture capital or buyout funds is severely limited.
4. Higher residual variance in the unspanned component of the private firm's cash flows results in a greater private cost of capital.

5. The duplication is mitigated somewhat by the ability of investors to free-ride on the information production of others, which is embodied in the stock price.
6. Barry et al. (1990) provides a comprehensive review of the role venture capitalists play in the creation of pubic companies.
7. Gompers and Lerner (1997) also examined the returns to venture capital, but looked only at a single fund.
8. The calculation assumed no taxes, a zero liquidity premium and risk free debt. These assumptions, especially the riskless debt, do not hold in practice. If they don't the debt–equity ratio would have to be even higher to eliminate the return premium to buyout funds.
9. Cochrane (2001) found a similar return pattern across the stages.
10. Moskowitz and Vissing-Jorgensen (2002) examined private equity as an asset class by using data on household investment. They found that private equity earned lower returns than the CRSP (Center for Research on Security Prices) value-weighted index of all public equity.
11. Berger and Udell (1998) estimate that about half of all small business debt is in the form of lines of credit.
12. If the bank debt is syndicated over a large number of banks this advantage is reduced.
13. Ransley (1984) found that 53 percent of issuers listed funds for growth by acquisition and 44 percent listed funds for organic expansion as reasons for going public. Marchisio and Ravasi (2001) surveyed the CEOs of Italian firms that had recently gone public. Access to cheaper and more plentiful capital were the top two reasons for the IPO.
14. See Fazzari, Hubbard and Petersen (1988, 2000) and Kaplan and Zingales (1997).
15. The markets were the Neuer Markt in Germany, the Nouveau Marche in France, and the Nuovo Mercato in Italy.
16. This quote originally appeared in Roell (1996).
17. A doubling of external financing decreased the predicted share of R&D financing by alliance partners from 44 to 41 percent.

4 Strategic behavior

Companies operate in competitive economic markets. Decisions related to and affected by a firm's product and input markets should be made with full regard to the response by its main competitors. Rational managers recognize the impact that an IPO has on the economic environment, anticipate the likely response by key players in the market and incorporate this into the going-public decision-making process. An IPO, as much as anything else, is a strategic decision and one that must be considered within the larger context of the entire market.

Strategic considerations inherent in the going-public decision can be classified into one of two categories. The first specifically relates to interaction with competitors in the industry. A firm will not voluntarily place itself at a competitive disadvantage vis-à-vis its rivals. The going-public decision must consider whether this action enhances or at least maintains the firm's competitive position. The second group of strategic factors pertains to the effect that going public has on the critical constituencies of the firm, namely suppliers, customers and strategic partners. An IPO produces information and conveys signals to these other parties, potentially benefiting the issuer's productivity, profitability and competitive strengths. These factors all directly enhance the firm's ability to compete with rivals.

4.1 INDUSTRY COMPETITION

Companies constantly seek out actions and opportunities that provide a competitive edge. Whether an IPO furnishes the strategic benefit a firm desires depends on a number of factors. One is the firm's competitive and financial health, and that of its rivals. Another is the specific industry characteristics. The nature of competition depends on whether the industry is relatively new and rapidly growing, or is stable and mature. In the latter case, competition is often a zero-sum game; one firm gains market share and profit at another firm's expense. In new industries the total profit pie is growing rapidly. Firms are as interested in growing the pie and staking their claim as they are with taking away a piece from a rival.

4.1.1 Competitive Environment

Industrial economics research has articulated ideas and theories for the strategic interaction of firms within an industry. Characterizing the basic nature of competition is an important step towards analyzing the strategic aspect of the going-public decision. Industries vary in their structure, stage of development and competitive dynamics. Three properties stand out for their impact on competition.

Industry life cycle: The life cycle of an industry is usually broken up into four stages: nascent, growth, mature and declining. The nascent stage is distinguished by uncertainty about the industry viability, firms that are just emerging from the start-up phase, and a small but growing market size. Once the industry viability has been established it enters a rapid growth phase. Market demand expands at a tremendous rate, new firms enter the industry and firms concentrate on growing their business. Mature industries converge to a stable and moderate level of growth, competition has whittled the pool of firms down to a core group and firms focus on competing for market share. Industries in decline exhibit shrinking aggregate demand, fierce competition for a remaining slice of the pie and market exit.

Concentration: Industry concentration is measured by how much of the market is allocated to each of the competitors. A highly concentrated industry might consist of only a few large firms, each with considerable market power, and some fringe competitors. At the other end of the spectrum is a perfectly competitive market, dominated by numerous small firms lacking any market power. In between are industries comprised of both large and small competitors without a clear dominant market leader.

Product differentiation: An industry is characterized by product differentiation if each firms' products are not perfect substitutes for those of competitors. A differentiated product enables a firm to carve out a niche and grants it some degree of market power. A homogeneous good industry forces firms to compete aggressively on price for market share, driving excess profits down to zero.

The combination and interaction of these three properties determines the nature of competition. Industries in the early growth stage likely have low concentration as more firms enter to satisfy the growing demand. Firms may be oriented towards satisfying the growing demand without competing as intensively with rivals. The competition should grow more severe in maturing industries as firms fight to retain their market share. Consolidation is often inevitable, especially if firms produce relatively similar products. Firms producing differentiated products will temper their competition because their market position is somewhat isolated from rivals.

The nature of competition is affected by the presence of large, dominant firms. If only a few large firms are competing, they may engage in collusive behavior. While explicit collusion is possible, it is more likely that they tacitly agree to set high prices or not encroach on each other's market. Large firms might also engage in predatory behavior to drive the smaller competition out of business. A sustained price war designed to hurt the profitability of weak rivals can force them to exit the market, and may deter entry in the first place.

The optimal competitive strategy can be different for public and private firms. The decision to go public is thus influenced by the existing strategic competition and, in turn, alters the status quo competition within the industry. IPOs can occur in any number of competitive environments, but the specific strategic motivation for going public will depend on the unique circumstances.

4.1.2 Information Disclosure

A major disadvantage of an IPO is that the issuer is required to disclose all materially relevant information necessary to value the firm. The information is contained in the prospectus and other major press releases that are freely available to the firm's competitors. Complete disclosure continues after the IPO as the company regularly updates shareholders about the latest developments. In a survey of chief financial officers (CFOs) of recent issuers, Ryan (2001) confirmed that disclosure is a negative aspect to going public. About 66 percent of respondents cited lack of confidentiality as a disadvantage of an IPO, while nearly 70 percent identified public scrutiny as another deterrent.

The disdain that companies have towards disclosing private information depends on the type of information and the circumstances. Disclosing information that is not value-relevant, but is time consuming and costly to release, should not be a significant factor in the IPO decision. More critical is information that can have an impact on a firm's competitive position and strength. The disclosure of three types of information could affect the IPO decision.

Product technology: Firms try to keep private any information pertaining to the results from R&D and new product design. A superior differentiated product or a lower cost of production confers a competitive advantage when rivals are prevented from copying the technology or process. Going public requires that such private information be disclosed to competitors sooner rather than later, cutting into the firm's advantage. The opposite incentive holds if the firm has good information about its product quality or production cost that will enhance its competitive position. The optimal disclosure policy would then favor an IPO.

Market conditions: The attractiveness of entering a new market depends on the profit opportunity. Potential entrants may decide it is not worth the cost and effort to enter if the expected demand is not large. A firm that is producing a new product should have some sense of the market demand based on its own sales effort. A private firm does not have to reveal its information about the potential market size and customer demand, thus providing it with a temporary advantage. Disclosure concerns may dictate remaining private longer in new industries to delay further entry.

Internal operations: Private companies do not have to disclose any information to the public regarding its operations. For example, information on the firm's financial health, the efficiency of its operations, its customers and its relationships with strategic partners can remain private. The advantage of keeping such information private is that competitors do not know the strengths and weaknesses of the company, which inhibits their aggressiveness in competing with the firm.

4.1.2.1 Disclosure and financing

A public listing requires more disclosure than bank financing or private equity, which both involve bilateral negotiations that minimize the diffusion of information to competitors (Bhattacharya and Chiesa 1995). Whether an IPO is optimal from a disclosure perspective depends collectively on the type of private information, the characteristics of the issuer and the potential competitive response of rival firms. Disclosure is not limited to the direct release of information by a firm. Financing choices can also signal private information to outsiders (Gertner, Gibbons and Scharfstein 1988).[1] To illustrate, an IPO could come to symbolize good private information, regardless of the actual content, if the 'good' firms go public and the 'bad' ones stay private.

The competitive response by rivals to divulged information is contingent on the type of information disclosed and the revealed quality of the issuer. In simple terms the rivals' response could be either passive, acquiescing to the threat posed by the firm or aggressive if they feel threatened. An aggressive response could include starting a price war, developing an intensive new marketing campaign or directly targeting the issuer's consumers. Cut-throat competition is damaging to all firms, unless only one survives and earns monopoly profits. The more attractive option is for competitors to tolerate each other's presence or, better yet, tacitly collude to keep prices and industry profits high.

The optimal disclosure policy will influence the going-public decision. The optimal policy hinges on the assumptions made about the likely response of rivals to the disclosure. Yosha (1995) assumed that rivals are more aggressive against issuers that disclose good information about their quality. The logical consequence is that good firms are more likely to remain private. Rivals, unable to determine the true quality of a private firm, compete based on the expected quality level. Thus, they are more passive than they would have been had the firm actually gone public. Low quality firms would go public to reveal their true condition to diminish the aggressiveness of rivals.

An equally valid but diametrically opposite assumption is that rivals respond more aggressively against firms disclosed to be of low quality. Whereas rivals would try to drive the low quality firms out of business, they find it more profitable to share the market with high quality firms. Under this scenario high quality firms have the incentive to go public to induce passive behavior among rivals. Low quality private firms would only bring forth even fiercer competition by going public and must still incur the IPO costs.

Theory suggests that more transparent firms have high average profits, whereas opaque firms exhibit comparatively less variability in profits and output. The intuition for this conclusion is as follows. Opaque firms reveal less of their characteristics to rivals; for example, rivals do not know if the firm has a high or low production cost. Consequently rivals' expectation for the opaque firm's output is either too high or too low. In general, rivals are less aggressive when competing against low cost firms and restrain their output. But with poor transparency rivals overestimate the cost and are too aggressive. The low cost firms are then forced to restrain output. High cost firms benefit from opaqueness because rivals are too passive, allowing them to preserve their output and profitability. The output and profits of high and low cost firms are more alike than they would otherwise be because of the poor transparency.

Applying the preceding logic, the preference over the degree of transparency depends on the firm's financiers, implicitly affecting the IPO decision. Perotti and von Thadden (2003) argued that there is a natural preference among lenders for less information dissemination since they do not gain from higher profits, while they suffer from higher risk associated with profit variability. Equity-dominated firms prefer greater transparency because it increases both profitability and risk, and therefore the call option value of equity. Private firms that are primarily equity financed have a stronger disclosure incentive to go public than bank financed firms.

4.1.3 Externalities and Herding

The frequent intra-industry clustering of IPOs is often a consequence of some type of externality. Chapter 2 discussed the ways in which informational externalities from past offerings can induce more firms to go public. Externalities lower the cost of public equity, making an IPO more attractive because investors have to produce less new information. Past IPOs could also be a positive signal for the payoff to investment options within the industry, leading more firms to go public to exercise them.

The two scenarios described could result in an IPO cluster, although neither explicitly relies on strategic interaction among the issuers. A strategic element would arise when issuers try to free-ride on the information produced by others. By delaying the IPO decision, an issuer can observe the success of past offerings and reduce its issuing costs. Such strategic delay could prevent an IPO cluster from ever arising, as each issuer waits for other firms to go public first.

4.1.3.1 Payoff externalities

A different type of externality that has strategic implications is one that is payoff-relevant. A payoff externality occurs when the actions of one firm affect the profits of all other firms in the industry, in either a positive or negative manner. The value of private firms can be adversely affected if competitors go public to invest and grow. This type of externality creates a strategic motive for going public.

Payoff externalities arise naturally in many settings. A classic example is a bank run. Any time an individual withdraws his deposit from a bank the probability of insolvency increases, generating a negative externality for other depositors. A bank run can start if each individual believes that many other depositors are going to withdrawal their savings and consequently decide to withdrawal as well, leading to a herd. An example of a positive payoff externality is the provision of liquidity in financial markets. Each additional investor adds liquidity, making it more attractive for other investors to participate in the market.

Payoff externalities directly affect the IPO decision and can result in clustering. An IPO provides a firm with cash and a stock currency, which can be used to finance growth either organically from within or through acquisitions. Firms that are able to grow rapidly gain market share at the expense of competitors. After a few firms in an industry have gone public, the remaining private firms may have little choice but to follow suit to remain competitive. The strategic motive for an IPO caused by payoff externalities is prevalent in new and rapidly growing industries.

The Internet sector offers a good case study of how payoff externalities and the need to grow impacted the IPO decision. Internet commerce grew at astounding rates in the late 1990s. The key to success for many firms was developing a critical mass of operations and attracting visitors to their web site. Schultz and Zaman (2001) reported that Internet firms were much more likely to merge or acquire other firms – the bulk of which were private – post-IPO, as compared to non-Internet companies. The market reacted favorably to the announcement of acquisitions, supporting the belief that rapid growth was crucial. Internet firms also entered into far more strategic alliances, usually with a marketing and distribution characteristic. The need to acquire cash and a liquid stock currency to grow the business appears to be the primary IPO motive for most of these companies.

Payoff externalities also affect the strategic timing and delay of IPOs, and thus the possibility of clustering. Innovator firms produce and adopt new technologies first, while imitator firms follow and in some cases improve upon the innovator's technology. Innovators face a dilemma when they are considering an IPO (Maksimovic and Pichler 2001). A public listing reveals to imitators valuable information about the technology, causing a rush of imitators to the market sooner rather than later. This eats into the innovator's profits. Financing expansion privately, while more costly, enables the innovator to hold off imitators a little longer and earn higher short term profits.

Two famous examples of innovator firms are Genentech and Netscape. After both firms went public – Genentech in 1980 and Netscape in 1995 – investors and entrepreneurs learned about the profit potential of the two industries. What followed was a stampede of new start-ups that went public shortly thereafter.

4.1.4 Financial Structure

A firm's financial structure influences its ability to compete against rivals, providing another rationale for an IPO. High leverage can be competitively harmful because it reduces financial slack during difficult economic periods and makes a firm vulnerable to predatory behavior by rivals. The infusion of equity from an IPO immediately lowers the leverage ratio and is often used to repay debt.

The importance of leverage on the IPO decision depends on the nature of competition, which is contingent on the financial structure of competitors. A private firm with little or no debt gains minimal competitive benefits from the equity supplied by an IPO. The situation for a highly levered firm is quite different. Three theories on the interaction between industry financial structure and competitive behavior have been proposed.

Predation: Unlevered companies can benefit from preying upon their levered rivals by increasing output and lowering prices to drive them out of business (Teslar 1966). Predation of this sort requires 'deep pockets' to survive the brutal competition necessary to bankrupt the rivals. The potential threat of predatory behavior against levered firms affects initial financing decisions. Bolton and Scharfstein (1990) showed how debt minimizes agency costs by motivating managers to avoid the poor performance that can result in firm liquidation. However, the optimal amount of debt from an agency perspective will invite predatory behavior. Financing with more equity lowers the possibility of liquidation and predation, offsetting the additional agency costs.

Credible commitment: Competition within an industry in which all firms have high leverage can result in higher output, lower prices and lower profits than if the industry was less levered. This occurs if managers maximize shareholder value, not profits, and shareholders have limited liability when the firm is levered. Since the payoff to equity is a call option, increasing output only in good times maximizes shareholder value. Brander and Lewis (1986) demonstrated that managers could credibly signal their intent to maximize shareholder value by taking on a large debt position. However, all firms would all be better off if they restrained output and split the tacit collusion industry profits. Each firm has an incentive to issue equity to break out of this bad equilibrium.[2]

Financial constraints: Firms that are financially constrained, possibly because of a high debt level, could face more or less competition relative to unconstrained firms. Highly levered firms cannot fund investment for future growth because the free cash flow is used to service the interest obligations. Rivals may behave less aggressively today knowing the firm will not be able to compete as effectively in the future (Phillips 1992). Alternatively, financial constraints weaken a firm's competitive position, allowing rivals to produce more and gain market share at its expense (Povel and Raith 2000). The two scenarios make opposite predictions about the desirability of an equity offering, which is more attractive when the competition is severe.

Although not specific to issuers, the intuition from these three theories can be applied to analyzing the IPO decision. For starters, only highly levered firms derive a financial structure benefit from going public. Considering first that case in which a firm's rivals are also highly levered, competition can be either intense or restrained. An IPO could be optimal in both cases, but for opposite reasons. When the competition is intense, an issuer with less leverage now has an incentive to be less aggressive in an attempt to increase industry profits. The IPO decision is reinforced if the levered private competitors also go public. An IPO serves less purpose in the restrained case. An IPO may signal to a firm's rivals that it will compete more aggressively. The end result is fiercer competition and lower profits.

Rivals with low leverage are more inclined to engage in predatory behavior, which would induce levered firms to go public and avoid such a threat. The potential for predation can also lead to clustering. The levered firm that goes public could prey on its private levered rivals. Industries that experienced a number of leveraged buyouts (LBOs) might exhibit a clustering of reverse LBOs for this very reason.

4.1.4.2 Evidence

The limited evidence on the relationship between leverage and competition supports the claim that too much debt is harmful. Opler and Titman (1994) found that highly levered firms lost market share to, and had lower operating profits than, their less levered competitors during industry downturns. The loss appeared partially attributable to customers who were reluctant to do business with the levered firm for fear that they would not receive product support in the future. The loss was also greater in concentrated industries, suggestive of predatory behavior.

Evidence from industries that experienced LBOs suggests that levered firms were more passive than and subject to predatory actions by less levered rivals. Chevalier (1995a) documented that unlevered supermarkets were more likely to open stores and less likely to exit markets in which competitors had recently gone LBO. Likewise, Chevalier (1995b) reported that prices in the supermarket industry decreased if rivals of the LBO firm were not highly levered and there was a single large competitor with low leverage that controlled a large share of the market. Prices increased if, at the time of the LBO, rivals were also highly levered. In other industries firms that increased leverage behaved more passively, investing less and losing market share (Phillips 1995; Kovenock and Phillips 1997). The less levered rivals of LBO firms invested more and increased market share, with the effect most pronounced in concentrated industries.

The possible interaction between leverage and the IPO decision was considered in two different studies. Repayment of outstanding debts is frequently listed as a primary use of the IPO proceeds. Akhigbe, Borde and

Whyte (2003) examined the share price reaction of rival firms at the announcement of a competitor filing to go public. The announcement CARs were significantly negatively related to the issuer stating that the proceeds would be used to repay debt. This is consistent with lower leverage enhancing the competitive position of the issuer and thus providing a motive for going public. Helwege and Packer (2001) tested the leverage motive for going public using a sample of private firms that had issued publicly traded bonds. The private firms had five times more leverage than the average public firm and one and a half times the leverage of industry- and size-matched comparison firms. The private firms also had lower interest coverage ratios. Surprisingly, regression analysis found that leverage was not related to whether a firm went public, after controlling for other factors. However, the analysis did not control for industry competition, which drives the financial restructuring motive.

4.2 REPUTATION AND VISIBILITY

The long-term success of a firm is dependent on its reputation with its customers, suppliers, employees and even rival companies. A firm known for producing high quality products, good customer service, prompt payment of outstanding debts and job security for employees has a competitive advantage. Executives routinely cite the desire to enhance the company's image and reputation as a motivating factor for the IPO. Marchisio and Ravasi (2001) surveyed the CEOs of Italian firms that had recently gone public. The third and fourth most popular reasons for the IPO were to improve the company's image and status, and to increase the company's visibility. Rydqvist and Hogholm (1995) examined IPO prospectuses and found that reputation factors appeared as a reason for going public 67 percent of the time. The chief operating officer of J.D. Edwards put it succinctly, 'privately held companies get no respect', in response to why his company went public (Brown 1997, p. 244).[3]

4.2.1 Reputation Development

Developing a good reputation that can increase a company's profitability, either by raising its market share or giving it pricing power, takes time and effort. A firm must be willing to incur a potentially high cost in order for its reputation to actually be valuable. Proclamations that the firm produces high quality products are not credible because any other firm can do the same, whether true or not.

Two options exist for developing a good reputation. The first is to produce a high quality product and have the market gradually learn the true quality through repeated experimentation. This option is costly because the firm earns low profits in the short term while the market is still learning and the probability of the product failing is greater when customers do not know the true quality.

The second way to develop a good reputation is by signaling the quality through a costly action. Typical examples include offering a product warranty or money-back guarantees. These actions signal high quality because lower quality firms find it too costly to offer the same terms. The act of going public is a signal for high quality for two different reasons.

IPO costs: An IPO involves multiple costs to all affiliated parties, effectively limiting the pool of potential issuers to only those of high quality. The issuer incurs IPO costs – filing and registration fees, compensation to its advisors and underpricing – and ongoing listing, auditing and investor relations fees. The indirect IPO costs to going public can be an even bigger deterrent. Management must devote considerable time and effort to the offering and is exposed to outside scrutiny at the IPO and beyond.

Other participants in the IPO process also face potential costs, but in the form of lost reputation. The underwriter performs due diligence of the issuer and stakes its reputation with investors on the fact that the firm is worth the offer price. Auditors attest to the veracity of the firm's financial situation and are exposed to legal liability if there are material misstatements. The fear of a damaged reputation from being associated with a low quality issuer increases the probability that only good firms are able to complete an IPO. Venture capitalists have similar reputation concerns. The value of the portfolio companies they take public depends on the VC's reputation with investors. Collectively, the real and potential costs of the IPO send a strong signal that the company is of high quality.

Bonding: Going public creates an incentive to maintain a good product market reputation because the shareholders now receive more of the benefits. Maksimovic and Titman (1991) argued that highly levered firms have a lower incentive to maintain a good reputation since the reputation's payoff accrues over many periods. The shareholders of levered firms receive less of this benefit for two reasons. First, the probability of bankruptcy is greater, lowering the expected shareholder payoff. Second, debtholders receive a larger fraction of the future profits when leverage is high. A reduction in the product quality increases the current profits accruing to shareholders at the expense of future debtholder claims.

Customers recognize the adverse affect of leverage on product quality and scale back their demand accordingly. Going public to reduce debt is a credible signal to customers that the firm cares about its reputation for producing high quality products.

4.2.1.1 Market visibility

The value of a good reputation is a function of the number of people who actually know about the company. The pool of customers, suppliers, employees and investors aware of the company pre-IPO is often limited to those who have direct dealings with it. Going public enhances the value of an already good reputation by expanding the company's public profile. Increased coverage by the media and a large following in the financial industry leads to greater public awareness. An IPO is valuable because it directly improves the reputation and it amplifies an already good reputation.

The mechanism that best conveys a public firm's reputation is not available to private companies: the stock price. The price is the market's assessment of the firm's quality. Potential customers and suppliers can interpret a high stock price as a signal of good quality and decide to do business with it. The additional business that a high stock price engenders fuels further increases in the valuation. A high stock price can become a self-reinforcing piece of information among investors and consumers because it confirms that the positive experiences each have had individually is an accurate indication of quality (Stoughton, Wong and Zechner 2001).

The improved reputation from going public and the increased exposure enhances a firm's ability to compete effectively. The company becomes a member of an elite group of businesses that are publicly traded. The status that is conveyed by a public listing increases the number of opportunities available to form strategic industrial partnerships. One anecdote captures the strategic benefits of an IPO quite clearly. The managing director of a producer of gas stove components based in Italy stated:

> Being public really helped us in our external relationships. Now we are not one out of many anymore: we are a listed company and we are treated as such by our clients. Their respect for us has increased and we are regarded as trustworthy counterparts. Now we negotiate with them as peers. (Marchisio and Ravasi 2001, p. 6–7)

The increased credibility for this particular company led to a number of companies in contiguous industries contacting management in the following months, proposing so many joint development projects that they had problems 'keeping track of all of them'.

4.2.2 Marketing

A vital part of any successful business is the marketing plan that promotes the company and its products to key strategic partners. Going public enhances an existing marketing plan by increasing the visibility and reputation of a company. At the same time, an IPO and a public listing can be a deliberate part of a marketing strategy, providing a direct motive for going public. The marketing benefits from an IPO can be achieved in various ways and serve different purposes of the firm's objectives.

4.2.2.1 Entering new markets

Companies, particularly those not based in the US, commonly cross-list their shares on exchanges in multiple countries. Cross-listings provide an ideal setting in which to examine the marketing motive for going public. A public company based in one country can cross-list its shares on an exchange in another country without raising capital, although sometimes they do. Since the companies are already public and the cross-listing is a cashless transaction, the action isolates the marketing motive from the other considerations associated with an IPO.

Anecdotal and empirical evidence reveals quite clearly that marketing objectives influence the cross-listing decision. A survey conducted by Bancel and Mittoo (2001) found that 16 percent of European cross-listed companies rated easier implementation of global marketing and production as a motive for cross-listing. The marketing aims of cross-listers are not limited to relatively unknown companies. Decker (1994, p. 512) discussed the decision of Glaxo, a major British pharmaceutical company, to cross-list in the US:

> When we helped Glaxo into the U.S. markets for the first time, they weren't interested in raising funds; they were just interested in raising their name recognition and market following here in the United States. Believe it or not, at that time, hardly anyone had ever heard of Glaxo in the United States, and now it is pretty much a household name.

Formal empirical analysis by Pagano, Roell and Zechner (2002) further supports the marketing motive for cross-listing. Non-financial European companies could cross-list either within Europe or in the US. Companies that cross-listed in the US pursued a strategy of rapid, equity-funded expansion. They relied heavily on export markets, both before and after listing, and tended to belong to high-tech industries. Companies that cross-listed in Europe did not rely on foreign sales to the extent that US cross-listers did, and were less likely to be in a high-tech industry. The US cross-listing decision was driven in large part by the tech-heavy NASDAQ and a desire to increase the marketing presence.

4.2.2.2 Branding

The IPO event can itself be a valuable marketing tool. IPOs have attracted greater media attention in recent years, largely stimulated by the Internet bubble. The CEOs of issuers can be seen ringing the opening bell at the NYSE. The media coverage of the event provides the firm with publicity that it might not otherwise be able to afford. The value of the coverage depends on who the issuer's customers are. A defense contractor whose sole customer is the government will care little for the marketing benefits of an IPO. At the other extreme, a company that sells products aimed at individual consumers would stand to benefit from the marketing exposure brought by the IPO.

A good example of the IPO being used as a marketing event is the Internet industry. The exorbitant initial returns generated by many of these IPOs became front page news and instantly created mass recognition. The marketing benefit of a large initial return is most pronounced for business-to-consumer (B2C) companies. Demers and Lewellen (2003) examined the relationship between the initial returns and the traffic at these B2C web sites. They found that the initial return was a significant positive predictor of the increased web traffic after the IPO. The average cost, measured by underpricing, to attract a unique visitor to the web site was estimated to be $562, similar to estimates for conventional marketing methods.

4.2.2.3 Labor markets

Among the criteria used by investors to judge the quality of an issuer is the senior management. A firm that is run by experienced professional managers, preferably people who have managed in a public company, creates a positive impression with investors. Venture capitalists make a committed effort to 'professionalize' their portfolio companies prior to the IPO (Hellmann and Puri 2002). As part of this effort they use their control over the firm and their contacts in the industry to put in place an established management team.

The prospect of an IPO is often a necessary condition to attract successful managers. Quality executives operate in their own managerial labor market and prefer working for public companies because of the additional prestige associated with the position. Therefore, the reputation of a company in the labor market is critical to attracting and retaining quality employees, and that reputation is augmented if the company is public.

The growing use of stock options as a means of compensating employees, to say nothing of their ability to attract good employees, is another motivating factor for going public. Public equity is a liquid currency that can be used to attract and motivate workers. In industries like high technology, where skilled workers are sometimes scarce, stock options become an absolute necessity to lure employees away from competitors. Stock option grants to CEOs have increased more than tenfold from 1980 to 2000.[4] Option grants to regular employees have gone from virtually nothing to being a basic part of compensation at companies like Cisco. Being public or on the path towards an IPO has become a requirement to compete in the labor market.

4.2.3 Valuation Effects

Information conveyed by an IPO regarding the issuer's reputation and the competitive effect in the industry is indirectly revealed by share prices. Highly reputable firms could have large initial returns for two reasons. First, the issuer may know it is of high quality and try to signal this by intentionally underpricing. Second, investors acknowledge the issuer's good reputation by rewarding it with a high stock price (Stoughton, Wong and Zechner 2001). A better reputation should manifest as a larger market share in the future, implying a positive correlation between initial returns and future market share. To date there is no empirical evidence on this relation.

The announcement of an IPO will have an affect on the share prices of competitor firms. Stoughton, Wong and Zechner argued that the exact price response depends on the relative importance of two factors. Investors may be uncertain about the size and value of the total market for the industry. An IPO that indicates the market is growing would produce a positive reaction in competitors' share prices. The increased competition from newly public firms would reduce competitors' profits and stock prices. The rivals' share prices could rise or fall, depending on whether the positive information or increased competition factor dominates.

The evidence on the rivals' price reaction to IPO announcements is indicative of industry-wide implications. Slovin, Sushka and Ferraro (1995) reported an average announcement CAR of -0.9 percent. However, using a much larger sample Akhigbe, Borde and Whyte (2003) found the CARs to be insignificantly different from zero. This was a consequence of offsetting positive information and negative competition effects. The CARs were positively associated with an IPO being the first after a period of dormancy, indicating good information about the industry, and in regulated industries, which are populated with relatively homogeneous firms. The CARs were negatively related to relatively large IPOs in highly competitive industries, those in relatively risky industries, those in better performing industries and those in the technology sector. Ward (1997) documented that the rivals' price responses were negatively correlated with the subsequent initial return of the issuer. A good reputation for the issuer could be driving the share prices of rivals down and its own higher. A plausible alternative explanation to the negative reactions is that the IPO signals that the industry is overvalued. Evidence presented in Chapter 2 strongly suggested that equity offerings are most likely to occur when valuations are too high.

4.3 SUMMARY

The competitive environment in which a firm operates has a profound effect on the IPO decision. Obtaining or maintaining a competitive advantage vis-à-vis rival firms makes an IPO attractive. IPOs result in the disclosure of proprietary information that can benefit or harm the issuer, conditional on the type of information and response of competitors. Externalities created when firms go public can induce additional IPOs by competitors. The externality could be positive information about the investment value or it could adversely affect the payoff to a firm if it remains private. Highly levered firms may go public to reduce their debt and gain an advantage over levered rivals. Alternatively, the need to go public and reduce debt is necessary to avoid potential predatory behavior by rivals.

Going public has the strategic benefit of conferring a good reputation upon the issuer and enhancing its visibility with investors, customers, competitors and employees. The issuer can also use the IPO event as a way to market the firm to customers and employees. The reputation and marketing benefits of an IPO should allow the firm to compete more effectively against rival firms.

NOTES

1. Bhattacharya and Ritter (1982) developed a similar financing choice signaling model.
2. Maksimovic (1988) pointed out that maintaining collusion is harder when the debt levels increase because more profits go to service the debt obligation. The incentive to deviate by lowering prices and increasing output becomes more attractive.
3. This quote originally appeared in Stoughton, Wong and Zechner (2001).
4. This is based on Baker and Gompers (1999) and Engel, Gordon and Hayes (2002).

5 Control, monitoring and governance

Accessing external capital sources introduces the challenge of designing an efficient corporate governance structure. A self-financed entrepreneur is obligated only to himself and can use the resources in any manner he sees fit. External financiers need assurances that they will be repaid before committing any capital. To alleviate investor concerns, mechanisms and structures must be implemented to prevent the entrepreneur from absconding with the funds. Corporate governance embodies the rules and regulations that grant investors control rights over the use of corporate resources and decision-making. The enforcement of control rights benefits from the monitoring of management, either directly or indirectly through incentive alignment, to deter the expropriation and inefficient use of capital.

The IPO decision is fundamentally interrelated with the design of an efficient governance structure. The firm is making a choice between the external control and monitoring associated with concentrated private equity and that of dispersed public ownership. Controlling management may conclude that the firm value is maximized by a governance structure that includes public equity investors. Control and monitoring considerations are of second-order importance in the going-public decision. The need for external capital provides the initial impetus for an IPO, but at this point the governance implications of a public offering must be carefully considered.

The role of corporate governance in the IPO process can be examined in three distinct ways. First, a theoretical analysis of the optimal ownership and control structure in response to agency conflicts provides a basis for assessing the governance motive for going public. Second, the governance structure of some private firms directly affects the IPO decision. Venture capitalists are granted significant control rights and have a say in whether their exit will be through an IPO. Third, the actual governance and control mechanisms adopted by issuers provides a test for the theory.

5.1 OPTIMAL GOVERNANCE STRUCTURE

Efficient corporate governance serves the ultimate purpose of maximizing firm value. It does this by minimizing the agency costs that inevitably arise because of conflicts between managers and external investors over the appropriate actions. Two properties characterize any governance structure. One, investors must monitor management to ensure that value-maximizing actions are selected. Two, investors have control rights to punish management if monitoring reveals managerial shirking or expropriation of resources. Public and private ownership are two distinct options for the governance structure. The relative efficiency of each depends on the effectiveness of monitoring by concentrated versus dispersed shareholders, monitoring in liquid or illiquid markets and the strength of investor control rights in the two settings.

5.1.1 Agency Conflicts

The separation of ownership of a firm's assets and effective control over those assets is at the root of shareholder-manager agency conflicts. Dating back to at least Berle and Means (1932), it has been argued that managerial ownership, at least in large public firms, is too small to perfectly align managerial interests with the shareholder objective of profit maximization. Instead, managers pursue their own agenda that can strictly reduce firm value. Jensen and Meckling's (1976) seminal article demonstrated how debt could be used to mitigate this agency conflict through the threat of bankruptcy if the manager does not create sufficient value. On the other hand, too much debt can lead to excessive risk taking.

In an ideal world a complete contract specifying the appropriate managerial action in every possible contingency can be written and enforced by investors. Unfortunately, practical constraints prevent such contracts from ever being written and non-verifiability of actions limits the enforceability of contractual clauses. Furthermore, investors hire managers to make decisions that the investors themselves are not qualified to make. It is unavoidable that managers have effective day-to-day control over the firm.

The agency costs that stem from managerial control can take a number of forms. Managers can expropriate corporate resources by directly stealing them or conducting phony transactions; for example, selling the firm's products at below market prices to corporate shells owned by the manager. Managers may shirk on their effort level, thereby lowering the firm value. Since managerial effort is only one of many factors affecting profitability, investors are unable to perfectly detect and punish shirking. Jensen (1986) argued that managers of firms that generate excess free cash flow and have few profitable investment opportunities will pursue inefficient pet projects and empire-build. Diversifying acquisitions that increase the assets under managerial control often reduce firm value.

5.1.1.1 Private control benefits

The misalignment of managerial and shareholder objectives can be traced back to private control benefits. Entrenched managers who have consolidated their control over the company can consume, perhaps excessively, private benefits of control not available to outside shareholders. Control benefits can take many forms, though usually non-pecuniary in nature. Running a large corporation, with the power to appoint officers and directors, determine compensation and set the corporate agenda can fuel a manager's ego. Control grants managers the ability to implement the strategies they believe to be in the best interest of their investment. Controlling managers can engage in self-dealing by using corporate resources to benefit themselves at the expense of the outside shareholders.

The desire to consume private benefits motivates managers to entrench themselves into a position of control. An entrenched manager is immune to career concerns, the discipline of the product market, monitoring by large shareholders and value-enhancing takeovers, and is thus costly to shareholders.[1] However, private control benefits need not have a negative effect on value. If the sole private benefit is the personal satisfaction of managing a major corporation, then shareholders are no worse off. The more likely scenario is that managers destroy shareholder value when consuming private benefits. The threat of lost private benefits may deter an entrepreneur from taking his firm public or, at the very minimum, motivate him to implement a governance structure that ensures his continued control after the IPO.[2]

The price an investor is willing to pay for a controlling interest in a firm should equal the value of the cash flow rights plus the expected private benefits. The private benefit is the difference between the cash flow value and the share price. Three approaches have been used to estimate the control premium.

1. The first measure is the premium paid in takeovers. Estimates for the premium are typically in the range of 20 to 45 percent (Schwert 1996). These estimates provide an upper bound to the control benefit because other factors, like efficiency gains, account for some of the premium.

2. The second measure is the premium paid in block transactions, which avoid some of the confounding effects of a takeover. Barclay and Holderness (1989; 1991) reported average premiums of 20 percent relative to the post-announcement share price. Hanouna, Sarin and Shapiro (2001) estimated premiums ranging from 7 to 51 percent in the US, but only 5 to 20 percent in most foreign markets.

3. The third measure compares the prices of two classes of shares in a company that differ only in their voting rights. The class with superior voting rights in US companies has traded at a 5 percent average premium (DeAngelo and DeAngelo 1985, Zingales 1995b). Although small, Zingales showed that the premium rose sharply when control was contested. Other estimated premiums include 45 percent in Isreal (Levy 1983), 20 percent in Switzerland (Horner 1988) and 82 percent in Italy (Zingales 1994).

5.1.2 Efficient Governance

The owner-managers of private firms benefit from the implementation of optimal governance structures. The definition of optimal, of course, depends on one's perspective. Managers interested in entrenching their position and retaining control would define less intrusive monitoring as optimal. However, managers are also large shareholders who directly benefit from the adoption of monitoring structures that maximize firm value. The choice between public and private ownership is also a choice between two distinct monitoring regimes. Independent of the choice, the securities sold and the control rights embedded within them should provide investors with the right incentives to monitor and the power to take action in response to managerial failure.

5.1.2.1 Optimal monitoring

The nature of external monitoring is fundamentally different between public and private ownership. Private companies are dominated by a few large blockholders. Those outside the core management group have a strong incentive to monitor because of their large equity position. Public ownership includes small, dispersed shareholders who are unlikely to actively monitor and possibly a few outside blockholders.

All external monitoring can be characterized by a few basic properties. Monitoring is a costly activity for investors, involving the collection and analysis of information that is used to spur on management to improve performance. Firm value should increase with the amount of external monitoring, but at a diminishing rate. The expected cost of monitoring is borne by the firm in the price it receives in the sale of equity. Finally, the efficient level of monitoring equates the marginal gain of shareholder value with the marginal cost of additional monitoring.

Four aspects of monitoring influence the choice of ownership structure and implicitly the IPO decision. Definitive conclusions about the optimal monitoring structure are not possible; only the potential benefits and costs of each structure can be assessed.

Duplication: The presence of too many blockholders results in the costly duplication of monitoring, reducing firm value. The failure of blockholders to coordinate their efforts means that each incurs the set-up cost to monitor, but the marginal value to the incremental monitoring can quickly fall below the cost. Pagano and Roell (1998) argued that a firm could achieve efficient monitoring if it went public and allocated shares to one monitoring blockholder and many small non-monitoring shareholders. A private placement may result in an unavoidably large number of monitors.

Managerial incentives: In lieu of costly direct monitoring, shareholders can write incentive contracts designed to align managerial interests with those of investors. A public listing creates an observable share price on which an incentive contract can be written (Holmstrom and Tirole 1993). The stock price aggregates information about the consequences of managerial actions, thus making equity-based compensation a powerful incentive mechanism for managers. Incentive contracts in private companies must be based on accounting measures, which are subject to managerial manipulation and thus are less powerful.

Expropriation: Large blockholders have the ability to expropriate corporate resources for their own personal benefit. An example is the demand for favorable terms for new finance after a successful performance by the firm. The inability of a large blockholder to pre-commit to not expropriate resources from the manager *ex post* adversely affects the *ex ante* managerial incentives to put forth the efficient effort (Burkart, Gromb and Pununzi 1997). Public ownership reduces or eliminates excessively large shareholders and the threats they pose to firm value.

Free ride: All investors share the benefits produced by monitoring, but only the monitoring investors have to incur the cost.[3] Each investor has an incentive to free-ride on the efforts of others, resulting in inefficiently low monitoring. Concentrated ownership with only a few blockholders – typical of a private firm – overcomes this problem and increases firm value. The free-rider problem may be the most important individual factor in determining the optimal monitoring regime. Advocates of leveraged buyouts point to the monitoring benefits of concentrated ownership. An entrenched manager who prefers less monitoring will instead seek out dispersed public ownership.

5.1.2.2 Optimal securities

Well-designed securities are the foundation of a governance structure that maximizes firm value. The equity contract with shareholders is a major component of the governance relationship. Equity cash flow rights provide the incentive to monitor management and the control rights, primarily in the form of voting rights, can be exercised to effect change following poor performance.

The strength of investor control rights depends on the effectiveness of the voting rights. Small investors have essentially no direct control because individually their votes are largely irrelevant and coordinating their votes is difficult. Shareholders are represented by the board of directors, which has a fiduciary duty to act on their behalf. However, since management usually appoints the board, its ability to independently monitor is often weak. A large investor with a significant fraction of the voting rights can overcome the free-rider problem, especially if he tries to acquire a majority position. Corporate charter anti-takeover provisions delay, and can effectively prevent, an outside acquisition of control. In this case the market for corporate control, an implicit control right for shareholders, loses out to entrenched managers.

Theory suggests that the value-maximizing governance structure for equity at the time of the IPO is one share one vote (Grossman and Hart 1988). The intuition is fairly straightforward. The manager wants to make it costly to deter a change in control, especially one that increases the cash flow value to all shareholders, just to protect his or her private benefits. The credible commitment to accept change, if it is warranted, maximizes the share price received in the IPO. By similar reasoning issuers should not adopt corporate charter provisions that impede takeovers.

The firm could implement a dual class structure in place of one-share-one-vote rules. The controlling owners retain the high vote shares and sell the low vote shares. When a dual class structure is implemented the optimal design is to assign high cash flow rights to the low vote shares. This increases the cost to the controlling owners of matching a bid by a rival who produces higher cash flow value for the firm, thus resulting in more efficient transfers of control.

Deviating from the efficient one-share-one-vote rule is optimal under some circumstances. Dual class structures can mitigate underinvestment problems. Managers may avoid issuing the required external equity to finance investment if it dilutes their voting rights (Attari and Banerjee 1999). In addition, managers may underinvest in costly firm-specific human capital if their access to private control benefits is at risk (Fischel 1987; Denis and Denis 1994).

5.1.3 Liquidity and Control

Liquidity plays an important role in the choice and efficiency of governance structures. The cost of equity falls with the liquidity in the secondary market, favoring public ownership. At the same time, a liquid secondary market undermines the incentive for investors to monitor management, lowering the firm value, because selling underperforming shares is relatively costless. Consequently, the IPO decision must compare the benefits and costs of liquidity in public and private markets. The optimal number of shares to sell in a public offering must also trade off the loss of control with the incremental benefits of liquidity.

5.1.3.1 Liquidity versus control

Liquidity is generally thought to be a virtue of well-functioning capital markets. Investors incur smaller transaction costs when the bid-ask spread narrows because of greater trading activity. Share prices increase because a narrow spread lowers the required rate of return (Amihud and Mendelson 1986). Yet there is a dark side to liquidity. Investors can sell their stake at low cost in liquid markets if the firm is not performing well, rather than incurring the cost of monitoring management and demanding an improvement to the operating returns. When liquidity is poor, and a quick, cheap sale is not possible, an investor's best option is to closely monitor to increase the value. Thus, the net effect of liquidity on firm value is ambiguous.

   The policy environment does not favor good corporate governance in the liquidity versus control debate. Many have argued that political considerations have helped shape the development of US capital markets toward higher liquidity and lower investor activism (see Coffee 1991; Bhide 1993; and Roe 1994). Chief executive officers who benefit personally from less monitoring of their actions and investors who prefer liquid markets have effectively lobbied policy-makers against adopting laws and regulations that give large investors greater ability to effect reform of the corporation.

5.1.3.2 Speculation

The information investors acquire during their monitoring activities can be used either for their own speculative gain or to prod management to improve performance. An investor is better able to 'hide' his speculative trades from other investors as market liquidity increases, thereby increasing his abnormal profits. Alternatively, exhorting management to improve performance results in a capital gain as the share value increases. Greater liquidity may tip the balance in favor of speculative trading, further weakening the advantage of public governance (Kahn and Winton 1998).

Liquidity-induced speculative trading need not be detrimental to effective control and can result in indirect monitoring through a more informative stock price (Holmstrom and Tirole 1993). Managerial incentive contracts based on the stock price act as a substitute for direct investor activism in the firm's operations. Private information is impounded into the stock price in the course of speculative trading. The stock price then becomes a barometer of managerial performance. The quality of the stock price signal improves with liquidity because informed speculators acquire more information and trade more aggressively on it. A refined price signal increases the power of the incentive contract, leading to more effective indirect monitoring.

5.1.3.3 Initial concentration

Two decisions made by managers at the IPO have direct bearing on aftermarket liquidity and the efficiency of the governance structure. First, the fraction of the firm sold in the offering must be chosen. Selling more shares, all else being equal, increases liquidity. Short-term liquidity traders should lose on average when trading against informed speculators. The anticipation of these losses at the time of the IPO means the offer price must be discounted to induce these investors to buy shares.[4] The optimal offer size trades off the benefits of increased speculative trading with the additional intentional underpricing (Holmstrom and Tirole 1993).

The second decision is whether to allocate a large block to a single outside investor, perhaps in a joint private placement, to ensure that there is sufficient post-IPO monitoring. The virtue of creating a large monitoring blockholder at the outset depends on the ease with which similar blockholders can arise on their own in the secondary market. Greater liquidity facilitates the accumulation of a block position and anything less than wide distribution at the IPO hampers this process.

When the exogenous level of liquidity is low, possibly because the stock receives little publicity or analyst coverage, the best option is to create a blockholder. Further supporting this position is the adverse effect of the free-rider problem (Bolton and von Thadden 1998).[5] Accumulating a block in the aftermarket can be costly if investors anticipate the increased monitoring and higher firm value. Investors will only sell at the expected post-monitoring price, extracting the value gains that should accrue to the large blockholder.[6] A large initial block alleviates the disincentive to monitor for two reasons (Maug 1998). First, a large stake means the shareholder receives a sufficient fraction of the monitoring-induced capital gain to cover the monitoring cost. Second, the lower liquidity due to the blockholding reduces the potential for speculative trading profits, further biasing the investor towards active monitoring.

A dispersed initial ownership becomes attractive once the exogenous liquidity exceeds a certain threshold. A large blockholder can emerge in the secondary market at relatively low cost to monitor management, yet the firm still retains the benefits of high liquidity.[7] Bolton and von Thadden (1998) argued that the efficiency of a dispersed ownership rises when the potential gain from monitoring increase. The reason is that concentration is now easier to achieve in the secondary market because investors recognize the benefit to intervening in management.

5.1.4 Change of Control

An IPO begins the dilution of insiders' ownership of the firm, which may actually culminate in a complete change in control. A transfer of control might even be efficient. The total surplus – firm cash flow value plus the private control benefits accruing to the majority owner – could increase if new owners control the firm. Owners looking to cash out would be well advised to take their firm public before selling out completely. A two-stage process beginning with an IPO would allow them to maximize the total proceeds from the sale. Three reasons suggest why this is the case.

Adverse selection: Asset sales are adversely affected by asymmetric information. The original owners may try to exploit their superior knowledge about the firm by demanding a price above the true value. Buyers, anticipating this possibility, pull out of the market. Completing an IPO before selling the firm gives potential buyers a stock price that reflects the beliefs of many informed traders. The informative stock price reduces the adverse selection cost to selling the firm. The original owners can maximize the sale proceeds by selling a small number of shares in the IPO and then the rest in a seasoned offering (Ellingsen and Rydqvist 1997).[8]

Surplus extraction: A two-stage sale is optimal if the old owner can use the IPO to extract the additional value generated by the new owner (Zingales 1995b). The old owner starts by selling cash flow rights to small, individual shareholders in the IPO, while retaining control with a majority of the voting rights. He then bargains directly with the buyer over the retained cash flow and control rights in the second stage.

The key to this process is that the small IPO investors anticipate the second-stage sale. The investors will accept an offer price equal to the cash flow value expected under the new owner. If the value is expected to increase, the old owner can extract the gain at the IPO. A direct private transaction between the old and new owners involves bargaining over the entire incremental surplus created by the new owner. The fraction received by the old owner depends on the relative bargaining skill of each. By completing an IPO first, the bargaining is over the smaller residual cash flow value not sold in the IPO. The old owner is able to increase his share of the surplus by selling the firm in two stages.

Price discrimination: A two-stage transaction could be the optimal way to create a large monitoring blockholder (Mello and Parsons 1998). The basic procedure follows the surplus extraction argument, with the change that the second stage is now a private placement to a large investor. The price the blockholder is willing to pay is a function of his expectation for the share value and the private control benefits derived from his position. The benefit to two stages is that the market price provides information about the firm value produced by the small investors. The manager uses this information to extract a higher premium from the blockholder in the private placement.

5.2 CONTROL AND EXIT

The decision to go public is one that is made by jointly by the principal shareholders. Reaching agreement among the few controlling shareholders should be fairly easy. The inclusion of a venture capitalist (VC), however, adds a complicating twist to the decision-making process. Neither the entrepreneur nor the VC has complete authority to make the final decision without agreement of the other. Venture capitalists make their initial investment on the expectation of exiting in relatively short order. The need to exit and the options available could create tension between the VC and the entrepreneur over the fate of the firm. Therefore the allocation of control rights to the VC affects whether or not a firm goes public.

5.2.1 Exit Options

A VC can exit from his investment in a portfolio company in one of five ways. The most desirable exit is an IPO. The VC can sell shares in the IPO or wait anytime from six months to a couple of years before selling. The general partner of the VC fund normally does not sell the shares; instead they are distributed to the limited partners who decide independently when to sell. The second exit option is an acquisition of the portfolio company by another firm. Acquisitions are commonly referred to as liquidation events.

The VC could receive cash in the transaction, shares in the acquiring firm, or other assets. If the acquirer is a publicly traded firm, the VC can sell the shares on the open market and exit immediately. Any conflicts over the exit decision usually involve the choice between an IPO and a takeover.

The remaining three exit options are a repurchase of the VC's shares by the firm, a complete liquidation of the company and distribution of the resultant cash to the shareholders, and a secondary sale of the VC's shares to a strategic buyer. Secondary sales without a full sale of the entire firm are uncommon. Formal liquidations differ from acquisitions in that the assets of the firm are sold off piecemeal to individual buyers. Repurchases and liquidations usually grant the VC priority in the distribution of the proceeds, conditional on the availability of sufficient funds. The exit event cannot be contractually specified *ex ante* and must be jointly chosen by the entrepreneur and VC in the future.

5.2.2 Optimal Contracts

The allocation of control rights in the VC contract is made with two considerations in mind. First, control should be allocated between the entrepreneur and VC in a manner that leads to efficient exit decisions. Second, the contract should minimize the agency costs for the duration of the relationship. Venture capitalists are active in their portfolio companies, sitting on the board, advising management and developing business relationships with third parties. This level of involvement reduces the potential for agency conflicts, but the high degree of uncertainty over future outcomes ensures that the entrepreneur retains considerable discretion over his actions.

The agency costs discussed earlier – shirking, expropriation and private control benefits – are present in start-up firms. Two additional costs are the entrepreneur's desire to continue investing in a project that has little chance of success and the hold-up problem. The viability of a firm often hinges on the specific skills and talent of the founder. Continual threats by the founder to leave unless the VC offers better terms could be the firm's undoing.

Financial contracting theory has proposed a number of properties that an optimal contract should possess, with results that are applicable to VC investment. The entrepreneur and VC must have financial incentives that are closely aligned. Entrepreneur compensation – stock options and cash flow rights – should be made contingent on output or profit signals (Holmstrom 1979). The pursuit of private control benefits can distract the entrepreneur from pure profit maximization. To realign the entrepreneur's incentives, control rights should be allocated on a state-contingent basis (Grossman and Hart 1986; Aghion and Bolton 1992). The VC gains control when the financial performance is poor, while the entrepreneur retains control when results are good. Payoffs and actions are frequently non-verifiable and thus cannot be contracted upon. The optimal contract is an easy to verify hard claim, such as debt, that transfers control to the VC following a poor outcome (Gale and Hellwig 1985; Hart and Moore 1994).

Explicit theoretical analysis of the entrepreneur–VC relationship has built on these general models to design optimal VC contracts. The theory has also examined how control should be allocated throughout the relationship to resolve the exit problem for the VC. Three key characteristics of optimal VC contracts stand out.

Convertible securities: The optimal contract for the VC is a convertible security.[9] The VC initially has a hard claim, most likely preferred shares, which receives a fixed payoff. The preferred shares are converted into common shares following a specific event or good performance. The entrepreneur receives common equity from the start, making him a residual claimant. Preferred shares are senior to common equity, granting the VC control in the bad states when the hard claim in not met and conversion does not occur. Conversion dilutes the control rights of the VC in the good states. The contract gives the entrepreneur a strong incentive to maximize profits and retain high cash flow and control rights.

Staging: The optimal supply of capital should occur in stages.[10] Each additional capital infusion is based on past performance and specific benchmarks being achieved. Staging minimizes agency costs because the capital supplied at each stage is limited and contingent on good outcomes. Staging also provides the VC with an implicit right to exit the company by refusing to supply any more capital.

Accumulating control: The optimal contract should allocate greater control rights to the entrepreneur at the beginning of the relationship and transfer more control to the VC as time passes (Hellmann 2002, Smith 2001). The staging of finance does result in the VC accumulating additional control rights at each stage. Allocating greater control over the exit event to the VC will allow him or her to optimally redeploy his or her capital. The entrepreneur, if in control, might prefer to keep the firm private and independent to preserve his or her private benefits.

5.2.3 Contractual Provisions

The contracts signed by VCs and entrepreneurs are extensive and spell out in great detail the rights of both parties. The final contract is based on the

91

non-binding term sheet presented by the VC to the entrepreneur when the financing is sought. The term sheet lists the rights and obligations of the two parties and the financial terms of the investment.

The standard security held by the VC is convertible preferred equity (CPE), while the founder and angel investors own common equity. Deviations from this template are not unusual, especially in Europe where VCs hold combinations of common equity and straight debt or preferred shares (Cumming 2002). The CPE has two types of conversion provisions: optional conversion of preferred into common at will and automatic conversion at specified events, including the IPO. The preferred stock is sometimes entitled to dividends, which accumulate over time if unpaid. The preferred shareholders receive a liquidation preference – their initial investment plus any unpaid accrued dividends – in the event of an acquisition or liquidation before common shareholders are compensated.

The conversion privileges afforded the VC can create different cash flow rights in the event of an IPO and an acquisition, which can lead to conflicting preferences relative to the entrepreneur. Most acquiring companies allow the VC to convert its preferred into common shares, in addition to receiving the liquidation preference. The VC's shares are converted at an IPO, but without receiving the preference. Assuming that an IPO and an acquisition garner equal total proceeds, the VC prefers an acquisition, whereas the entrepreneur wants to go public. A frequently used security called participating convertible preferred equity resolves this conflict, although not to the benefit of the entrepreneur. Upon both exits, the VC receives the liquidation preference for the preferred stock and the conversion of the preferred into common equity, effectively 'double-dipping'.

The control wielded by the VC over the exit decision and other general operational issues depends on the explicit contractual provisions. The preferred stock does come with voting rights. Seats on the board of directors are the most effective method of controlling the exit. The board is charged with managing the affairs of the corporation and initiates the most important exit decisions. While shareholder approval is required for certain transactions, they typically do not initiate exit events. Additional contractual provisions are listed in Table 5.1.

5.2.4 Contractual Features

Real venture capital contracts should provide the proper financial incentives for the entrepreneur, allocate control rights to achieve the optimal continuation and exit decisions, and efficiently allocate the payoff risk

Table 5.1 Contractual provisions pertaining to VC control rights

Clause	Description
Negative covenants	Veto rights over certain transactions, including mergers and charter amendments, the latter being a precursor to an IPO
Redemption ('put') rights	The VC can redeem his or her shares by having the company repurchase them for an amount specified in the contract. The rights can be mandatory or optional, but kick in only after a few years
Demand registration rights	Contractual right to initiate an IPO, contingent on certain ownership conditions being met. The provision provides almost no practical control because forcing an IPO with the management support is not credible
Right of first refusal	The VC has the right to purchase up to 50 percent of the shares that the company proposes to offer to any person
Co-sale agreement	Shares held by the entrepreneur/manager cannot be sold, transferred or exchanged unless each owner of the preferred stock (the VC) has had an opportunity to participate in the sale
Anti-dilution provisions	The conversion price of any convertible security will be adjusted to reduce any dilution that results when the company sells additional equity. The price is also adjusted for stock splits, stock dividends, etc.
Protection rights against new issues	Consent by a majority of preferred shareholders is required for any action that alters or changes the rights, privileges, seniority, or number of shares held by preferred shareholders

between the two parties. Detailed examination of real contracts by Kaplan and Stromberg (2003a, 2003b) and Cumming (2002) enable a comparison between theory and practice. Their main results are summarized below, but an overall assessment is that actual contracts possess many theoretically desirable properties.

Cash flow rights: The allocation of cash flow rights is highly sensitive to the performance outcome. For example, the average entrepreneur cash flow rights in Kaplan and Stromberg (2003a) increased eight percentage points when all, as opposed to none, of the performance targets were met. The entrepreneur's equity stake was far more contingent on performance when the VC had control, consistent with the VC adopting powerful incentive compensation. Entrepreneurial compensation was also more contingent-based when uncertainty about the firm and its environment was high.

Control rights: The two principal forms of control are voting rights and board control. The cumulative VC voting rights increased with the financing round, but that did not necessarily translate into board control. The entrepreneur retained/obtained more control rights as company performance improved. If the company performed very well, the VCs retained their cash flow rights, but relinquished most of their control and liquidation rights. Venture capitalist control rights were stronger when the investment uncertainty was high, suggesting that the VCs want more control to prevent an entrepreneur from continuing poor projects.

Complementarities: Cash flow and control rights were separated and used as complements. However, the VC's cash flow, voting and board rights generally increased with each financing round, inducing correlation in their terms. Cumming (2002) found that VCs typically had fewer control rights when common equity was used and more with mixes of preferred and common stock. He reported that VCs indicated deals with simple payoff structures were typically associated with fewer contractual provisions because the important distinguishing aspect of the deal was its simplicity.

Convertible use: The dominant form of financing, used 95 percent of the time in the Kaplan and Stromberg (2003a) sample, was a convertible security, with participating convertible preferred used frequently.[11] Automatic conversion provisions were common, almost always at the IPO, but they usually required certain performance targets to be attained.[12] The VC gives up many of his control rights upon conversion if the performance targets are met. Schwienbacher (2002) reported that convertibles were used less than a third as often in Europe relative to the US.

Contingencies: Cash flow and control rights and future financing rounds were often contingent on observable and verifiable measures of financial and non-financial performance. Contingencies were most common in early stage rounds. A financial contingency might specify that the VC obtains voting control if the firm's earnings fall below an agreed upon level. A non-financial contingency might be the hiring of a new executive. Greater uncertainty internal and external to a firm resulted in more contingent financing within a round and shorter duration between rounds, respectively. These patterns suggest an attempt to minimize agency and monitoring costs.

Hold-up problem: Two provisions were often included to mitigate the hold-up problem. Non-compete clauses prohibited the entrepreneur from working for another firm in the same industry for a certain period if he or she left. Vesting provisions restrict the entrepreneur's access to his or her shares until he or she is with the firm a specified amount of time. Such clauses were most common in early financing rounds. Vesting provisions were used in complex environments where the entrepreneur's human capital was critical because standard financial incentives were not effective.

5.2.5 Exit Patterns

The exit patterns of VCs from their portfolio companies can be used to answer a number of important questions. Can the initial investment be classified as a success based on the exit event? Did the choice of exit reflect the control rights of the VC and was there conflict with the entrepreneur? Finally, what strategy did the VC follow in liquidating his or her position and how did it affect the duration of the exit?

5.2.5.1 Method

A clear pattern has emerged in the exit of VC investments across a diverse range of countries.[13] Roughly 25 to 30 percent of portfolio companies are exited through an IPO, about 25 to 30 percent are acquisition exits and the remaining 40 to 50 percent of investments are written off or have unknown outcomes. In 2002 VentureOne reported that in five of the preceding six years in the US there were more VC exits via acquisition than IPOs. The number of exits of both types were near or a little above 200 over the 1996–2001 period. IPOs are thought to be the pinnacle of a successful investment, but acquisitions can connote success as well; Cisco's purchase of Cerent for $6.9 billion being the most striking example. Laine and Torstila (2003) reported that large VC firms had significantly higher rates of successful exit – either an IPO or acquisition – as did larger funds, suggesting that size and reputation confer a certification benefit that improves a company's prospects.

The IPO/acquisition choice can engender conflict between the VC and entrepreneur. The latter is able to retain control after an IPO and would generally prefer this option. Disagreement might arise when the IPO market is closed. If the VC needs to exit, he or she will push for an acquisition, whereas the entrepreneur prefers to wait for the IPO window to open. Brau, Francis and Kohers (2003) did find that the probability of an IPO exit in the US increased in the 'hotness' of the IPO market relative to the takeover market. Observing actual conflict over the exit is rare. However, Cumming (2002) noted that five of the ten IPO exits for which he had data involved a conflict about timing and one involved a conflict about valuation. The true amount of conflict could be far higher, but that is unknowable.

The allocation of control rights appears to be related to the exit event. Cumming (2002) observed that the amount of control and veto rights granted to VCs were positively associated with acquisition exits. These acquisitions appeared to be pre-planned and the control rights could have helped expedite the takeover. IPOs were related to the use of common equity (in Europe) for VCs, which would give the entrepreneur more control. The tentative conclusion based on this limited data is that contracts are simpler when the objective is to give control back to the entrepreneur.

5.2.5.2 Exit duration

The exit event provides the VC with the opportunity to cash out, but that does not mean that a full exit is completed immediately. A partial exit, with only some of the VC's shares sold in the event or shortly thereafter, could constitute an optimal divesting strategy in the presence of asymmetric information (Cumming and MacIntosh 2003). Potential investors risk purchasing overpriced equity and could interpret the VC's decision to sell everything at the event negatively. Just as the entrepreneur retaining a large fraction of the equity conveys a positive signal about the value, so too does the VC's decision to hold off on immediate liquidation.

Partial exits are more attractive when asymmetric information is severe. Secondary sales and buybacks involve informed, perfectly in the latter case, buyers. Acquisitions are targeted to strategic buyers who will conduct a thorough due diligence review before the takeover. IPOs, however, involve retail and institutional investors who possess only limited knowledge of the issuer. Cumming and MacIntosh (2003) documented that partial exits were most common in IPOs and surprisingly secondary sales and buybacks, and were rare in write-offs.

Venture capitalists can partially overcome the asymmetry cost by developing a good reputation. Venture capitalists with a track record of backing issuers that were properly priced and that performed well in the aftermarket have credibility with investors that their current offerings are fairly priced. Reputable VCs can use this to their advantage by selling more shares in the IPO. In fact, Lin and Smith (1998) observed this very relationship. They also reported that reputable lead VCs sold fewer shares as the initial return decreased, which they conjectured was the VC's attempt to protect his or her reputation by not selling potentially overpriced shares.

5.3 ISSUER GOVERNANCE STRUCTURES

Implementing an effective corporate governance structure at the IPO is critical for a number of reasons. Since the firm value is a function of the governance structure adopted, the amount of proceeds that can be raised from the offering is directly affected. The future firm performance depends on the incentive and control mechanisms in place for management. Selecting the appropriate incentives to align managerial interests with those of shareholders is fundamental to minimizing agency costs. Lastly, the legal reorganization of the issuer that precedes the IPO is decided by a small group of shareholders. Subsequent changes to the governance structure also require shareholder approval, but this is more difficult to attain with a large, dispersed investor base. The structure implemented at the IPO is likely to persist indefinitely and should be chosen wisely.

5.3.1 External Regulations

The foundation of effective corporate governance starts with investor access to the information needed to evaluate managerial performance. The management of a public company is legally obligated to provide investors with timely and accurate information about the firm's operations and performance, a burden not placed on private companies. The SEC requires US public companies to file quarterly and annual audited financial statements. Public disclosure statements must also be issued following specific actions or events, such as an acquisition or the sale of shares by officers and directors.

The external regulations for public companies provide shareholders with information that would be difficult and costly to acquire through their own independent review. Without the assurance of receiving accurate information, investors will be reluctant to supply capital.[14] The large concentrated shareholders in a private company should have the resources, incentives and sophistication to effectively monitor management without recourse to publicly disclosed documents.

The aftermath of the late 1990s stock market bubble revealed glaring examples of corporate malfeasance, most notably Enron and Worldcom. Much of the blame for the failure of these and other companies was attributed to a breakdown of effective corporate governance. Unscrupulous accounting tricks, manipulated transactions and skewed financial incentives for senior management all contributed to the eventual downfall of these firms. In response, lawmakers passed the Sarbanes-Oxley Act, which was designed to combat the real and perceived failures of existing corporate governance rules.

The implementation of the Sarbanes-Oxley Act has two implications for the IPO decision. First, the additional burden it places on management will deter some marginal companies from going public. The surge in interest among small public companies to go private shortly after the Act was passed corroborates this conjecture. Second, external governance regulations are uniformly imposed on all public companies. The firm-specific aspects of corporate governance – the allocation of cash flow and control rights – are still decided individually by issuers at the IPO. However, Sarbanes-Oxley will undoubtedly affect the self-imposed structures that define a firm's corporate governance.

5.3.2 Control Rights

Control rights in a public firm are synonymous with voting rights. A simple majority of the voting rights is sufficient to grant control to a shareholder in most companies. Inside shareholders – the executives, officers, directors and other large shareholders – must decide how much control to relinquish after the IPO. The choice involves a trade-off: retaining more control better preserves private benefits but with the potential loss in firm value. The power of outside investor voting rights is reflected in their ability to influence the board of directors, which has the responsibility of representing the interests of all shareholders.

5.3.2.1 Retained ownership

The pattern of retained control has been fairly constant across issuers and time.[15] The typical issuer floats one-third of the post-IPO outstanding shares, with the remaining two-thirds retained by pre-IPO shareholders, although considerable variation does exist. The consistency of this percentage suggests that investment bankers use it as a benchmark for an optimal initial ownership structure. Field (1999) examined the breakdown of insider ownership immediately before and after the IPO. In her sample the chairman, CEO and president collectively owned 26 and 18 percent of the total shares pre- and post-IPO, respectively. The combined ownership of officers and directors was 73 and 50 percent pre- and post-IPO.

The ownership stake of the pre-IPO shareholders further declined with the duration from the IPO. Mikkelson, Partch and Shah (1997) documented the long-term decline in ownership of officers and directors in a sample of 1983 IPOs. The pre-IPO ownership started at 67.9 percent, fell to 43.7 percent immediately after the IPO and, finally, to 28.6 and 17.9 percent five and ten years later. The long-term managerial ownership decline is due to VCs liquidating their holdings, management selling their shares in follow-on offerings and the open market, and additional primary equity offerings diluting their stake.

The gradual decline in insider ownership does not necessarily translate into a loss of control over the firm. Effective day-to-day control can be had with as little as 20 percent of the votes if the remaining shareholders are small and dispersed. For the pre-IPO insiders, the slow disbursement of their majority position allows them to retain their access to the private control benefits.

5.3.2.2 Dual-class stock

Inside owners can maintain control after the IPO by implementing a dual-class share structure. The standard structure involves class A shares being sold to investors on a one share one vote basis. The typical class B shares retained by the controlling owner each has ten votes, although the number can vary. Both share classes have the same cash flow rights. The following example illustrates how the separation of cash flow and control rights alters the ownership structure. The issuer could sell ten one-vote shares and retain nine ten-vote shares. The insider would have 90 percent of the votes, but just under 50 percent of the cash flow rights.

The use of dual-class shares has increased over time, with nearly one in nine issuers adopting this structure in the late 1990s (Smart and Zutter 2003). The typical dual-class IPO involved a sale of 8 percent of the voting rights and 28 percent of the cash flow rights (Field 1999). Dual-class shares cannot be easily transferred. Almost without exception, the high-vote shares lose their superior voting rights if an insider sells them to another party, unless that party is also an insider. Field (1999) found that 22 percent of dual firms were family controlled, where control is presumably highly valued, compared to only 3 percent for single class firms.[16] The dual firms were also concentrated in the communication, printing and publishing industry, reflecting a desire for editorial control.

The use of a dual-class structure is limited by investors' willingness to buy low vote shares. Benefits other than control are needed to attract them. There is evidence that dual-class issuers were of higher quality relative to single class firms. Dual firms were usually more profitable, larger, hired more prestigious underwriters, more likely to pay immediate dividends, generated normal to above-normal market and operating performance, and traded at a 20 percent discount all relative to similar single class firms (Boehmer, Sanger and Varshney 1995; Field 1999; Smart and Zutter 2003).

5.3.2.3 Board of directors

The board of directors has a fiduciary duty to shareholders to monitor the actions and decisions of management, remove management if necessary and consider corporate control transactions that will increase shareholder value. Board members are one of three types: executive, instrumental and monitoring (Baysinger and Butler 1985). Executives are the officers, retirees and other insiders. Instrumental directors are the bankers, lawyers, accountants and consultants who provide services to the firm. Instrumental directors are quasi-outsiders who lack a true ability to be objective monitors of management. Monitoring directors are outsiders who do not have any other affiliation with the firm.

The median issuer board at the IPO has had six members, which is less than half the size of a typical public corporation (Field 1999; Baker and Gompers 2003). The boards were roughly split with half being inside directors and the other half consisting of an equal number of outsiders and quasi-outsiders. Financiers made up the largest fraction of quasi-outsiders, with an average of 0.6 seats. Venture capitalists were the largest non-insider holder of seats with 0.66.

Board independence, measured by the number of outsiders, is a sign of good corporate governance. Venture capitalists should understand that this positively affects the firm value at the IPO and therefore lobby for greater independence. Venture capital-backed firms had larger boards compared to non-VC firms, 6.2 versus 5.9, but with fewer insiders, 2.4 versus 3.2, and quasi-outsiders (Baker and Gompers 2003). As expected, VC-backed firms had greater representation of VCs on the board; 1.6 versus 0.1 seats for non-VC firms. The value-added services provided by the VC led to a substitution away for instrumental directors. Hochberg (2003) similarly found that the percentages of outsiders on the board for VC and non-VC-backed firms were 65.1 and 42.9 percent, respectively.

Hochberg examined two other measures of board independence. First, the audit and compensation committees were far more likely to be free of insiders if the firm had VC backing. Second, the CEO served as chairman in 46.5 and 72.7 percent of VC and non-VC firms, respectively. Separating the jobs of chairman and CEO should lead to a more objective evaluation of the managerial performance and therefore better accountability.

The final board composition is the outcome of bargaining between the CEO and the VC. The CEO and other officers prefer to place 'friendly' candidates on the board to reduce monitoring. Baker and Gompers (2003) conjectured that the longer the CEO's tenure with the firm and the more skilled he or she is relative to the board's alternative candidates, the greater the bargaining power he or she possesses. Likewise, the VCs' power to determine the board rested on their reputation and ability to attract superior alternative CEO candidates. Sure enough, the number of VC board seats fell with CEO tenure and voting control, but rose with the VC reputation.

5.3.3 Monitoring Incentives

Direct monitoring of management by outside investors is rarely possible. The marginal benefit to small investors is unlikely to compensate for the time and expenditure required. The managerial control of the information flow further complicates matters. An alternative and indirect way to minimize agency costs is to align the financial incentives of managers with shareholders. Compensation can take three forms: fixed salary, capital gains from equity ownership and stock options.

Total compensation: The primary source of CEO compensation is capital gains. The typical CEO owns approximately 20 percent of the post-IPO outstanding shares. The second largest form of compensation is stock options. The base salary is the smallest component of compensation and is not very responsive to the firm performance. In a sample of IPOs from 1996 to 1999, Engel, Gordon and Hayes (2002) estimated the average total CEO compensation to be $8.6 million in the IPO year and $3.6 million in the year after. They also found some evidence that firms tried to achieve a target level of compensation. Chief executive officers with small equity stakes prior to the IPO, in the range of 10 to 15 percent, did not sell shares in the offering and received option grants. In contrast, CEOs with larger stakes, 25 to 45 percent, sold shares but did not receive options.

Monitoring: The elasticity of CEO compensation to a change in shareholder wealth is one measure of how closely aligned CEO and shareholder interests are. The elasticity measures the change in CEO wealth – based on the equity stake, stock options and salary – for a $1,000 change in total shareholder value. Engel, Gordon and Hayes (2002) reported an elasticity of $186 for IPOs occurring from 1996 to 1999. A similar study by Baker and Gompers (1999) for the 1979–87 period estimated an elasticity of $220.[17] The equity stake wealth elasticity was much lower in the later period, $138 to $211. The difference was partly made up by the much larger recent use of stock options, with respective option wealth elasticities of $46 and $2.8. Baker and Gompers found that the wealth elasticity was lower for VC versus non-VC issuers, $144 to $254. The direct VC monitoring of management could be reducing the need for CEO financial incentives.

Performance measures: Ideal incentive contracts should tie CEO compensation to the firm performance. Stock options are the obvious choice, but exogenous factors weaken the link between stock prices and performance. Compensation contracts based on accounting data removes much of the noise. However, accounting returns are subject to managerial manipulation and may not be a good measure of performance among young firms. Stock-based incentive compensation is more attractive when the quality of accounting information is poor.

Engel, Gordon and Hayes (2002) compared the incentive contracts used in the Internet, non-Internet technology and manufacturing industries. They assumed that the quality and transparency of accounting information increased monotonically across the preceding industry ordering. Specifically, they analyzed the relationship between post-IPO CEO compensation grants and the information content of earnings and stock returns. Total compensation was positively related to earnings for manufacturing firms and stock returns for Internet firms, but not vice versa. This pattern suggests that firms relied on the relatively more precise performance measure to create stronger incentives.

5.3.4 Control and Defenses

The effectiveness of voting rights depends on when and under which circumstances the votes can be exercised. Minority shareholders sometimes have little recourse against entrenched managers who produce poor stock returns. One option is to take over the firm in the market for corporate control and remove management, thus increasing shareholder value. Pre-IPO inside owners anticipate such an eventuality and respond by revising the corporate charter before going public. Specific anti-takeover provisions (ATPs) can be adopted to prevent unsolicited acquisition attempts. This further diminishes the control rights of minority shareholders.

5.3.4.1 ATP benefits and costs

A debate over the merits of ATPs has been ongoing since the mid-1980s when they first appeared. On one side are mostly practitioners arguing that ATP use is justified because of the negative consequences of hostile takeovers. The other side, usually academics, argues that ATPs do more harm than good and should be avoided. Each side can point to specific benefits and costs to support their position. The first three points in the following list are purported benefits, the latter three are costs.

Bargaining power: An ATP can enhance management's bargaining power when negotiating with a bidder, increasing the premium paid to target shareholders if an acquisition occurs (DeAngelo and Rice 1983; Stulz 1988). The benefit is a direct consequence of the collective action problem; dispersed target shareholders may tender at a price below the maximum attainable because coordinated action is not possible. Attracting multiple bidders to compete for the firm also alleviates this problem.

Managerial myopia: The lower likelihood of a hostile bid when ATPs are used increases the managerial incentives to invest in good long-run projects whose value may not be reflected in the stock price (Stein 1989: Shleifer and Vishny 1990). In the absence of ATPs, managers may sacrifice long-term value to boost current earnings in order to increase the share price and prevent shareholders from being 'ripped off' by a raider.[18]

Social cost: A hostile bid is disruptive and costly to a firm as management wastes time engaged in a proxy fight for shareholder approval. The target firm is often subject to a substantial reorganization after acquisition. Assets are sold off and socially harmful layoffs are frequent. Defenses can deter a hostile bid from arising, avoiding these costs.

Reduced premiums: Anti-takeover provisions prevent takeovers that produce immediate profits for shareholders. Target shareholders earn substantial returns – 30 to 45 percent in Schwert (1996) – from a tender offer. The share price of most stocks includes an implicit takeover premium to reflect the possibility of a high-return acquisition. The premium is reduced when ATPs are in place.

Managerial entrenchment: Defenses can further exacerbate agency costs because managers are no longer disciplined by the market for corporate control. They can continue to pursue value-reducing activities, extract above market compensation and consume excessive control benefits.

Inefficient allocation: Social welfare dictates that the firm should be sold to the bidder with a higher total surplus, even if the cash flow value is lower under the new owner. Anti-takeover provisions restrict the efficient allocation of resources if a bidder has a higher total valuation for the firm than the current owners.

The theory fails to offer a convincing prediction, one way or another, for the affect of ATP adoption on shareholder value. Empirical analysis has proved no more helpful in resolving the debate. Based on a large number of studies, the price reaction to the adoption of ATPs is not significantly different from zero.[19] Anti-takeover provisions did not reduce the frequency of hostile bids, although they helped to entrench management (Comment and Schwert 1995). Managers protected by ATPs were more likely to resist a hostile bid and received higher compensation (Daines 2001).

5.3.4.2 Defense mechanisms

Issuers have a wide range of ATPs to choose from prior to the IPO. The ATP could be an explicit corporate charter provision designed to impede a takeover. Alternatively, a charter provision could limit the ability of management to adopt an ATP in the future. The absence of such a provision is equivalent to adopting an ATP. Individual states also have their own anti-takeover statutes that limit the feasibility of hostile takeovers. Firms can include provisions that allow it to opt out of state anti-takeover statutes.

The strength of an ATP is measured by the delay it imposes on a hostile bidder from acquiring the firm. Dual-class voting structures offer the inside owners complete protection against a takeover. Other ATPs are not as strong, but can cause a sufficiently costly delay – anywhere from a few months up to two years – so as to make an initial bid pointless.

A hostile bidder must acquire a majority of the voting rights and control of the board of directors in order to take over a firm and remove management. Anti-takeover provisions used in conjunction with a poison pill severely impeded the takeover process. A poison pill, also known as a Shareholder's Rights Plans or blank check preferred stock, works by allowing rights-holders to purchase shares in the bidding company at a low price if the bidder acquires control of the target. The threat of dilution deters potential bidders. The ability of a poison pill to prevent a takeover by itself is limited because the board can revoke it at any time. Strong ATPs delay a bidder's ability to gain board control and remove the pill. Table 5.2 lists the most common ATPs, roughly in order of their strength.

5.3.4.3 Issuer ATPs

The belief among some academics is that issuers adopt the governance structure that maximizes the firm value and IPO proceeds, and thus avoid value-destroying ATPs. Easterbrook and Fischel (1991, p. 204–5) stated, without evidence, that 'firms go public in easy to acquire form: no poison pill securities, no supermajority rules or staggered boards. Defense provisions are added later'. Studies of ATP use show that this belief is way off the mark.[20]

1. Approximately half of all issuers adopted the most restrictive defense measures – dual-class stock and staggered boards – and upwards of two-thirds adopted at least one ATP (Field 1999; Field and Karpoff 2002; Daines and Klausner 2000). Firms never committed to avoiding subsequent adoption of ATPs and only 5 percent opted out of state anti-takeover laws. The ATP adoption rate increased throughout the 1990s.

Table 5.2 Anti-takeover charter provisions

Defense	Description
Classified (staggered) board	Directors are divided into separate classes, usually three, elected to overlapping terms. It may take up to two years for a hostile bidder to gain board control
Shareholder meeting requirements	Restrictions are placed on shareholder's ability to call a special meeting to conduct a vote or to vote without a meeting by 'written consent'
Fair price provision	A hostile bidder is required to pay each of the target's shareholders a similar price for their shares, regardless of whether a shareholder tenders in the bidder's offer or is 'frozen out' in a subsequent merger
Stakeholder clause	This clause gives the board permission to evaluate a takeover bid by considering the likely effects on employees, bondholders, suppliers, customers and other stakeholders
Anti-greenmail provision	Prevents a company's management from agreeing to repurchase the stock held by a large shareholder, usually at a premium, in exchange for the shareholder's agreement not to launch a takeover bid
Control share acquisition	Suspends the voting rights of a shareholder whose portion of a corporation's outstanding equity surpasses a predetermined threshold
Supermajority voting requirement	These provisions establish approval levels (say 75 percent of outstanding votes) for actions that otherwise would require simple majority approval

2. Issuers had fewer takeover defenses than established public companies in spite of the fact that the public firms' much larger size acts as a defense (Field and Karpoff 2002). The average issuer had 1.2 ATPs, excluding poison pills, versus 2.5 for the public firms. The lower ATP use could reflect the insiders internalizing the potential cost of ATPs on their equity stake.

3. The relationship between potential control benefits and ATP adoption is ambiguous. Field and Karpoff (2002) reported a negative relation between insider ownership and defense adoption, whereas Daines and Klausner (2000) found a positive relationship.[21] A negative relationship may reflect insiders internalizing the ATP cost on their own shares. The large stake already poses a deterrent to a takeover attempt. Insiders with small stakes may want to entrench their position with the use of

ATPs. A positive relation implies that insiders are trying to protect the greater control benefits they receive from their large stakes.

4.   Daines and Klausner (2000) argued that managerial self-interest was a primary motive for ATP adoption. Firms that adopted ATPs had little need for additional bargaining power because there was a high number of potential bidders. Myopia was not a concern either, as the firms did not invest heavily in R&D. Anti-takeover provisions were most common where takeovers were frequent and thus a threat to the manager's position.

5.3.4.4 Puzzles

The pattern of ATP adoption at the IPO is somewhat puzzling. Institutional investors are largely indifferent to issuers adding ATPs to their corporate charters. Yet these same investors are hostile to public corporations that try to do the same. This contradictory behavior may reflect different concerns. IPO investors focus on the short-run returns and the future potential of the issuer, and less so on the governance structures. Anecdotal evidence supports this view. One lawyer asserted that 'in strong markets, antitakeover provisions are not normally a problem, but in weaker markets … such provisions are more difficult to sell' (Simmons 1997, p. 95).[22]

A second puzzle is why only half of the issuers chose to adopt a rigorous ATP. Defenses either increase or decrease firm value, implying that half of all issuers have chosen a value reducing governance structure. Coates (2000) suggested that the puzzle results from a failure in the corporate law market. The quality of the legal advice provided to issuers varies with the experience, size and location of law firms serving as company counsel.[23] Coates found that the takeover experience and size of a law firm was positively correlated with the number and strength of ATPs adopted by its clients. Following this logic, low quality law firms failed to provide their clients with the advice to adopt ATPs.

A second explanation for the ATP variation, proposed by Hannes (2001), is based on the effect of externalities. Bidders in a given industry have a pool of potential target firms they could attempt to acquire. A firm that adopts an ATP is less likely to receive a bid and any successful takeover will require a higher purchase price. This biases bidders towards non-ATP firms. Consequently, non-ATP firms have higher takeover premiums priced into their stock. Each additional firm that adopts ATPs reduces the pool of attractive targets, further driving up the takeover premium. In equilibrium, an issuer should be indifferent between adopting and foregoing ATPs because the payoff to shareholders is the same in either case – high built-in premiums pre-takeover for non-ATP firms versus high expected acquisition premiums for ATP firms.[24]

5.3.4.5 Subsequent takeovers

The pattern of takeovers in the post-IPO period suggests that potential control changes were part of the IPO planning process. Only a handful of firms were acquired within a year of the IPO, increasing to about 2 percent within two years and 15 percent within five years (Field 1999; Field and Karpoff 2002; Smart and Zutter 2003). The probability of a takeover was negatively related to the percentage of votes controlled by officers and directors and positively related to the voting rights of corporate investors with board representation. The probability also increased in the proportion of outsiders on the board, consistent with outside directors' acting in the interest of shareholders.

Issuers that were subsequently acquired sold a significantly larger fraction of their shares in the IPO (Field and Karpoff 2000). Such firms might have prepared for a takeover by allowing the bidder to get a toehold. Alternatively, non-acquired firms may have deliberately tried to avoid a takeover by issuing a smaller number of shares. Defenses also reduced the probability of a takeover. Firms with at least one ATP were acquired 11.3 percent of the time, less than the 16.6 percent for issuers without any takeover defenses (Field and Karpoff 2000).

The valuation effect from a takeover within five years of the IPO was roughly the same for firms with and without ATPs, confirming that at the margin issuers should be indifferent about adopting ATPs. Field and Karpoff (2002) reported average takeover announcement abnormal returns of 18.4 and 14.8 percent for firms with and without ATPs, respectively. The corresponding market-adjusted returns from the day of announcement to either de-listing or six months later were 8.9 and 14.2 percent. Additional bidders for the non-ATP firms may have driven up the price. The total abnormal returns starting 42 days prior to and ending six months after the announcement were not significantly different at 33.3 and 38.4 percent.

5.4 SUMMARY

Efficient corporate governance indirectly has an impact on the IPO decision. External investors need to monitor management to minimize agency costs and must possess control rights to effect change when necessary. Public and private ownership involves different monitoring regimes, with no clear advantage for either option. The greater liquidity resulting from a public listing can increase share value, but it also diminishes the incentive to monitor. An IPO is also an effective first stage in a planned change of control.

The allocation of control rights in private companies with VC-backing can affect the IPO decision. Venture capitalists are allocated control through convertible securities, contractual provisions and the staging of financing. Other contractual features are designed to provide the entrepreneur with strong financial incentives. IPO and acquisition exits are equally common. The VC does not exit immediately following an event, especially an IPO, because of reputation and asymmetric information concerns.

Governance structures adopted at the IPO affect the proceeds received in the offering and are not easily modified in the future. Insiders retain control after the IPO, either by retaining a large stage or by implementing a dual-class share structure. Managerial incentives are a big part of external monitoring, with the CEO wealth highly sensitive to changes in shareholder value. Half of all issuers adopt strict ATPs in their corporate charter; their primary purpose being to protect managerial interests, although shareholder value seems largely unaffected.

NOTES

1. See Fama (1980), Shleifer and Vishny (1986) and Jensen and Ruback (1983).
2. The newspaper industry offers an interesting example of this consideration. Publishers likely derive benefits from having editorial control over the paper's content and may have an incentive to increase circulation at the expense of profit maximization. Schargrodsky (2001) showed that newspaper prices rose when the publisher went public, perhaps representing a shift to profit maximization to satisfy new shareholders.
3. The monitoring shareholder will be partly compensated with a lower purchase price. If, however, the equity is not placed exclusively with the monitor, other shareholders also benefit from the underpricing.
4. Stoughton and Zechner (1998) argue that underpricing an IPO is necessary to induce an investor to acquire a block position that allows for effective monitoring. The gross proceeds in the IPO are larger because the gain from monitoring exceeds the additional underpricing.
5. Admati, Pfleiderer and Zechner (1994) take a similar perspective as Bolton and von Thadden on the benefits of large shareholder intervention.
6. This argument is reminiscent of the Grossman and Hart (1980) free-rider problem for takeovers.
7. Bhide (1993) argued that the combination of a thick secondary market and the presence of a large controlling block could potentially solve the corporate governance problem.
8. IPOs are frequently followed by seasoned offerings in which initial owners cash in (Brennan and Franks 1997; Rydqvist and Hogholm 1995).
9. See Cornelli and Yosha (2003), Rupello and Suarez (2002) and Hellmann (1998).
10. See Berglof (1994), Admati and Pfleiderer (1994) and Bergemann and Hege (1998).

11. Existing models cannot explain why VCs in different countries use a variety of forms of finance. Gilson and Schizer (2002) explain the prevalent use of CPE in the US as a response to the fact that US tax practice enables more favorable entrepreneurial incentive compensation.
12. It is generally understood, although not necessarily formally written, that control will transfer back to the entrepreneur if the firm goes public.
13. See Gompers and Lerner (1999), Cochrane (2001), Cumming (2002), Cumming and Fleming (2002), Schwienbacher (2002), Cumming and MacIntosh (2003) and Laine and Torstila (2003).
14. Bottazzi and Da Rin (2002) found that a significant factor in the ability of issuers listing on the German Neuer Markt to increase their offer size was the adoption of US generally accepted accounting principles (GAAP) or international accounting standards (IAS), considered to be more investor friendly than German standards.
15. See Field (1999), Field and Karpoff (2000) and Mikkelson, Partch and Shah (1997) for post-IPO ownership data.
16. Close to 30 percent of dual-class structures are motivated by a non-control reasons and are concentrated among bank holding companies that are constrained from owning more than 5 percent of the firm (Field 1999). The voting rights of the retained class B shares in these cases are less than 1 vote per share.
17. CEO compensation for issuers was far more sensitive to shareholder wealth than the $3 elasticity for the typical CEO of a public company (Jensen and Murphy 1990).
18. The evidence on the myopia hypothesis is mixed. Meulbroek et al. (1990) found that R&D declined after the adoption of an ATP, but Pugh, Page and Jahera (1992) found the opposite.
19. See Comment and Schwert (1995) for poison pill adoption; Partch (1987) for price reactions to dual class recaps; McWilliams (1990) for stock price reactions to ATP charter amendments; and Collins, Black and Wansley (1993) for price effect of state anti-takeover statutes.
20. The SEC regulation SK requires the disclosure in the issuing prospectus of any 'provision of the registrants' charters or by-laws that would have an effect of delaying, deferring, or preventing a change in control of the registrant'.
21. The latter study used more recent IPOs and may better reflect current trends.
22. This quote originally appeared in Coates (2000).
23. Coates (2000) found a number of legal gaffes in the issuers' prospectuses. Several companies used 'form' charters published by third-party service providers for generic corporations, with no effort to tailor the forms to the firm or the fact that it was going public.
24. The indifference at the margin between adopting an ATP and not is supported by the negligible announcement return. For the marginal firm, the costs and benefits are roughly equal.

6 The external market: an international comparison

The choice of public over private ownership is a valid decision only if a stock market listing is a viable and attractive option. The well-developed US capital markets certainly satisfy this necessary condition. However, it is not universally true that all private companies have a realistic option to go public. Western European countries like France, Italy and Germany have stock markets that are disproportionately small – measured by total market capitalization and number of listed firms – relative to the US and the UK. Stock market underdevelopment does not preclude private firms from going public, but it reduces the attractiveness considerably.

Stock market quality directly influences the IPO decision and thus indirectly impacts the design of economic policy. Promoting stock market development, both for its own sake and to induce additional firms to go public, may be a desirable public policy objective. The social optimality of an active, liquid stock market depends on whether it fosters economic growth and efficiency. Assuming that it does, a government can adopt specific policy measures to stimulate market development. One policy is to create a legal and political environment that supports the good corporate governance practices necessary to raise external finance. A more direct policy is a privatization program of state-owned enterprises (SOEs). Privatizations are important in their own right as an IPO decision. They constitute a large fraction of all IPOs and the total stock market capitalization in many countries.

6.1 THE STOCK MARKET AND GOING PUBLIC

Stock market quality and the IPO decision are intimately intertwined. Quality is measured along many dimensions, including price efficiency, market depth and liquidity. The quality of these attributes affects the optimality of an IPO as an exit option for shareholders. Similarly, the advantage of an informative stock price is contingent on the market being efficient and investors researching the companies. The quality of the market is in turn affected by the collective outcome of firms independently deciding whether to go public.

6.1.1 Exit Opportunity

Shareholders exit their investment in a company because of liquidity concerns, portfolio diversification objectives or the need to cash out. As a rule, it is more time consuming and costlier to exit an investment in a private company as opposed to a public firm. The relative advantage of public ownership is positively related to the liquidity and depth of the stock market. An IPO is a desirable first step that allows investors to begin exiting, assuming that the market is of sufficiently high quality.

An active stock market that welcomes IPOs by young risky companies is vital to the success of the venture capital industry. Venture capitalists make investments in start-up firms on the condition that they will have attractive exit options. Black and Gilson (1998) suggested three reasons why the option of a public listing contributes to the growth of venture capital. First, VCs provide informed capital to start-ups that includes the provision of specific industry knowledge and contacts, managerial skill and a valuable reputation. An IPO allows for the recycling of this limited supply of capital from firms that have succeeded to new start-ups. Second, IPOs enable limited partners to evaluate a VC's ability and determine whether capital should be reallocated to more successful VCs. Neither of these two benefits is exclusive to IPOs; acquisitions offer the same virtues. The final and unique benefit of an IPO is that it enables control to be transferred back to the entrepreneur. The implicit agreement to transfer control at the IPO helps to facilitate the initial financing agreement.

The effect of the IPO exit option on VC funding was directly examined by Jeng and Wells (2000). The contemporaneous volume of IPOs was found to be the most significant determinant of VC funding for start-ups and for the amount of capital raised by new funds. This held for both North American and European countries. Late stage investments responded strongly to the IPO volume, whereas early stage investments were unaffected. Later rounds are usually intended to tie the firm over until its IPO, but when the IPO market is cold and a potential offering is unlikely the funding may not arrive.

6.1.2 Market Feedback

Investment and strategic decisions made by a firm depend on the available information. Practical time constraints prevent managers from gathering all possible information, assessing it and then making decisions. Investors

111

provide an alternative and cheap source of information because they analyze a company before and after investing in it. The virtue of being public is that the stock price aggregates all relevant information gathered by investors. The manager can simply look at the price to get an independent assessment of the firm's prospects, an option not available to private firms.

Investors indirectly provide two types of information, according to Subrahmanyam and Titman (1999). The first type relates specifically to the quality of the firm's operations. The second type of information is serendipitous and free. Investors come across it by chance in their day-to-day activities. Examples include the popularity of a restaurant or the sales of a new toy. Serendipitous information is most relevant when product demand is uncertain or in industries with products aimed at the mass consumer market. A broad consumer base results in more potential investors receiving serendipitous information. The benefit of this information only accrues to public firms because it is based on the aggregation of many individual random assessments.

The feedback from informative stock prices can be used to improve the efficiency of investment decisions. The post-IPO level of capital expenditures was positively related to the initial return and the subsequent stock returns (van Bommel and Vermaelen 2001). All else equal, firms with the same amount of capital supplied by the IPO invested different amounts based on the aggregate assessment of the market. The probability of a follow-on equity offering increased with the post-IPO stock returns (Jegadeesh, Weinstein and Welch 1993; Garfinkel 1994). Positive returns signal investor approval of the managerial actions and the growth prospects, thereby motivating the firm to raise additional capital for investment.

6.1.3 Externalities

When a firm goes public it generates externalities that affect the IPO decision of other firms. Earlier chapters discussed how direct informational or payoff-related externalities could induce more firms to go public. An indirect externality is the effect that a public listing has on the stock market quality. Better markets subsequently induce more firms to go public. Three indirect externalities affect the IPO decision.

Market depth: Public equity markets that are 'thick' with many participating investors offer two clear advantages over the 'thin' private equity market. First, greater liquidity in thick markets reduces trading costs, benefiting investors and lowering the cost of capital (Amihud and Mendelson 1986). Second, investors are encouraged to produce more information because speculative trading is easier to hide and more profitable in a liquid market, and that increases the informativeness of stock prices. Investors' willingness to incur the set-up cost of becoming an informed trader increases directly with the opportunities for speculative investment. Each additional firm that goes public attracts new investors to the market, further enhancing liquidity, creating a virtuous cycle in which more firms and investors enter the public equity market (Pagano 1989; Subrahmanyam and Titman 1999).

Risk diversification: An IPO enables the founding entrepreneur to shed risk by selling shares and diversifying his portfolio. The benefit from this strategy is contingent on there being other securities available for purchase. A poorly developed stock market with few listed companies offers limited risk diversification options. Each additional firm that goes public improves the diversifying benefits of an IPO for all remaining private firms, attracting incremental public listings (Pagano 1993).

Managerial labor market: The skills required to found a start-up firm – specific scientific or technical knowledge – are often quite different from those needed to manage a large, rapidly growing company. The mismatch in managerial skills demanded by firms and supplied by employees results in inefficiencies. The economy is better off if some workers develop specific managerial talent. A market of public firms, in which ownership and day-to-day control are separated, creates a demand for managerial talent (Maug 1996). As more firm go public and the supply of managerial labor grows, a public listing becomes more important in attracting professional managers.[1]

The presence of externalities results in coordination failures and potentially the stock market underdevelopment. The liquidity, risk sharing and human capital benefits to an IPO are small when there are few publicly listed firms. After weighing the small benefit against the high cost of an IPO, firms will opt to remain private. The stock market can get stuck in a low-listing trap with few public companies. The economy would be better off if the private firms could coordinate and all go public, but in the absence of a social planner such coordination is not likely. The core problem is that each firm fails to internalize the effect it's IPO decision has on other private firms.

The relative lack of development of Western European stock markets could be the consequence of coordination failures. Government policy designed to stimulate market development may be necessary to push the economy out of the bad equilibrium. Simple actions – reducing brokerage or other trading costs, improving information disclosure or streamlining the listing process – would improve the attractiveness of the stock market to firms and investors. More complex and sophisticated policy options examined in the following sections include changing the legal and political environment, and implementing a privatization program.

6.2 STOCK MARKET DEVELOPMENT

Governmental policy towards stock market development should be subsumed within the broader objective of promoting economic growth and efficiency. The merits of market development and a general reliance on capital markets should be judged on the consequences. If a causal link between stock market and economic growth can be demonstrated, then the next step is to decipher the role played by the legal and political environment in this relationship. The conclusions will illuminate the policy measures that best serve the government's objectives.

6.2.1 Economic Growth

Drawing a causal link between stock markets and economic growth is an empirical issue. However, theory offers some guidance on the likely relationship and the pros and cons of stock markets relative to bank-based financial systems.

6.2.1.1 Pros

There are numerous efficiency benefits to stock markets that should translate directly into higher long-run economic growth. Share prices quickly aggregate and disseminate information that is valuable in guiding investment decisions (Boot and Thakor 1997; Allen and Gale 1999). Without efficient price signals investors may continue to finance firms with low return projects (Rajan and Zingales 2003).

Developed stock markets are efficient at spreading risk and offer investors superior diversification opportunities (Levine 1991). A direct consequence is a lower cost of capital, which can encourage investment in high-risk, high-return projects (Morck and Nakamura 1999). Thus stock markets should do a good job of encouraging innovative, growth-enhancing activities (Allen and Gale 2000).

Liquid stock markets lead to increased information production and more efficient prices because informed investors can profit from speculative trading. Greater liquidity improves the incentive to fund long-term projects because investors can easily cash in their shares before the project reaches maturity (Levine 1991; Bencivenga, Smith and Starr 1995).

Stock markets can improve corporate governance. Informative stock prices can be used to design efficient incentive contracts, aligning managerial interests with shareholders (Holmstrom and Tirole 1993). The market for corporate control spurs on managers to improve performance and avoid hostile takeovers (Jensen and Murphy 1990).

6.2.1.2 Cons

There is a dark side to the benefits of stock markets. A more efficient allocation of resources should increase the returns to savings, potentially lowering the savings rate. It is possible that a lower overall level of savings, and thus feasible investment, offsets the gains from efficient allocation. Long-run growth is actually lower as a result. Furthermore, stock prices that are too efficient reveal information too quickly, reducing the incentive for individuals to acquire costly information and seek out innovative projects (Stiglitz 1985). Liquid markets can worsen corporate governance because it might be easier for an investor to sell his stake if the firm performs poorly, rather than actively monitoring management (Bhide 1993).

Stock markets may not perform as intended, further undermining their usefulness. Considerable evidence suggests that the market is not informationally efficient, with prices deviating from their intrinsic values for long periods of time (Campbell and Shiller 1988; DeBondt and Thaler 1995). Resource allocation is distorted as a result, lowering the economy's growth rate. Stock markets appear to be prone to short-run instability. Short-term excess volatility increases the risk to investors instead of reducing it (Allen and Gale 2000).

Capital markets can be inferior to bank financing in multiple ways. Banks form long-term relationships with borrowers that enable them to efficiently acquire information and improve capital allocation and corporate governance (Diamond 1984). Banks are good at mobilizing capital to exploit economies of scale (Sirri and Tufano 1995) and are better than uncoordinated stock market investors at monitoring firms and reducing post-lending moral hazard (Boot and Thakor 1997). Powerful banks are more effective at forcing repayment of debts than dispersed creditors, especially in countries with weak legal enforcement, thereby increasing the willingness to lend in the first place (Rajan and Zingales 1998).

6.2.1.3 Markets and growth

A growing body of research has examined the relationship between the development of stock markets and banks on the one hand and economic

115

growth on the other. The general findings are grouped into three main categories.

Financial market development: The evidence overwhelmingly indicates that both bank and stock market growth is positively related to future economic growth, although financial development and growth typically emerge at the same time.[2] Bank growth is usually measured by the level of bank credit supplied to private borrowers, adjusted by the gross domestic product (GDP). Stock market development is proxied by the turnover ratio – the dollar volume of all trading activity in a year divided by the market capitalization.[3]

The economic impact of financial development is large. Beck and Levine (2003) estimated that if Mexico's turnover ratio during the 1996–98 period had equaled the Organization for Economic Cooperation and Development (OECD) average of 68 percent instead of the actual 36 percent, the economy would have grown 0.6 percent faster per year. Similarly, if Mexican bank credit equaled the 71 percent OECD average and not 16 percent, economic growth would have been 0.8 percent faster.

Micro-level growth: Aggregate level growth is directly attributable to individual firms and industries growing. Access to external finance facilitates faster growth. Demirguc-Kunt and Maksimovic (1998) estimated a growth rate for individual firms assuming that they were constrained to finance their growth internally. They found that countries with more active stock markets and larger commercial banking centers had a higher proportion of firms growing above the estimated constrained rate. Rajan and Zingales (1998) showed that industries that were externally financed in the US – deemed to be naturally heavy users of capital – grew faster in more financially developed countries.

Well-developed stock markets also appear to allocate capital more efficiently. Wurgler (2000) reported that investment increased (decreased) more in growing (declining) industries in financially developed as compared to less developed countries. The overall investment level was not necessarily higher in financially developed countries, but the capital was allocated more efficiently. A high level of state-ownership was associated with relatively poor capital allocation. These countries neither increased capital in growing industries nor decreased it in declining industries.

Financial services: The evidence suggests that the debate between stock market and bank-based financial systems is somewhat irrelevant. According to Levine (2002), neither bank- nor market-based systems consistently produced superior economic growth relative to the other. Levine advocated an alternative way of thinking about financial development, stressing that contracts, markets and intermediaries arise to ameliorate market imperfections and provide financial services. The efficiency with which these financial services are provided determines how effectively a financial system promotes economic growth

The financial services view stresses the importance of a well-functioning legal system on the operation of markets and intermediaries in creating a growth-promoting financial sector (La Porta et al. 1997; 1998). Levine demonstrated that the component of financial development defined by the legal rights of investors and the efficiency of contract enforcement was very strongly associated with economic growth.

6.2.2 Law and Finance

The discussion of optimal ownership and governance structures in Chapter 5 took for granted that the financial contracts and their legal rights therein are strictly upheld. Reality suggests otherwise. Countries vary in the legal rights and enforcement afforded to investors. The legal recourse of minority investors in the event of expropriation by majority owners determines their initial willingness to invest. Therefore the implementation of specific corporate governance policies is subject to the legal support for such a structure.

6.2.2.1 Legal systems

A pioneering group of papers by La Porta et al. (1997; 1998; 2000a; 2000b; 2002) emphasized the importance of the legal system in corporate finance. La Porta et al. argued that the legal protection afforded outside investors is a primary determinant of the amount of external capital raised by firms and consequently determines the size and development of financial markets. They went even further by claiming that the strength of the laws enacted and the level of enforcement are a function of the legal tradition. The legal system in every country can be traced back to English, French, German or Scandinavian legal traditions, which spread throughout the world either by conquest, colonization or imitation.

English law is common law, written by judges and subsequently incorporated by the legislature. Common law is inherently dynamic, as judges reinterpret and rewrite existing laws to better reflect the current circumstances. The French and German civil codes, formally written at the start and end of the 19th century, respectively, solidified state dominance of the courts. The French civil code was written with the goal of being the perfect, immutable legal doctrine. The judiciary was given little freedom to interpret the code or make new laws and was to apply the law in a very literal manner. The German civil code was enacted much later than the French civil code and the writers recognized the importance of allowing the judiciary to modify and amend laws as circumstances changed. This placed German law somewhere between English and French law in granting power to the state and acting as a defender of individual rights.

La Porta et al. (1998; 1999) argued that common law countries have stronger legal protection of investors for three reasons. First, legal systems that evolve faster to meet the needs of the economy are more effective at fostering financial development by protecting investors' rights. Common law is the most flexible in that respect. Second, the French and German codes supported the strengthening of the nation. Thus, the civil law tradition tends to concentrate state power and takes a skeptical stance towards financial development. Third, well-developed financial markets can undermine political agendas, motivating powerful governments to create laws that constrain financial development. The civil code is more amenable to such constraints.

Legal traditions by themselves do not protect investors; rather it is the specific laws and regulations written that do. Investor protection rights differ for shareholders and creditors, with the main ones listed in Table 6.1. Equally as important as the specific laws is the quality of legal enforcement. The greatest legal protections are nothing more than a theoretical abstraction if they are not enforced. A regular survey of the quality of law enforcement, called the 'rule of law', is an assessment by investors of the law and order environment in different countries.

Empirical analysis indicates a strong correlation in both the strength of investor protection and the quality of enforcement with the presence of a common law tradition (La Porta et al. 1997). Beck, Demirguc-Kunt and Levine (2001) found that countries with a French civil law tradition tend to have less transparent financial statements, poorer property rights protections and weaker protection of the rights of shareholders and debtholders. Common law countries generally have particularly strong accounting systems and strong protection of the rights of outsiders. German civil law countries have strong protection of property rights and effective contract enforcement.

The legal tradition view of corporate finance and financial development has attracted substantial criticism. Legal scholars have argued that the crude distinctions between French civil law and English common law mask a far more complex reality. Common law countries, such as the US, have written formal commercial codes, whereas the French judiciary has been granted more freedom to interpret existing laws and offer comments on decisions.

Table 6.1 Investor rights

Shareholder rights	Creditor rights
Shareholders are allowed to mail their proxy vote	Restrictions on the managers' ability to unilaterally seek bankruptcy protection from creditors
Shareholders retain control of the shares during the shareholders' meeting	Secured creditors gain possession of their assets once the bankruptcy petition has been approved
Cumulative voting for directors is allowed	Managers do not retain their control over the assets during a reorganization
Shareholder can call for an Extraordinary Shareholders' Meeting with under 10 percent of the share capital	Secured creditors have priority in the distribution of the proceeds from the sale of assets in bankruptcy
Mechanisms that allow oppressed minority shareholders to make legal claims against the directors (e.g. class action lawsuit)	

Source: La Porta et al. (1997).

Critics have also challenged the underlying economic logic of the legal traditions' impact on financial development (Berglof and von Thadden 1999). The primary focus of this research has been on the rights of minority investors, which assumes a widely held corporation. Yet outside the US and UK this corporate structure is rare, even though many other countries have strong investor rights. In addition, the legal theory implies that there should be more, not less, blockholders in the US because minority shareholders are less concerned with large shareholder expropriation.

Legal traditions may be correlated with observable differences in investor rights, but a policy of adopting stronger protections seems unlikely to have much affect on financial development. Reforming weak investor protection rights in developed countries would be difficult because modern corporations evolved jointly with the current legal and financial structure. Only wholesale changes to the legal system would fundamentally alter the reliance on external financial markets. The adoption of stronger investor rights in developing economies is probably neither the most important nor the most effective policy initiative.

6.2.2.2 External finance

Agency costs are an inevitable consequence of external finance. Entrenched managers can expropriate corporate resources to consume private control benefits. The willingness of external investors to monitor management to prevent such value-reducing activities depends on the strength of their legal rights. Investors with few protections against expropriation have little incentive to incur the monitoring cost. Shleifer and Wolfenzon (2002) examined theoretically the implications of poor shareholder protection, due to either weak legal rights or indifferent law enforcement, on corporate financing decisions and the broader capital markets.

Stronger protection lowers the mangerial diversion of corporate resources by making it more costly (caught more often) and reducing the benefit (consume resources less frequently). Lower diversion means that the marginal cost to the firm from selling additional shares, measured by the expected punishment, is smaller. Simultaneously, better protection lowers the cost of capital because investors require less *ex ante* compensation for the expected diversion. The optimal fraction of the firm sold to outside investors increases with shareholder protection because the marginal cost falls and the marginal benefit increases.

The theory makes additional predictions about the relationship between investor protection and corporate finance patterns. Large fractions of equity sold to outside investors results in lower ownership concentration among public firms. The larger fraction sold at a higher price provides the issuer with more capital, leading to additional investment and bigger firms. Reduced diversion means that firms are more valuable and have higher market-to-book value ratios. They also pay out more of the cash flow as dividends. The combination of more firms going public, selling larger equity stakes and being more valuable results in larger capital markets. These predicted relations have received strong support in the data.

External capital: La Porta et al. (1997) reported that firms' reliance on external capital increased with the level of investor protection, based on a sample of 49 countries. The ratio of the total market value of external investor shareholder equity to the gross national product (GNP) increased with shareholders rights and was lowest in civil law countries. The same patterns held for the number of domestic firms listed on the exchange and the number of IPOs relative to the population. The relationship between creditor rights and debt levels was more tenuous. Indebtedness increased with the shareholders rights index, but was only weakly related to creditor rights. Debt financing was generally, but not always, lower in countries with civil law traditions.

Legal tradition: Legal tradition explained some of the cross-country variation in financial development (La Porta et al. 1997, Beck, Demirguc-Kunt and Levine 2001). Countries with a French civil law tradition tended to have comparatively weak financial institutions and lower levels of stock market and bank development. Common law countries had larger equity markets, whereas German civil law countries had well-developed banks.

Ownership and control: La Porta, Lopez-de-Silanes and Shleifer (1999) found that firms had lower ownership concentrations in countries with better investor protection. They examined the ownership of the 20 largest public companies in 27 countries. A firm was deemed closely held if there was a shareholder that controlled at least 20 percent of the voting rights. The percentage of widely held firms in countries with strong and weak shareholder protection was significantly different at 48 and 27 percent, respectively. This difference held at the 10 percent critical ownership level and for mid-sized firms.

Valuation: La Porta et al. (2002) showed that firm valuation was higher in countries with better investor protection. High cash flow ownership by the controlling shareholder improved valuations, especially in countries with poor protection. The incentive to expropriate is low when the controlling shareholder already receives a large fraction of the cash flows.

Dividends: La Porta et al. (2000a) documented that firms paid out larger dividends in common law rather than civil law countries. Common law countries had dividend-to-earnings payout ratios 10 to 15 percent higher, after controlling for other factors. In common but not civil law countries high growth firms paid lower dividends than low growth firms. This suggests that investors used their superior legal rights to extract larger dividends from firms with poor investment options.

Investment: Wurgler (2000) reported that strong minority investor rights were associated with better capital allocation. The allocational benefits appeared to work mainly by limiting overinvestment in declining industries, and less so from improving the supply of finance to growing industries. Declining industries are apt to suffer from the free cash flow problem; managers with access to excess cash and few investment opportunities. Strong investors force the managers to pay out the free cash flow, thereby limiting agency costs.

6.2.3 Political Environment

The commitment to a policy of implementing and enforcing laws designed to protect investors is contingent on the political culture within a country. Even well-designed legal systems will be unsuccessful in promoting financial development without the political support for private property and investor rights. This implies that political factors are the root determinant of market development, relegating legal issues to a second-order effect.

The weakness of the legal tradition hypothesis stems from the incongruity between the static tradition and the dynamic variation in financial development. Rajan and Zingales (2003) compared the level of financial development in common and civil law countries starting in 1913 and ending in the 1990s. The development in many civil law countries in 1913 was comparable to or exceeded that of the common law countries. Development declined in most countries in the 1930s, largely because of the Great Depression, but it fell most precipitously in civil law countries. Only by the 1980s did the situation reverse and return to pre-1930s levels, with convergence in the level of development in civil and common law countries observable by the 1990s.

6.2.3.1 Political interests

The historical patterns of financial development may be best explained by continually evolving political cultures. Rajan and Zingales (2003) argued that there are groups in a society that wield disproportionate power in the government. Once a group has power it will shape the institutions and policies to its own advantage. When the special interests find it to their advantage to suppress financial development, they pressure the government to avoid reforms that liberalize the market. A powerful centralized state is more responsive and efficient at implementing the interests of an elite group than a decentralized, open and competitive political system.

The groups in society that have the most to lose from financial development are the dominant industrial and financial elite. Incumbent financial institutions benefit from a lack of competition from other suppliers of capital.[4] The major industrial firms that possess sufficient capital will be against development that facilitates the entry of new competitors into their market. These institutions possess considerable political clout, which may explain the evolution of financial markets.

Rajan and Zingales (2003) conducted an interesting test of their political theory. The test was based on the notion that the openness of a country to trade and foreign capital is an indirect proxy for the strength of the incumbents to prevent financial reform. They reported a strong positive correlation between measures of financial development and the openness to trade over most of the 20th century. The Great Depression and the signing of the Bretton Woods agreement in 1948 dramatically curtailed openness during the 1930–70 period. This enabled dominant incumbent groups to exert their influence to suppress development. The effect was a weakening of the correlation between openness and development during this period. Civil law countries in particular were less responsive to trade openness and the impetus to reform financial markets when capital inflows ebbed.

6.2.3.2 Ideology

The political and social values held by a society will influence the development of financial markets. Roe (2003) argued that social democracies, which place greater emphasis on social equality than on pure wealth creation, are less likely to have well-developed capital markets. The conjecture rests on the consequence and response to agency costs. Mechanisms designed to deal with agency costs in widely owned American corporations – the norm of shareholder value maximization, incentive compensation, strong accounting disclosure rules and the market for corporate control – all emphasize the pre-eminence of shareholder wealth creation. An unyielding focus on shareholder value is not acceptable in social democracies, creating an impediment to resolving agency conflicts. Investors who fear that maximizing the value of their shares is not the top priority of the company will either not supply capital or do so at prohibitive terms. The aggregate implication is poorly developed capital markets.

Different beliefs about what constitutes efficient governance could account for the diversity of investor protections. Holmen and Hogfeldt (2001) make the case that governments in civil law countries seek to reinforce majority shareholder rights, weakening minority protection as a by-product. Such a policy is designed to encourage the formation of controlling blocks, which, the policy makers believe, leads to strong stable ownership that can more efficiently plan for the long-term. Holmen and Hogfeldt report that in Sweden, a country that has adopted this policy stance, 90 percent of firms go public with dual-class structures and issue low vote shares. The previously documented ownership and control structures of public companies in civil law countries could reflect the preferred outcome among policy makers, as opposed to the unintended consequence of weak investor rights.

6.3 PRIVATIZATIONS

Privatizing state-owned enterprises is an important policy tool that is an under-appreciated aspect of the economics of IPOs. The IPO market is directly affected by the privatization of SOEs through a public offering. These privatization IPOs account for a significant percentage of all IPO activity, measured both in number and total proceeds, in some developing economies. Privatizations also indirectly affect the IPO decision of private firms by stimulating stock market development. New investors are attracted to the stock market, helping poorly developed markets break out of a bad, low-listing trap. A privatization program is the most direct tool available to the government to spur on market development and IPOs.

6.3.1 The History of Privatizations

A brief review of the modern history of privatizations provides some perspective on the current thinking on SOEs. Megginson and Netter (2001) date the current privatization era to the 1979 election of the Thatcher government in the UK. Conventional wisdom at the time held that many of the soon-to-be-privatized enterprises should be owned and operated by the government. This opinion was based on the fact that the SOEs were either in industries characterized by natural monopoly or, in the interest of national and economic security, the SOEs should be owned by the government. There was even skepticism amongst economists about the mechanics of selling a billion-dollar enterprise.

The success of the British Aerospace, Cable and Wireless, and British Telecom privatizations proved the skeptics wrong. It also demonstrated to other governments around the world that privatizations were not only viable, but were an attractive policy option. Privatization programs spread throughout Western Europe, to Latin America, Southeast Asia, Sub-Saharan Africa and, in the 1990s, to Eastern Europe and Russia.

The sheer magnitude of the privatization programs and the effect they have had on the industrial structure of economies are quite substantial. The cumulative value of proceeds raised by privatizations exceeded $1 trillion sometime in the second half of 2000 (Gibbon 2000). Annual proceeds in the late 1990s were around $150 billion. The contribution of SOEs to GDP in high-income countries declined significantly from 8.5 percent in 1984 to less than 6 percent in 1991, and that percentage has continued to fall (Sheshinski and Lopez-Calva 2003). The reduction is even more dramatic in developing countries, dropping from 16 to 7 percent by 1995.

The significance of privatizations is captured by the fact that they account for nine of the ten largest IPOs in history. There were 112 privatizations that raised over $1 billion each between 1984 and 1997; private firm IPOs are rarely this large. Table 6.2 lists the largest privatization IPOs in history, their country and the size of the offering.

Table 6.2 Largest privatization IPOs[5]

Date	Company[a]	Country	Amount ($mil)[b]
11/1999	ENEL	Italy	18,900
10/1998	NTT DoCoMo	Japan	18,000
2/1987	Nippon Telegraph & Telephone	Japan	15,097
11/1996	Deutsche Telekom	Germany	13,300
11/1997	Telstra	Australia	10,530
12/1990	Regional Electricity Companies	UK	9,995
7/2000	Telia	Sweden	8,800
12/1989	UK Water Authorities	UK	8,679
12/1986	British Gas	UK	8,012
11/1984	British Telecom	UK	7,360
10/1993	Japan Railroad East	Japan	7,312
10/1997	France Telecom	France	7,080
7/1999	Credit Lyonnais	France	6,960
10/1998	Swisscom	Switzerland	5,600

a. Includes all privatizations as of April 15, 2000.
b. All amounts in nominal $US.

Source: Table 12 in Megginson and Netter (2001).

6.3.2 Why Privatize?

A government decision to adopt a policy of privatizating SOEs is motivated by one or more of four possible factors. The first consideration is a straightforward goal to generate politically cheap revenue for the state without raising taxes or cutting programs. The second factor is a change in philosophy about the government's role in the economy. Due either to a revision in beliefs or a change in the governing party, the preference for less government interference in the economy and greater private sector competition motives the privatization of SOEs.

A third, less ideological factor is a desire to promote economic efficiency by subjecting SOEs to market discipline. There is a widely held perception that government owned enterprises are poorly run and inefficient because the fear of being driven out of business is absent. The final motive combines the preceding two factors to produce the objective of developing the national capital markets. The policy is a conscious shift towards a market-based economy and privatizations help by promoting wider share ownership and stock market growth.

6.3.2.1 Economic efficiency

The economic success of a privatization program can be evaluated at the firm level by measuring the change in SOE performance and at a national level for its impact on stock market development. The current section focuses on individual SOE performance; a later section considers the aggregate market.

There are a number of reasons why SOEs produce inferior operating returns compared to similar private companies. The primary objective of an SOE is not always profit maximization. Politically motivated objectives, such as appeasing a particular voting constituency, can take precedence over pure economic interests. One consequence is that SOEs tend to have inefficiently large workforces. Political interference by the government is much more difficult in a private company, assuming that private property rights and market forces are respected. State-owned enterprises have 'soft' budget constraints, as the government will usually bail out a failing firm, further undermining the profit maximization incentive.

Studies have consistently found that privatized SOEs' operating and financial performance improves after a privatization IPO.[6] Gains were observed in profitability, sales and productivity, and were related to specific characteristics of the SOE post-privatization. Performance improvements were greater when the government sold a larger fraction of the SOE and foreign investors participated in the IPO. State-owned enterprises that faced increased competition in the product market exhibited larger productivity gains (D'Souza, Megginson and Nash 2001). Overall, the evidence on efficiency gains supports the economic justification for privatizations.

Privatizing an SOE does not itself cause operating improvements; the gains result from the restructuring and reorganization. In fact, D'Souza, Megginson and Nash (2001) showed that SOEs that were restructured prior to the privatization showed significantly larger improvements compared to non-restructured SOEs. This raises the question of whether the performance improvements could be achieved without a privatization. Some evidence suggests the answer is yes. The Polish government adopted a privatization program in the early 1990s, but not before instituting regulatory changes that included a hard budget for the SOEs, enforcing a 'no bailout' rule and allowing import competition. The result was performance improvement even before privatization (Pinto, Belka and Krajewski 1993).

6.3.3 Privatization Methods

Governments have many different methods of privatizing SOEs at their disposal, which is helpful considering the highly politicized environment encompassing the process. The optimal privatization method must take into account a number of concerns. The first is the overall feasibility of the privatization. Specifically, the SOEs' financial health and competitive strength determine how best to sell the assets, while the sophistication of potential investors influences the marketing approach.

The second concern is the political interests that must be assuaged. Politically sensitive groups could include the prior owners of the SOE's assets, individuals or groups who expect to suffer a loss as a result of the privatization and the entire population if foreign investor participation is being considered.

The final concern is the government's commitment to promoting stock market development. The government must credibly commit to respecting investors' property rights after the sale. It must also be willing to implement and enforce the institutional framework that supports good corporate governance practices.[7]

There are four major methods of privatization (Brada 1996). The most common is the sale of state-owned assets for an explicit cash payment. The assets can be sold whole or in part directly to an individual, an existing corporation, or a group of investors. The alternative is a share issue privatization (SIP), in which some or all of the government's stake is sold through a public equity offering. The second method is a voucher program, whereby eligible citizens use vouchers that are distributed free or at a nominal cost to bid for stakes in the SOE. Voucher-based privatizations have only been used in Central and Eastern Europe. Restitution is the third method. The assets and capital of the SOE, which had been confiscated, are returned to the original owners or their heirs. Finally, there is privatization from below; new private businesses in formerly socialist countries are allowed to compete with the SOEs.[8]

Privatization sales involve more than just a divestiture of state-owned assets. The government must implement and adhere to a set of procedures that support the privatization program (Gibbon 1997). The first step requires setting up a legal structure for the privatization. Next is the release of adequate performance records and accounting data for the SOEs to investors. New regulatory agencies, if required, must be established. Finally, the appropriate post-sale relationship between the firm and the government is determined.

6.3.3.1 Choice of sale method

The choice between a SIP and a direct asset sale is influenced by economic, political, legal and firm-specific factors (Megginson et al. 2002). Share issue privatizations have the advantage of promoting stock market development by creating a large new shareholder class. But if the stock market is insufficiently developed a public listing may not even be feasible. A direct asset sale is not a practical choice for larger SOEs because no individual or group of investors could raise the necessary capital to purchase the entire enterprise. A SIP may not be attractive if the overall income level in the country is low or if there is considerable inequality because it would be too costly, in terms of lost proceeds, to induce low income individuals to participate.

Investor-related considerations further influence the sale method. Investors need to see proof that purchasing shares in a SIP is a good investment. This biases the potential SIP candidates toward higher quality SOEs to ensure the long-term success of a large-scale privatization program. A direct asset sale is more likely when the law, and the government's commitment to it, offers strong protection of private property rights. This minimizes buyers' fear of expropriation and re-nationalization. Investors in a SIP immediately become a large voting constituency that effectively deters the government from violating property rights. Therefore, investor rights do not need to be as strong for a SIP.

Along with the sale method, the government must decide how to structure the entire privatization program and the sale of an individual SOE. Perotti (1995) argued that the sale of SOEs should proceed in stages to build domestic support for the privatization program, develop reputational capital with investors and to identify the bidders who will maximize the future efficiency of the firm. Reputational concerns suggest that the SIP of a single SOE should occur in stages as well, which also makes it easier for the market to absorb a large offering.

Summary statistics on SIPs and direct sales provide some sense of how privatization programs have been structured.[9] Megginson et al. (2002) documented a total of 938 SIPs raising $745 billion and 1539 direct asset sales raising $445 billion, representing 108 countries, from 1977 to 2000. The average SIP (direct sale) generated $794 ($289) million. About 90 percent of the privatizations occurred in the 1990s, accounting for almost 70 percent of the total proceeds. Prior to 1990 direct sales accounted for 38 percent of the privatization transactions and 8 percent of the value of privatized assets. After 1990 these numbers increased to 64 and 42 percent, respectively.

Specific studies have examined the choice between SIPs and direct sales and the structure of individual SIPs. The two main conclusions follow.

Sale method: Megginson et al. (2002) reported that SIPs were more likely when the stock market was less developed, there was less income inequality, the larger the offering size and the more profitable was the SOE.

These patterns are consistent with the predictions and support the market development objective of a SIP. Furthermore, the greater the government's ability to commit to protecting property rights, the more likely a direct sale was used.

Sequential sales: Perotti and Guney (1993) documented that privatization programs generally started slowly. Proceeds from privatizations increased over time, suggesting gradual selling to build investor confidence. The SIPs of individual SOEs were completed in stages. The average IPO stage generated between $500 million and $700 million, with a typical follow-on offering of $1 billion.[10] On average 44 percent of the equity was sold in the IPO and 23 percent in the follow-on.

6.3.4 Investor Returns

The long-term success of a privatization program is contingent on investors' continued willingness to buy the assets for sale. The short- and long-run returns generated by SIPs provide a gauge for how well the program has performed and thus its continued viability in the future.

6.3.4.1 Initial returns

A consistent finding in privatization studies is the significant initial return. The average initial return for privatization IPOs has been in the 30 percent range and even follow-on SIPs were underpriced an average of 7 to 9 percent.[11] Huang and Levich (1998) found the average returns in OECD and non-OECD countries to be 11 and 66 percent, respectively. The difference may reflect the need for greater underpricing in developing economies with less stable political environments and uncertainty regarding the government's commitment to the privatization program. They also found that initial returns for IPOs early in the privatization process averaged 39.4 percent, compared to 24.5 percent for later SIPs. The decline, although not statistically significant, could reflect the resolution of uncertainty.

The criteria used by a government to price and allocate the shares in a privatization IPO differ from those used by a private firm. It is possible that the government deliberately underprices the IPO to attract a large investor base and signal its beliefs about the SOE's value (Perotti 1995; Biais and Perotti 2000). Ljungqvist, Jenksinson and Wilhelm (2003) documented that privatization IPO initial returns were about nine percentage points higher than private sector IPOs, after controlling for issuer characteristics. As predicted, underpricing increased with the degree of income inequality within a country. Finally, Jones et al. (1999) found that the initial return was negatively related to the level of government spending as a fraction of GDP, a proxy for the government's budget constraint. If the need to raise revenue is the primary motive for the privatization, then less underpricing will be tolerated.

6.3.4.2 Long-run returns

Investors in privatization IPOs continue to receive good returns over horizons beyond the first trading day. The abnormal returns for privatized SOEs – measured by comparing the actual raw stock return against a benchmark return – over one, three and five-year horizons were significantly positive (Megginson et al. 2000; Boardman and Laurin 2000; Dewenter and Malatesta 1997). The positive abnormal returns were robust across time horizons and various benchmarks, and stand in stark contrast to the negative abnormal returns found for private firm IPOs (see Chapter 13).

There are few convincing explanations for why SIPs earn excess returns, but Perotti and Huibers' (1998) political risk premium explanation is the most plausible. The expected returns are initially high because investors are not sure how committed the government is towards the privatization program, thus driving down share prices. The political risk premium falls in time as the privatization uncertainty is resolved. The subsequent increase in the valuation results in excess returns.

6.3.5 Stock Market Development

Privatization programs have become an important policy tool for stimulating stock market development and, in turn, greater economic growth. Measures of stock market activity in developing countries have shown dramatic growth over the past 20 years. Drawing a causal link between privatizations and stock market growth is, however, confounded by the many other factors that could have contributed to the growth. Nonetheless, an examination of the correlation can establish a lower bound for the significance of privatizations and focus on the specific properties that encourage market development.

6.3.5.1 Market growth

The growth in stock market capitalizations and trading volume in developing countries during the 1980s and 1990s was nothing short of astounding.[12] Market capitalization grew from $83 billion in 1983 to $2.18 trillion in 1999, a twenty-sixfold increase.[13] The annual trading volume

Table 6.3 Largest privatized SOEs

Country	Company	Market value[a]	Market rank[b]
Australia	Telstra	$37,814	1
Brazil	Petrobras	20,435	1
China	China Mobile	44,899	1
Finland/Sweden	TeliaSonera	18,415	2
France	Total	103,779	1
	France Telecom	57,448	2
Germany	Deutsche Telekom	62,850	1
Italy	Telecom Italia	60,123	2
	TIM (Telecom Italia Mobiliare)	44,761	3
Japan	NTT DoCoMo	105,306	1
	Nippon Telegraph & Telephone	55,578	3
Korea	SK Telecom	13,343	2
Mexico	Telefonos de Mexico	19,442	1
Netherlands	ING Groep	32,407	3
Spain	Telefonica	56,802	1
	Banco Bilbao Vizcaya Argentaria	31,574	4
UK	BP	153,240	1

a. The market values are as of May 31st, 2003 in $US
b. The company's rank on its national stock market, based on market capitalization

Source: The market value and rank are taken from Business Week Global 1000 and the Top 200 Emerging Market Companies.

increased from $25 billion to $2.3 trillion, a ninety-twofold increase. The World Bank calculated the total proceeds from privatizations in developing economies to be $154.5 billion over the 1988–96 period.

A direct measure of the effect privatizations have had on market growth is the fraction of the total market capitalization attributable to privatized SOEs. In many developing and developed countries either the largest or second largest public firm is a former SOE. These privatized SOEs account for a sizable percentage of the total market capitalization of their respective national stock markets. Table 6.3 lists the largest privatized SOEs in 13 countries, their market value and their rank in terms of size on their respective national stock markets.

Privatizations are indirectly responsible for stock market growth because of their substantial impact on liquidity and the increase in diversification opportunities for investors. These two benefits have a positive effect on risk sharing and lead to a deepening of the market, which can help it to break out of its low-listing trap. Of course, the gains in market deepening could occur from private listings as well, there is nothing special in that regard about privatizations. However, two unique aspects of this policy provide additional impetus for market growth: a reduction in political risk and the implementation of legal rights to protect minority shareholders.

6.3.5.2 Political risk

The unique feature of a privatization program that stimulates market development is the gradual resolution of regulatory and legal uncertainty (Perotti and van Oijen 2001). Investors incur the risk of future interference and expropriation of their assets in an economy dominated by government intervention. A privatization program leads to a reduction of this risk because of the necessary strengthening of property rights and institutional reliability needed to broaden the appeal and confidence in equity investing. Only after the program has been sustained over time will the political uncertainty be resolved. The reduction in risk should be especially large in countries with less developed legal systems and that privatize in periods of economic difficulty, and when entrenched political interests are hit hard.

The theory raises two empirical questions. First, do privatizations in developing countries lower the perceived political risks? Second, does a reduction in political risk lead to stock market development? Perotti and van Oijen (2001) found that many developing countries have gradually reduced their political risk over the post-1987 period through a course of sustained privatization. The conclusion was based on an assessment of political risk by international investors. However, the risk was only resolved if the privatization program was implemented, not just announced, and only in the later stages of the program.

Perotti and van Oijen showed that the resolution of political risk was strongly correlated with growth in stock market capitalizations, the value of trading activity and excess returns. A major factor in the growth was the decrease in market segmentation, as the developing countries became more integrated into global capital markets. Political risk appears to be a priced factor for which investors are rewarded with a higher return.[14] A one-percentage point improvement in the political risk factor led to a 4 percent increase in the ratio of traded market value to GNP.

6.3.5.3 Legal development

Major legal reforms usually accompany or even precede a privatization program. The primary motive for legal reform is the desire to avoid the political fallout from unsuccessful privatizations. Many governments make a concerted effort to increase the participation of small investors in the privatized SOE to improve the political viability of the sale. When over a million investors participate in the SIP, the government is acutely aware of the damage caused by poorly performing shares due to weak investor protection.

The simultaneous implementation of legal reform and a privatization program is one reason why it is difficult to draw conclusive inferences on the link between privatizations and stock market development. The privatizations might be proxying for the legal reforms, which really drive the growth. However, the government typically would not engage in any reforms unless there was a policy change towards privatization.

The legal reforms adopted by the government fall into one of two categories. The first group tries to improve the reputation of the capital markets. The government will establish or augment a regulatory body similar to the SEC in the US. Stock exchanges tighten weak listing and disclosure requirements. Regulatory agencies must be created when utilities and other natural monopoly SOEs are privatized. The second major reform is the strengthening of shareholder legal protection. Investors are reluctant to supply their capital if they do not have sufficient legal recourse against the threat of expropriation.

The failure to implement strong shareholder protection and governance rules can prove devastating. Poor governance practices are perceived by many to have played an important role in the East Asian economic contraction that began in July 1997 (Claessens, Djankov and Lang 2000; Johnson et al. 2000). A similar failure of corporate governance accounts for the difficulty the former communist countries in Central and Eastern Europe have had in transitioning to market-based economies (Sachs, Zinnes and Eilat 2000; Djankov and Murrell 2002).

6.4 SUMMARY

The development and quality of stock markets has a major effect on the IPO decision. Stock markets offer an attractive exit opportunity for pre-IPO shareholders, which stimulates venture capital financing. A public listing provides market feedback through the stock price about the firm's investment options. Public listings create positive externalities for the market development, inducing more firms to go public. Markets with few listings get stuck in a poor listing trap in which no firms want go public.

Government policy is useful for promoting stock market growth. There are pros and cons to relying on stock markets as a primary financing vehicle in the economy, but the evidence confirms the positive impact financial development has on economic growth. The law and finance view argues that enforcing strong legal rights for investors is critical to the development external capital markets. There is a persuasive correlation between measures of financial development and legal protection, although political and cultural factors may be even more significant.

A direct policy measure that stimulates market development is a privatization program for SOEs. Privatizations result in operating efficiency gains, directly benefiting the economy. The two most common privatization methods are SIPs and direct asset sales, with the former used to stimulate market development. The adoption of privatization programs in many developing countries corresponded with the onset of tremendous growth in the stock market. The primary impact of privatizations works indirectly through the resolution of political uncertainty and the adoption of legal and institutional reforms designed to protect minority shareholders.

NOTES

1. Hiring professional managers with a known reputation is often done prior to an IPO. Investors prefer that issuers have managers with experience in a public firm. Similarly, professional managers join a private firm with the understanding that it will go public soon to protect their own reputation.
2. See Levine (1999), Levine and Zervos (1998), Carlin and Mayer (2003), Levine, Loayza and Beck (2000) and Beck and Levine (2003).
3. The turnover ratio explicitly captures market activity and how attractive the market is as a financing vehicle. Market capitalization might be high because investors expect future growth to be high, but this does not provide a link for financial development to influence growth.
4. Banks that literally controlled the debt markets in Japan are a good example of incumbent institutions exerting their clout. Only when major Japanese companies gained access to the Euromarkets in the 1980s did the banking system open up a bit.
5. Re-printed from the *Journal of Economic Literature*, Vol. 39, Megginson, W. and J. Netter, "From State to Market: A Survey of Empirical Studies on Privatization," pp. 321-89, Copyright (2001) with permission.
6. See Megginson and Netter (2001), Djankov and Murrell (2002) and Shirley (1999).
7. Another factor is the stock market conditions. An IPO is only feasible when the market is performing well.
8. Other government policies that have an affect similar to privatizations include the outsourcing of services once provided by government employees and the deregulation of industries or monopolies.
9. The numbers were tabulated for the sample in Megginson et al. (2002) and were compiled from Privatization International, a regularly updated database, and the World Bank Privatization database.
10. See Jones et al. (1999), Huang and Levich (1998) and Dewenter and Malatesta (1997) for more specific results.
11. See Dewenter and Malatesta (1997); Ljungqvist, Jenkinson and Wilhelm (2003); Huang and Levich (1998); Jones et al. (1999).

12. Attention is restricted to developing countries because they are more likely candidates to adopt a privatization program to stimulate stock market development.
13. The data is from the World Banks' *Emerging Markets Fact Book.*
14. Erb, Harvey and Viskanta (1996) showed that expected returns are positively related to the magnitude of political risk.

7 Corporate restructuring

IPOs are synonymous with small, privately owned start-ups reaching a size and level of maturity that culminates with them tapping the public equity market. This description is certainly true for a subset of all IPOs, but it excludes an important avenue for the creation of new public companies: corporate restructuring. Large diversified public corporations frequently divest divisions or subsidiaries that become independent companies. The divestiture does not have to involve an IPO, although in many cases it does.

Examining corporate restructuring as a means of creating new public firms is important for three reasons. First, a significant fraction of new public companies are the consequence of some type of restructuring. These firms are generally much larger than conventional private issuers and account for a disproportionately large fraction of the total market capitalization of new public firms. Second, the IPO motives for a conventional start-up – market timing and information effects, financing options, private control benefits and the competitive landscape – are applicable to a diversified parent corporation considering the divestiture of a subsidiary. Examining divestitures provides an 'out-of-sample' verification of the IPO motives. Third, the desire to restructure is itself a motive for creating a new public company, driven by the belief that doing so increases total shareholder value.

Two major types of restructuring result in new public firms. The first involves the divestiture of assets by a parent firm either through a spin-off or a carve-out. A new legal entity that is at least partly separated from the parent is created in both cases. The second type of restructuring involves two events: a leveraged buyout in which a public firm is taken private, followed by a reverse LBO with the firm sold back to public investors.

7.1 CARVE-OUTS AND SPIN-OFFS

Divesting a subsidiary involves a decision-making process similar to the IPO decision for private firms, with a few notable differences. A subsidiary is a division of a diversified conglomerate and therefore may already publicly owned. However, the subsidiary is not an independent entity and its managers cannot decide to 'go public' on its own through a divestiture. The non-subsidiary component to the conglomerate – the parent firm – has control over the subsidiary and the CEO of the conglomerate decides whether to divest. The decision to divest is usually made jointly with the divestiture method. Carve-outs and spin-offs are of interest in the current context because both result in the subsidiary becoming a new public corporation. Subsidiaries are also frequently sold directly to a third company, which does not result in a new firm.

7.1.1 Definitions

The following briefly describe the process, structuring and consequences of spin-off and carve-out restructuring events.

Spin-off: A spin-off is a pro rata distribution of the subsidiary's shares to the shareholders of the parent firm and does not involve cash. The spun-off subsidiary is a distinct legal entity with its own board of directors and management team, with no connection to the parent firm on an operating level. The subsidiary and parent share the exact same group of shareholders immediately after the distribution, but secondary market trading can lead to significantly different groups within a year.

A spin-off has the advantage of being a tax-free transaction if three conditions are met. The dividend distribution must constitute at least 80 percent of the outstanding shares of the subsidiary and the shares retained by the parent should not confer 'practical control' over the subsidiary. The parent and subsidiary must both be engaged in an active trade of business for at least five years prior to the ex dividend date. Finally, the spin-off is done for sound business reasons and not as a means to avoid paying taxes. Not surprisingly, most large spin-offs are structured to satisfy these criteria.

Carve-out: A carve-out is a sale of the subsidiary's stock in an IPO, which consists of either secondary shares owned by the parent, new primary shares in the subsidiary or both. The IPO proceeds are split between the parent and subsidiary contingent on the secondary/primary make-up of the offering. Unlike a spin-off, a carve-out involves an infusion of cash and immediately establishes a new set of shareholders. Carve-outs frequently result in no more than 20 percent of the subsidiary's shares being held by new investors, with the parent retaining the remaining 80-plus percent. This enables a subsequent spin-off of the retained shares to be a tax-free transaction. In addition, the financial statements of the parent and subsidiary can be combined for tax consolidation purposes if the parent retains at least 80 percent of the shares.

137

Carve-outs and spin-offs differ in the degree of separation between the parent and subsidiary post-divestiture. A spun-off firm is completely separate from the parent, whereas the carved-out subsidiary is controlled or heavily influenced by the parent. The CEO of the carved-out subsidiary is often the former division manager for the parent and the subsidiary board includes at least one board member from the parent. A carve-out also involves significantly greater out-of-pocket expenses and is subject to stricter disclosure requirements by the SEC than a spin-off.

7.1.2 Motivation and Price Effects

The common theme underlying the multiple motives for divesting a subsidiary is the desire to increase total shareholder value. The potential sources of the value gain are varied: improved information flow to investors, increasing focus of the parent's operations, devising more effective compensation contracts and improved financing and investment opportunities. The preceding motives all involve, to one degree or another, a strategic or informational element. Less strategic, but no less important, considerations also motivate divestitures.

Regulation: A company that has surpassed a threshold level of market share may be required by the federal trade commission (FTC) or the Department of Justice to divest some assets to reduce its monopoly power. Studies by Schipper and Smith (1983) and Hite and Owers (1983) reported that up to 30 percent of spin-offs were motivated by the regulatory environment. Many of the divestitures occurred when two firms merged on the condition that some assets would be sold off.

Wealth transfer: A restructuring can increase shareholder value by transferring wealth from bondholders to shareholders. The evidence, with some exceptions, does not support this motive. Schipper and Smith (1983) found that the announcement of a spin-off did not have a negative effect on the price of bonds. Parrino (1997), however, provided a contrary example. Marriott Hotels engaged in a reverse spin-off that reduced the collateral for its existing debt and lowered the bondholder claims on cash flows from the business. The effect of these combined changes was a decrease in the debt value and a corresponding large increase in the stock price.

Taxes: Restructuring the company in a manner that minimizes taxes will benefit shareholders. The restructuring could be done by spinning off a subsidiary in a corporate form, like a REIT or master limited partnership, which reduces the tax burden. There is little empirical evidence to suggest that taxes are a significant motive for divesting.

Conflict of interest: A conglomerate might divest a subsidiary to avoid a conflict of interest with its customers. For example, one division of a vertically integrated firm might produce a product that is serviced by another division. The product could be sold to a company competing with the service division to supply product support to independent customers. The rival service firm would be reluctant to buy the product from a competitor. Shareholders of the conglomerate may be better off if the product division is spun off as a separate entity.

Risk: Parent firm managers might prefer that the conglomerate have a low level of risk exposure. A subsidiary involved in a risky venture that does not fit into the desired risk profile could motive a divestiture.

Clientele effect: Shareholder value can be adversely affected by the clientele effect. Investors who are only interested in a particular division, perhaps a high-tech venture, shun the diversified conglomerate, thereby lowering the share price. Divesting such a division could attract additional investors to both the parent and the subsidiary, driving up their valuations.

7.1.2.1 Announcement returns

Rational investors should anticipate the value gains that are expected to accrue because of a divestiture. The stock price will jump immediately at the restructuring announcement to reflect the expected increase in shareholder value. The price effect at the announcement is measured by the cumulative abnormal return.

The conjecture that restructuring the conglomerate increases shareholder value is supported by the positive announcement CARs. The value gains are estimated to be in the range of 2.5 to 4 percent for spin-offs, 1.5 to 2.5 percent for carve-outs and 1 to 2 percent for direct asset sales (sell-offs).[1] The announcement CARs for all three events were positively related to the size of the subsidiary relative to the parent and were larger if the spun-off or carved-out subsidiary was subsequently purchased by another company. The difference in the CARs across the three types of divestitures reflects investor beliefs about the efficacy of the restructuring. Within each divestiture method the CARs vary depending on the motive and perceived effectiveness of such an action.

7.1.3 Information Effects

Practitioners frequently cite the desire to 'unlock the hidden value' in the complex organizational structure of a diversified corporation as a reason for divesting a business unit. Deciphering the value of individual business segments from aggregate financial data can be difficult for outside observers. When analysts and investors are unable or unwilling to fully comprehend the sources of value within a company, the entire firm can be undervalued. Separating the large diversified company into individual 'pure plays' helps the market overcome this informational barrier, thereby increasing shareholder value.

The hidden-value divestiture motive is only valid if firm management is cognizant of the undervaluation. This implies that managers have superior information relative to investors. Increased information production can overcome the asymmetry between management and investors, but that first requires the divestiture of the subsidiary. Information asymmetries also affect the divestiture method choice by altering the appeal of a carve-out versus a spin-off.

7.1.3.1 Information production

To unlock the hidden value in a conglomerate, investors must possess more and better information after the restructuring. A divestiture is an immediate step in that direction because both the parent and subsidiary issue separate audited financial statements. Of course, a divestiture is not necessary for the conglomerate to release the same financial information. The shortcoming of voluntarily disclosed information is that the numbers are subject to cross-subsidization between the parent and subsidiary, lowering their credibility. Other value-relevant information, such as the subsidiary's dividend policy and capital structure, is only revealed by a restructuring.

The primary source for the improved information flow post-divestiture is increased coverage by research analysts. Gilson et al. (2001) estimated that the average number of analysts covering a conglomerate prior to the restructuring was 17. This increased to a combined 24 for the parent and subsidiary two years after the divestiture. There was also substantial turnover among analysts. Two-thirds of the analysts covering either the parent or the subsidiary one year after the divestiture did not cover the conglomerate prior to the break-up. The change in composition likely reflects industry-specific analysts now willing to cover the focused firms.

The increased quantity of information produced is positively correlated with the quality. Analysts issue forecasts for future earnings. One proxy for information quality is the difference between forecasted and actual earnings. The size of earnings forecast errors and the standard deviation of forecasts for the parent dropped by over 50 percent from the pre- to post-divestiture fiscal years (Gilson et al. 2001; Krishnaswami and Subramaniam 1999). The benefit of greater analyst coverage and precision is a more efficient share price and increased liquidity, thereby raising the firm value.

The provision of increased analyst coverage is costly for investment banks, which implicitly expect compensation in return. Restructuring firms pay for the increased coverage with larger future underwriting fees. Subsidiaries can no longer be cross-subsidized with excess cash from another division. The frequency of equity issues and the total amount of capital raised increased significantly in the two years after the divestiture, for the subsidiary as well as the parent (Krishnaswami and Subramaniam 1999; Vijh 2002). Lower information asymmetries reduce the cost of a public equity offering, making it more attractive to both firms.

7.1.3.2 Asymmetric information

The expected valuation gain from a divestiture must be sufficient to cover the cost of the restructuring. The combined time spent by management planning and executing the divestiture, and the direct compensation paid to lawyers and bankers who advised on the deal can be quite costly. Conglomerates that proceed with a divestiture for information production reasons should be those that suffer from the most severe asymmetries.

The evidence does suggest that conglomerates are more apt to divest when asymmetric information is severe. Krishnaswami and Subramaniam (1999) examined analysts' forecast errors and the dispersion of forecasts, and conjectured that both would increase with the asymmetry. Conglomerates that subsequently spun off a subsidiary were found to have forecast errors and a dispersion that were up to three times larger than the equivalent forecasts for industry and size-matched comparable firms. The positive relationship between the announcement CARs and the forecast errors suggests investors anticipate an improved information environment.

A divestiture may be motivated by a desire to exploit information asymmetries, not lessen them. Chapter 2 presented data showing a consistent pattern of private-firm IPOs occurring after abnormally positive industry and market returns, followed by a subsequent downturn in valuations. The timing patterns certainly implied that issuers exploited their private information to go public when they are overvalued.

Carved-outs subsidiaries are sold through an IPO and exhibit the same opportunistic timing patterns as their private firm counterparts. Hand and Skantz (1999) reported that the average market return in the year prior to the carve-out was 17.9 percent, greater than the 11.3 percent average annual return over the 1960–95 period. The average one-year post-carve-out return was 11.9 percent. The pre- and post-carve-out industry returns were 27.3 and 17.7 percent, respectively. The market return prior to the carve-out announcement, the interim market return between the announcement and offer date, and the number of carve-outs in the prior six months were all strongly negatively related to post-carve-out returns. All three relationships point to overvaluation.

7.1.3.3 Divestiture method: theory

The value of a conglomerate is the sum of the individual values for the parent and the subsidiary. Mis-valuation can occur because one or both of the two units are not properly priced. Since the majority of a conglomerate's assets are usually affiliated with the parent, the conglomerate's mis-pricing follows that of the parent. While asymmetric information results in mis-pricing, there is no *a priori* bias towards under or overvaluation. The direction and the source of the mis-valuation determines the desirability of a particular divestiture method.

The models of Nanda (1991) and Nanda and Narayanan (1999) worked through the possible combinations of parent and subsidiary mis-valuation to reveal the scenarios in which each divestiture method is optimal. The analysis was aided by assuming that the conglomerate would like to raise equity finance for an investment project in the subsidiary. Overvalued parent assets results in conglomerate overvaluation. The existing shareholders prefer a seasoned equity offering by the conglomerate over a divestiture because it transfers wealth from the new to the old shareholders. Parent and conglomerate undervaluation makes divesting preferable to selling equity. A carve-out is optimal when the subsidiary assets are overvalued. The direct sale of equity goes to the subsidiary to finance the investment. An undervalued subsidiary should be first spun off. Increased information production resolves the asymmetry problem and eliminates the undervaluation. The subsidiary can then sell properly priced equity.

The reduction of information asymmetries begins even before analysts' increase their coverage because the financing decision made by management signals its private information. The seasoned offering indicates that the conglomerate is overvalued, causing the parent firm stock price to drop. Both types of divestiture signals undervaluation, causing the stock price to rise upon announcement. The positive reaction should be larger following a spin-off announcement because a carve-out signals that the subsidiary is overvalued, whereas the spin-off indicates undervaluation.

7.1.3.4 Divestiture method: evidence

The pattern of price responses by the conglomerate's shares predicted by the theory corresponds exactly with actual announcement returns. Seasoned equity offering announcements result in an immediate average share price decline of 2 to 3 percent. Spin-off announcements produce positive abnormal returns of 3 to 4 percent and carve-out returns are 1 to 2 percent.

The conjecture that carve-out subsidiaries are overvalued and spin-offs are undervalued cannot be directly tested because there is no observable subsidiary stock price at the announcement. An indirect test was proposed by Slovin, Sushka and Ferraro (1995), who looked at the share price response of rival firms. Firms in the same industry have a common component to their valuation. The timing of carve-outs certainly suggests that industry overvaluation is relevant. Slovin, Sushka and Ferraro reported that the average carve-out announcement return for rival firms was a significant -1.1 percent, consistent with subsidiary overvaluation.

The negative price reaction for rivals could be explained by another factor, increased competition. The restructuring allows the subsidiary to operate more efficiently and compete more effectively. The threat of greater competition causes the rivals' stock prices to fall. Of course, the same competitive effect would apply to spun-off and sold-off subsidiaries. Yet Slovin, Sushka and Ferraro found that rival firms' price reactions to those two alternative divestiture announcements were an insignificant 0.6 and 0.4 percent, respectively. The best explanation for the price patterns is that the carved-out subsidiaries were overvalued due to asymmetric information.[2]

The theory predicted that a divestiture would only occur if the parent and conglomerate were undervalued. The positive price reaction to divestiture announcements is consistent with the prediction. Once again, however, the reaction could reflect a belief that the parent will now operate more efficiently. If so, a more competitive parent would negatively impact rivals' share prices. Slovin, Sushka and Ferraro reported that the average price reaction for parental rivals was in the range of 1.2 to 1.7 percent, although not statistically significant. The positive reaction favors undervaluation due to asymmetric information.

7.1.4 Operating Efficiency

The second major divestiture motive cited by practitioners is the need for a conglomerate to refocus on core business lines and improve operating efficiency. The implicit assumption behind this motive is that the value of the conglomerate is less than the sum of the divisional values if operated individually. The positive divestiture announcement CAR is justified by a belief that total shareholder value will increase after the break-up. Researchers have found evidence of a so-called 'diversification discount'; conglomerates trade at a price less than the value of an equivalent portfolio of single-line firms. Multiple explanations for the discount have been proposed, which provide an indication of the source of efficiency gains post-restructuring.

The value gain due to increased efficiency is quite distinct from the hidden-value information explanation. The firm value is fixed but not known precisely by investors in the latter case. The divestiture signals inside information to investors and improved information production *ex post* enables the market to accurately value the firm. The restructuring is the source of the value gain under the efficiency hypothesis, which is anticipated by investors at announcement.

7.1.4.1 Diversification discount

The initial discovery of a diversification discount challenged the belief that conglomeration has many value-increasing benefits. Managerial economies of scale in running multiple line businesses, increased debt capacity, tax savings and valuable internal capital markets were all thought to increase firm value. Yet Berger and Ofek (1995) estimated that diversified conglomerates traded at a 13 to 15 percent discount from an equivalent portfolio of stand-alone firms.[3] Similarly, Lang and Stulz (1994) found that multi-segment firms had low q ratios – the market value of the firm's assets to its book value – compared to single line businesses.[4] The impact on shareholder value from the discount is enormous. Graham, Lemmon and Wolf (2002) estimated the aggregate value loss due to diversification was $800 billion in 1995.

The potentially huge cost to shareholders from diversified firms has led many researchers to ask whether diversification does indeed destroy firm value. Some have disputed even the existence of a discount on methodological grounds. The validity of estimated discounts is contingent on the measured diversification actually equaling the true amount of diversification, which may not hold because of disclosure and accounting issues.[5] Villalonga (2003) used data that she claimed accurately measured diversification and doing so turned the discount into a significant premium. Other researchers have treated the discount as a given and tried to explain it as a consequence of the conglomerate organizational structure. Two such explanations are examined in the next sections. Finally, some researchers have argued that diversification *per se* does not cause the discount; rather the discount is a function of the diversifying firm's characteristics. Two possibilities are considered below.

Endogenous discount: Factors that cause a firm to initially diversify could also be related to the discount. Failure to control for the diversification decision leads to biased inferences about the discount. Campa and Kedia (2001) and Villalonga (2004) both showed that the discount always declined, and sometimes turned into a significant premium, after controlling for the endogenous diversification decision. The companies that diversified were already discounted prior to diversification and they differed considerably from specialized firms.

The discount was also partly due to the acquisition of already discounted firms, according to Graham, Lemmon and Wolf (2002). The typical target firm was discounted 10 percent in its last year of stand-alone operation. The average discount for the diversifying acquirer increased seven percentage points in the two years after the purchase and the value loss was almost entirely attributable to the target. The general conclusion is that diversification itself is not responsible for the discount.

Risk and expected return: Firm value is based on future expected cash flows and the expected return. Lamont and Polk (2001) reported that discounted conglomerates and single-line firms trading at a premium have had relatively high and low, respectively, subsequent stock returns. Since actual returns were consistently higher for discounted firms, they argued that expected returns should also be higher for conglomerates. The higher cost of capital would then account for the initial discount.

The discount could be a function of the way in which risk is affected by diversification. Conglomeration reduces risk to shareholders because the cash flows across segments are not perfectly correlated. Lower risk reduces the equity value if shares are priced as call options on the firm's assets, with the exercise price equal to the debt obligation. The equity value is more sensitive to cash flow risk when the debt level is high. Thus the discount should be most pronounced among highly levered firms because lower conglomerate risk causes a greater loss in the call option value. Mansi and Reeb (2002) found that this was indeed the case. In contrast, all-equity conglomerates exhibited no discount.

7.1.4.2 Internal capital markets

The primary cause of the value loss associated with conglomeration appears to be inefficient internal capital markets. If anything, firm value should increase with the presence of a well-functioning internal capital market because the costs of raising external finance are avoided and financing constraints are overcome. However, two agency problems stemming from the internal capital markets can destroy more value than the market creates.

The first agency cost stems from the free cash flow problem. Conglomerate executives that have access to excess cash flow may over-invest in poor projects or pursue empire-building that destroys value. A diversified conglomerate provides management with more internal growth options and the cash needed to finance them that would be difficult to obtain externally. Based on this agency argument, managers actively pursue diversification strategies to satisfy their own personal objectives, but simultaneously reduce firm value.

Evidence on managerial behavior is only partly consistent with this agency hypothesis. Denis, Denis and Sarin (1997) and Villalonga (2004) both documented a negative relation between the equity ownership of insiders and outside blockholders and the degree of diversification. Low-ownership managers may fail to internalize the diversification cost on other shareholders. However, Denis, Denis and Sarin found no relationship between any of their ownership structure variables and the discount. Market disciplinary forces such as acquisition attempts, blockholder pressure, financial distress and management turnover were shown to diminish the extent of diversification.

The second agency cost is caused by internal conflicts. Divisional managers compete for corporate resources by lobbying central management (Stein 1997). Such rent-seeking behavior directly wastes resources and partly causes the value loss. Scharfstein and Stein (2000) suggested that senior executives might try to deter costly rent-seeking by bribing managers with less costly preferential capital budget allocations. The net effect is that strong divisions tend to subsidize weak ones. The evidence of inefficiently low investment in high q industry divisions and overinvestment in low q divisions corroborates the prediction of value-reducing cross-subsidization (Lamont 1997; Scharfstein 1998; Shin and Stulz 1998).

Expected cross-subsidization can affect the initial investment decisions. Managers in good divisions may underinvest in the best investments because the profits will be split with weaker divisions. Rajan, Servaes and Zingales (1999) predicted that the greater the diversity in the quality and potential profits among the conglomerate divisions, the worse the conglomerate performs and the larger the discount. They showed that capital allocations to relatively low q divisions outweighed the allocations to high q divisions as the dispersion in opportunities increased. Hence, the conglomerate diversity and discount were positively related, with low diversity firms actually trading at a premium.

The blame heaped on inefficient internal capital markets could be misguided, just as diversification might not be the cause of the discount. Whited (2001) found no evidence of inefficient resource allocation in diversified firms after controlling for measurement problems associated with defining high and low growth segments. The investment inefficiency ascribed to cross-subsidization in diversified firms was found by Chevalier (2000) to be present in pairs of firms prior to their merger. Poorly managed firms may try to diversify in a mistaken attempt to improve performance and it is this attribute that causes the discount.

7.1.4.3 Investment efficiency

Inefficient conglomerate investment facilitated by internal capital markets is eliminated or reduced by a divestiture. Comparisons between pre- and post-spin-off investment patterns showed a marked improvement in capital allocation (Gertner, Powers and Scharfstein 2002; Ahn and Denis 2004). Industry-adjusted investment levels were negative in the conglomerates' high q industry segments prior to the spin-off and close to zero in the low q segments. Following the spin-off, investment increased (decreased) significantly in high (low) q subsidiaries. The change in the discount from pre- to post-spin-off was positively related to the change in investment efficiency over the period, with the discount eliminated on average. The improved efficiency was most pronounced when the subsidiary operated in an industry unrelated to the parent.

The evidence on investment efficiency must be interpreted with caution. The samples were limited to those conglomerates that voluntarily chose a spin-off. Factors motivating a spin-off could be related to the inefficient investment, biasing the sample towards finding significant improvements. The most that can be claimed is that for some firms the diversification discount appears to be caused by inefficient investment. It is natural to conclude that poor internal capital markets caused inefficient investment, although there are alternative explanations for the improved investment efficiency. Better information flow about the subsidiary after the divestiture could improve managerial decision-making and provide stronger managerial incentives.

7.1.4.4 Incentive alignment

The strengthening of managerial incentives post-divestiture is made possible by the creation of stock that specifically tracks the performance of the subsidiary. The subsidiary stock provides a cleaner measure of managerial productivity than the parent stock price. More efficient and powerful incentive contracts can be implemented as a result, which should lead to improved investment efficiency and operating performance.

The limited evidence does not support the proposition that value gains are derived from improved incentives. Vijh (2002) reported that designing better compensation contracts is rarely mentioned in the *Wall Street Journal* as one of the factors motivating the divestiture. Nevertheless, performance-based compensation plans are implemented regularly after the divestiture. Seward and Walsh (1996) found that the subsidiary had a board of directors and compensation committee composed of a majority of outside directors and the CEO compensation was typically performance contingent. However, operating gains following spin-offs were not statistically related to the improvements in contract efficiency.

7.1.4.5 Operating performance

The divestiture value gains that investors expect from improved investment and operating efficiency are derived from increased managerial focus and the elimination of negative synergies. Any efficiency gains will show up as improved operating performance. Divestitures can be classified as either focus-increasing or non-focus-increasing (henceforth referred to as focus and non-focus) to test whether reduced diversity and increased focus improves performance. A focus divestiture involves a subsidiary operating in a different two-digit standard industrial classification (SIC) industry than the parent or results in the parent sales becoming more concentrated in fewer industries. A divestiture is non-focus if neither condition is met.

A comparison between focus and non-focus divestitures reveals that the market expects greater operating improvements at focus firms. The announcement CAR for focus spin-offs was about 4.5 percent, much larger than the 1.5 to 2 percent for non-focus spin-offs (Daley, Mehrotra and Sivakumar 1997; Desai and Jain 1999). Carve-outs follow the same pattern, with Vijh (2002) reporting abnormal returns for focus and non-focus firms equal to 2.3 and 0.8 percent, respectively. The announcement CARs are justified only if the firms perform as expected.

Spin-offs: The accounting treatment of spin-offs enables a comparison between the pre- and post-divestiture operating performance of the parent, the subsidiary and the portfolio of the two.[6] Operating performance is measured using return on assets (ROA) and operating cash flow-to-assets (CFA). Daley, Mehrotra and Sivakumar (1997) showed that the median ROA for the parent and subsidiary portfolio increased by about three percentage points from one year prior to one year after a focus spin-off. Non-focus spin-offs did not result in any significant ROA gain. Desai and Jain (1999) similarly found that the CFA increased three percentage points following a focus spin-off, with no gain for non-focus spin-offs.

Separate examination of the parent and subsidiary reveals that focus parents are the source of the improvement. The ROA for focus parents increased a significant two percentage points from the spin-off year to one year later. None of the remaining parents or subsidiaries experienced any significant ROA improvement. The same conclusion holds for the CFA measure. Interestingly, Desai and Jain reported that the average CFA dropped by eight percentage points for non-focus subsidiaries post-spin-off. It appears that these spin-offs were motivated by a desire to shed an underperforming unit.

Carve-outs: Measuring the change in operating performance for carve-outs is possible because the IPO prospectus contains subsidiary accounting information for the preceding three years. Powers (2003) found that the subsidiary ROA peaked in the carve-out year with a mean of 18.7 percent. The mean ROA went from 15.8 to 12.8 percent from two years before to two years after the carve-out year.[7] The time series profile of the subsidiary ROA is consistent with management using its inside information to optimally time the carve-out. The operating performance of the parent firms showed no discernible change from pre- to post-carve-out. The analysis did not distinguish between focus and non-focus carve-outs.

7.1.5 Managerial Discretion

The preceding divestiture theories have assumed that managerial interests are perfectly aligned with those of shareholders. An equally plausible assumption is that managers act in their own self-interest and derive benefits from controlling a large firm. Consequently, managers try to avoid a divestiture that reduces the assets under their control, even if it would increase shareholder value. Management acquiesces to a divestiture only if a new more attractive opportunity becomes available and if a divestiture is the only source of capital for the financially constrained firm.

Management that is in control and maintains discretion over all operating decisions has, according to Allen and McConnell (1998), three consequences for divestiture behavior. First, the firm divests assets only when it is financially constrained, which is more likely if it is highly levered, recently suffered poor earnings performance, or both. Second, only carve-outs and sell-offs will be used to divest assets because they generate cash flow. Third, investors are aware of the agency costs stemming from managerial control. Thus they react much more favorably to carve-out announcements in which the parent firm commits to using the proceeds to repay debt or for dividends, as opposed to retaining the funds for discretionary purposes.

The predictions of the managerial discretion theory have received strong empirical support. Carve-out and sell-off parents had low interest coverage ratios, high leverage ratios, and low profits and profit margins prior to the divestiture (Lang, Poulsen and Stulz 1995; Allen and McConnell 1998). Carve-outs involving parent firms that intended to use the proceeds to repay debt or pay a dividend had announcement CARs of approximately 6.5 percent, whereas the CARs for firms retaining the funds were not significantly different from zero (Allen and McConnell 1998; Vijh 2002). The CARs for sell-off announcements were 2.8 and 1.3 percent for payout and retention firms, respectively (Slovin, Sushka and Ferraro 1995).

7.1.6 Choice of Divestiture Method

The decision to divest is often contingent on the divesting methods available. For example, a carve-out is not feasible if the IPO window is closed. Cost is another consideration. Carve-outs involve an expensive public offering that is avoided with a spin-off or sell-off. The following points summarize the factors affecting the method choice discussed thus far and present some additional evidence.

Asymmetric information: Carve-outs occurred when industry and market valuations were high, reflecting the positive excess returns that preceded the divestiture (Powers 2001; 2003). Spin-offs and sell-offs followed industry returns that were slightly below expectation, which left them properly priced. Parent firms exploit the mis-pricing caused by asymmetric information to carve-out overvalued subsidiaries, but must spin-off undervalued divisions.

Subsidiary quality: Carved-out subsidiaries were of higher quality than spun-off or sold-off divisions, measured by operating performance (Nixon, Rosenfeldt and Sicherman 2000; Powers 2001; 2003). The carved-out divisions were significantly more profitable and faster growing than spun-off units, which in turn dominated sell-off subsidiaries. IPO investors prefer high quality issuers, which biases the pool of potential carve-outs away from poorly performing subsidiaries.

Financial constraints: Carve-out and sell-off parent firms had worse operating performance and significantly higher leverage than spin-off parents, and were more likely to be financially distressed (Nixon, Rosenfeldt and Sicherman 2000; Powers 2001; 2003). A spin-off is not a practical option for these cash-strapped parents. Parents also conducted an abnormally large number of seasoned offerings after the carve-out and invested significantly less in capital expenditures than control firms (Vijh

2002). These financing and investment patterns suggest that the capital raised is used to repay debt or for other financial contingencies.

Focus and control: Spin-offs result in a clear separation between parent and subsidiary and are best able to reap the gains from focusing. Carved-out subsidiaries were usually still majority owned by the parent. Powers (2001) found that carve-out subsidiaries were more likely than spin-offs to operate in industries related to those of the parent. Conglomerate managers may find it easier and preferable to retain (partial) control of the subsidiary when it is in a closely related industry.

7.1.7 Sequential Asset Sales

A divestiture that ultimately ends in the subsidiary being sold to another firm might best be completed in stages. The two-stage mechanism proposed in Chapter 5 for the sale of a private firm is applicable to divestitures. The first stage is a carve-out IPO in which a minority of the subsidiary's shares is sold to dispersed investors. The second stage consists of direct bargaining between the parent and the buyer over the remainder of the subsidiary.

A majority of initial carve-outs are followed by a second event, either by design or in response to new developments. The parent firm sells the subsidiary to a third party 40 to 50 percent of the time, completing the second event within a few years of the IPO (Klein, Rosenfeldt and Beranek 1991; Vijh 2002). Spinning off the remainder of the subsidiary is the next most frequent event, followed by a reacquisition by the parent.

The anticipation of a second event increases the subsidiary's value at the announcement. Vijh (2002) reported that the announcement CARs to carve-outs that were subsequently sold or spun off were higher than for those with no second event, possibility reflecting the parent's ability to extract a higher price in the IPO. Cusatis, Miles and Woolridge (1993) concluded that larger announcement CARs for spin-offs were likely caused by subsequent takeover activity. Since the parent shareholders initially own the spun off subsidiary, they gain from a higher takeover premium.

7.1.8 Long-Run Returns

The expected and realized operating improvements following the divestiture only really matter to shareholders if the gains show up in the stock price. Long-run stock returns are the ultimate arbiter of a divestiture's success. The general finding on long-run returns is that they are consistent with the initial CARs; spin-offs produce positive excess returns that are much larger than those generated by carve-outs. The findings support the conclusion that undervalued subsidiaries are spun-off, whereas carve-outs are optimally timed when the valuations may be too high.

Spin-offs: Parents and subsidiaries both produced positive abnormal three-year returns. Desai and Jain (1999) estimated that the parents and subsidiaries generated excess returns of 15.2 and 32.3 percent, respectively, but only the latter was significantly different from zero. The abnormal returns for parents of focus and non-focus spin-offs were 25.4 and -10.5 percent, respectively, and for subsidiaries 54.5 and -21.9 percent. These returns are at least partly driven by efficiency gains from improved focus. Cusatis, Miles and Woolridge (1993) found that all of the abnormal performance was associated with a subsample of spin-offs that were involved in takeover activity within three years of the divestiture.

Carve-outs: The three-year abnormal returns for parents and subsidiaries were not significantly different from zero (Vijh 1999; Powers 2003). The carve-out long-run excess returns offer an interesting contrast to conventional IPOs. The three-year annual raw return for carve-outs was 14.3 percent, far larger than the 3.4 percent for IPOs reported in Loughran and Ritter (1995). The superior performance by carve-out subsidiaries could reflect opposing forces. Optimal market timing observed for both IPOs and carve-outs negatively biases the excess returns. The increased focus that leads to efficiency gains only occurs following a carve-out IPO, producing a positive excess return bias. The net effect is no abnormal return for carve-outs and negative excess returns for conventional IPOs.

7.2 LEVERAGED BUYOUTS

The path between private and public ownership is not one-way. A public company can be taken private if an investor or group of investors purchase all of the outstanding shares. The new owners borrow heavily to finance the acquisition in a transaction called a leveraged buyout. The group of investors could be led by a management team (MBO), or a specialist buyout firm, such as Kolhberg Kravis Roberts, that sponsors the acquisition.

A LBO is a major corporate restructuring event on par with a spin-off or a carve-out and offers a different perspective on the going-public decision. The characteristics and virtues of an LBO organizational structure highlight the benefits of remaining private. In particular, the corporate governance properties of the LBO structure point to the weakness of public ownership. However, the LBO structure is usually only temporary, with the firms being sold back to the public in a secondary IPO. These reverse LBOs constitute a sizeable fraction of the total IPO volume and proceeds.

7.2.1 Why LBO?

Advocates of the LBO structure argue that public ownership is not the best organizational form for firms in mature industries with excess capacity.[8] Leverage buyout candidates in these industries operate below their capability and have depressed valuations.[9] Taking these firms private through a LBO results in a major restructuring designed to refocus the business on its core activities, eliminate waste and inefficiency, and divest assets. The subsequent improved operating performance raises the firm value, giving the LBO investors a positive return on their investment.

Two characteristics of mature public corporations are at the core of the inefficiencies resolved by a LBO. The first is excess free cash flow. Managers that are even moderately entrenched could consume excess private control benefits with the available cash or pursue unwarranted acquisitions to increase the assets under their control. The second is that managerial incentives are not perfectly aligned with the objective of maximizing shareholder wealth.

The LBO structure has two properties that create strong incentives for managers to improve the operating efficiency. First, the managers, who may be retained from the pre-LBO period, acquire a significant ownership stake. This gives them the necessary incentive to pay out the excess cash flow, as opposed to investing in poor projects, and to wring out the maximum possible return from the existing assets. In addition, the concentrated ownership structure ensures that non-managerial owners actively monitor management. Second, the debt used to finance the purchase of the firm absorbs much of the excess cash flow. The constant requirement of meeting interest obligations further disciplines management into maximizing operational efficiency.[10]

Critics of LBOs as an optimal organizational structure counter with the claim that a LBO is only a temporary deviation from public ownership. The constraints imposed by the debt obligations hinder the firm's ability to adapt to changing circumstances and remain competitive. The illiquidity of private equity severely limits the ability of investors to cash in on the value gains the LBO brings forth. The LPs of the buyout fund, and especially the firm managers, bear a significant amount of undiversified risk when the firm is private. All these factors point to an LBO firm returning to public ownership, either through an IPO or an acquisition, after a relatively short time period. The evidence straddles the middle ground between LBOs being a permanent and a temporary structure. Kaplan (1991) found that about 40 percent of LBOs remained private even after six years.

7.2.2 Characteristics and Performance

The defining feature of a LBO is the heavy use of debt. The pool of potential LBO candidates is therefore limited to those firms capable of servicing high interest obligations through cash flow. Firms in mature industries that generate stable cash flows, have sufficient tangible assets for collateral, limited growth opportunities and little need for heavy investment in R&D are the best targets. The firms also need to have unused debt capacity, generate cash flow in excess of working capital requirements and have non-core assets that can be divested for cash without too much trouble. Companies in manufacturing, retailing and food-processing industries, to name a few, have been frequent targets of LBOs. Undervaluation and inefficient operations are additional firm attributes necessary for the LBO to generate substantial returns. The principal characteristics of a LBO are its leverage, managerial ownership and initial acquisition premium.

Leverage: The typical debt-to-total capital ratio has ranged from 90 percent in the 1980s to about 70 percent in the late 1990s. Kaplan (1991) estimated a median leverage ratio of 88 percent at the time of the buyout, far higher than the 19 percent pre-buyout. The leverage does not change much while the firms are private. Holthausen and Larcker (1996) reported a median debt-to-capital ratio of 86 percent immediately prior to the reverse IPO.

Managerial ownership: Kaplan (1991) reported that managerial ownership in MBOs increased from 8.3 percent of outstanding equity before the buyout to 29 percent afterwards. Holthausan and Larcker (1996) found a similiar management stake post-buyout, 36 percent, and the holdings of all insiders – officers, directors and employees – totalled 75 percent.

Premiums: The expectation of improvements in operating efficiency and abnormal returns on investment is captured by the acquisition price. The premium paid to the target shareholders exceeded 40 percent in studies that examined LBOs in the 1970s and early 1980s (DeAngelo, DeAngelo and Rice 1984; Lowenstein 1985; Lehn and Poulsen 1988).

7.2.2.1 Performance

The purpose of the LBO to stimulate operating efficiency gains is borne out in the data. Kaplan (1989) found that operating income increased faster in

LBO firms than comparable industry firms in the first two post-LBO years. Holthausen and Larcker (1996) reported that the real value of sales increased 9.4 percent and operating profits by 45 percent from the LBO announcement to the reverse IPO date. Since these LBOs were able to go public again, the gains likely overstate the improvements in all LBOs. A positive correlation between the fraction of equity held by the officers and directors and the gain in operating performance and shareholder value was also documented (Holthausen and Larcker 1996; Muscarella and Vetsuypens 1990). This is consistent with powerful managerial incentives promoting efficient operations.

The documented returns to LBO investors are significantly positive, but come with a number of caveats. The median annualized return during the first three post-LBO years was 36.6 percent in Muscarella and Vetsuypens (1990) and 26 percent in excess of the S&P 500 return in Kaplan (1991). These estimated returns again likely overstate the true median return to LBO investors because they were based on the subsample of LBOs that subsequently went public. The reported returns did not adjust for the high leverage ratio, which drives up the expected returns. The leverage-adjusted expected return should be much higher for LBOs than the S&P 500. The returns to buyout funds (see Chapter 3) provide the most complete measure of returns to LBOs and these have generally been average at best on a risk-adjusted basis.

7.2.3 Reverse LBOs

Taking the LBO firm back public is often an explicit part of the initial objective. Buyout firms purchase companies they believe are undervalued and underperforming, restructure them to bring about performance gains and then liquidate their position with a public offering or sale to another firm. Sometimes a secondary IPO is completed for the simple reason that the firm needs equity capital to pay down the heavy debt burden. Whatever the motive, secondary IPOs are completed an average of 2.5 years after the LBO date (Kaplan 1991; Holthausen and Larcker 1996).

The early 1990s experienced a surge in reverse LBOs as the companies taken private during the 1980s started to go public when the IPO window opened. Ang and Brau (2003) documented that 334 LBOs completed an IPO sometime from 1981 to 1996, with most, including 70 in 1992, in the 1990s. The sample of LBOs included 124 firms that were once public, 144 that were subsidiaries of public corporations and 66 that were private firms. The average initial return for the reverse LBOs was in the range of 2 to 5.5 percent, far less than the 18 percent average for all IPOs (Holthausan and Larcker 1996; Ang and Brau 2003). Ang and Brau suggested that the relatively low initial returns reflect less severe asymmetric information. The LBOs are more transparent and less risky to IPO investors because the firms were once publicly owned and are required to release financial information if they have public debt outstanding.

The two defining properties of LBOs, high leverage and concentrated managerial ownership, are at least partly reversed by the public offering. The evidence that both factors were positively correlated to the LBO efficiency gains suggests that the performance might consequently decline post-IPO. A public corporation could easily mimic the high leverage and managerial ownership of an LBO, if that is indeed the source of operating improvement. The post-IPO data suggests that may be happening.

Post-LBO structure: Holthausan and Larcker (1996) reported that the median debt-to-capital ratio immediately fell from 83 to 56 percent from pre- to post-IPO. The leverage ratios of the reverse-LBO firms remained on average 17 percent higher than the median ratio for firms in the same two-digit SIC industry. Holthausen and Larcker also documented that the mean ownership of all insiders declined from 75 to 49 percent after the IPO and from 36 to 23.7 percent for managers. These ownership percentages are far above that of a typical public firm.

Operating performance: The accounting performance of reverse LBOs was significantly better than that of the median firm in their industry in the year prior to the IPO, the IPO year and for at least four years after the offering (Holthausan and Larcker 1996). The post-IPO change in accounting performance was unrelated to the change in leverage, but the performance decline was positively correlated with the decline in managerial ownership. These relationships confirm that optimal governance structures, whether the firm is public or private, are important determinants of operating success.

7.3 SUMMARY

Corporate restructuring is a major source of new public companies. Conglomerate subsidiaries can be divested through a carve-out, spin-off or sell-off. Investors react favorably to the announcement of divestitures, which are motivated by non-strategic reasons such as regulation and risk preferences. Divesting to increase the quantity and quality of information produced about the firm to unlock the hidden value is one strategic motive. Focusing on core business lines and removing inefficient investment policies increases firm value and is another divestiture motive.

A carve-out is more likely when the subsidiary is performing well, when the industry stock returns have been abnormally positive and if the parent is financially constrained and needs capital. Spin-offs occur when the subsidiary is undervalued and before any equity is raised, and when it operates in a different industry than the parent. In that case, parent firms want to focus on core operations. The undervaluation of spun-off subsidiaries is captured by the positive abnormal long-run stock returns, while carve-outs generate normal returns.

Leveraged buyouts offer a unique perspective on the going-public decision. They are characterized by very high leverage ratios and concentrated managerial ownership, both of which align manager's interests towards maximizing operating efficiency. Operating performance does improve post-LBO and continues after the secondary IPO. The managerial incentives appear to be partly responsible for the valuation gains.

NOTES

1. See Hite and Owers (1983), Schipper and Smith (1983) and Krishnaswami and Subramaniam (1999) for spin-offs; Schipper and Smith (1986), Klein, Rosenfeld and Beranek (1991) and Vijh (2002) for carve-outs; and Alexander, Benson and Kampmeyer (1984) and Hite, Owers and Rogers (1987) for sell-offs.
2. The same negative reaction by the stck prices of rival firms following the announcement of private firm IPOs was documented in Chapter 2.
3. The discount was calculated by comparing the actual conglomerate value to an imputed value found by summing up estimated divisional values, assuming they are unique. Divisional values are computed by capitalizing the sales for each division using the median value-to-sales ratio for stand-alone firms in the industry segment.
4. A high q ratio is synonymous with numerous growth options and a greater ability to extract value from the existing assets.
5. Most studies use segment data from Compustat, which is an imprecise measure of the diversification.
6. Spin-offs are recorded at book value. The total reported value of assets held by the parent and subsidiary immediately following the spin-off is identical to the total book value of the assets recorded by the conglomerate immediately before the spin-off.
7. Powers (2000) showed that the high carve-out year ROA, nor the subsequent decline, was not the result of earnings management.
8. See Michael Jensen's controversial 1989 article entitled 'The Eclipse of the Public Corporation', published in the *Harvard Business Review*.
9. The depressed value could reflect industry undervaluation. Slovin, Sushka and Bendeck (1991) found a comparable positive one percent intra-industry response to going-private announcements.
10. Kaplan and Stein (1993) found that buyouts in the late 1980s had some difficulty in meeting debt payments. The prices paid for many firms were driven higher by bidding wars and the resulting interest obligations ate up too much of the cash flow.

8 Valuation

Deriving a valuation for an issuer is a necessary and critical part of the going-public process. A company's value should differ when it is publicly versus privately owned, a factor that must be weighed in the IPO decision. On a practical level, issuer management must have a good expectation for the share value in order to set the terms of the IPO. Similarly, investors need to know what the company is worth before agreeing to buy shares in the offering. A further benefit to developing a valuation framework is that it enables management to compare the benefits of various strategic and financial decisions.

A sequence of steps is discussed in this chapter that build towards a valuation methodology suitable for the IPO decision. The first step is a review of the standard equity valuation models. The second covers the special issues associated with valuing IPOs. The prospectus is often the sole source of public information available about the issuer prior to the offering. Analysis of the accounting statements must be judicious, as there is no benchmark against which the numbers can be compared. The third step evaluates the usefulness of the valuation methods for IPOs. The accuracy of the methods and the information reflected in the stock price provide a guide on how best to value potential issuers. The last step considers some of the unique ways of valuing private firms.

8.1 VALUATION METHODS

Valuing the shares of a company is as much art as it is science. Theoretically correct valuation formulas are no better than *ad hoc* back-of-the-envelope calculations when the inputs to the formula are themselves the outcome of an educated guess. Thus, the applicability of a valuation method will depend on the particular characteristics of a firm and the rigor of the formula. This section provides a brief taxonomy of the valuation methods either used or appropriate for potential issuers.[1]

The variety of firms considering a public offering demands that a broad array of valuation methods be at our disposal. The choice of method invariably involves a trade-off between simplicity and ease of use with theoretical correctness. Models that have been shown theoretically to derive the 'true' value are difficult and costly to implement in practice, whereas simple formulas are based on weaker foundations.

8.1.1 Discounting Methods

The theoretically correct value of equity is the sum of all future expected cash flows accruing to the shareholders discounted to the present using the appropriate cost of capital. A number of discounting valuation models exist, each making different assumptions about the correct measure of cash flows and implementation. Two methods are used most frequently.

Discounted free cash flow (DCF): The workhorse model for discounting is the DCF method. Free cash flow is defined as cash flow from operations after investment in working capital, less capital expenditures. The free cash flow in each period is discounted using the appropriate risk-adjusted rate. The discount rate is estimated using a standard asset pricing model, such as CAPM or the Fama-French three-factor model (see Chapter 13 for details).

Firm value is the sum of the debt and equity values. The value can be calculated by discounting cash flows accruing to all liability holders at the weighted-average cost of capital. Alternatively, the cash flow to shareholders and creditors can be valued separately by discounting the respective cash flows at the cost of equity and debt, and then summing. The use of cash flows is appealing because it is generally believed that they are a less subjective measure of firm performance than accounting earnings and capture the true payoff to the initial investment.

A firm can produce cash flows in perpetuity. Forecasting them beyond a few years is difficult and subject to considerable error. The DCF method is made tractable by discounting the expected cash flows for five to ten years and then assuming a terminal value for all remaining years. The following formula is the general model for discounted free cash flow and produces the estimated firm value V. The variables in the equation are the discount rate r, the expected free cash flows in period t, $E(c_t)$, and the terminal value T.

$$V = \sum_{t=1}^{10} \frac{E(c_t)}{(1 + r)^t} + T \qquad (8.1)$$

Residual income model (RIM): The DCF method requires accounting numbers to be converted into cash flows. Mapping accounting numbers directly into a valuation was thought to be inappropriate because the numbers fail to reflect the timing of cash flows and investment, are subject to manipulation and are influenced by accounting choices. The RIM method works because it includes earnings and book values, which are both affected in the same way by accounting choices and thus leave the valuation estimate unaffected.

The RIM method is similar to DCF in that future abnormal earnings, or residual income, are discounted at the risk-adjusted rate. The residual income in each period equals the difference between the realized earnings and the expected earnings, with the latter equal to the cost of equity times the start-of-period equity book value. The equity market value equals the equity book value plus the present value of all future residual income. The equity value calculated from RIM is then added to the value of debt. The market value of equity equals the book value if no abnormal profits are expected. The RIM method should yield the same valuation as the DCF method when implemented properly (Penman 1999). The formula for RIM is below. The new variables are the period t equity book value bv_t and abnormal earnings ern_t.

$$V = bv_1 + \sum_{t=1}^{10} \frac{\left(E\left(ern_t\right) - r * bv_t\right)}{\left(1+r\right)^t} + T \qquad (8.2)$$

Weaknesses: Discounting methods suffer from weaknesses that limit their practical applicability, especially for IPOs. The valuation formulas rely on forecasts for future cash flows and earnings. Beyond a few years the forecasts can become very imprecise and small changes in assumed growth rates have a large effect on the estimated value. Companies with the short operating histories and high growth rates typical of many issuers compound the problem. The lack of sufficient historical data prevents the extrapolation of past trends into the future because growth will revert to an unknown 'normal' level. The formulas also require an estimated discount rate. Since issuers do not have the stock price history necessary to estimate an expected return, an industry cost of capital must be used instead, with *ad hoc* adjustments to capture firm-specific effects. All this leaves aside the tricky problem of choosing the appropriate asset pricing model.

8.1.2 Comparable Multiples

The valuation method used most frequently by investment banks, especially for IPOs, is the comparable multiples approach. The issuer is matched up with comparable firms, or 'comps', which possess the same fundamental characteristics – risk, growth prospects and profitability – and are from the issuer's industry. Valuation multiples for the comparable firms are then used to compute a value for the issuer. A valuation multiple consists of a value measure, like the share price P, and an accounting measure, such as earnings per share E, and is measured as a ratio, P/E. The issuer's corresponding accounting measure is then capitalized into a value using the multiple for the comparable firm. For example, the per share value of firm i can be estimated using the P/E ratio of the comparable firm:

$$V_i = \left(\frac{P}{E}\right)_{comp} * E_i \tag{8.3}$$

The simplicity of the comparables approach makes it both easy to apply and intuitively straightforward. The most commonly used valuation multiple is the P/E ratio, followed by price-to-sales (P/S). Other multiples like the market-to-book equity ratio (M/B) are used less frequently, but are still applicable.

The success of the comparables method depends critically on choosing the appropriate comp. There are no formal rules for selecting the comps, although certain approaches have been recommended. One approach is to mechanically select a half dozen comparable firms from the industry and use the group's median multiple of interest to value the issuer. The second and most popular approach is to select companies that are most similar to the issuer and who are probably direct competitors. The IPO prospectus includes a discussion of who the issuer believes are its closest competitors. Using the multiples of firms that have recently gone public is a third option; the idea being that all issuers share a common valuation multiple. Finally, aggregate market multiples can be used when there are an insufficient number of similar firms to choose from. This would apply to relatively thin capital markets with few listings.

An advantage to using the comparables approach is that it is a commonly used method. Uncertainty over the market price of an issuer is reduced when everyone knows that investors will capitalize the issuer's accounting measures using the same multiples to arrive at similar valuations. This is one reason why the final offer price often falls within the initial price range in the preliminary prospectus.

The comparables method does suffer from a number of drawbacks. First, there is relatively little theoretical justification for the values imputed from the method. Consequently, a firm can be priced correctly relative to the comparable firms, but collectively they can all be mis-priced on an intrinsic basis. Second, the method does not take into account firm-specific risk, and *ad hoc* adjustments must be made if earnings and sales growth or profit margins differ significantly from the comparable firms. Third, finding appropriate comparable firms is difficult if there are few publicly traded companies, which limits the methods usefulness outside the US and a few other large markets. Finally, the comparables approach is susceptible to manipulation by issuers. Adjusting earnings to the high end of the acceptable range increases the potential offer price.

8.1.3 Real Option Analysis

In recent years a new valuation tool called real option analysis (ROA) has emerged to challenge the theoretical supremacy of standard discounting models. The fundamental idea behind ROA is that firms have flexibility in making operating decisions, including the option to expand, contract or abandon an investment project. The option to adjust the parameters of investment in response to newly discovered information about the project payoff is valuable and should be incorporated into a valuation framework. Unlike the standard DCF analysis, ROA accounts for the value of flexibility, yet still embeds the NPV calculation inherent in DCF analysis.

The ROA method can be used to value issuers with high growth rates and considerable uncertainty about future prospects. The basic intuition is conceptually straightforward, but the method is computationally complex.[2] To illustrate the basic idea, suppose a start-up firm can invest in a new, unproven technology. The technology can either fail, in which case the firm is worthless, or it can take off, with potentially unbounded profits for the firm. The firm value essentially resembles the payoff to a call option. Basic option pricing theory states that the value of a call increases with the uncertainty and, thus, so should the firm value.

The all-or-nothing nature of the payoff scenario just described seems perfectly suited for many issuers. In an attempt to explain the astronomical valuations of Internet firms like Yahoo and Amazon, Schwartz and Moon (2000) developed a real option model that captured the extreme uncertainty and growth emblematic of these firms. They estimated a value for Ebay of $22.40 per share using the option pricing equation. The price at the time of estimation, April 2000, was $39.17. While too low, the ROA estimate exceeded the DCF estimate of $12.42.

The development of ROA is still in its early stage and it remains unclear what role it will play in valuation problems in the future. The valuation formulas are close relatives of the Black-Scholes option pricing equation, with considerable additional complexity. The high cost of learning and implementing the model, with uncertain benefits, could limit its broad acceptance.

8.1.4 Miscellaneous Methods

There are other common valuation methods, although they have limited applicability for the typical issuer. Asset-oriented methods, such as tangible book value and liquidation value, are useful in specific circumstances. A firm with highly liquid assets, like a financial services company, could be valued by adding up the value of the existing assets. The liquidation value is the sum of the current market value of the individual assets, less the cash value of the liabilities. Asset-based methods fail to capture the value of the assets operating together as a going concern and the intangible growth options that account for a large percentage of IPO valuations. Another approach values the firm based on the cost of replacing the assets at current market prices, less the present value of the liabilities. This method also fails to take into account growth options and the going-concern value.

Unorthodox valuation methods have been used when the firm lacks the necessary inputs for the conventional models. Many Internet firms in the late 1990s did not have positive earnings or cash flows. Practitioners tried developing other metrics on which to base a valuation, often relying on non-financial data. One school of thought was that value should increase with web traffic, and there is some weak evidence that this was the case (Hand 2000; Rajgopal, Venkatachalam and Kotha 2003; Demers and Lev 2001). Another case study found that the primary determinant of valuations in the wireless communication industry was the population in the franchise territory, rather than financial variables (Amir and Lev 1996). The drawback to unconventional valuation methods is that there is no theoretical basis for any particular model and it is not obvious which method is best *ex ante*.

8.1.5 Valuation Accuracy

The choice of method should ultimately be determined by how well it performs in practice. The benchmark against which the predicted valuations should be judged is the actual prices observed in the marketplace. Valuation prediction errors are the difference between the estimated value and the observed price. An accurate valuation method is one that produces consistently small prediction errors.

The two valuation methods, discounting and comparables, that are of primary interest have been shown to have roughly equal accuracy in forecasting market prices. In the case of LBOs, Kaplan and Ruback (1995) found that both methods generated valuation estimates that came within 15 percent of the actual transaction value between 37 and 47 percent of the time. Gilson, Hotchkiss and Ruback (2000) found that 21 to 27 percent of estimated valuations using both methods were within 15 percent of the actual value for firms emerging from Chapter 11 bankruptcy protection. Alford (1992) reported that comparable firms selected based on industry classification produced fairly accurate value estimates when using the P/E multiple. Liu, Nissim and Thomas (2002) showed that using P/E multiples based on forecasted earnings resulted in the most accurate valuation estimates. Value estimates were within 15 percent of the stock price for about half of their sample of public companies.

8.2 IPO-SPECIFIC INFORMATION

The quality of any valuation estimate is only as good as the information investors have at their disposal. Accounting data taken from an issuer's financial statements are the explicit inputs into the valuation formulas. Unfortunately, the problem is not so simple that an investor can take the most recent earnings and capitalize them into a value using a comparable multiple. Issuers have considerable latitude in managing earnings in the pre-IPO period. Therefore, how well the data represents the issuer's financial health is open to interpretation. Accounting data is also historical, yet the valuation is based on future earnings. Forecasting into the future requires non-financial information that enables investors to formulate an overall picture of the issuer's risk, growth potential and quality.

8.2.1 Non-Financial Information

The prospectus is usually the first source of information about the issuer available to investors, as there is rarely anything published prior to the IPO (Rao 1993). The prospectus provides a thorough overview of the firm, its operations and structure, competitive environment, risk factors, financial information, intended use of proceeds and terms of the offering. Investors can comb through the information in this document, anywhere from 50 to 100 pages long, and determine an appropriate valuation. Surprisingly, this is not often done, even though there is no market price offering a consensus estimate of the issuer's worth. Only a quarter of IPO investors who responded to a questionnaire distributed by Shiller (1990) said they performed any kind of fundamental analysis to derive a valuation.

Non-financial information available to investors provides a lens for interpreting the financial data. A statement that the proceeds will be used for specific investment projects or acquisitions could alter calculations for expected growth rates in earnings and sales. Discussion of the issuer's products and the competitive environment provides an indication whether and for how long the issuer can earn abnormal profits. A review of the executive team reveals their experience and inferences about their ability to manage a public company successfully can be drawn. Issuers obviously have every incentive to portray themselves in the best possible light in the prospectus. Nonetheless, this intangible information is useful in shaping investors' overall impression about the issuer.

Specific quantifiable non-financial information is contained in the prospectus and it could reflect a deliberate attempt by management to signal their private beliefs about the firm. Credibly conveying positive information to investors increases the share value. Investors can look for the following pieces of information to improve their valuation estimate.

Share retention: The prospectus lists the current shareholders, the percentage of the post-IPO outstanding shares floated and the combination of primary and secondary shares sold. Leland and Pyle (1977) argued that managers can signal that their firm is of high value by retaining a large fraction of the equity. The action is credible because it is to costly for managers of low value firms to mimic and hold an undiversified portfolio dominated by the firm's shares. Klein (1996), among others, documented a positive relationship between the fraction of shares retained by insiders and the IPO and market price.

Reputation: A credible way to signal a high quality is to put valuable reputational capital on the line. Private firms have no reputation with investors and must borrow the capital of others. Investment banks and venture capitalists are the two most likely candidates because both are regular participants in the IPO market. Banks and VCs that build a reputation for being affiliated with high quality firms confer a value premium on future issuers. To avoid damaging their valuable reputations, banks and VCs only bring high quality firms to the market. Klein (1996) supported this conjecture by finding a positive relationship between the offer and market prices and the underwriter reputation and the presence of VC-backing.

Risks: The prospectus includes a listing of all possible risk factors associated with investing in the issuer. Some of them are called boilerplate because they are standard in all prospectuses and refer to the general risks of investing. Other factors pertain specifically to the issuer. A long list of potential risks could signal management's own uncertainty about the firm's prospects. Investors demand a lower offer price in return for their participation in riskier IPOs. Klein (1996) and Bartov, Mohanram and Seethamraju (2002) reported that both the offer and market prices were lower when the prospectus cover displayed an explicit reference to the risk of the offering.

Corporate governance: Firm value is affected by the governance structures implemented at the IPO. Smart and Zutter (2003) found some evidence that firms with dual-class share structures were of higher quality, which was a necessary condition for investors because of the diminished control rights and reduced takeover premium. Incentives in the form of stock options can skew managerial preferences when it comes to setting the offer price. Taranto (2003) documented that issuers that had granted more options to the CEO and other top executives had larger underpricing, which he attributed to the tax incentive to lower the offer price.

8.2.2 Accounting Information

The SEC requires all issuers to include, at a minimum, the three most recent annual balance sheets and the two most recent income statements in the prospectus. An accredited auditor must attest to the veracity of the financial statements. The financial information is vital to an investor's ability to value the issuer. The statements include current and past sales and earnings, facilitating the calculation of expected growth rates in both variables. Financial ratios like the profit margin, the return on assets and the interest coverage ratio collectively provide evidence on how efficiently the firm is operated. Leverage ratios measure the issuer's financial health and are necessary to estimate the equity cost of capital.

Two aspects of the current accounting rules increase the difficulty for investors to draw correct inferences about the firm value. The first is unique to IPOs. The Accounting Principles Board (APB) Opinion 20 allows issuers to retroactively change prior accounting choices for all the financial statements in the prospectus. The ruling exempts issuers from reporting the cumulative effect of the change as a component of current income.

The second challenge is a consequence of the accrual accounting system. Firms have fairly wide discretion under GAAP to adjust current earnings by deciding when to recognize revenues and expenses. These two aspects combined give issuers an exceptional opportunity to manage the pre-IPO time series profile of accounting earnings to place the firm in the best possible light. The effectiveness of earnings manipulation depends on whether investors see through the accounting tricks to decode the issuer's true financial health. The finding that few investors perform fundamental analysis suggests that they do not.

8.2.2.1 Earnings management

The GAAP accounting system is designed with the intent to produce financial statements that give a representative picture of a company's financial health. This goal is achieved through the use of accruals, which gives management discretion in recognizing the timing and amounts of revenues and expenses. Accountants and market participants alike advocate the use of accruals to present a more accurate picture of the true economic condition of the firm.

Granting firms such accounting discretion means that there is a fairly wide range of acceptable earnings. The incentive for issuers to report the highest possible earnings is obvious; it can increase the potential offer price. The drawback to managing income higher is that it inevitably leads to false expectations about future earnings. Greater current income usually requires an equal trade-off with lower future income. The challenge for investors is to tell the difference between accurate high earnings and aggressively managed earnings.

The accounting and operating choices made by a firm can be classified as either income-increasing or income-decreasing, contingent on the affect on current earnings. There are three primary ways in which a firm can manipulate earnings.

Accounting choices: Firms make specific accounting choices that have a direct affect on reported earnings. Long-term assets can be depreciated using either straight-line, accelerated, or a combination of both methods. Straight-line is income-increasing relative to accelerated because less depreciation is charged against current revenue. Issuers must disclose the depreciation method used and indicate if a recent change in the method has been made. Earnings management through depreciation charges is rather limited. Firms must account for inventory using either the last-in-first-out (LIFO) or first-in-first-out (FIFO) cost methods. The latter is income-increasing because older goods are booked at lower cost, resulting in a smaller charge against revenue. The inventory accounting method is also disclosed.

Accruals: Reported earnings consist of cash flows from operations and accounting accruals that can be decomposed into long-term and current accruals, that latter of which involve short-term assets and liabilities. The use of accruals is an attempt to recognize the economic effect of transactions in the period in which they occur, rather than exclusively in the periods in which cash is received or paid out. Among the ways managers can increase current accruals are to recognize revenues from credit sales before cash is received or to delay the recognition of expenses for goods not yet received even if cash is advanced to suppliers. Non-current accruals can be increased by decelerating depreciation or realizing unusual gains.

Total accruals for each time period are defined as net income minus cash flows from operations. The decomposition of accruals into current and non-current parts is relevant for examining earnings manipulation because management has more discretion over current accruals. Current accruals are defined as the change in non-cash current assets minus the change in operating current liabilities:

$$
\text{Current Accruals} = \qquad\qquad (8.4)
$$
$$
\Delta \text{ [accounts receivable + inventory + other current assets] } -
$$
$$
\Delta \text{ [accounts payable + tax payable + other current liabilities]}
$$

where Δ measures the year-over-year change. Studies of IPO earnings management focus almost exclusively on current accruals.

Operating decisions: A firm can affect current earnings directly through the timing of operating decisions. The firm may wait until after the end of the current fiscal year before purchasing supplies to delay the expense showing up on the income statement. The sale of assets could be completed before the end of the quarter to increase current revenue. It is difficult to determine the extent to which earnings are managed through the timing of operating decisions, but it could potentially be quite large for some firms.

There are limits to just how much earnings can be managed. An external accounting firm must audit reported earnings to verify that they are compliant with GAAP. Issuer management, the auditors and the investment bankers are all legally liable for any misstatements or misrepresentation in the prospectus. While these considerations no doubt limit earnings management, they do not prevent it from happening. The GAAP-approved earnings can fall within a wide range. Investment bankers rarely audit the firm's financial statements during due diligence. They instead rely on the auditor's opinion, who in turn generally defer to management's judgement on discretionary accrual items.

8.2.2.2 Measuring managed earnings

Verifying the accuracy of financial statements is critical for deriving an unbiased expectation of the issuer's value. Unfortunately, there is no easy and sure fire way to determine if the issuer used accounting tricks to overstate earnings. The task of sorting through the data to find abnormal earnings is especially difficult for IPOs. There are no prior financial reports that enable investors to cross-check the prospectus data, and the few years of statements are not sufficient to detect any long-term accounting patterns.

Methods have been designed by researchers to detect earnings management. One method classifies a firm as either aggressive or conservative based on the collective accounting choices it makes. For example, a firm that uses straight-line depreciation and FIFO is aggressive, whereas firms using accelerated depreciation and LIFO are conservative in their accounting measures.

An alternative method test for earnings management tries to estimate the abnormal accruals. Abnormal accruals are the difference between an expected level of accruals that a firm should have, conditional on the economic climate, and the actual accruals. Jones (1991) first proposed the now standard procedure for estimating abnormal accruals, which has been subsequently updated and revised. The basic approach is to regress the current accruals of each firm in the same two-digit SIC industry as the issuer on the year-over-year change in their sales. The expected accruals for the issuer are then calculated by plugging the issuer's change of sales into the estimated regression equation. Abnormal accruals are not explained by firm and industry conditions, and are considered discretionary.

8.2.2.3 Evidence of management

The time series of abnormal accruals, earnings and cash flows starting in the IPO year and continuing on for five years is consistent with deliberate earnings management. The following stylized facts emerged from studies by Teoh, Wong and Rao (1998) and Teoh, Welch and Wong (1998a).

1. Abnormal current accruals peaked in the IPO year and then declined monotonically over the next three years. They started at 4 to 5 percent of the IPO year assets and fell to a level not significantly different from zero. The expected accruals also declined, but by a much less significant degree.

2. Cash flows from operations began poorly in the IPO year compared to similar non-issuers and steadily improved over the next five years, although remaining relatively low. Firms that were conservative in their use of abnormal accruals had worsening cash flows in the post-IPO period, while aggressive firms had improving cash flows.

3. Earnings peaked in the IPO year and declined over the next four years. The median net income was initially positive, but was not significantly

different from zero four years later. The median return on sales (ROS) also peaked in the IPO year, but equaled only 28 percent of that total four years later. The decline in earnings performance was not driven by falling cash flows, strongly implying that earnings management through abnormal accruals was the cause.

4. Subdividing the issuers into quartiles based on abnormal accruals revealed stark differences in earnings performance. The post-IPO earnings were benchmarked against non-issuers with similar IPO-year performance. The most aggressive issuers consistently underperformed for six years, whereas the conservative quartile did not. These patterns held despite the fact that cash flows improved for aggressive issuers, but worsened for the conservative quartile. The earnings decline of the aggressive quartile was due to the fall in abnormal accruals, which could not be sustained at the IPO level indefinitely.

5. The IPO-year abnormal current accruals had a significant negative relation to the post-IPO earnings, measured by both the level and change in performance. The expected accruals, both current and long term, did not predict future earnings performance.

The evidence strongly suggests issuers that were most aggressive in managing accruals were overstating current earnings.[3] Since abnormal accruals cannot be high indefinitely, their inevitable decline pulls down future earnings. Teoh, Wong and Rao (1998) reported that other accounting choices made by issuers were consistent with them being too aggressive. Most issuers used the same depreciation method as their matched non-issuers, but when they did deviate it was usually to an income-increasing method. Issuers also made significantly smaller allowances for bad debts than their matches in the year preceding and the year of the IPO.

Deliberate manipulation to increase reported earnings only makes sense if it results in a higher share price. The limited evidence suggests manipulation pays-off. Neill, Pourciau and Schaefer (1995) found that firms that chose aggressive over conservative accounting methods were priced higher at the IPO. Jindra (2000) found similar evidence in a sample of SEO issuers. The highest abnormal accruals quintile had the greatest mis-valuation, which helped the firms sell overvalued equity.

8.2.2.4 Non-opportunistic earnings

Claiming that managers intentionally manipulate reported earnings is a serious charge and a difficult one to prove. If true, there should be greater post-IPO evidence of such manipulative behavior, including litigation, than is currently the case. Other plausible explanations exist for what appears to be abnormally high reported earnings. IPOs are biased towards young growth firms that could be issuing stock after unusually good performance. The models for expected accruals cannot perfectly distinguish between abnormal accruals and exogenous influences on firm performance not motivated by any malicious intent.

The threat of litigation arising from improperly stated earnings could provide a sufficient deterrent to opportunistic earnings management. Hughes (1986) suggested that income-increasing accounting choices might be deliberately chosen to signal insider beliefs about the firm value. Only managers of high-quality firms choose aggressive accounting measures because the potential litigation cost is sufficient to deter low-quality firms from trying to overstate earnings. Thus abnormally high earnings could signal high value, not intentional manipulation.[4] The signaling theory also justifies why some firms voluntarily choose conservative accounting measures and understate earnings.

Aggressively managed earnings, if done at all, may be less a consequence of opportunistic behavior and more a rational response to investor expectations (Shivakumar 2000). Investors could assume that issuers manage earnings higher, even if the issuers did not initially intend to. This leads investors to rationally discount the accounting valuation. The issuers must respond by actually manipulating earnings higher to avoid undervaluation. Evidence produced by Shivakumar on the share price around seasoned equity offerings supports these myopic equilibrium beliefs. There was a strong inverse relationship between the aggressiveness of earnings management prior to the SEO announcement and the negative announcement return. The strong pre-SEO share price run-up, perhaps due to the overstated earnings, was partly undone at announcement as investors recognized the earnings manipulation.

8.3 IPO VALUATION

Armed with a valuation tool-kit and knowledge of the unique challenges to pricing issuers, the next step is to see IPO valuation in action. This begins by examining how well the valuation methods work in practice. A comparison between the value estimates made by each method and the actual prices tests for method accuracy. The variables that drive the valuation of issuers are then determined. The stock price is a function of accounting and non-financial variables, but the relationship mapping these variables into a price is not *a priori* obvious. Understanding the value-drivers is important for the issuer because it focuses on the criteria investors use to price a stock.

8.3.1 Valuation Accuracy

Evaluating the accuracy of valuation estimates requires three inputs: the predicted value, the observable price and a measure of accuracy. The discounting and comparables valuation methods are the only two used with any frequency, so attention is restricted to them. Two prices are of interest, the IPO offer price and the initial market price.

Accuracy is measured by the difference between the estimated value and the observed price. The difference must be scaled – either dividing by the observed price or taking the natural log – to eliminate the effect the price level has on the errors. The absolute value or square of the difference is used to ensure that positive and negative errors do not cancel out in the average. To illustrate, the absolute prediction error, measured in percentage terms, would be 25 percent when the value estimate is $15 and the price is $20. Another common measure of accuracy is the percentage of estimated values within 15 percent of the observed price.

8.3.1.1 Comparable multiples

Clear patterns have emerged from the analysis of comparable multiples accuracy. The generality of the results is, however, limited by the fact that the studies have been restricted to issuers that had positive earnings and book value in the year prior to issue. This tilts the sample toward larger, more stable firms, enhancing the accuracy of the comparables method. Notwithstanding these caveats, the following conclusions can be drawn.

1. The valuation accuracy improved when the comparable firm was chosen carefully (Kim and Ritter 1999; Yetman 2003). Matching issuers based on pre-IPO growth rates, profitability, risk properties and industry improved the predictive power of the comparable method.

2. The accuracy improved when forecasts for future earnings were used in lieu of past earnings. Kim and Ritter (1999) found that the mean absolute prediction error for the offer price fell from 55.0 to 43.7 to 28.5 percent when historical earnings, current year earnings forecasts, and next year forecasted earnings were used, respectively. This relationship is expected because stock prices reflect the present value of future earnings.[5] Corroborating evidence was found for Belgium IPOs (Deloof, De Maeseneire and Inghelbrecht 2002). Prediction errors

were smaller when the one-year-ahead earnings forecasts made by management were used instea of IPO year forecasts.

3. The accuracy was better for mature firms than for younger growth firms. Kim and Ritter (1999) estimated the mean absolute prediction errors for old and young firms, based on next year forecasted earnings, to be 23.0 and 31.9 percent, respectively. Accuracy should improve as earnings become more stable and there is a longer earnings record to project into the future. The best valuation errors in Belgium and New Zealand – two countries biased toward older, relatively large issuers – were lower than their US counterparts (Deloof, De Maeseneire and Inghelbrecht 2002; Berkman, Bradbury and Ferguson 2000).

4. The use of market and transaction multiples in thin stock markets with few listings resulted in the best accuracy. Berkman, Bradbury and Ferguson (2000) documented that the median absolute error for industry comparables was 38.3 percent in New Zealand, but only 20.5 and 19.7 percent when market and transaction-based multiples, respectively, were used. The accuracy of recent IPOs for pricing the issuer could reflect the clustering of IPOs by similar firms, which provide the best comps. Indeed, Kim and Ritter (1999) found that selecting comparables from recent US IPOs led to smaller errors than industry-based comparables.

5. Valuation accuracy improved when adjustments were made to reflect the different sales growth rates and profitability between the issuer and comparable firm. Kim and Ritter (1999) estimated that a 20 percent premium over the comparable-derived value is necessary for fast-growing issuers or those twice as profitable as the average comp.

6. The accuracy was better when the estimates were compared to the offer price, rather than the market price. For example, Deloof, De Maeseneire and Inghelbrecht (2002) found that the best prediction error for the offer price in Belgian IPOs was 10 percent, but that increased to 20 percent for the market price. Two factors account for the accuracy difference. First, investment banks set the offer price using the valuation estimates as an initial guide, so they should be quite close. Second, speculative trading in the secondary market introduces noise into the price, decreasing the accuracy.

7. Yetman (2003) claimed that the accuracy was inversely related to the investor sentiment toward IPOs. The early market prices did not

efficiently incorporate the available accounting information during positive sentiment periods. A few possibilities explain this pattern. Hot markets are associated with large initial returns and easy money for investors. The need to conduct fundamental analysis is thus weakened. The large returns also attract new investors to the IPO market, many of whom may be speculators or uninformed retail investors. These investors bring additional noise to the price, further diminishing the accuracy of valuation estimates.

8.3.1.2 Discounting methods

Analysis of the valuation errors produced by discounting methods leads to two conclusions. First, the method does not work well for young, fast-growing firms. The absence of a history of stable earnings makes forecasting future cash flows highly subjective and produces large valuation estimate errors. Yetman (2001) is the lone study to apply the discounting method to US IPOs and she found that the value estimates using the RIM model had little correlation with market prices. The second conclusion is that when discounting methods can be applied they work as well, if not better, than the comparables approach.

The sample of Belgian IPOs in Deloof, De Maeseneire and Inghelbrecht (2002) provided a unique opportunity to see the discounting methods in action. The regulatory environment in Belgium allows the lead investment bank to include valuation estimates in the prospectus. The bank states both the estimate and the method used in the calculation.[6] The median DCF valuation error for the offer price was 9.8 percent, but it was close to zero for the market price, making it an unbiased estimator.[7] Underwriters seemed to consciously underprice the IPO by emphasizing a conservative valuation estimate. Overall, the discounting methods consistently produced smaller valuation errors than the best comparable multiple valuation.

The application of discounting methods to New Zealand IPOs by Berkman, Bradley and Ferguson (2000) resulted in valuation errors of the same magnitude as the comparables method. The median absolute error when the market return was used as the discount rate was 20.1 percent, almost exactly equal to the 20.5 percent error for the market multiples model. Regression analysis showed that the market-based DCF valuation estimates explained 75 percent of the variation in the actual share prices.

8.3.1.3 Underwriter value-added

An IPO's success is at least partly dependent on the choice of offer price. A price set too high increases the chance of a failed offering, whereas too low a price costs the issuer valuable proceeds. The job of setting the offer price belongs to the underwriter, in consultation with the issuer. The underwriter uses the same valuation methods that anyone else could use. Given the high cost of underwriting fees and the relatively low cost of estimating an issuer valuation, it is worth asking whether the bank adds sufficient value to the pricing process to justify its role.

In the banks' defense, underwriters do contribute significantly by improving the accuracy of the offer price. A bank's unique knowledge of the IPO market and the information it gathers from investors during the marketing phase enables it to tweak the initial value estimate to set a more appropriate offer price. Proof of the underwriter's ability to refine the value estimates is provided by the pattern of errors throughout the IPO process. The median absolute prediction errors reported by Kim and Ritter (1999) for the preliminary offer price (the mid-point of the initial filing range), the final offer price and the initial market price were 43.6, 49.9, and 58.0 percent, respectively.[8] The increasing errors reflect the fact that the prices incrementally incorporate more value-relevant information not captured by the valuation formulas.

8.3.2 Pricing Information

Mapping available information, financial or otherwise, into a stock price requires an understanding of the factors that drive the valuation. Discounted cash flow analysis may be correct in that cash flows ultimately determine the value, but it offers little guidance into what drives expected cash flows. A useful first step is to break down the cash flow into its accounting components to understand how they relate to value. Next, non-financial information can be used to guide the formation of expectations for future performance. For example, the link between the growth in current market share and future revenues and cash flows can be derived. A valuation framework built on these two steps can be used to price IPOs, along with any other public firm.

8.3.2.1 Accounting valuation

Accounting research in the 1990s showed a renewed interest in examining the influence of accounting data on stock valuations. Surprisingly, there had been relatively little empirical evaluation of the standard valuation models. Papers by Ohlson (1995; 2001) sparked much of the change by developing a parsimonious theoretical model that linked basic accounting data to the market value of equity.

The Ohlson model built on the conventional RIM model by assuming clean surplus accounting and specifying a recursive dynamic evolution for future residual income.[9] Residual income follows a modified autoregressive process that relates next period abnormal earnings to the current period and 'other information' v. The decay inherent in an autoregressive process means that residual income tends to revert to zero, producing the economically pleasing result that abnormal earnings are temporary. The v term represents other information about future abnormal earnings that is reflected in the price, but not in the current financial statements.

The basic RIM model is greatly simplified by the autoregressive process assumption because current residual income can then be recursively substituted into all future expected residual income. The implication is that the current value of a stock is a function of only three variables: current equity book value, current residual income and v. Formally, v is the difference between the expectation for next period's residual income and the purely autoregressive forecast for residual income. The current value V_t is thus a linear function of the current equity book value bv_t, current residual income ern_t and v:

$$V_t = bv_t + a_1 ern_t + a_2 v_t \qquad (8.5)$$

The Ohlson model has the benefit of a simple structure and requires inputs that are readily available from financial statements. The information term v has been proxied with some success by analysts' forecasts for abnormal earnings. Equity book value, net income and dividends all have well-defined economic relationships with the market value under this model. Book value and current income can also be decomposed into their contingent parts – contributed capital, retained equity, treasury stock, revenues, cost of goods sold, general selling and administrative expenses, and R&D – to allow for greater examination of the relevant variables.

8.3.2.2 Decomposing value

The efficient price for equity should reflect all available information. Accounting data is one component to the information set and equation (8.5) provides a theoretical model for the financial value drivers. Non-financial information is also important and potentially value-relevant variables can be added to those already included in (8.5). Only recently have researchers conducted in-depth analysis of how well the valuation models and variables explain stock prices. The limited evidence on the decomposition of recent IPO market valuations produced three main findings.

1. Equity book value per share and earnings per share were both positively related to the share price (Klein 1996). A similar conclusion was reached by Hand (2003a) using a log-linear relationship between the pre-income book value and core net income (net income less special items) and the equity market value. The log transformation was an attempt to control for the high degree of skewness in the valuations and accounting variables. For both Internet and non-Internet IPOs from 1997 to mid-1999, the market values were linear and increasing in book equity, but concave and increasing (decreasing) in positive (negative) core net income.

2. Financial performance appears to be the principal determinant of equity valuations. Hand (2000a) estimated that accounting data explained a majority of the cross-sectional variability of the market prices – between 65 and 85 percent based on adjusted-R^2 measures in regression analysis – for Internet and non-Internet IPOs. Hand (2003b) similarly reported that 70 percent of the valuation variability in the biotechnology industry was attributable to financial data. This good explanatory power left relatively little room for non-financial information. A number of studies tried to determine the value-relevance of web traffic and similar measures for Internet companies (Hand 2000; Rajgopal, Venkatachalam and Kotha 2003; Trueman, Wong and Zhang 2000). These measures were, at best, a marginal value driver after controlling for financial performance.

3. Decomposing net income into revenues and the sub-components of expenses reveals how investors interpret the performance of the issuers. Hand (2003a) showed that revenues for Internet firms were positively priced in a concave manner. The valuations were also increasing and concave in marketing, selling and R&D expenditures when net income was negative. This is consistent with investors interpreting marketing and R&D as intangible assets, even though they are treated as period expenses for accounting purposes. In a study of biotechnology firms, many of which had recent IPOs, Hand (2003b) reported that market values were significantly more sensitive to R&D spending when it grew faster and the earlier in the development stage it occurred.

The basic conclusion to take from these findings is that market valuations are determined by the financial performance of companies, as the theory predicts, although the relationships are not always simple. It is somewhat reassuring that even issuers with suspect revenues and earnings, such as biotech firms, can still be valued using straightforward models. The ultimate determinants of a firm's value, such as the outcome from R&D or the success of a marketing program, are clearly important, but are not obviously valued by the market beyond the measurable financial impact.

8.4 PRIVATE FIRM DISCOUNT

Valuing a private firm is a necessary and important part of the entire IPO process. The decision to go public requires a careful comparison between the share value if the company remains private and the price that could be garnered if the shares were publicly traded. The choice between an IPO and being acquired by another firm can hinge on the fairness of the acquisition price, which demands an estimate of the firm's value. Private investors and venture capitalists need a valuation estimate before they agree to the terms of the investment. The valuation tools applied to issuers and public companies can be used for private firms.

The task of valuing a private firm is made more difficult by the absence of market prices and rigorous accounting records, and the private firm discount. The value of two otherwise identical companies will differ if one is publicly owned and the other is private. The private firm discount is due to restrictions on the liquidity and marketability of the shares. Both factors diminish the attractiveness of private equity to investors, who will demand a higher return on private investments. Direct estimates of private firm valuations are not possible because the data is simply not available. The discount has been estimated through three indirect methods. Armed with this knowledge, it is possible to value private firms assuming they were public and then adjusting the value to reflect the discount.

8.4.1 IPO Approach

The price of shares sold prior to the IPO can be compared to the post-IPO market price. The estimated private firm discount using this measurement method is in the 50 percent range, which has been fairly uniform across time (Emory 1985; see Williamette Management Associates in Pratt 1989). Discounts of this magnitude seem to vastly overstate the value loss due to private ownership. The private sales took place within five months of the IPO in one of the studies, which translates into a return of close to 100 percent in only a few months.

Two other considerations argue against discounts of 50 percent (Bajaj et al. 2003a). First, the discounted purchase price for private equity investors also reflects the compensation for the consulting, managerial and networking services provided by the investors. Second, the estimated discount is inflated by a serious sample selection bias. Only successful firms are able to complete IPOs. The poor investments are not included in the total returns to investors who buy private equity. Factoring in the low return investments would produce a smaller discount estimate.

An analysis of returns to venture capital financing conducted by Das, Jagannathan and Sarin (2002) provides a clearer picture of the discount. They calculated exit multiples – the ratio of the firm value at successful exits to the value at the time of financing – adjusted for dilution and industry returns between the financing and exit dates. An estimate of the discount can be imputed from the expected exit multiple at the time of financing. The discount equals one minus the inverse of the expected multiple. Das, Jagannathan and Sarin estimated that an appropriate discount would be 11 percent, based on the exit multiples for late stage financing.

8.4.2 Restricted Stock Approach

A share offering that is registered with the SEC can be publicly traded without restriction by the shareholders. Shares placed privately with accredited investors by a public firm do not have to be registered with the SEC. The trade-off is that the unregistered shares cannot be sold by the investors for up to two years.[10] The discount at which the unregistered but restricted shares are sold provides a reasonable measure of the cost of illiquidity. Early studies found that private placements involved discounts averaging between 20 to 35 percent, with considerable cross-sectional variation (Wruck 1989; Silber 1991; Hertzel and Smith 1993).

It would be incorrect to assume that the discount is strictly due to liquidity constraints. The discount could be compensation for monitoring services provided by the new blockholder. One way to control for potential blockholder compensation is to compare the discounts of private placements that involve restricted and unrestricted shares. The incremental discount for restricted placements, after controlling for firm and issue characteristics, has been estimated to be from 7 to 14 percent (Hertzel and Smith 1993; Bajaj et al. 2003a). The restricted stock approach provides the best estimate for the liquidity discount, but it may not capture all the aspects of a private firm discount. For example, a minority stake in a closely held business may be worth even less than the liquidity discount implies.

8.4.3 Acquisition Approach

A comparison of the acquisition prices of similar target firms that were privately and publicly owned provides another estimate of the discount. If private firms are worth less, holding all other characteristics constant, they should be cheaper to acquire. Koeplin, Sarin and Shapiro (2000) estimated the discount by calculating the ratio of enterprise value, based on the acquisition price, to earnings.[11] The ratios for the private and public acquisitions were then compared. The private firm enterprise value-to-EBITDA (earnings before interest, taxes, depreciation and amortization) ratio, at 8.08, was about 20 percent less than the 10.15 ratio for matched public acquisitions. Similar discounts were obtained for enterprise value-to-EBIT ratios. Even after controlling for characteristics that could account for the valuation difference, including size, growth and industry, the private firm discount still came out to 20 percent.

The acquisition approach measures the private firm discount and not a liquidity discount specifically. Interpreting the finding as a pure private firm discount does raise an interesting puzzle. The acquiring firm purchases assets that will contribute to its cash flow and profitability. Whether these assets were publicly or privately owned prior to the acquisition should not alter their performance as part of the new corporate structure. The discount could reflect the different bargaining power possessed by target management and its ability to extract concessions from the acquirer.

8.5 SUMMARY

Deriving a valuation for an issuer is an important part of the going-public process. The two most common valuation methods are comparable multiples and discounted cash flow. IPOs present unique valuation challenges because there is little information available aside from the prospectus. Non-financial information on the ownership and governance structure, risk factors and advisor reputation can signal insider beliefs about the firm value. Accounting data provides the basic inputs for the valuation models. Issuers have a fair amount of discretion in reporting their earnings and have a strong incentive to manage them higher to increase the offer price. The best evidence suggests that at least some issuers manage earnings higher through the use of discretionary accruals and that these firms produce the worst earnings performance post-IPO.

The comparable multiples valuation method works quite well when the comps are chosen carefully, either from the industry or preceding IPOs, when forecasted future earnings are used and if market multiples are used in thin stock markets. Valuation accuracy declined in hot markets as positive investor sentiment introduced additional noise into the pricing process. Discounting methods work best when the firm is mature and has stable earnings; the same is true of the comparables method. Over 70 percent of the cross-sectional variation in recent issuer's stock prices was explained by the financial variables – current equity book value and net income – leaving only a small role for non-financial variables. Private firms can be valued using the same methods, with the additional adjustment for the private firm discount. The best estimate for the discount is 20 percent and is found using the acquisition approach.

NOTES

1. A number of good sources provide a more thorough treatment of the valuation techniques. Practitioner oriented discussions include Weisman (1999) and Damadaran (2002). Textbooks covering equity valuation include Penman (2000) and Benninga and Sarig (1997).
2. Copeland and Antikarov (2001) is an excellent demonstration of real options methods and how to apply them to practical problems.
3. Morsfield and Tan (2003) produced evidence consistent with the claim that venture capitalists offer credible certification of issuer quality. They reported that abnormal discretionary accruals were significantly lower for VC-backed issuers compared to non-VC-backed issuers. The VC presence was related to lower income-increasing discretionary accruals, with no relation to income-decreasing accruals.
4. An interesting corollary to this relationship is the affect on underpricing. Firms with higher initial prices are more likely to be the target of litigation. Consequently, firms that are overly aggressive in reporting earnings are at greater risk for being exposed. Increased intentional underpricing reduces the litigation risk. Neill, Pourciau and Schaefer (1995) did find a positive relation between accounting aggressiveness and underpricing.
5. Purnanandam and Swaminathan (2004) compared the IPO offer valuation to an estimated value based on accounting data from the fiscal year prior to the IPO. The IPOs were estimated to be 50 percent overvalued. The high forecast error could be due to the use of historical rather than forecasted earnings.
6. The bank-supplied estimates could bias the errors towards zero because investors use them to formulate their own valuation for the issuer.
7. These are not absolute errors, but an average of positive and negative errors. A zero mean error reflects an unbiased estimate for the price. The mean absolute error was 10.5 percent.
8. The first comparable P/E was based on the market price on the day before the IPO is filed and the latter two use the price on the day before the offer date.
9. Clean surplus accounting holds if current equity book value equals last period book value plus net income minus net dividends (total dividends plus net capital flows).
10. The investors can sell a limited number of shares during the two years, but are completely unrestricted after that.
11. Enterprise value is defined as the purchase price of the acquisition multiplied by the total number of outstanding shares, plus the book value of liabilities.

9 Preparing for the IPO

Going public is a time-consuming, expensive endeavor that demands meticulous preparation. The need to 'get it right' is critical because a company has only one opportunity to go public. The process begins with senior management preparing the organization for public ownership. An internal accounting system must be implemented to produce regular financial statements for external shareholders. Appropriate incentive compensation for employees needs to be adopted. Executives with experience in the management of a public company should be hired. These actions, among others, constitute the 'professionalization' of the firm, which is fundamental to any success the company will have as a publicly owned enterprise.

A different set of preparations for going public, which is the focus of the current chapter, involves navigating the actual IPO process. An issuer must make decisions about the expert advisors – the underwriter, the auditor and legal counsel – to be hired, the type and terms of the offering and the exchange it will list on. The importance of selecting the right advisors cannot be overstated because of the economic impact these choices can have on the offering's success. Lawyers guide a company through the legal steps involved with the IPO. Auditors attest to the financial status of the company. The investment bank is, by far, the most economically relevant advisor. The bank is solely responsible for selling the offering to investors and how well it performs this job shows up directly in the IPO proceeds.

9.1 THE TIMELINE

Internal preparations for the IPO can begin up to two years prior to the offer date. The external preparations begin a little later than that, usually with the hiring of an auditor. A long lead time helps the issuer develop the accounting structure necessary for public reporting and it gives the auditor sufficient time to attest to three income statements and two balance sheets. The latter is required by the SEC and alleviates concerns public investors may have about the financial health of the issuer.

Figure 9.1 Timeline of events for the firm commitment IPO process

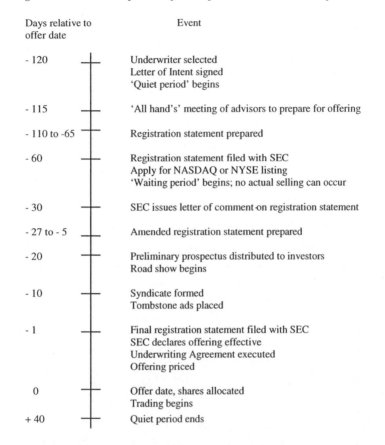

Days relative to offer date	Event
- 120	Underwriter selected Letter of Intent signed 'Quiet period' begins
- 115	'All hand's' meeting of advisors to prepare for offering
- 110 to -65	Registration statement prepared
- 60	Registration statement filed with SEC Apply for NASDAQ or NYSE listing 'Waiting period' begins; no actual selling can occur
- 30	SEC issues letter of comment on registration statement
- 27 to - 5	Amended registration statement prepared
- 20	Preliminary prospectus distributed to investors Road show begins
- 10	Syndicate formed Tombstone ads placed
- 1	Final registration statement filed with SEC SEC declares offering effective Underwriting Agreement executed Offering priced
0	Offer date, shares allocated Trading begins
+ 40	Quiet period ends

A private company likely retains legal counsel even in the absence of an IPO. However, at some point between two years and six months pre-IPO, an issuer may switch to a law firm that has IPO experience. Legal advice is split between amending the corporate charter to make it suitable for public ownership and assisting in the preparation of the registration forms. Finally, three to six months prior to the desired offer date the issuer hires an investment bank. Figure 9.1 presents a detailed timeline of events from this point foward.

Once the underwriter has been hired attention turns to preparing the S-1 registration statement that must be filed with and approved by the SEC. Each advisor has a complementary role in the preparation of the registration statement. Accountants audit the issuer's financial records. The registration statement must include an observation of inventory, confirmation of accounts receivable and an *auditor's opinion*. The auditor provides a 'comfort letter' to the underwriter to provide assurances of the auditor's examination of the client's financial records. Lawyers advise on the disclosures required in the narrative sections of the registration statement based on SEC Regulation S-K. These include management discussion and analysis, use of proceeds and risk factors.

The underwriter coordinates the drafting of the registration statement and ensures that it presents the issuer in the best possible light. After the registration statement is filed, a portion of it becomes the preliminary prospectus, which is sent to potential investors. The prospectus must disclose all relevant information pertaining to the issuer that a reasonable investor would require to accurately value the shares.

9.1.1 Exchange Listing

An issuer must choose which stock market to list its shares on and then submit an application to the exchange around the same time it files with the SEC. There are three major options in the US: the NYSE, the NASDAQ National Market System (NMS) and the American Stock Exchange (AMEX). Each market has specific minimum listing requirements that an issuer must meet. Table 9.1 presents these requirements for the NYSE and the NASDAQ, the two dominant markets for IPOs. The NYSE requirements are more stringent, demanding that the issuer be larger, have a larger offering size and be more profitable.

The NASDAQ has attracted the majority of new listings – between 80 and 85 percent in the 1990s – due in part to the lenient listing requirements. Issuers that meet the NYSE requirements have the option of either market and should choose the one that offers the best economic advantage. Corwin and Harris (1998) reported that 57 percent of NYSE-eligible IPOs listed on the NYSE. Issuers on the NYSE were significantly larger, measured by total assets, and had higher operating earnings. Carve-out IPOs and larger, less risky issuers were more likely to list on the NYSE, whereas technology firms and those with VC-backing were inclined to choose the NASDAQ.

A number of factors influence the choice of market. Data presented in Chapter 3 showed that NYSE listing fees are considerably higher, a potential deterrent for smaller issuers. Corwin and Harris estimated that the average combined listing and underwriting fees were approximately $500,000 less for NASDAQ IPOs. Over the long run the NYSE may offer cost savings because of lower trading costs. Firms switching from the NASDAQ to the NYSE typically experience a positive price increase. Increased liquidity, greater investor recognition and reduced execution costs could all contribute to the value gains.

Table 9.1 Minimum listing standards for the NYSE and NASDAQ

Listing standard	NYSE	NASDAQ		
		Standard 1	Standard 2	Standard 3
Shares publicly held	1,100,00	1.1 m	1.1 m	1.1 m
Number of stockholders (round lot holders)	2,000	400	400	400
Market value of publicly held shares	$60 m	$8 m	$18 m	$20 m
Pre-tax income	$6,500,000 over last three years	$1 m	N/A	N/A
Assets and revenue	$40.0 m (net tangible assets)	N/A	N/A	$75 m and $75 m
Shareholders' equity	-	$15 m	$30 m	N/A
Minimum bid price	-	$5	$5	$5
Operating history	-	N/A	2 Years	N/A

Source: NYSE and NASDAQ.

The market's reputation may be the biggest consideration in the choice. In a survey of issuer CFOs, Ryan (2001) reported that the prestige of the Big Board was the biggest advantage to a NYSE listing. The CFOs of NASDAQ issuers felt that this market was better for new companies, reflecting the bias towards technology companies on the NASDAQ and in the IPO market. In addition, NASDAQ market-makers typically promote the securities they trade to investors through a process called sponsorship, with small and young companies the most likely beneficiaries.

9.1.2 Disclosure

The SEC requires that all materially relevant information about the issuer be disclosed in the prospectus. While remaining compliant with the regulations, issuers do have latitude in the detail of the disclosure. For example, when discussing the intended use of the proceeds the issuer can be vague and state that they are for general corporate purposes, or alternatively provide an itemized description of how funds will be used to repurchase debt and finance growth. Disclosure is not limited to the prospectus; the firm can issue press releases before and after the offering is filed regarding current developments like new joint ventures, results from R&D and the hiring of a new executive.

The optimal disclosure policy must balance the costs and benefits of releasing information. Additional disclosure reduces the asymmetric information between the issuer and investors, and amongst investors, which translates into a lower cost of capital. At the same time, disclosing proprietary information about the issuer's operations could strengthen the competitive position of rival firms.

IPO underpricing is a cost to the issuer that should increase in the severity of asymmetric information. In two different studies the initial return was negatively related to the frequency of pre-IPO disclosure, defined as manager-initiated announcements (Schrand and Verrechia 2002), and to the specificity of the intended use of proceeds (Leone, Rock and Willenberg 2003). Issuers appeared conscious of the consequences of disclosure, as they were less forthcoming when proprietary costs – measured by greater industry concentration and whether the issuer was a high-tech company – were high.[1]

9.1.3 Insider Sales

Before filing to go public the issuer has to decide how large the offering will be and the composition of shares sold. The offering can consist of two types of shares: primary, which are new shares in the company, and secondary, which are already owned by pre-IPO shareholders. The firm receives the proceeds from the sale of primary shares, whereas the funds go directly to selling shareholders. Capital requirements, and to a lessor extent control, determine the size of the primary component, but strategic considerations affect the number of secondary shares sold.[2]

Pre-IPO shareholders thinking of selling in the IPO must acknowledge the negative signal such an action would convey to investors. These shareholders are better informed about the firm's value and prospects than any potential investor could be. Investors would, justifiably, interpret the decision to sell as an indication that the insiders believe the firm is overvalued. Consequently, investors discount the price they are willing to pay in the IPO. Leland and Pyle (1977) demonstrated that insiders could avoid this 'lemons' problem if they retain a large fraction of their shares, thereby signaling their faith in the firm quality. The strength of the signal required increases in the severity of the informational asymmetry between existing and new potential shareholders. This applies to all existing shareholders, but the extent of the asymmetry varies within this group. Senior management knows more about the quality of the firm than general employees, so their selling decision carries more weight with investors.

The pattern of secondary sales in the IPO is consistent with the signaling theory. Dor (2003a) reported that only 40 to 45 percent of IPOs included a secondary component, and among those only 13 percent of the pre-IPO outstanding shares were sold. The fraction of pre-IPO shares sold was positively related to the firm age and volume of sales, both of which should be inversely related to the degree of asymmetry, and increased with the presence of VC-backing and a prestigious underwriter, which credibly certifies the firm quality. The shareholders likely to be better informed – CEOs, top executives and directors – sold an average of 8.6 percent of their holdings, compared to 30 percent for general employees.

9.2 THE UNDERWRITER

The investment bank is a vital cog in a successful IPO. Historically, the senior management of an issuer had rarely been through an IPO before, although it is now common for issuers to hire a CFO with going-public experience. What issuers will certainly lack is a detailed knowledge of investor interest in their offering. Consequently, the issuer/underwriter relationship is of paramount importance and must be structured wisely. The issuer should select the bank that will best serve its specific needs and requirements. Conditional on selection, the details of the relationship need to be ironed out, including the compensation and contractual obligations of the underwriter.

9.2.1 Selection Process

The bank provides up to three distinct services in the primary market – the period between the filing and offer dates. The first is origination and advisory, which includes administrative preparation of the prospectus and advice on setting the offering terms. Second, the bank underwrites the offering by committing to bear some or all of the risk associated with the issue proceeds. Distribution is the final service and involves placing the shares with investors. The distribution effort ranges from actively marketing the issue to simply filling orders as they come in.

The choice of an underwriter is a function of the specific issuer demands and the ability of a bank to provide the desired services. For example, a large offering will require greater distribution capabilities, thereby limiting the pool of potential underwriters. Before reviewing the criteria used by issuers to evaluate potential underwriters, it is helpful to understand how the underwriter is chosen.

Table 9.2 Underwriter rankings based on 2002 US IPOs

Bank	Total proceeds ($m)	No. of deals	Market share (%)[a]
Citigroup	8,369	17	19.1
Goldman Sachs	5,459	13	12.4
Merrill Lynch	3,995	17	9.1
CS First Boston	3,949	18	9.0
Lehman Brothers	3,078	8	7.0
Morgan Stanley	3,040	11	6.9
UBS	2,527	12	5.8
HSBC	1,427	2	3.3
Deutsche Bank	1,425	7	3.3
Credit Lyonnais	949	1	2.2
Subtotal	34,223	81	78.1
Grand Total	43,832	146	100.0

a. Total proceeds and market share are based on all IPOs for which the bank was the lead or co-lead managing underwriter.

Source: Dealogic.

9.2.1.1 The banks

Selecting an underwriter first requires identifying the banks that can lead manage the IPO process. The underwriting market for IPOs is dominated by traditional investment banks, whether independent like Goldman Sachs or Lehman Brothers, or bought by commercial banks, like First Boston (Credit Suisse). Considerable attention is devoted to the ranking of the banks based on deal flow. Table 9.2 ranks the top 10 banks based on total IPO proceeds for which they were the lead or co-lead managing underwriters in 2002. The data are from the *Investment Dealers Digest* and comprise the league tables that are used frequently in promotional materials. The banks that are regularly in the top half dozen or so comprise the 'bulge bracket' of the industry.

The underwriting market has changed considerably since the early 1980s. IPOs used to be underwritten primarily by boutique investment banks such as Alex. Brown and Montgomery Securities. The bulge bracket banks were not major players in this market. In the 1980s, Goldman Sachs underwrote only one technology IPO with annual sales of less than $20 million, inflation-adjusted to 2000 dollars (Loughran and Ritter 2002b). Goldman underwrote 37 such IPOs during the Internet bubble of 1999 and

2000. Two factors have contributed to the change. First, underwriting IPOs is a highly lucrative business that now appeals to mainstream investors, thereby attracting the big banks. Second, the larger banks bought many of the smaller boutique banks, mainly because they were profitable.

9.2.1.2 The 'beauty contest'

The process of selecting an underwriter is called the 'beauty contest' or 'bake-off'. The participating banks each have an opportunity to pitch their services to the issuer in a formal presentation. A bank emphasizes its expertise in the issuer's industry, its ranking in the league tables, the quality of its corporate finance advisory work and, at least until recently, the reputation of the analyst who will cover the firm. The issuer then chooses the bank that will act as lead manager on the IPO and negotiates the terms of the underwriting agreement.

The competition to be the lead manager, frequently called the bookrunner, and receive the substantial profits is fierce. Banks go to great lengths to win an IPO, which has resulted in unscrupulous behavior in the past. Prior to 2002, banks frequently allotted shares in hot IPOs to the CEOs of private companies in a practice known as spinning. The hope was that in return the CEO would select the bank for the IPO. Banks would also promise to provide positive analyst coverage of the issuer, setting up the potential for conflict of interests. Issuers are not naive at how the game is played. They occasionally demand loans at favorable terms and a bank's ability and willingness to meet this request can affect whether it is selected.

9.2.1.3 Syndicate structure

An issuer is free to select more than one bank to lead the IPO, designating two or more banks as co-lead managers. As a practical matter, only one bank really manages the IPO process. The bookrunner's responsibilities include managing the road show, determining the final offer terms jointly with the issuer, coordinating aftermarket price support and pooling together other banks to form the IPO syndicate. The syndicate is split into several brackets, with bulge bracket banks given top billing. The IPO Tombstone advertisements that appear in the business press list the syndicate members by bracket. The bookrunner decides how many shares each syndicate member will allocate, which is contingent on its ranking in the brackets.

A dramatic evolution in the structure of syndicates has taken place since the mid-1980s. Chen and Ritter (2000) documented that the percentage of moderately sized IPOs – $20 million to $80 million – with a single lead manager decreased from 37 percent during the 1985–87 period to only 4 percent from 1995 to 1998. In contrast, the percentage of IPOs that had three co-leads increased from 16 to 41 percent. Corwin and Schultz (2003) reported that the average number of bookrunners and co-leads per IPO was 1.03 and 1.93, respectively, in the late 1990s.

The change in the syndicate structure reflected the new economics of the underwriting industry.[3] Corwin and Schulz (2003) documented many of the new stylized facts. Issuers were able to buy additional analyst coverage at no cost by choosing more co-lead managers. Each additional co-manager resulted in 0.69 more analysts issuing reports within three months of the IPO. An issuer benefits if the additional co-managers 'whisper in their ear' about the pricing performance of the bookrunner, especially if the underpricing is severe. Co-managers have an incentive to do this because it could help to win new business in the future. Additional syndicate members can provide stronger certification of the issuer's quality, which reduces the IPO costs. Each additional co-managing (non-managing) syndicate member was correlated with 6.0 to 7.5 (0.6 to 1.7) percent less underpricing.

The average syndicate had 16 members, down from about 20 in the mid-1990s. Banks may be chosen for the syndicate to complement the strengths of the bookrunner. Underwriters vary in their distribution network, emphasizing different geographic regions and either retail or institutional investors. Relationships are even more important. An underwriter was much more likely to be included in another bank's syndicate if it had been in the past and if the other bank participated in the underwriter's past syndicates.

9.2.2 Selection Criteria

Issuers use multiple criteria to evaluate potential lead underwriters. The importance of each depends on their specific needs. A brief description of the main criteria follows; subsequent sections elaborate in greater detail.

Cost minimization: IPO costs can be decomposed into three parts: direct issuing expenses that include registration, filing, legal and auditing fees, underwriter compensation and underpricing. Direct expenses are fixed and largely independent of the chosen underwriter. The magnitude of the other costs is sufficiently large that an issuer cannot help but consider them in the choice of underwriter. Lee et al. (1996) measured the cost components for different size IPOs. The results of their findings are presented in Table 9.3. The combined direct expenses and underwriter compensation exhibited strong economies of scale, and the average underpricing declined with the offer size. The percentages are sample specific, but nonetheless provide an accurate snapshot of the IPO costs.

Table 9.3 IPO costs as a percentage of the gross proceeds[4]

Proceeds (millions $)	No. of IPOs[a]	Gross spread (%)	Direct expenses[b] (%)	Total direct costs (%)	Initial return (%)
2 – 9.99	337	9.05	7.91	16.96	16.35
10 – 19.99	389	7.24	4.39	11.63	9.65
20 – 39.99	533	7.01	2.69	9.70	12.48
40 – 59.99	215	6.96	1.76	8.72	13.65
60 – 79.99	79	6.74	1.46	8.20	11.31
80 – 99.99	51	6.47	1.44	7.91	8.91
100 – 199.99	106	6.03	1.03	7.06	7.16
200 – 499.99	47	5.67	0.86	6.53	5.70
500 and up	10	5.21	0.51	5.72	7.53
Total	1,767	7.31	3.69	11.00	12.05

a. The costs are based on IPOs during the 1990–94 period.
b. The direct expenses include filing, printing and advisor fees.

Source: Lee et al. (1996).

A judicious choice of underwriter can minimize the combined underpricing and compensation costs, thereby maximizing the proceeds received by the issuer. A more concerted underwriter selling effort will reduce the amount of underpricing. In return, the underwriter will demand greater compensation. The choice of lead underwriter should also allocate the cost between compensation and underpricing in the issuer's preferred manner. Thus, an issuer that wants to minimize underpricing will pay for superior underwriting services.

Analysts: Some issuers select the lead underwriter based on the prominence and reputation of the bank's analyst who will cover the stock. Anecdotal evidence supports this conjecture. During the Internet bubble many issuers chose Morgan Stanley because coverage by Mary Meeker, Morgan's Internet analyst, was known to have a positive impact on share valuations. Todd Wagner, former CEO of Broadcast.com, stated as such: 'Our rationale was, if we went with Morgan Stanley, we'd get Mary Meeker, and we'd get a lot of attention', (Elkind 2001, p. 76).[5]

Formal evidence of the importance of analysts in the underwriter choice was offered by Krigman, Shaw and Womack (2001). They used both data and survey questionnaires of CEOs and CFOs to determine the factors motivating firms to switch underwriters following their IPO. The primary factor was dissatisfaction with the quantity and quality of the research coverage by analysts. The mean number of analyst research reports issued by the IPO lead underwriter in the six months prior to the follow-on equity offering were 1.3 and 3.1 for switching and non-switching firms, respectively. Firms also traded up to better perceived research quality; the percentage of *Insititutional Investor* All-Star analysts covering the firms increased from 13 before the switch to 20 percent after. Cliff and Denis (2003) reported corroborating evidence. Issuers were more likely to switch underwriters for the follow-on if the lead did not have a buy recommendation outstanding one year after the IPO.

The importance of analysts as a selection criterion grew in the 1980s and 1990s. Morgan Stanley did not have a single equity analyst in the early 1970s, even though it was a major player in the IPO market.[6] By 2000 the premier investment banks were spending upwards of $1 billion annually on equity research. Analysts were involved in pitching the bank to prospective issuers and later in the IPO process. The dual task of aiding investment bankers in the service of issuers and providing recommendations to the investors buying IPOs naturally led to a conflict of interests for analysts, which were revealed after the stock market bubble burst in 2000 (see Chapter 11 for more details). Reforms of the investment banking industry that resulted from an investigation of the conflicts limit the involvement of analysts in the IPO process. Consequently, the future role of analysts in the underwriter selection remains in doubt.

Reputation and certification: A bank's reputation is another factor in the underwriter selection. An issuer that has its IPO underwritten by a bulge bracket bank automatically attains a higher status among investors. A prestigious bank puts its reputation on the line with an offering and will try to avoid bad companies to reduce the potential damage inflicted by a poorly performing IPO. The certification that an issuer receives from a reputable bank should enable it to increase the offer price. The gain in gross proceeds derived from a prestigious underwriter will be offset to some extent by the higher compensation such a bank demands. Ljungqvist, Marston and Wilhelm (2003) demonstrated that the reputation of a bank and its analysts were important factors in winning a firm's equity underwriting business.

Information specialization: An underwriter's ability to market an IPO depends on the quality of information it possesses about the issuer and investors. In the case of follow-on equity offerings, James (1992) found that a firm was more likely to stay with its IPO underwriter if the bank had spent time acquiring relationship-specific knowledge about the firm's operations and requirements. Similarly, Ljungqvist, Marston and Wilhelm (2003) showed that a strong prior underwriting relationship was a significant determinant in a bank's ability to win future equity underwriting business from a company. Such a relationship is not likely to exist pre-IPO, but a bank can compensate by specializing in certain industries. This gives them a superior understanding of the characteristics necessary for a successful IPO from these industries, which perhaps tips the balance in their favor (Booth and Chua 1996). Smaller banks and those that operate in a specific geographic region are more likely to specialize.

Monitoring: An intangible service that a firm might demand from its underwriter is external monitoring. The bank's analyst provides an independent evaluation for the board of directors to use in assessing managerial performance. Such monitoring can improve corporate performance and reduce agency costs. Each level of underwriter monitoring is associated with a different certifiable firm value. Reputation concerns suggest that prestigious underwriters may be better monitors because they have a greater stake in the issuer continuing to perform well in the aftermarket. Jain and Kini (1999) found some evidence that issuers desire monitoring and that this leads them to choose higher quality underwriters.

9.2.3 Underwriter Compensation

The primary form of underwriter compensation is the spread – the percentage of the offer price retained by the underwriter. A 5 percent spread means that for each dollar of IPO proceeds the underwriter retains 5 cents. Occasionally underwriters receive additional warrants to buy shares in the firm at a predetermined exercise price. When the spread is the only form of compensation, the underwriters' financial interests are more closely aligned with the issuer objective of maximizing the proceeds.

9.2.3.1 The spread

The spread is composed of three parts.[7] The first is the management fee – typically 20 percent of the spread – paid to the lead and co-managing underwriters, with the split tilted towards the lead. The second is the underwriting fee, also equal to about 20 percent of the spread. All syndicate members receive a fraction of the underwriting fee, net of the underwriting and stabilization costs, in proportion to the number of shares each underwrites. The final part is the selling concession. Syndicate members receive the concession for each share that they are credited with underwriting.

The number of credits earned need not correspond to the number of shares allocated. The *Capital Markets Handbook* states that the standard practice in recent years has been to credit each syndicate member with selling 10 percent of its allocation.[8] Corwin and Schultz (2003) reported that the lead underwrote on average 41 percent of the shares, the co-leads 38 percent, leaving 21 percent for the other syndicate members. Consequently, the lead takes home as much as 80 percent of the spread fees.

The normal spread charged by banks for firm commitment IPOs is 7 percent, although there are economies of scale.[9] The data in Table 9.3 reveal that spreads start at about 9 percent for IPOs under $10 million and fall to about 5 percent for the largest IPOs. By way of comparison, the average spread for SEOs was about 5 percent, and only 1.5 percent for straight bonds. Higher IPO spreads are at least partly justified by the greater uncertainty over the offering's outcome and the additional selling effort required.

By the late 1990s a 7 percent spread was used almost exclusively. Chen and Ritter (2000) documented that 26 percent of IPOs in the 1985–87 period with proceeds between $20 million and $80 million had exactly 7 percent spreads. This percentage increased to 91 in the 1995–98 period. The clustering at 7 percent for IPOs above $80 million was less pronounced, but also increased over time. These percentages probably understate the current usage of the new industry standard 7 percent spread.

The convergence to 7 percent spreads essentially eliminates compensation cost as an underwriter selection criterion. However, even prior to this development spreads were not a major consideration. Krigman, Shaw and Womack (2001) reported that CFOs ranked fee structure as the lowest decision criteria when selecting the lead manager. Companies were also willing to pay higher fees to a bank with whom they had an extended relationship, whereas firms that opportunistically switched between underwriters paid lower fees (Nanda and Warther 1998). Nonetheless, high spreads are a deterrent to going public. Ryan (2001) surveyed the CFOs of issuers from 1996 to 1998 and found that 60 percent thought the underwriting spread was a disadvantage to going public and was a cause of some concern.

9.2.3.2 Underwriter collusion

The fixation on a 7 percent spread has led many observers to suggest that collusion might be behind the underwriter compensation.[10] Adding fuel to the fire is the fact that spreads in Europe and Asia average between 2.5 and 4 percent.[11] Even underwriters admit that spreads are high (Chen and Ritter 2000). However, a pattern of high and uniform spreads is not sufficient evidence of collusion. What is needed is proof that spreads are above the competitive level. A cursory examination of the data seems to suggest that this condition holds. Both $20 million and $80 million IPOs have 7 percent spreads. If spreads were determined solely by costs, the need to earn a fair return on capital and the risk, then they should decline with the issue size.

Collusion among underwriters, if it exists, could be either explicit or implicit. The possibility of explicit collusion seems highly unlikely, given the number of people involved in setting spreads at the different banks. The more plausible scenario advocated by Chen and Ritter is implicit collusion. High spreads can be maintained because of the dynamic interaction between underwriters (Chen 1998). A bank can deviate from the implicit agreement by charging a spread less than 7 percent. Deviation increases short-run profits if the gain from attracting new issuers compensates for the lower spread on existing deals. In the long run, profits are reduced because other banks respond by lowering their spreads. The threat of smaller long-run profits acts as a sufficient deterrent to lowering the spread below the collusive level. The fact that spreads are not a major factor in the underwriter choice serves to reinforce the implicit collusion because there is little gain to deviating.

Hansen (2001) tested for collusive spreads by examining the investment banking market structure. He found little evidence in support of explicit collusion. The market concentration for underwriting services has been low and unchanging during the 7 percent spread era. There were a high number of new entrants who also charged 7 percent. The use of 7 percent spreads did not decline after the Department of Justice investigation was announced.[12] Finally, spreads for SEOs exhibit no tendency to cluster on one number. Hansen also rejected the claim that 7 percent spreads were non-competitive, in fact suggesting they may be too low to contain abnormal profits, except for IPOs in excess of $100 million. He instead argued that constraining the spread to 7 percent is efficient because it reduces the number of terms to be negotiated with the underwriter, including underpricing and marketing effort.[13]

The international evidence raises further doubts about collusion. Spreads in many countries tend to cluster at a single number. For example, 95 and 86 percent of spreads in Hong Kong and India, respectively, cluster at 2.5 percent (Torstila 2003). The country-level data indicates that clustering is most severe in low spread countries. If clustering indicated collusion, one would expect it to occur at higher spreads, not lower.

9.2.3.3 Underwriter warrants

Warrants are another form of compensation, used in addition to the spread, that give the underwriter the right, but not the obligation, to buy new shares in the issuer. Warrants cannot be exercised within one year of the IPO, have a duration longer than five years, have an exercise price below the offer price or be exercised for more than 10 percent of the shares sold in the IPO. Some state security laws specify that the exercise price must equal 120 percent of the offer price. The warrants are granted to the underwriter at fractions of a penny per warrant. Warrants mostly appear in best efforts IPOs, but sometimes are used in small firm commitment IPOs as well. Warrants are a significant additional cost to going public; Barry, Muscarella and Vetsuypens (1991) estimated they cost between 4.5 and 7.75 percent of the gross proceeds when they are granted.

The use of costly warrants is justified on a number of grounds. Barry, Muscarella and Vetsuypens suggested that they provide a way to circumvent regulatory guidelines. The NASD requires underwriter compensation to be fair and reasonable, but does not set specific quantitative guidelines. Many states do impose compensation limits, usually not more than 15 percent of the gross proceeds. The NASD uses a simple formula for the calculation of warrant value that leads to a significant underestimation of the true value. Thus, an issuer can get around the 15 percent compensation constraint without technically violating the law.

A second rationale for warrants is that they alleviate investor concerns about overpaying for shares. The reason being is that the underwriter now has an incentive to underprice the IPO or create aftermarket demand to raise the warrant value. Barry, Muscarella and Vetsuypens reported that IPOs with warrants had initial returns three percentage points higher than non-warrant IPOs, and Dunbar (1995) reported a ten percentage point differential. By the same token, since investors are less concerned about overpricing when warrants are granted, they should tolerate less underpricing, reducing a different IPO cost.

Granting the underwriter warrants can be optimal if the total costs of going public are lower as a result. Dunbar tried to test whether issuers self-select into the lowest cost warrant-use option. He estimated that the initial return for warrant-issuing firms would have been 36.4 percent if they had not been granted, compared to the actual 23.3 percent. Simultaneously, direct issuing costs would have fallen from 23.9 percent to an expected level of 14.6 percent. The estimated total cost of 51 percent of IPO proceeds without warrants was significantly larger than the actual cost of 47.2 percent. Based on this analysis, warrants offer a cost-minimizing way to go public for some issuers.

9.2.3.4 Underwriter services

Applying the adage 'you get what you pay for' to the IPO market would imply that issuers paying higher spreads receive better service from their underwriter. Better service could manifest as superior certification ability or greater marketing effort, both at the time of the IPO and afterward through analyst coverage. Paying for better service is justified if it increases the net IPO proceeds received by the issuer and improves the aftermarket price performance. As the following evidence suggests, issuers that pay higher fees are rewarded with better service and greater IPO proceeds. Constraining the spread to 7 percent means that the level of service must be traded-off with the amount of underpricing. In fact, Cliff and Denis (2003) showed that issuers that increased their underpricing were able to 'buy' more and better analyst coverage.

The growing international use of the US-style book-building mechanism to sell IPOs – the mechanism now accounts for 80 percent of IPOs outside the US (Ljungqvist, Jenkinson and Wilhelm 2003) – provides a good opportunity to test whether higher fees translate into greater underwriter selling effort. A defining feature of book-building is the active role the underwriter plays in trying to sell the IPO.[14] The 7 percent spread in the US is consistently higher than spreads elsewhere. If a causal relationship between compensation and effort exists, it should result in superior outcomes for US IPOs.

Non-US firms have the option to market and list their IPO in the US. Their decision to do just that could reflect a favorable trade-off between the higher spread and better service. Ljungqvist, Jenkinson and Wilhelm (2003) examined over 2,000 IPOs that varied in their use of US banks as lead managers, marketing to US investors and listing in the US. They found that the combination of hiring US banks and marketing to US investors lowered underpricing relative to foreign IPOs. The additional cost to hiring an American bank was more than offset by the reduced underpricing cost. The superior outcome could result from a greater effort or greater skill and experience with the book-building procedure; either way issuers were better off paying more.

An indirect measure of underwriter effort is the offer price revision. The preliminary offer price chosen at the start of the IPO process is subsequently revised conditional on information gathered from investors. Greater marketing effort should translate into a positive price revision. Barondes, Butler and Sanger (2000) found that increasing the spread one percentage point above the average was correlated with a positive 5.7 percent revision of the offer price. A one-percentage point decrease was associated with a downward revision of almost 6 percent. For a $100 million IPO, the $6 million increase (decrease) in proceeds would overwhelm the $1 million increase (decrease) in compensation.

Some issuers demand monitoring services from their underwriter, usually in the form of analyst coverage. Hansen and Torregrosa (1992)

197

examined seasoned equity offerings consisting entirely of primary shares. Investors could be concerned that the proceeds will be used inefficiently. The concern is mitigated if either the managers have high ownership stakes to align their interests with those of shareholders or the underwriter monitors the managers. Hansen and Torregrosa found that spreads were inversely related to the managerial stake and concluded that this was evidence that issuers pay for monitoring services.[15]

The pay-for-service relationship exists in other countries. Ljungqvist (2003) examined IPOs in the UK, where compensation takes a different form: a fixed fee and a spread component. Other aspects of the underwriting agreement – the option to price stabilize, underwriting cover, marketing to US investors and retail participation – can be negotiated. Ljungqvist estimated for each issuer the required compensation based on the explicit services demanded. Excess compensation – the difference between actual and estimated compensation – suggests that the issuer paid for more effort and less underpricing. Consistent with this conjecture, Ljungqvist showed that a 1 percent increase in excess compensation reduced underpricing by 11 percent.

9.2.4 Underwriting Contract

A formal contract between the issuer and the underwriter must specify the bank's obligations regarding origination and advisory, underwriting and distribution services. The compensation terms are also spelled out. In theory, there are an infinite number of contracts that could be signed by the two parties. Reality limits this set of contracts to only a few.

9.2.4.1 Optimal contracts

An IPO is a sale of securities from an issuer to investors. Ideally, the issuer and investors would deal directly with each other at no cost. Information would be perfect in the sense that issuers know the extent of investor demand and investors have all value-relevant information. The real world is obviously far from this perfect environment. Issuers and investors would incur prohibitive expenses trying to find each other and agree to terms. To correct for potential market failures, investment banks act as an intermediary between issuers and investors.

An underwriter can help an issuer minimize three problems present in a direct offering to investors. First, the underwriter bears the IPO proceeds risk. Transferring risk from the issuer to the underwriter is efficient because banks have a larger capital base, can better diversify across investment opportunities and can shed risk to other syndicate members. Second, underwriters possess better information about the state of market demand because of their frequent contact with investors. A private firm would have difficulty ever acquiring such information. Third, underwriters have the organizational structure and experience to efficiently sell the IPO that issuers cannot easily duplicate.

An issuer's optimal underwriting contract is one that simultaneously maximizes the expected IPO proceeds, while minimizing the risk.[16] Implementing a contract that achieves these objectives is generally not possible. The underwriter's incentives are not perfectly aligned with those of the issuer because the bank incurs the full cost of marketing the IPO, but only receives a fraction of the proceeds. At the margin, the underwriter will prefer to shirk on the effort level required to maximize proceeds. Issuers cannot perfectly observe and verify the underwriter's effort and private information regarding the state of investor demand. Consequently, an issuer cannot be certain if a poor IPO is the result of low investor interest or insufficient underwriter effort.

An efficiently designed contract can overcome some, but not all, of the information and agency problems. The optimal outcome can still be achieved when the underwriter effort is unobservable. The efficient contract entails the underwriter buying the entire offering from the issuer for a fixed payment and reselling the shares to investors at whatever price it can garner. Since the bank receives the full marginal benefit from its effort, it will supply the efficient effort level and maximize the proceeds (Baron 1979; Baron and Holmstrom 1980). The fixed payment is chosen to give the underwriter a fair expected return on its effort.

Problems arise when the underwriter has private information about investor demand prior to signing the contract (Baron 1982). The bank can get the issuer to accept a lower offer price, which attracts more investors and reduces the required selling effort, by understating the true level of demand. The fixed payment mechanism no longer achieves the optimal outcome because the issuer has no way of knowing if the reported state of demand is true. The next best contract involves intentional underpricing. A lower offer price reduces the required effort level and this cost saving to the underwriter is compensation for revealing the true state of demand to the issuer.

Agency-induced underpricing has mixed support. Muscarella and Vetsuypens (1989) looked at bank IPOs, where agency conflicts are not an issue because the bank is both underwriter and issuer. They found no difference in the initial returns between bank and non-bank IPOs. In contrast, Li and Masulis (2003) found that the initial returns decreased as the underwriter's ownership stake in the issuer – due to venture capital investments – increased, thereby aligning their interests.

9.2.4.2 Actual contracts

The set of actual underwriting contracts available to issuers in the US is limited to three. The firm commitment contract is by far the most prevalent, used almost exclusively for IPOs in excess of $10 million. The best efforts contract is one alternative, but its use dwindled in the 1990s. A new contractual development in the late 1990s is the advent of Internet-based auctions. The investment bank W.R. Hambrecht, for one, conducts a uniform price auction for the IPOs it underwrites, which affect its contractual obligations to the issuer. To date auction contracts have been used sparingly. An in-depth discussion of auctions is left for Chapter 10.

Firm commitment: The firm commitment contract, referred to as book-building in preceding sections, begins with an initial letter of intent that specifies the arrangement between the issuer and underwriter. The initial agreement protects the underwriter against any uncovered expenses in the event the offer is withdrawn, but does not guarantee a final offer price or number of shares. A registration statement for the IPO is filed with the SEC and the preliminary prospectus is distributed to investor. The underwriter then begins to actively market the issue to investors. The SEC reviews the registration statement and once it is approved the issue becomes effective. The underwriter and issuer have a final pricing meeting, typically the night before the offer date, and set the final offer terms. At this point the letter of intent is replaced with a formal underwriting agreement. The underwriter guarantees to the issuer the net proceeds specified in the final prospectus by buying the entire issue at the offer price, net of the spread, and bearing the risk of re-selling the shares to investors.

The firm commitment contract exhibits some resemblance to the optimal contract. The underwriter buys the entire offering for a fixed price and re-sells it to investors. However, the fixed payment is based on the final offer price and the underwriter is paid a proportional spread, not the residual proceeds. The contract is also inefficient in terms of risk sharing. The underwriter guarantees the proceeds only at the end of the primary market. By this point, the underwriter has a good idea of the full subscription offer price. Thus, the bank bears very little pricing risk with the IPO and it is the issuer who is exposed to the proceeds risk throughout the primary market.

The typical firm commitment underwriting agreement contains a number of boilerplate conditions. The underwriting spread is usually 7 percent. Pre-IPO shareholders agree to not sell, or lockup, their shares for 180 days after the offer date without prior consent from the underwriter. The underwriter agrees to affect price stabilization in the aftermarket, if necessary. The terms of the relationship that are negotiated are usually not explicitly included in the agreement; for example, the amount of acceptable underpricing and the tone and intensity of analyst coverage.

Best efforts: The underwriter does not guarantee the proceeds or actively sell with a best efforts contract. The registration statement filed with the SEC includes the final offer price, whereas it only includes a preliminary price range for a firm commitment IPO. The underwriter waits for final SEC approval before distributing the prospectus and giving a 'best effort' to sell the offering in order to avoid the cost of multiple mailings that would occur if there were revisions. Best efforts IPOs are sold almost exclusively to retail investors. Firm commitment IPOs, by comparison, are geared primarily toward institutional investors.

The best efforts contract has a fixed selling period, usually 90 days. During this period investors indicate their interest by depositing money for the desired number of shares in an escrow account set up by the bank. The registration statement specifies the maximum and a minimum number of shares that can be sold, the latter of which is referred to as the minimum sales constraint (MSC). Many best efforts contracts are all-or-none; all shares must be sold for the IPO to be completed. If the MSC is not reached within the specified time period, the offer is withdrawn, investors' money is refunded and the firm gets nothing. The underwriter bears no responsibility for a withdrawn offer, or for shares above the MSC not sold.

9.2.4.3 Use and cost

The firm commitment contract is used almost exclusively today, but that was not always the case. Best efforts contracts were used regularly in the late 1970s and 1980s – accounting for 15 to 30 percent of all IPOs – according to Ritter (1987) and Chua (1995). The types of issuers and offering characteristics for the firm commitment contract differed significantly from the best efforts IPOs. Ritter reported that firm commitment issuers were older, had more sales, a higher book value of equity and had a less speculative value. They also had a larger offer size and higher offer prices.[17]

The two contracts differed in their IPO costs, based on the data in Ritter. The average underwriter compensation for best efforts and firm commitment IPOs equaled 11.9 and 8.9 percent, respectively, of the total proceeds. The best efforts compensation understates the true cost because it does not include warrants granted to the underwriter, which are less common in firm commitment IPOs. The respective average underpricing for best efforts and firm commitment IPOs were 47 and 11 percent.

9.2.4.4 Contract choice

At first glance it seems odd that an issuer would choose the best efforts contract, given that it has a high relative cost. Circumstances beyond the issuer's control partly explain this choice. Investment banks tend to specialize in one of the two methods, with large prestigious banks only underwriting firm commitment IPOs. Top-tier banks also avoid underwriting risky offerings for reputation reasons and small IPOs because the low compensation is not worth their effort. Some issuers may have to use the best efforts contract because they are frozen out of the firm commitment contract market. Supply-side constraints alone cannot explain the use of the best efforts contract because some issuers do have a choice.[18] A number of factors could justify the use of a best efforts contract.

Efficient investment: The best efforts contract can help the issuer improve its investment efficiency (Sherman 1992). Investors evaluate the issuer's projects before deciding whether to subscribe to the IPO. Those investors who reach a positive assessment for the issuer will invest, while other investors abstain. The MSC increases the probability that only high-quality projects that produce good evaluations receive enough subscriptions for a successful offering.

Adverse selection risk: The all-or-nothing nature of the best efforts contract alleviates adverse selection risk for investors. Better-informed investors avoid overpriced IPOs, leaving the less informed with large allocations in lackluster offerings. A high MSC constraint ensures that only offerings with sufficient informed demand are completed, implying that they are not overpriced. The offer price can now be increased because the participation risk is reduced. This pricing advantage of the best efforts contract increases in the issuer risk. In fact, Ritter (1987) found best efforts IPOs to be associated with higher levels of risk and, among all completed IPOs, best efforts were more likely to have positive initial returns, consistent with the overpriced IPOs being withdrawn more frequently.[19]

Underwriter services: The firm commitment contract demands greater selling effort from the underwriter and forces it to bear some re-sale risk. The bank can certify the quality of the issuer to reduce the re-sale risk, but in return for higher compensation. Since low quality issuers do not benefit from certification, yet still have to pay for it, a best efforts contract is a cheaper alternative (Bower 1989). The bank could also try to increase underpricing to reduce the required selling effort and re-sale risk. The incentive to underprice increases in the riskiness of the issuer.

Consequently, small risky firms may find that the best efforts contract is a more cost-effective way to go public (Benveniste and Spindt 1989).

Divergence of opinion: The best efforts contract gives the issuer greater say in setting the offer price. This attribute is beneficial when the underwriter disagrees with the issuer's assessment of the firm value and wants to set a lower offer price. Chua (1995) suggested disagreement is more likely when a large fraction of the value is determined by speculative intangible growth options, which she proxied with the ratio of the market value of IPO proceeds to the book value of total assets. The ratios in her sample of best efforts and firm commitment IPOs were 19.6 and 6.5, respectively. The ratio was positively related to the probability of using a best efforts contract.

Probability of withdrawal: Underwriters demand greater compensation when the probability of the IPO failing is high in order to keep the expected compensation at the desired level. The contract selected should minimize the expected cost associated with failure. Dunbar (1998) found that the greater the difference between the predicted probability of IPO success with a firm commitment and a best efforts contract, the higher the probability the firm commitment contract was used. The finding supports the hypothesis that issuers cost minimize, but offers no insight into why success varies with the contract type.

9.2.5 Reputation and Pricing

An investment bank's ability to perform its intermediary function is contingent on its reputation with investors and issuers. A bank that cannot be trusted to complete its tasks at least adequately will not last long in the underwriting industry. On the other hand, an underwriter with a good reputation will attract strong interest from issuers and investors alike. Reputation is an important factor in the underwriter decision, primarily because of the certification benefit. An IPO underwritten by a bulge bracket bank attains a privileged status among investors, translating directly into higher IPO proceeds.

9.2.5.1 Certification

Underwriter certification is fundamental to resolving market failures caused by severe adverse selection in the new issues market. The due diligence review conducted by the underwriter ferrets out relevant information about the issuer's operations, management's ability and the firm value. Individual investors would find it prohibitively expensive to perform a similarly thorough review. Without an underwriter to certify that the reported firm valuation is accurate, there is little to deter an issuer from overstating its true worth. Rational investors understand the issuer's incentives and abstain from purchasing overpriced shares, leading to a breakdown of the IPO market.

The enduring presence of underwriters overcomes potential market failures. The repeated interaction between an underwriter and investors is predicated on a bank's reputation for verifying that IPOs are accurately priced. An issuer can bond itself to not overprice by temporarily borrowing an underwriter's reputation (Beatty and Ritter 1986; Booth and Smith 1986). The bonding cost is contingent on the bank's reputation. A prestigious underwriter will earn abnormal profits because its certification confers a higher firm value. Higher compensation reflects the greater risk the underwriter bears, measured in terms of lost future abnormal profits caused by a damaged reputation. Investors can be more confident that the offer price accurately reflects the firm value, reducing the 'lemons' discount applied to the issuer.

The choice of underwriter reputation must weigh the benefit of higher expected proceeds against the cost of additional compensation. Titman and Trueman (1986) argued that the prestige of the underwriter selected would increase in the issuer quality. High value issuers have their true quality certified, and the resulting gain in the offer price is sufficient to cover the additional cost. Low quality firms will not mimic their high value counterparts because their true value is revealed, yet they would still have to pay high compensation.

9.2.5.2 Underpricing

Prestigious underwriters increase the net IPO proceeds received by an issuer either directly by certifying a higher firm value or indirectly by reducing the required underpricing for investor participation. The latter consequence of a good reputation can be achieved for two reasons.

Bonding: The feared loss in profits due to a lower reputation is an effective incentive for bank's to prevent overpricing. Rational investors are cognizant of an underwriter's desire to avoid overpricing, which reduces their adverse selection risk and the required underpricing for their participation (Booth and Smith 1986). A prestigious bank has more reputation capital at stake and should be most diligent in ensuring that an IPO is not overpriced. The bonding hypothesis predicts that underpricing and underwriter reputation will be inversely related.

Risk signaling: Underpricing increases in the riskiness of the issuer (Draho 2001a). Low risk firms that want to avoid unnecessary underpricing need to credibly signal their risk profile to investors. Hiring a reputable underwriter could achieve this objective because these banks try to avoid riskier issuers and the threat they pose to their reputation (Carter and Manaster 1990). The greater compensation demanded by prestigious banks could outweigh the benefit of lower underpricing for risky issuers. Risk signaling therefore predicts an inverse relation between reputation and underpricing.

Empirical tests of the reputation/underpricing relationship have made use of three reputation proxies. First, underwriters have been alloted into four quality-tiers, the top group corresponding to the bulge bracket banks (Johnson and Miller 1988). Second, a bank's reputation has been based on its share of all IPO proceeds (Meggison and Weiss 1991). Third, reputation has been proxied with Tombstone rankings that reflect the 'company' an underwriter keeps (Carter and Manaster 1990). Early studies, using IPOs from the 1980s, found all three reputation proxies to be negatively related to the initial return.[20]

More recent studies examining IPOs from the 1990s have found the opposite; a positive correlation between reputation and initial returns.[21] Loughran and Ritter (2002b) attribute the reversal to a change in issuer objectives. Issuers became more tolerant of the excessive underpricing that came with hiring a prestigious bank, especially if it meant getting coverage by a prominent analyst. In addition, prestigious banks started to underwrite the IPOs of risky and unproven issuers that they had avoided in the 1980s. Habib and Ljungqvist (2001) questioned the new found positive correlation. They argued that the reputation level chosen by issuers is the outcome of a value-maximizing allocation of IPO costs between compensation and underpricing. After controlling for issuer preferences over the costs, they found reputation and initial returns to be negatively related.

9.2.5.3 Reputation development

A bank with a consistent record of high priced IPOs that are not overpriced will satisfy both issuers and investors, and contribute to the development of a good reputation. The bank's challenge is to not play one group against the other, say by underpricing too much to please investors at the expense of issuers. If the respective reputations with investors and issuers diverge to far apart, the underwriter will be unable to operate effectively.

Investors: An underwriter must do two things to please investors; screen out the bad issuers from the good and ensure that IPOs are not overpriced.

Failure to do both satisfactorily will damage the bank's reputation with investors, making it more difficult to sell IPOs in the future. Underwriters with the best reputation apply the strictest evaluation standards to potential issuers because they have the most to lose from an IPO gone bad (Chemmanur and Fulgheri 1994a).

The prediction that prestigious banks only underwrite high quality IPOs is difficult to test directly because it requires a pre-IPO measure of issuer quality. Foster-Johnson, Lewis and Seward (2000) instead deemed an issuer low quality if it was de-listed shortly after the IPO. They showed that lower quality banks were indeed more likely to underwrite IPOs that subsequently failed. Firms that reputable banks refuse to underwrite go public with a low quality bank, which occurs primarily during hot markets.

Issuers: To maintain a good reputation with issuers a bank must consistently raise the expected amount of proceeds. Failure to do this will result in a loss of market share over time. Firms that switched underwriters for a follow-on offering were found to have received fewer IPO proceeds than initially expected, whereas non-switching firms received more than expected (James 1992; Krigman, Shaw and Womack 2001). Dunbar (2000) reported that the future market share of prestigious banks was negatively related to the level of underpricing for their current IPOs.[22] Initial returns had little impact on the market share of low reputation underwriters. The one dissenting study is Clarke, Dunbar and Kahle (2002). They reported that among underwriters that lost a star analyst, past underpricing was positively related to market share growth.

Underwriters can do a number of things to improve their reputation and gain market share. One is to specialize in a particular industry. Information spillovers from one IPO to another help the underwriter improve its marketing skills, which should lead to increased pricing accuracy (Booth and Chua 1996). Studies have documented a positive relation between reputation and offer price revision in the primary market, a proxy for pricing ability (Benveniste et al. 2003; Ljungqvist and Wilhelm 2003).[23] Better pricing skills acquired through specialization will enable a bank to gain market share, something Dunbar (2000) documented for low prestige underwriters.

Another way to increase market share is to hire a reputable analyst to cover the bank's IPOs, although the new restrictions on analyst participation in IPOs will diminish this benefit. An analyst's reputation can be measured by his or her ranking in *Institutional Investor's* All-American Research Team. Clarke, Dunbar and Kahle (2002) estimated that acquiring a star analyst increased a bank's overall market share a significant 1.26 percentage points. The market share in the analyst's industry increased 4.3

percentage points if a first, second or third team all-star was hired. On average, the gain in market share translated into an additional $22 million in underwriting fees.

9.3 AUDITORS AND LAWYERS

The services provided by auditors and lawyers to the issuer during the IPO process are necessary and vital for a successful public offering. However, the economic impact of these services and the intangible qualities auditors and lawyers provide are minor next to the underwriter. Advisors are not hired independently and the selection of one can influence the choice of the others. For example, a firm that has experienced legal counsel may feel greater freedom to choose a less experienced underwriter.

9.3.1 Legal Liability

Fair and accurate prices are critical for the continual operation of the IPO market. The reputation concerns of underwriters and auditors go a long way towards ensuring that offer prices meet this condition. Unfortunately, reputation alone is not sufficient to assuage all investors concerns about buying shares in an unproven company. Granting investors legal protection against misrepresentation by the issuers and its advisors is an additional carrot to induce their participation. Exposure to legal liability has an impact on the entire IPO process, including the offer price and the selection and compensation of the advisors.

9.3.1.1 Securities law

The Securities Acts of 1933 and 1934 require that participants involved in IPO preparations disclose any material fact that a 'reasonable' investor would consider in deciding whether to invest. The reporting of material untruths or omissions in the prospectus is the basis on which investors can bring forth a lawsuit against the members of the issuer and its advisors. Almost all IPO-related lawsuits are filed under Sections 11 and 12 of the Securities Act of 1993. Section 11 lists the individuals subject to legal liability as the issuer, persons signing the registration statement, directors, partners, individuals that 'expertised' portions of the registration statement (including auditors) and all underwriters. Under Section 11, maximum damages for shares purchased directly in the IPO are based on the difference between the offer price and either the subsequent sale price or the share price at the time of the lawsuit. Lawsuits must be brought within three years of the IPO.

Section 11 mandates that the 'experts' are jointly severally liable for damages resulting from false or misleading information presented in the prospectus. Thus, the issuer and its advisors are collectively liable for the actions of each and every participant involved in preparing the prospectus. Defendants in a lawsuit are permitted the defense of 'due diligence'. The expert must only show that he or she undertook an investigation that would allow a reasonable person to conclude that there were no untrue statements or material omissions. As a practical matter, the legal counsel is held to a much lower standard than the auditor and underwriter. The auditor is fully liable for any material omission in the financial statements and is a primary target of lawsuits.

9.3.1.2 Underpricing deterrence

Lawsuits are time-consuming and potentially very costly to issuers and advisors, who have at their disposal methods to minimize the probability of litigation. Releasing all relevant information and pricing the IPO accurately are minimal first steps. Listing more risk factors in the prospectus further insulates against a lawsuit. The drawback is that it shifts risk to investors, reducing the marketability of the IPO and the offer price. Another tactic, suggested by Ibbotson (1975) and Tinic (1988), is to underprice the IPO as a means of insurance. Underpricing is particularly effective because a lower offer price reduces the probability of future litigation and the potential damages the plaintiff can recover. Alexander (1993) emphasized that the amount of the expected settlement reward is a major determinant of the probability of being sued.[24]

Preliminary tests of the underpricing/insurance hypothesis were inconclusive. Tinic (1988) compared the initial returns of IPOs from 1923 to 1930 to the 1966–71 period, pre- and post-Securities Act periods. As predicted, the average initial return was significantly higher in the latter period. However, Drake and Vetsuypens (1993) reported that the 1972–77 period actually had the lowest initial returns of all three periods. Furthermore, the average initial return of 93 sued issuers was greater than that of similar non-sued issuers.

More recently, Lowry and Shu (2002) pointed out that firms with higher litigation risk would underprice more as insurance against a lawsuit, producing a positive relation between initial returns and litigation risk. But firms that underprice more should be sued less often, generating a negative relation between initial returns and actual litigation. Lowry and Shu examined 84 Section 11 lawsuits.[25] The average initial returns of sued and non-sued issuers were not significantly different at 13.2 and 14.5 percent, respectively. But the underpricing did increase significantly with the litigation risk, after controlling for the joint determination of underpricing and lawsuit probability.

Exposure to legal liability obviously increases the underpricing cost of going public, but it also leads to higher underwriter fees because of the potential damage to the bank's reputation (Beatty and Welch 1996). An issuer can try to minimize the total IPO costs, or at least allocate them most efficiently, by listing more risk factors and uses of proceeds in the prospectus. This lowers the litigation risk and, as a corollary, underpricing and fees. But it also makes the offering more difficult to sell, which drives up the fees. The net overall effect on total costs from this strategy could be positive or negative.

9.3.2 Auditor Selection

The process of selecting accountants should, in theory, involve careful consideration of the economic benefits and costs of each potential auditor. Reality is much more mundane. To start with, there are few auditors to choose from. Four firms dominate, collectively accounting for over 90 percent of all IPOs in the US: Ernst & Young, PriceWaterhouseCoopers, Deloitte and Touche, and KPMG. The rest of the market consists of a large group of relatively small homogeneous auditors. The auditor decision is really only a choice between a Big-4 and a non-Big-4 firm. The choice may not even be one the issuer is free to make. Investment banks frequently make the selection, either through tacit approval of the issuer's current auditor or by requesting a change to a Big-4 firm.

One could legitimately argue that the economic impact of the auditor is not large enough to justify a time-consuming and costly selection process. Auditors do not produce new information, they only attest to the veracity of the existing financial statements. Beyond their reputation it is not obvious what service benefit prestigious auditors provide.[26] Nevertheless, an examination of the costs and benefits of hiring a prestigious auditor is a useful exercise, as not all issuers use a Big-4 firm and the auditing market is continually evolving.

Costs: The audit cost is made up of two components, a production cost and an expected loss component (Beatty 1993). The production cost increases in the traditional measures of audit complexity: the firm size, the number of consolidated subsidiaries, the percentage of the value in foreign subsidiaries, and inventories and receivables relative to total assets (Beatty and Welch 1996). The loss component is a function of the litigation risk and the damage done to the auditor's reputation from a lawsuit.

Liability is a very real concern for the auditors of IPOs that have gone bad. Bunsis and Drake (1995) reported that from 1980 to 1989 auditors were attached to 45 of 119 IPO lawsuits, although the number dropped to only seven of 92 during the 1990–94 period. Since lawsuits are costly, compensation should be higher when the *ex ante* probability of litigation is greater. Beatty (1993) documented that issuers subject to a post-IPO lawsuit were charged higher audit fees pre-IPO. However, Beatty and Welch (1996) found no relation between audit fees and liability risk after controlling for other factors affecting compensation.

Big-4 auditors have the most reputation capital at stake when they attest to the accuracy of an issuer's financial statements and therefore should charge a premium. The compensation should also increase in the riskiness of the issuer, as the potential damage to the reputation and probability of litigation increase. Not surprisingly, Beatty (1989; 1993) reported that top-tier audit firms charged higher fees, all else being equal. Mayhew and Wilkens (2002) found that auditors that had a significantly higher IPO market share within an industry than their competitors – suggestive of a good reputation – charged a premium.

Benefits: The principal benefit of a prestigious auditor is the certification it conveys about the issuer quality. Prestigious auditors demand that the financial statements provide the most accurate reflection possible of the issuer's financial health to avoid a potential lawsuit. This minimizes the adverse selection risk for investors, leading to a higher offer price. Certification can also reduce the required underpricing, producing a negative correlation between auditor reputation and initial returns, a fact documented by a number of studies (Balvers, McDonald and Miller 1988; Beatty 1989; Beatty and Welch 1996).

The choice of auditor should reflect the trade-off between the cost of higher quality and the benefit of additional net proceeds. Titman and Trueman (1986) argued that, similar to selecting an underwriter, high quality issuers hire more prestigious auditors because they receive the most benefit for the expense. In essence, the issuer selects the auditor that minimizes the combined underpricing and compensation costs. Hogan (1997) estimated that issuers that hired high (low) quality auditors would have increased their total costs had they instead chosen low (high) quality auditors, thus providing some evidence that issuers think strategically about the auditor selection.

9.3.2.1 Risk-quality trade-off

There is an ongoing debate in the accounting literature over the type of relationship between issuer risk and auditor quality. One group argues for an inverse relationship because as the risk increases, the compensation for high quality auditors goes up faster than the benefit from certification (Titman and Trueman 1986). Others who advocate a positive relationship believe that the insider owners of the riskiest issuers benefit most from a high quality auditor (Datar, Feltham and Hughes 1991). Insiders have conflicting objectives at the IPO; diversify their portfolio and signal the firm quality. Hiring a prestigious auditor is an attractive way to signal firm quality that avoids the alternative of retaining a large fraction of the risky shares.

The evidence offers qualified support for the positive relationship camp. Early studies generally found a negative relation and concluded that the supply-side effect – higher compensation – dominated the selection decision as risk increased (Beatty 1989; Simunic and Stein 1987; Feltham, Hughes and Simunic 1991). The initial findings were challenged along two fronts. First, inferences are sensitive to the measure of issuer risk. Using Altman's Z-score for bankruptcy risk, Copley and Douthett (2002) reported a positive relation.

The second challenge emphasized the effect of the legal environment. The litigiousness of US investors drives up the expected loss component of auditor fees, which may account for the negative relationship. Countries with lower litigation risk provide a cleaner test of the theory. Clarkson and Simunic (1994) found a positive relationship between issuer risk and auditor quality, and a negative relation between quality and managerial retained equity in Canada. Lee et al. (2003) drew the same conclusion for small Australian IPOs that did not hire a Big-6 auditing firm.

9.3.3 Legal Counsel

Legal counsel offers little in the way of certification benefit to issuers, but their negotiating skills and experience can have an impact on the IPO outcome. Experienced lawyers, especially those who have dealt with post-IPO litigation, may be inclined to argue for more risk factors in the prospectus and a more negative overall tone to protect the issuer from legal liability. Such actions will undoubtedly lower the attractiveness of the IPO to investors. Beatty and Welch (1996), in contrast, speculated that lawyers, relatively insulated from legal liability, allow issuers to be more aggressive in the prospectus.

An indirect test of the hypothesis that experience will be negatively correlated with the overall tone was conducted by Barondes and Sanger (2000). They argued that one manifestation of the influence of experienced lawyers would be a smaller positive offer price revision. Legal experience was proxied with the law firm's IPO market share. A significantly negative relationship between the experience of the underwriter's legal counsel and the offer price revision was found, but there was no relationship for issuer legal counsel. Underwriter counsel generally had a much larger market share, which may explain their greater influence in advocating caution when setting the offer price.

9.4 SUMMARY

The IPO process begins many months before the actual offer date. As part of the IPO preparations, an issuer must hire the necessary advisors: an underwriter, an auditor and legal counsel. The underwriter is the most important advisor because of the intermediary role it plays between the issuer and investors. Various criteria are used to select an underwriter, including its ability to minimize the costs of going public, the quality of analyst coverage, its reputation, industry specialization and monitoring services.

Underwriter compensation, the contractual provisions of the underwriting agreement and the certification provided by the underwriter are all interrelated. The underwriting spread for most US IPOs is now 7 percent. There is little evidence that the high spread is the result of collusion, and underwriters appear to provide better service when the spread is higher. The firm commitment contract dominates the US market, although best efforts contracts have been used with some frequency in the past and auctions may be used more in the future. Prestigious banks put their reputation on the line and certify the quality of issuers, thereby raising the issuer's net proceeds. Superior certification does come at the cost of higher compensation.

Auditors and lawyers also play important roles in the IPO process. Part of their responsibility is to ensure that all materially relevant information is disclosed and accurate to minimize the probability and cost of post-IPO litigation. Underpricing is one means to reduce the litigation risk, another is more risk factors in the prospectus. The choice of auditor usually comes down to selecting one of the Big-4. Prestigious auditors can increase the IPO proceeds through their certification, but this comes with a higher cost.

NOTES

1. Schrand and Verrechia (2002) reported that the post-IPO disclosure frequency positively related to underpricing, suggesting that issuers took measures to reduce their high cost of capital.
2. Huyghebeart and Van Hulle (2001) reported that Belgian firms usually chose the number of primary shares to sell first based on capital needs, and then adjusted the secondary portion to achieve sufficient aftermarket liquidity.
3. The purpose of the syndicate has changed over time. Historically, it was intended to satisfy regulatory capital requirements, obtain risk-sharing benefits, and create a larger distribution network.
4. Re-printed from the *Journal of Financial Research*, Vol. 19, Lee, I., S. Lochhead, J. Ritter and Q. Zhao, "The Costs of Going Public," pp. 59-74, Copyright (1996) with permission.
5. This quote fist appeared in Das, Guo and Zhang (2002).
6. This was reported by Loughran and Ritter (2002b), who were quoting Bruce Foerster of South Beach Capital.
7. The breakdown of the spread is based on analysis in Chen and Ritter (2000). They provide a thorough example of how the spread is paid out to syndicate members.
8. See Burch and Foerster (2002).
9. Altinkilic and Hansen (2000) found evidence of a u-shaped relationship between compensation and offer size, challenging the conjecture of economies of scale.
10. After the Chen and Ritter (2000) article was circulated in 1998, the US Department of Justice began an investigation into the 'alleged conspiracy among securities underwriters to fix underwriting fees'. It also inspired a class action lawsuit against 27 banks for not competing on price. The Justice Department subsequently dropped the case, while the lawsuit was dropped following a judge's ruling in favor of the defendants.
11. A direct international comparison of spreads is misleading because different mechanisms are used, such as auctions and fixed-priced offerings, that require different levels of underwriter service.
12. Bankers who felt they were not colluding would have no reason to change their pricing practices. In contrast, Christie and Schultz (1994) documented collusive practices among NASDAQ dealers to avoid odd-eighth quotes, which stopped after their paper was circulated (Christie, Harris and Schultz 1994).
13. Supporting this conclusion, Bajaj et al. (2003b) documented that average spreads declined from 8.31 to 6.94 percent during 1980–98. The increased clustering at 7 percent was due mostly to a decline in spreads above 7 percent.
14. See Chapter 10 for a detailed description of book-building.
15. Hansen and Torregrosa (1992) reject other possibilities for this relation. There is no obvious relation between the stake and underwriter marketing effort. Certification costs and the spread should, if anything, increase with the stake because the managers benefit from misleading investors to buy overpriced equity.
16. Efficient risk-sharing dictates that the bank should underwrite IPOs by the riskiest firms, but only distribute the shares of low risk issuers when the fixed cost of underwriting is too high (Mandelker and Raviv 1977).
17. The data in Ritter (1987) and Chua (1995) cover the period 1977-88. Firm commitment and best efforts IPOs varied in offer size ($15.3 vs $2.9 million), offer price ($9.5 vs $1.5) and age of issuer (10.6 vs 3.8 years).
18. Based on the data in Ritter (1987) and Chua (1995), 28 percent of all IPOs for less than $2 million were firm commitment offers. Presumably, at least some of best efforts issuers could have used the firm commitment contract.
19. Welch (1991) found that the MSC was unrelated to the level of risk, when in fact the two should be positively related for the adverse selection argument to hold.

20. The reputation proxies could be capturing distinct aspects of underwriter quality. Bates and Dunbar (2002) found that the Tombstone proxy was negatively related to underpricing after controlling for market share, which was positively related to the first-day return.
21. See Loughran and Ritter (2002b), Cooney et al. (2001) and Beatty and Welch (1996), whose analysis pre-dates the hot market of the late 1990s.
22. Nanda and Yun (1997) argued that the market share proxy was a poor measure of reputation because market share evolves exogenously with changes in the type of issuers coming to the market.
23. Logue et al. (2001) found that reputation had almost no effect on the initial returns after controlling for the offer price revision, suggesting that reputable underwriters affect the initial return through their superior services and not some intangible quality.
24. The high cost of mounting a lawsuit means that they should be targeted only to those firms with sufficiently 'deep pockets'. In fact, sued IPOs were significantly larger in terms of issue proceeds and market valuations, had higher quality underwriters and were more likely to have VC-backing (Lowry and Shu 2002).
25. The average payment was $4 million in the 60 suits that were settled, or about 13 percent of the IPO proceeds.
26. Lee, Taylor and Taylor (2002) indirectly test auditor ability by examining the accuracy of management earnings forecasts in Australian IPOs. They found only weak evidence that forecasts attested to by the former Big-6 auditors were more accurate, but the forecast bias was significantly less optimistic.

10. IPO mechanisms: allocations and pricing

An IPO, at its core, is the sale of commodities from a seller to multiple buyers. The seller is the issuing firm, the buyers are investors and the commodities are shares in the firm. An IPO mechanism defines the rules and procedures issuers and underwriters must follow to sell the offering to investors. The set of possible mechanisms is almost limitless, with each having a slightly different effect on the final outcome of the IPO.

An optimal mechanism for issuers is one that maximizes the expected IPO proceeds. Two questions naturally come to mind when thinking about this issue. What does an optimal mechanism look like and how does it work? And do any of the mechanisms used in practice resemble the theoretically optimal mechanism? Mechanisms differ in how shares are priced and allocated, the role of the underwriter and investor participation. The current systems can be appraised by comparing the empirical patterns of actual IPOs to the theoretical optimum. Understanding how IPO mechanisms work is more urgent than ever because of the hot IPO market of the late 1990s. Revelations of unscrupulous and illegal practices by investment banks have led to calls for major reforms. An important corollary to the operation of IPO mechanisms is the underpricing puzzle. Any explanation for underpricing must be viewed within the context of mechanism efficiency and the objectives of the issuer.

Defining the optimality of a mechanism based solely on its ability to maximize proceeds is rather narrow and excludes other important considerations for policy-makers. Regulators may care about how fairly a mechanism treats different classes of investors. Another criterion for mechanism optimality is that it results in a socially efficient number of firms going public. Assessing mechanisms based on these other criteria is beyond the scope of this chapter.

10.1 IPO MECHANISMS

All IPO mechanisms fit into one of three categories: book-building, auctions or fixed-price offerings. Variations occur within each category, with differences in when and how the offer price is set, when and which investors can submit orders and the allocation rule for distributing shares. By and large, issuers do not get to choose their IPO mechanism. Either regulatory constraints limit the choice or market forces dictate that certain types of issuers must use a particular method. The following sections review the general properties of the three mechanisms.

10.1.1 Book-building

The major distinguishing characteristic of book-building is the discretion afforded to the underwriter and issuer to price and allocate the shares. The term book-building is used to describe firm commitment IPOs because the underwriter markets the offering to investors and attempts to 'build the book' of orders. The marketing phase begins after the registration statement is filed with the SEC. The first step is to distribute the preliminary prospectus, or 'red herring', to the underwriter's sales force and potential investors. The preliminary prospectus states the expected offer size and may include the expected number of shares and a preliminary offer price range. The underwriter also prepares a selling memorandum, which is given to the sales force. The selling memo usually has earnings and revenue forecasts and comparable firm multiples.

The issuer's executives and its underwriter promote the IPO through a 'road show', traveling around the country to pitch the offering to investors. The typical road show lasts two to three weeks, with multiple presentations a day to institutional investors. The road show is an opportunity for two-way communication between the issuer/underwriter and investors. The presentation elaborates on the material contained in the prospectus. If any new materially relevant information is disclosed at one of the presentations, the prospectus may have to be revised and resubmitted for SEC approval.

The road show enables the underwriter to learn about investor demand through indications of interest. An investor could specify the number of shares he or she would like to buy, set a limit price for the purchase or provide only general interest. The indications are not legally binding orders and can be rescinded without a formal penalty. The offer terms are revised based on investor interest. An amended registration statement must be submitted to the SEC stating the revised terms.

Pricing the IPO is as much art as it is science. The science part makes use of the issuer's comps and the limit prices supplied by the investors. The art of pricing IPOs involves gauging the true investor interest based on the multiple conversations leading up to the offer date. Skilled underwriters have a well-developed ability to read the mareket and are able to combine the two parts. The Penny Stock Reform Act of 1990 imposed severe restrictions on IPOs with offer prices below $5 in an attempt to curb fraudulent security issues, effectively limiting the price to be above $5.

Following SEC approval of the registration statement, the underwriter files a request to accelerate the effective date of the statement. Shares can only be sold once the offering is effective. Company executives and the lead underwriter set the final offer price and number of shares immediately prior to the effective date, which is when the IPO occurs. The underwriter concurrently decides on the allocation of shares.

The book-building method in many European countries differs from the aforementioned US approach in two major ways. First, investment banks actively solicit investor interest prior to the issuer actually filing to go public, something that is strictly prohibited in the US. Consequently, the preliminary price range already incorporates much of the investor information that is only revealed later for US IPOs. Second, a gray or forward market for the issuers' shares is open concurrently with the marketing phase. The gray market price is informative about the likely market price and can influence the final offer price.

10.1.2 Fixed Price Mechanisms

The fixed-price mechanism – called an open offer, public offer or universal offer – differs from book-building in two major ways. First, the final offer price is chosen prior to soliciting orders from investors. The offer price is included in the preliminary prospectus and is set anywhere from two weeks to two months prior to the offer date. Second, the underwriter does not actively sell fixed-price IPOs. It distributes the prospectus to potential investors, collects order applications and allocates the shares.[1]

Fixed-price mechanisms constrain the underwriter's pricing and share allocation discretion. The issuer and underwriter are free to choose the offer price, but it is not conditional on investor demand. The underwriter must treat all investor share applications, whether institutional or retail, equally in the allocation due to fairness rules. The lone exception is discrimination based on order size. The 'fill-rate' policy is stated in the prospectus. An even-handed policy leads to a pro rata share allocation when the issue is oversubscribed. Deviations from an even-handed policy almost always favor small orders, a bias likely to benefit retail investors. Investors are usually required to send in a check for the requested shares along with their application. The money for the unfilled orders is refunded to the investor. The underwriter earns the interest float for the one to two weeks between the order submission and the offer date.

Hybrid mechanisms that combine book-building with an open offer have gained popularity. The underwriter uses book-building to price and allocate shares to institutional investors and an open offer for retail investors. Variations exist in the exact structure of hybrid methods. France uses one method in which the book-building and open offer portions run simultaneously. Instead of a fixed price, the open offer uses the book-building offer price range, with the final offer price still determined by book-building.

10.1.3 Auctions

Auctions afford the issuer and underwriter the least amount of control in determining the IPO outcome. Investors submit orders specifying the number of shares and the limit price at which they will buy. In a uniform price auction – sometimes mistakenly referred to as a Dutch auction on Wall Street – the individual orders are aggregated into a cumulative demand curve. The offer price is determined by the intersection of the demand curve and the fixed supply. All investors who submitted a bid above the offer price have their orders filled; bids at the offer are pro-rated filled. An investor pays what he or she bid in a discriminatory price auction. The underwriter slides down the aggregate demand curve filling orders until the supply is exhausted. The underwriter is once again passive in the IPO. The bids are effectively anonymous, as shares are allocated in a non-discriminatory basis to institutional and retail investors.

Hybrid mechanisms exist that combine auctions and an open offer. Japan and Taiwan both use a mechanism that begins with a discriminatory price auction for 50 percent of the offer size, followed by an open offer for the remaining shares. A minimum bid price is specified for the auction and any unsold shares are included in the open offer. In Taiwan, the open offer price equals either the quantity-weighted average winning bid price in the auction or 1.5 times the minimum bid price, whichever is lower. The open offer price in the Japanese method used to equal the weighted-average bid, but now the issuer and underwriter are freer to negotiate discounts.

Some auction rules grant the underwriter a small amount of pricing discretion. A reservation price specifies the minimum acceptable bid. The prospectus could include a price range the underwriter believes the offer price should fall within, guiding investors in their bids. The underwriter can sometimes disregard bids with limit prices far in excess of the market-clearing price. These bids are an attempt to guarantee an allocation, without providing a reasonable assessment of the share value.

So-called 'dirty auctions' use the allocation rules of a formal auction with the twist that the underwriter has some discretion in setting the final offer price. The *offre a prix minimum* (OPM) method in France has this property. Investors submit price-quantity bids and a market-clearing price is determined, but the underwriter can select a final offer price below the auction price.

The advent of the Internet has created the possibility of conducting low-cost auctions online. W.R. Hambrecht created an online auction called OpenIPO, which has sold seven IPOs as of May 2003. The OpenIPO web site states that investors are instructed to 'make a bid at the maximum price at which they are comfortable owning shares of the issue'. The use of a uniform price auction ensures that 'IPO offering prices are set by the market', and reflect 'what people are truly willing to pay for the stock'.

10.1.4 Mechanism Use

Book-building is becoming the dominant mechanism worldwide. Ljungqvist, Jenkinson and Wilhelm (2003) estimated that book-building now accounts for 80 percent of all IPOs outside the US and Canada. The gain in popularity of book-building has come at the expense of auctions and, to a lessor extent, fixed-price methods. Few countries rely on auctions exclusively. Table 10.1, taken from Sherman (2001) with slight modifications, lists the mechanisms currently used in a large cross-section of countries.

The growing popularity of book-building has been aided by changing regulatory environments, as more governments are allowing it as an alternative to auctions and fixed-price methods. The gains made by book-building also reflect market forces at work. Countries such as France and Japan that had used auctions, and only recently allowed book-building, are now dominated by book-built IPOs. Issuers, underwriters and institutional investors appear to universally favor book-building when given the choice.

10.2 MECHANISM EFFICIENCY

An efficient IPO mechanism is one that maximizes expected proceeds. The subsequent analysis looks for the properties of an efficient mechanism and examines the efficiency of the three main methods. Issuers can and do have multiple objectives they would like to achieve with the offering, not all of which are compatible with proceeds maximization. These other objectives and their impact on the offer price are reviewed later in the chapter in the section on underpricing.

The challenge confronting all mechanisms is the opposing interests of the issuer and investors. While the issuer wants to maximize the offer price, investors want to minimize it. Complicating matters is the presence of

Table 10.1 IPO mechanism use across countries[2]

	Book-building	Fixed Price Past	Fixed Price Today	Auctions
Europe				
Austria	Yes	Yes		
Czech Republic		Yes	Yes	
Finland	Yes	Yes	Yes	
France	Yes	Yes		Sometimes
Germany	Yes	Yes		
Hungary	Yes	Yes	Yes	
Ireland		Yes	Yes	
Italy	Yes	Yes		
Netherlands	Yes	Yes		
Norway	Yes	Yes		Sometimes
Portugal	Yes	Yes	Yes	
Spain	Yes			
Sweden	Yes	Yes	Yes	
Switzerland	Yes	Yes		
United Kingdom	Yes	Yes	Yes	
N & S America				
Argentina	Yes			
Barbados		Yes	Yes	
Brazil	Yes	Yes	Yes	
Canada	Yes			
Chile	Yes			Hybrid
Mexico		Yes		
Paraguay		Yes	Yes	
Peru	Yes	Yes	Yes	Sometimes
United States	Yes			Sometimes
Asia/Pacific				
Australia	Yes	Yes		
Bangladesh		Yes	Yes	
China	Yes	Yes	Yes	
Hong Kong	Yes	Yes	Yes	
India		Yes	Yes	
Indonesia		Yes	Yes	
Japan	Yes			
Korea	Yes	Yes		
Malaysia		Yes	Yes	
New Zealand	Yes	Yes	Yes	
Philippines	Yes	Yes		
Singapore		Yes	Yes	
Taiwan		Yes	Yes	Yes
Thailand		Yes	Yes	
Other				
Kenya		Yes	Yes	
Israel		Yes	Yes	Yes
Jordan		Yes	Yes	
South Africa		Yes		
Turkey		Yes	Yes	

Source: Sherman (2001).

private information. Issuer management knows far more about the true firm value than investors. Underwriter reputation concerns and legal liability are sufficient to prevent the issuer from exploiting its inside information and setting too high a price. Investors also have private information, the maximum price each is willing to pay. Collectively, investors want to understate their interest in the IPO to drive the offer price down. The ability of a mechanism to induce investors to pay their private valuation determines its efficiency.

The participation of two distinct types of investors – institutional and retail – in the IPO throws another twist into the mechanism design problem. The economic environment and regulatory constraints could dictate that both investor types participate. Institutional and retail investors are differentially informed, with institutions possessing more precise information about the issuer value. An optimal mechanism must take into account the heterogeneous nature of the potential IPO investors.

10.2.1 Book-building Efficiency

The key to maximizing the offer price is getting investors to truthfully reveal their private value to the underwriter. Economic theory has examined in detail the optimal selling mechanism in general settings of trade when buyers have private information. Benveniste and Spindt (1989) were the first to apply these ideas to the IPO context. They started with basic assumptions about the information and institutional environment likely to characterize the book-building primary market. From these assumptions, efficient pricing and share allocation rules were derived that maximized the expected IPO proceeds.

The properties of the optimal mechanism derived by Benveniste and Spindt and the intuition for the results are best illustrated by working through a simple scenario.[3] An issuer is selling shares with a true value of either $8 or $12; the exact value is unknown by the underwriter. Investors evaluate the issuer at a cost to form a more precise expectation for the value. If the true value is $12, an investor will assign greater probability to the value being $12 than $8, and vice versa if the true value is $8.

The underwriter solicits interest from the investors in the primary market, asking what price they would be willing to pay. Investors have an incentive to state $8 even if they believe the more likely value is $12. The practice of understating the value creates a problem for the underwriter. Since the bank cannot differentiate between $8 and $12 firms, it must set a price close to $8 for all IPOs, otherwise too few investors will participate when the true value is $8. Investors profit from their private information – called informational rent – when the value is $12 and the price is near $8.

Benveniste and Spindt demonstrated that there are pricing and allocation rules the underwriter could use to increase the expected IPO proceeds. The optimal rules look something like the following. Investors who report a value near $8 receive the smallest share allocation possible, contingent on the IPO being completed, whereas investors who report a value close to $12 receive large allocations. The offer price is set equal to the expected share value, conditional on all values reported by investors. If the number of investors reporting a high value exceeds a critical level, the underwriter intentionally underprices. For example, the offer price will be $8 if all investors report $8, but it will equal $10 if they all report $12.

The mechanism maximizes expected proceeds because it induces truthful revelation of private information. An investor who deliberately understates his or her value to drive the offer price down also reduces his or her allocation. The offer price will be set slightly lower, but without underpricing he or she only makes a small profit on the allocation. The risk to the investor from lying is that many other investors report high values, further reducing his or her allocation in what could be an underpriced IPO. Truthfully reporting the value substantially increases the allocation in underpriced IPOs without significantly increasing the price. The *ex ante* commitment to intentionally underprice actually maximizes the proceeds received, despite any appearance to the contrary.

The underwriter can further improve the mechanism efficiency by including more investors in the IPO. The information of any one investor becomes less important, reducing the underpricing necessary for truthful revelation. The number of shares that must be allocated to investors reporting a low value decreases, further reducing underpricing, strengthening the incentive to be honest. The model makes a number of predictions for the pricing and allocation patterns in book-built IPOs.

1. Intentional underpricing increases with the level of informed investor interest – captured in the scenario by the number of investors reporting a high value – leading to a 'hot' offering.

2. Starting from the preliminary offer price, positive information revelation leads to an upward revision of the price. The price is only partially revised for hot IPOs, producing a positive covariance between the price revision and the initial return. The price is fully revised downward when negative information is revealed.

3. Informed investors, usually institutions, receive priority in the share allocation. The institutional allocation increases with the amount of

underpricing because the two are jointly determined by the positive information revealed by the institutions.

The simple scenario described above can be enriched to provide a more realistic characterization of the primary market. The book-building mechanism possesses properties that allow it to further improve performance in this richer environment. For these reasons, many academics believe that book-building is the best mechanism.

Discretion and flexibility: The ability to discriminate between investors in the share allocation increases the expected proceeds (Biais and Faugeron-Crouzet 2002).[4] Investors who reveal their private valuation expect a certain amount of informational rent in return. The rent can be effectively provided through any number of allocation/underpricing combinations. Allocation discretion enables the underwriter to minimize underpricing by giving large allocations to investors who report high values. The underwriter has less incentive to even canvass investor interest when they cannot be effectively compensated, compounding the problem caused by lack of discretion.

Flexibility to adjust the offering terms at the last moment also lowers the underpricing cost (Benveniste and Busaba 1997). The underwriter can increase the number of shares offered if investor interest is strong. Since investors have already revealed their values, the rent is fixed. Issuing more shares reduces the required per share underpricing. A standard feature of most book-built IPOs is the over-allotment option (OAO), which gives the underwriter the option to increase the offer size by up to 15 percent. Exercising the option only when demand is strong will reduce underpricing.

Repeated interaction: The benefit to allocation discrimination is enhanced by repeated interaction between the underwriter and institutional investors over multiple IPOs. The underwriter can promise an investor access to all IPOs, including those that are underpriced. The threat of exclusion from future hot offerings empowers the underwriter to demand lower underpricing in the current IPO (Benveniste and Spindt 1989). The implicit threat also forces regular investors to accept allocations in poor offerings. The pool of regular investors generally consists of institutions, but the threat of exclusion for regular retail investors can further reduce underpricing (Sherman 2001).

Efficient information production: A positive by-product of forming a pool of regular informed investors is that the underwriter can indirectly control the amount of information produced. Investors are not endowed with knowledge about the issuer; they must exert costly effort to evaluate the firm. Issuers can ultimately bear the evaluation costs through a lower offer price. The optimal size of the informed investor pool is determined by a trade-off between the additional underpricing cost and the benefit of more information (Sherman and Titman 2002). Greater information production results in a more accurate aftermarket price, provides feedback about the value of investment projects, confirms the underwriter's certification ability, improves liquidity and reduces the possibility of a lawsuit. Lack of allocation discretion can result in either too much or too little information being produced and higher issuing costs.

Winner's curse: Asymmetric information between different groups of investors can result in additional underpricing. Informed investors use their superior knowledge to 'cherry-pick' underpriced IPOs and avoid overpriced issues. Uninformed investors cannot differentiate issuer quality and indiscriminately participate in all IPOs. Consequently, the allocations to the uninformed are biased towards overpriced shares. As a result, these investors lose on average over a large number of IPOs – the winner's curse from receiving an IPO allocation. All IPOs must be underpriced if the participation of uninformed investors is necessary (Rock 1986). The expected initial return – the realized initial returns weighted by the probability of receiving an allocation – from the perspective of the uninformed should then equal the risk-free rate.

Book-building eliminates the winner's curse, reducing the required underpricing relative to the fixed-price method (Biais and Faugeron-Crouzet 2002). The fixed offer price is set before investors reveal any information, making it susceptible to overpricing. The book-built offer price adjusts to reflect the information revealed in the primary market and is never set above the conditional expected value. The uninformed do not have to worry about being receiving overpriced shares.

10.2.2.1 Underwriter objectives

The objectives to be achieved with an IPO differ between the issuer and its underwriter. The IPO is a one-time event for the issuer, who wants to maximize the proceeds. A typical bank underwrites multiple security offerings and interacts repeatedly with the same investors in different contexts. Maximizing the profits from all these activities is the bank's objective. The underwriter will undoubtedly use its influence in the IPO process to choose a pricing and allocation strategy that is biased towards achieving its goals, which may not include maximizing expected proceeds.

Trading commissions generated by institutional investors are a major source of bank revenue. Investors that have generated large commissions in the past, and presumably the future, expect to receive preferential IPO allocations (Fulghieri and Spiegel 1993). Favoritism shown by the underwriter towards a pool of regular investors could reflect a quid pro quo of trading commissions for underpriced shares.[5] The regular investors need not provide value estimates to receive their allocation. Regardless, underpricing can still be reduced if the underwriter has the discretion to exclude investors from the pool.

A quid pro quo arrangement between the underwriter and institutional investors could give rise to collusion against the issuer. In return for greater underpricing, the investors direct more commissions to the underwriter, benefiting both parties at the issuer's expense. Biais, Bossaerts and Rochet (2002) proposed a mechanism that would help the issuer overcome the collusion. For every price the underwriter reports that the institutions are willing to pay, the issuer will select the size of the retail allocation. The underwriter is induced to reveal the true institutional valuation if the retail allocation decreases in the reported value. The underwriter will admit when the value is high and set a high offer price, otherwise retail investors would receive too many underpriced shares.[6]

The allocation decision is also influenced by a bank's desire to win future business. Spinning is the practice of allocating underpriced shares to the senior executives of companies from whom the bank hopes to win new underwriting mandates. Maynard (2002) argued that spinning is a form of corporate bribery and may violate the legal doctrine of 'corporate opportunity'. Corporate executives have a fiduciary responsibility to their shareholders. When they select an underwriter because they received hot IPO shares, and not because it was the best candidate for the job, the executives are not acting in shareholders' interests. The settlement reached in April 2003 between the market regulators and the major investment banks imposed a ban on future spinning.

10.2.2 Fixed-price Methods: Theory

The fixed-price mechanism is essentially a restricted version of book-building. The underwriter does not collect information from investors prior to setting the offer price and shares are allocated in a non-discriminatory manner. The optimality of a mechanism that relies on discretion and information gathering naturally implies that the fixed-price method is sub-optimal. However, the fixed-price method does have some virtues that make it useful in appropriate circumstances.

Information cascades: An investor's decision to apply for shares is based on his private valuation and any information gleaned from the early

225

demand. Information leakages that indicate demand is heavy and the IPO is underpriced may lead an investor to ignore his low valuation and subscribe to the offering. An information cascade ensues if all subsequent investors ignore their respective private valuations and buy based on the revealed demand. Such herd behavior can result in a successful IPO, even if the private valuations are generally low. Welch (1992) argued that the underwriter could guarantee an IPO's success by underpricing sufficiently to induce early investors to buy, starting a positive information cascade. Information leakages are more likely when the subscription period is lengthy. Chowdhry and Sherman (1996b) predicted that the probability of either a vastly oversubscribed IPO generating high initial returns or an under-subscribed and withdrawn offer increases in this length.

Risk aversion: Book-building results in higher expected proceeds than the fixed-price method. However, fixed-price offers have the advantage of lower *ex ante* uncertainty over the issue proceeds (Benveniste and Busaba 1997). The offer price can be chosen to guarantee the IPO's success with known proceeds, whereas the proceeds from book-building are uncertain prior to the marketing stage. Highly risk-averse issuers may prefer the relative safety of a fixed-price offer.

Marketing costs: The fixed-price method does not require a costly selling effort by the underwriter, such as conducting a road show. The incremental cost of book-building over fixed-price methods may not be justified for small offerings. In addition, the advantage of developing long-term relationships is not likely to confer much benefit in a market with few IPOs. The fixed-price mechanism is probably the best alternative in small markets, such as Barbados and Finland.

10.2.3 Auctions: Theory

Economic theory argues that auctions are an efficient mechanism in many different markets. It seems logical to conclude that an auction would be efficient in the IPO context as well. Auctions also have appeal on fairness grounds. The underwriter's role in the IPO is greatly diminished, removing the possibility of self-serving behavior on the bank's part. The initial conjecture of IPO auction efficiency is not actually borne out by the theory. Auctions are essentially a constrained version of book-building, with the underwriter specifying the auction rules prior to investors submitting orders.[7] Consequently, auctions should, at best, generate the same expected proceeds as book-building.

An IPO is a common value auction because each share is worth the same to all investors. An IPO auction also involves a divisible good, as the equity sold consists of millions of shares. In this setting Ausubel and Crampton (1998) documented that a discriminatory price auction produces less expected proceeds than a uniform price auction, which generates less expected proceeds than a dynamic ascending price auction. In the latter, the winning bidders – those who are still bidding when the aggregate demand equals the supply – pay the final market clearing price.

Auctions are associated with underpricing, although it is not intentional on the underwriter's part. Whenever bidders have private information they earn rent as compensation for revealing their true valuations. Thus, the expected value of the issuer's proceeds will be less than the expected market value of the shares, with the difference equal to the amount of underpricing. Expected underpricing corresponds with the auction efficiency; discriminatory price auctions will be more underpriced than uniform price auctions. The intuition for underpricing in a discriminatory price auction is based on the winner's curse. Investors uncertain about the true value are concerned with overpaying, which causes them to shade their bids below their private valuations. A uniform price auction eliminates this problem because the offer price is the lowest winning bid; investors do not have to fear overpaying if they bid their valuations.

10.2.3.1 Tacit collusion

Underpricing in uniform price auctions could occur because of tacit collusion. Among the multiple bidding strategy equilibria that exist in a uniform price auction are some in which the investors symmetrically lower their demand. The offer price in such equilibria is far below the market-clearing level. Back and Zender (1993) derived the necessary conditions for low price equilibria and argued that investors will focus on these bidding strategies.

The intuition for the tacit collusion bidding equilibria is as follows. A bidding strategy consists of an entire demand curve, specifying the number of shares for each price. At low price equilibria the share offering is split among the investors. An investor could deviate by bidding a higher demand curve to increase his allocation, but without too much effect on the price. To enforce the collusive low bid equilibrium, the bidding demand curves must be steep. That way, in order for a deviating investor to significantly increase his allocation he would have to bid a much higher demand. The rise in the offer price would actually reduce the deviating investor's profits. Tacit collusion is difficult to maintain as more investors participate. The collusive allocation becomes smaller, whereas deviation leads to a larger allocation with less effect on the price. IPOs, with thousands of bidders, seem to be an unlikely candidate for collusion.

10.2.3.2 Inefficient information production

Proponents of IPO auctions point to their practical implementation as a reason why they should replace book-building. In theory, auctions may not generate greater expected proceeds than book-building, but they will work better in practice because the optimal pricing and allocation rules are not subject to manipulation by the underwriter. A major flaw in this argument is the narrow perspective it takes of the IPO. It assumes that investors are already informed about the issuer and that the mechanism only has to get investors to pay the maximum price. A more accurate characterization is that investors start the IPO process relatively uninformed. A mechanism's efficiency is then be judged by how much information it produces and how effectively that translates into higher proceeds. An auction consisting of uninformed bidders is far less attractive than a book-built IPO. Auctions can result in inefficient information production for three reasons.

Primary market supply: Book-building involves a more active underwriter marketing effort compared to auctions, which should result in a greater transfer of private information from the issuer to investors. Book-building also indirectly signals quality. The high cost of a book-built IPO will only be incurred if the issuer has positive information to convey. Restricting issuers to auctions leads to an insufficient amount of information revelation and possibly too few firms going public (Kutsuna and Smith 2003). Small and risky issuers who likely suffer from the most severe information asymmetries would benefit from being able to reveal private information through a book-built IPO.

Primary market production: The underwriter has no control over which investors bid in an auction. Consequently, either too little or too much information is produced (Sherman 2001). The most likely outcome is too little because of the free-rider problem. Investors want to avoid costly information production, yet still receive an allocation. Placing a high, uninformed bid in a uniform price auction guarantees an allocation without any cost. The offer price is uninformative when too many investors free-ride. Book-building avoids the free-rider problem because the underwriter can discriminate against uninformed investors.

Secondary market production: Continued information production in the aftermarket is critical for the long-term success of the issuer because it leads to greater price accuracy and liquidity. Since institutional investors do not receive preferential treatment in auctions, they could end up with small allocations. A position of only a few thousand shares is not a practical use of funds in a billion-dollar portfolio. Without a guarantee of a minimum-sized allocation, an institution might decline to participate in an IPO.[8] Reduced information production results from fewer institutions participating and the diminished analyst coverage that engenders.

Issuers who expect at the time of the IPO to complete a follow-on offering desire price accuracy in the aftermarket and the information production is requires. Underpricing the IPO could create price momentum and compensate investors for future information costs. The flexibility of book-building to underprice makes it an attractive alternative to auctions for issuers who have a dynamic issuing strategy (Chemmanur and Liu 2001).

10.2.3.3 'Dirty auctions'

The conventional uniform price auction can be modified to help it overcome some of its deficiencies regarding information production. Dirty auctions, like the OPM method in France, allow the underwriter to select an offer price below the market-clearing level, but shares are still allocated on a pro-rated basis. Excessively high bids can be ignored, which reduces the free-rider problem. The intentional underpricing should result in greater aftermarket information production.

In addition, tacit collusion is harder to sustain because the underpricing reduces the sensitivity of the offer price to total demand. An investor can deviate and increase his demand without affecting the price too much (Biais and Faugeron-Crouzet 2002). However, a dirty auction is still not as efficient as book-building. Uninformed investors earn informational rent in underpriced IPOs; an issuing cost that can be eliminated when the underwriter can discriminate against them.

10.3 ALLOCATIONS AND PRICING

Taking the theory to data serves two purposes. First, the explicit predictions made about the pricing and share allocation patterns in each mechanism can be tested to see if investors and underwriters behave in the manner expected. The insights garnered from this first stage of empirical analysis can then be used to resolve the question of mechanism efficiency. Theory argues that book-building is efficient because the underwriter can implement specific pricing and allocation rules that maximize the expected proceeds. Evidence that underwriters follow these rules, which implies that they are acting optimally, and that any deviation from them results in inferior outcomes supports the conjecture that book-building is the efficient mechanism.

10.3.1 Book-building: Evidence

The theoretically optimal book-building mechanism has a number of empirically testable properties. The offer price is set conditional on information collected from investors, although the price is only partially revised upwards when the information is positive. IPOs that attract strong investor interest are the most underpriced. A core group of regular institutional investors is favored in the allocation and individual allocations are larger when the investor expresses a positive assessment of the issuer. A word of caution is necessary before proceeding. Much of the data comes from the bubble period of the late 1990s, which is not representative of all past and possibly future IPOs. Any inferences about mechanism efficiency and the book-building pricing and allocation rules must bear this in mind.

10.3.1.1 The offer price

A virtue of book-building is that the offer price can and should incorporate valuation information revealed by investors. Cornelli and Goldreich (2003) provided explicit evidence that underwriters do indeed set the offer price conditional on investor information. They examined the order books – each bid submitted by institutional investors and the limit price, if specified – for 63 international equity issues occurring in the late 1990s.[9] They found that the average of the limit prices, weighted by the order size, explained about 80 percent of the variation in the offer prices. The offer prices increased approximately one-for-one with the average limit price and the limit bids from frequent bidders and favored investors carried the most weight. Oversubscription of the offering influenced the price to a lessor degree, although still led to deviations from the average limit price.[10]

The precision of the offer price is contingent on the amount of information the underwriter collects, which is a function of the bank's effort. Offer prices can either be on the whole dollar, say $9, or a fractional price, like $10.50. Fractional prices are relatively refined and precise, and may indicate that the underwriter was more thorough in gathering investor information to correctly price the offering. Consistent with this notion, Bradley et al. (2004) found that the average initial returns for whole and fractional priced IPOs were 25.5 and 8.1 percent, respectively. Chiang and Harikumar (2002) reported whole and fractional IPO initial returns of 16.2 and 10 percent, respectively. They also showed that the three-year post-IPO abnormal returns of fractional priced issuers exceeded those of whole priced issuers by 12 to 30 percent, implying that a greater effort in the primary market can reduce mis-pricing.

10.3.1.2 Partial adjustment phenomenon

The prediction of a partially revised offer price in response to positive information has strong support. Hanley (1993) first documented that the initial return for IPOs priced below, within and above the preliminary filing range had average initial returns of 0.6, 10 and 20.7 percent, respectively, a pattern corroborated by Loughran and Ritter (2002a). As a rough rule approximately half of all IPOs are priced within the range, with a quarter each above and below, and almost all priced above the range have a positive initial return (Ritter 1998).[11]

The offer price should only be partially revised in response to information supplied by investors. New public information that is revealed during the marketing phase would be fully incorporated into the offer price, as no investor needs to be compensated for it. Yet Loughran and Ritter (2002a) showed that the market return in the three weeks prior to the offer date was positively related to the initial return. Bradley and Jordan (2002) also found that initial returns were predictable based on information public at the IPO. Lowry and Schwert (2002) refined this result by demonstrating that negative market movements were fully impounded into the price to avoid an overpriced issue, but positive returns were not. Loughran and Ritter attributed this phenomenon to issuers not bargaining hard for a higher offer price when unexpectedly positive information arrives.

10.3.1.3 Aggregate institutional allocation

Institutional investors collectively receive a majority of the shares and their allocation is positively correlated with the initial return. Aggarwal, Prabhala and Puri (2002) showed that the median institutional allocation for IPOs with negative initial returns, returns between 0 and 20 percent, and returns greater than 20 percent were 56.1, 72.8 and 75.8 percent, respectively. Boehmer, Boehmer and Fishe (2002) similarly reported that the institutional allocation averaged 76 (70) percent in IPOs with positive (negative) initial returns and that the two were positively correlated.[12]

Two equally valid explanations are compatible with the allocation patterns. The first, which supports the optimality of the book-building mechanism, is that institutions are compensated for revealing positive information about the issuers with larger allocations in underpriced offerings. The positive correlation between the institutional allocation and the offer price adjustment in the Aggarwal, Prabhala and Puri sample further supports this view. The second explanation is that underwriters reward institutions with larger allocations in better offerings, compensating them for their trading commissions. Boehmer, Boehmer and Fishe did find that IPOs with institutional allocations above the median level generated better one- to two-year risk-adjusted returns than IPOs below the median, suggesting they were of higher quality.

10.3.1.4 Asymmetric information

The common assumption that institutions are better informed than retail investors, enabling them to selectively participate in underpriced IPOs, is supported by the data. Aggarwal, Prabhala and Puri (2002) reported that institutions earned an immediate return of 15.7 percent on their IPO investments versus 13.9 percent for retail investors. The difference was due to the disproportionately large institutional allocation in the most underpriced issues. Overpriced IPOs were small in size and the negative return was close to zero, minimizing the loss to retail investors. Boehmer, Boehmer and Fishe (2002) demonstrated that the long-run returns of the institutional allocation – measured over horizons of up to three years – were almost always higher than the retail allocation returns.

Determining which theory for the allocation patterns – information revelation, underwriter rewards or asymmetric information – is most appropriate is a difficult task. Aggarwal, Prabhala and Puri argued that if the institutional allocation was determined by the information revealed, which is then incorporated into the offer price, the allocation should have no additional predictive power for the initial return after controlling for the price update. What they found was the opposite; the institutional allocation was still positively related to the initial return. They interpreted this to mean that both information revelation and asymmetric information are factors influencing the institutional allocation.[13] Evidence presented shortly reveals that underwriter rewards may have been the most important factor.

10.3.1.5 Individual institutional allocation

The allocation patterns to individual institutions are generally consistent with the predictions. Two studies have examined the complete order books for over 70 recent equity offerings: Cornelli and Goldreich (2001) and Jenkinson and Jones (2003).[14] The findings in both studies were mostly in agreement, with one notable exception. Bids in Cornelli and Goldreich that included a limit price received larger allocations, measured relative to the bid size. Higher limit price bids, relative to the weighted average limit

232

price, obtained still larger allocations. Jenkinson and Jones did not find that bids with limit prices were favored. Furthermore, the fraction of all bids in their sample that included a limit price was 18 percent, but it was only 3.5 percent for bids in hot IPOs. This runs counter to the prediction that more information is revealed in a hot offering.[15]

The remaining allocation patterns were similar in both studies. Large bids had a greater fraction of their order filled compared to small bids. A large bid could signal positive information, justifying a higher fill rate. Frequent bidders were favored with larger allocations and they were especially favored when over-subscription was high. Jenkinson and Jones reported that bids from high quality investors – those deemed more likely to hold the shares for the long term – received larger allocations, which again increased in oversubscribed offerings.

The favoritism shown towards frequent bidders is consistent with the underwriter forming a pool of regular investors. James (2001) examined institutional investors' 13f filings with the SEC that disclosed their holdings in the quarter after an IPO. He concluded that underwriters did form a stable coalition of investors who participate regularly. Using similar data, Binay and Pirinsky (2003) showed that the percentage of the total allocation given to these regular investors increased with the initial return and size of the offering. Consistent with the theory, underwriters with a larger pool of regular investors had lower average underpricing. Whether the frequent bidders earn abnormal profits is debatable. Cornelli and Goldreich found that they did not earn additional profits beyond that of an average investor, whereas Jenkinson and Jones reported that frequent, high quality and large bidders all received above normal profits.

The limited evidence from actual order books suggests that allocations at least conform to the rules of the optimal book-building mechanism. However, many other factors could account for the patterns. In particular, allocations during the IPO bubble were clearly a consequence of underwriters maximizing their own objective functions. Investigations into the practices at some of the top-tier banks began in 2000 after the bubble burst, providing anecdotal evidence on the factors that determined allocations. Not surprisingly, banks loathe revealing how they allocate shares, so getting hard data is a challenge. Three practices were particularly influential in the allocation decision.

Commissions: Allocations to many institutional investors were largely dependent on past and future trading commissions. A more troubling and illegal practice was the requirement that the institutions return part of the extraordinary first-day return to the bank in the form of excessively high commissions when the shares were sold. A quid pro quo allocations-for-commissions is in violation of NASD rule 2110 on 'Free Riding and Withholding'.[16] Since the underwriter has an economic interest in the IPO after it has been allocated, the security is not in 'full distribution'. The economic effect is equivalent to withholding shares and selling them at a price higher than the offer.

The extent of the profits made from higher commissions is illustrated by a real case. In December of 1999 Credit Suisse First Boston (CSFB) underwrote the IPO of VA Linux.[17] The IPO priced at $30 and closed the first day at $239.25. The commissions received by CSFB totaled between 33 and 66 percent of the initial profits that some investors received from certain hot IPOs. An investor who flipped his allocation in VA Linux at the end of the first day would have a capital gain of $209.25. Even if CSFB received only a third of that as commissions it would still make a per share profit of $70.

Spinning: IPO shares were frequently allocated to the decision-makers of current and future investment banking clients. The pervasiveness of spinning is best illustrated with the case of CSFB. Frank Quattrone headed technology banking at CSFB and allegedly had control over the banking, research and even share allocation for technology IPOs. So-called 'Friend of Frank' brokerage accounts were set up for decision-makers at still private companies. As Elkind and Gimein (2001, p. 118) describe it:

> (I)n the 1990s firms also began offering shares to potential clients ... Typically, IPO shares would be flipped for a quick – and riskless – windfall. 'The stock would go into the hands of venture capitalists and the managements of companies that were going to go public next,' notes a Silicon Valley fund manager.[18]

The success of the spinning program may have been responsible for CSFB's climb up the underwriting rankings. However, it is unclear just how useful spinning was to win new business. Elkind and Gimein refer to two anonymous Silicon Valley CEOs who stated that 'because several competing investment banks were offering them cheap IPO shares, they could not have been influenced when choosing between them'.

Laddering: Allocations were sometimes made contingent on the investor agreeing to buy additional shares at a higher price in the aftermarket. The SEC began an investigation in 2002 into this illegal practice – known as laddering – at Goldman Sach and Morgan Stanley. Laddering could have artificially stimulated additional demand in the aftermarket, contributing to the huge first-day returns. Laddering is also a deliberate attempt to manipulate the market in a manner that injures ordinary investors who lack access to the IPO allocation.

While the banks denied any wrongdoing, the anecdotal evidence suggests otherwise. A defense attorney who represented witnesses in the SEC probe admitted that brokers would ask customers how much they would be willing to pay in the aftermarket if they got IPO shares (Smith 2003). Some brokers demanded that for every IPO share they received, investors had to buy one, two or three additional shares in the aftermarket. A hedge fund employee who was shown a spreadsheet prepared by Goldman for the Marvell Technologies IPO asserted: 'You could easily see that the investors that put in the large aftermarket orders had gotten larger IPO allocations' (Smith 2003, p. C4).

10.3.1.6 Optimality

The overall evidence on pricing and allocations in book-built IPOs produces two contrasting perspectives. On the one hand, the evidence that pre-dates or excludes the Internet bubble is consistent with the predicted behavior. From this perspective, the evidence indirectly implies that book-building is an efficient mechanism. Underwriters voluntarily choose pricing and allocation rules that are in accordance with the optimal rules.

A more direct test of book-building efficiency was conducted by Ljungqvist and Wilhelm (2002). The theorized efficiency is derived from the underwriter's discretion to select the price and allocation rules that maximize the expected proceeds. Constraints on the discretion should result in suboptimal outcomes. Comparing IPOs across regulatory environments that impose different constraints provides a test for the value of discretion.

Ljungqvist and Wilhelm compared IPOs in Germany, France, the UK and the US. Three patterns emerged from their analysis. First, allocation constraints tended to reduce the percentage of shares allotted to institutions. Second, the constraints resulted in less revision of offer prices.[19] Third, initial returns were negatively related to the institutional allocation and positively related to the price revision. Investors require a fixed amount of compensation for revealing their information, which can be paid through any number of underpricing/allocation pairs. The three patterns collectively imply that allocation restrictions necessitated additional underpricing. The conclusion is that less discretion produces inferior outcomes, which favors the optimality of book-building.

The evidence from the Internet bubble offers a completely different take on the book-building mechanism. There is little doubt that offer prices were not chosen to maximize proceeds, although, in the banks' defense, setting offer prices near the overvalued first-day closing prices would not have been in the issuers' best interest either. Underwriters gave institutions large allocations in IPOs they know would be hot – easy to predict when these institutions were required to buy shares in the aftermarket – in return for exorbitant commissions. This could easily account for the allocation patterns observed in the data. Underwriters clearly abused the discretion afforded them to line their own pockets at the expense of issuers and retail investors. Many critics argue on fairness grounds alone that book-building is not optimal.

The challenge for market regulators and economists trying to determine the best IPO mechanism is to decide how much emphasis to place on the bubble IPOs. Are these patterns indicative of how book-building will work in the future or was it an aberration? The three practices that largely determined the allocations – spinning, laddering and high commissions – are all illegal under current regulations. If banks follow the rules, it does appear that book-building can be an efficient mechanism. Only time and further analysis of future data will tell if this is true.

10.3.2 Fixed-price Methods: Evidence

The information environment associated with the fixed-price mechanism leads to two empirical predictions. First, information can leak out about the state of demand during the subscription period. Potential information cascades produce investor herding, generating either vast over-subscription or an undersubscribed offering. Second, asymmetric information between investor classes leads to the winner's curse. The uninformed investors should break even from their IPO participation.

10.3.2.1 Herding

Compelling evidence implies that information leakages do cause herding. News reports in Hong Kong about investor sentiment towards an IPO are common. In addition, a gray market for IPO shares sometimes begins trading during or before the subscription period. According to Harrison (1994, p. 273): 'It becomes apparent whether or not the offer is a good buy at the offer price. Consequently, issues tend to either flop or to be massively oversubscribed'.[20] Fueling the excess demand is the rule of proportional allocation. An investor has to increase his order size as total demand increases just to ensure that he continues to receive his desired allotment. McGuinness (1992) confirmed this formally, documenting that the subscription rate in Hong Kong averaged between 2.7 and 59.5 times the offer size on an annual basis from 1979 to 1989. Rates between 200 and 300 were not uncommon.

Figure 10.1 The distribution of allocation fill rates for Isreali IPOs[a]

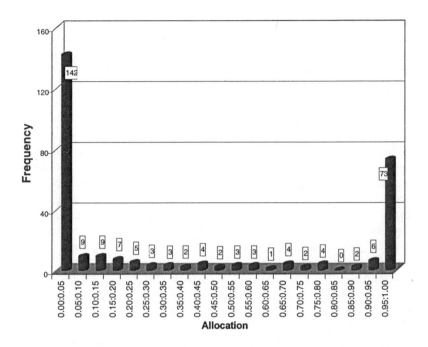

a. The allocation is the proportion that a subscriber receives of his or her order.

Source: Amihud, Hauser and Kirsh (2003)[21].

Israeli IPOs sold via a fixed-price/auction mechanism offer additional evidence of investor herding.[22] Amihud, Hauser and Kirsh (2002) found that the fill-rates were at either one of two extremes. Investors received less than one share for every 20 requested in half of the IPOs and at least 95 shares for every 100 requested in a quarter of the offerings. Figure 10.1, taken from their paper, graphically illustrates what appears to be the effect of herding. Investors submitted their orders on the morning of the offer date, making it unlikely that leakages about actual demand could occur. Instead, speculation and rumors prior to the offer date could lead to herding.

10.3.2.2 Winner's curse

Fixed-price IPOs must be underpriced to combat the winner's curse faced by uninformed investors. Rock (1986) predicted that the realized average initial return from bidding a fixed quantity in all IPOs would equal the risk-free rate. To test this prediction the initial return for each IPO must be weighted by the probability that the order for a share is filled. The evidence strongly supports this prediction. The average initial returns – weighted by the allocation fill-rate – were close to zero in a number of countries: Singapore (Koh and Walter 1989), the UK (Levis 1990), Finland (Keloharju 1993) and Israel (Amihud, Hauser and Kirsh 2002).

10.3.2.3 Asymmetric information

The winner's curse hypothesis assumes that institutional investors are better informed than retail investors. If true, institutions should bid more aggressively in IPOs that they believe are underpriced. Lee, Taylor and Walter (1999) examined investor share applications in Singaporean IPOs and concluded institutions are indeed better informed. Large investors, most likely institutions, were aggressive in applying for and receiving large allocations in the IPOs that were most underpriced. Small to medium-sized investors submitted fairly uniform order sizes across offerings with varying levels of initial returns.

Rationing rules that favor smaller orders can benefit retail investors directly by filling more of their applications and indirectly by altering the incentive to become informed. The cost of evaluating an issuer is not easily recovered when large allocations are rationed heavily. Therefore, the incentive to become informed declines, and with it the asymmetry between investors. Keloharju and Torstila (2002) examined Finnish IPOs with rationing rules that favored small orders. They found institutions to be no more successful at picking underpriced IPOs than retail investors, although both types increased their demand for underpriced shares. Within each investor class larger orders were associated with the best performance, suggesting that informed investors still did better.[23]

10.3.3 Auctions: Evidence

IPO auctions have become a rare occurrence. Few countries rely on them exclusively anymore and, when given the choice, issuers choose book-building over an auction. The principal drawback to auctions, at least from a theoretical perspective, is that they are inefficient at producing information. The limited available data offers some insight into whether auctions actually suffer from this predicted malady and why they have lost favor to book-building.

10.3.3.1 Initial returns

Israel and Taiwan are two of the few remaining countries that use auction mechanisms for IPOs: uniform price in Israel and discriminatory price in Taiwan. Both auctions have produced positive average initial returns, consistent with the prediction that informed bidders earn informational rent. Kandel, Sarig and Wohl (1999) documented a 4.7 percent initial return in Israel. Lin, Lee and Liu (2003) reported an initial return of 2.39 percent in Taiwan measured from the quantity-weighted average winning bid price.

Kandel, Sarig and Wohl proposed an explanation for why underpricing occurs in the uniform price auction. Investors have heterogeneous beliefs and are uncertain about the likely market price. The resolution of this uncertainty could lead investors to reassess the risk associated with the issuer, causing the price to rise. Israeli authorities announce the aggregate demand at the minimum reservation bid after the IPO but before the start of trading. Investors can calculate the elasticity of demand at the offer price based on the available information. A high elasticity implies greater uniformity of investor beliefs and lower uncertainty. Kandel, Sarig and Wohl then demonstrated that the initial return was positively related to the elasticity, consistent with a confirming effect resolving much of the valuation uncertainty.

A similar analysis was conducted by Liaw, Lui and Wei (2001) for the Taiwanese IPOs. They too reported a positive relationship between the elasticity and the winning bidders' average market-adjusted initial return. The winner's curse that is thought to afflict discriminatory price auctions appears to have impacted the bidding strategies in these IPOs. Liaw, Lui and Wei showed that the most aggressive 5 percent of bidders lost only 1.64 percent on the initial market-adjusted return. This is not much considering they were the highest bids, which suggests that they were shaded.

10.3.3.2 Auctions versus book-building

The growing popularity of book-building has come at the expense of IPO auctions. This partly reflects regulatory changes, but mostly it is a consequence of issuers choosing book-building over auctions when given a choice. Japan had relied exclusively on the discriminatory price auction method until 1997 when book-building was first allowed, largely in response to its success in the US. In a matter of months only book-building was used, even though auctions were still allowed (Kutsuna and Smith 2003). A similar experience occurred in France. The OPM auction and book-building were used equally in the mid-1990s, but by 2000 book-building was used almost exclusively (Derrien 2002).

What explains these developments in two of the most financially advanced countries in the world? A simple comparison of issuing costs for the two mechanisms offers no obvious clues. The average initial return in France in the mid-1990s for OPM and book-built IPOs were 9.7 and 16.9 percent, respectively (Derrien and Womack 2003). The same held in Japan; the initial returns during 1996–98 for auctioned and book-built IPOs were 10.7 and 19.5 percent, respectively (Kutsuna and Smith 2003). Underwriter compensation was also higher for book-built IPOs in both countries.

Comparing total costs across the two mechanisms is misleading. Book-building involves a bundle of services, which is not the case in auctions. Underwriters put forth a greater selling effort in book-built IPOs and may agree to provide the issuer with analyst coverage, but will expect either additional underpricing or compensation in return. Furthermore, the positive correlations between the initial return, the price adjustment and investor interest in book-built IPOs implies that while the underpricing cost might be high, the net proceeds are greater than initially expected.

The source of the issuer preference for book-building can be found by digging a little deeper into the data. Kutsuna and Smith (2003) showed that the average total IPO costs in Japan masked the considerable economies of scale associated with book-building. They estimated that large, well-established firms realized a cost saving with book-building relative to what they would have paid with an auction. Therefore, the aggregate total issuing costs across all IPOs would actually be lower if all IPOs were book-built.

Economies of scale in book-building imply that smaller issuers pay the highest cost as a percentage of their proceeds. But this does not mean that they would benefit from an auction. Kutsuna and Smith argued that the small, risky firms that gravitated to book-building were shut out of the IPO market when only auctions were allowed. The reason was poor information production. These issuers had speculative values that required thorough due diligence and a way to communicate private information to investors. The auction mechanism failed to provide an effective communications channel and the incentive for investors to become informed.[24]

Poor information production adversely affects the outcome of auctions. After examining discriminatory price auctions in Taiwan, Lin, Lee and Liu (2003) made three observations. First, retail investors won a significantly higher proportion of the shares in IPOs with negative initial returns, although their average allocation-weighted returns were close to zero, consistent with the winner's curse. Second, the average institutional allocation was only 19 percent and institutions bid most aggressively in large offerings and avoided the smallest IPOs. Third, institutional investors targeted their bidding to win shares in hot IPOs and their allocation increased with the initial return they earned. The allocation-weighted average initial return for institutions was 10.5 percent.

These findings provide a rationale for the superiority of book-building. The auction did a poor job of pricing the IPO when institutions did not participate because retail investors were not informed; the average initial return was negative for these IPOs. Institutions will reveal their private valuations through their bids only if they expect to receive informational rent. The advantage of book-building is that the underwriter can give institutions large allocations to minimize the per share rent. The positive correlation between underpricing and institutional allocation in the auctions stands in contrast with the negative relation found by Ljungqvist and Wilhelm (2002) for book-built IPOs. Overall, book-building allows the issuers to benefit from lower costs and a more informative stock price.

10.4 UNDERPRICING

The positive initial return is one of the more enduring puzzles in financial economics. An estimated $27 billion was 'left on the table' during US IPOs over 1990–98, only to be surpassed by an even more staggering $63 billion in 1999 and 2000 (Loughran and Ritter 2002a; 2002b). Why is such extreme underpricing tolerated? This question was first asked in the 1970s and has since generated its own mini-industry of academic research.[25]

No single theory could possibly hope to explain the underpricing phenomenon. Instead, a number of independent theories coexist, each contributing one piece to the puzzle. The theories can be grouped into three general categories. Institutional explanations posit that underpricing is a response to imperfections in the IPO market and is an unavoidable cost of going public. Issuer, and to some extent underwriter, objectives to be achieved with the IPO that deviate from strict proceeds maximization form the second group. Lastly, less than fully rational behavior is invoked to explain the pricing patterns of IPOs.

Another aspect of the underpricing puzzle is the considerable time series variation. The average initial return was 7.4 percent in the 1980s, 14.8 percent during 1990–98 and an astounding 65 percent in 1999 and 2000, although it fell back to 11 percent in the immediate post-bubble period (Loughran and Ritter 2002b). The long-term increase in underpricing suggests that a fundamental change in issuers' objectives and the underwriting industry occurred. Loughran and Ritter claim that a changing composition of the type of issuers accounts for very little of the increased underpricing.

10.4.1 Institutional Underpricing

Imperfections abound in the IPO market. Informational asymmetries exist between the issuer and investors, and amongst investors. Underwriter and issuer incentives are not perfectly aligned. Uncertainty is pervasive. Intentional underpricing can be a best response to the imperfections because it actually maximizes the expected proceeds. Most of the institutional explanations have already been presented and are briefly reviewed below, along with a few additional ones.

Informational rent: An underwriter must commit to underprice book-built IPOs when the demand is strong in order to get informed investors to truthfully reveal their valuations. This increases the gross proceeds because investors reveal when they are willing to pay a high price. The underpricing is informational rent.

Winner's curse: Uninformed investors receive disproportionately large allocations in overpriced offerings because informed investors selectively purchase shares in only underpriced issues. Underpricing is necessary to ensure that the uninformed participate in the IPO. The winner's curse explanation is most applicable in the fixed-price method.

Information cascades: The expected proceeds in a fixed-price offering are maximized when underpricing creates a positive information cascade and herding. The offer price is lowered until the marginal benefit from a greater probability of a fully subscribed offering equals the marginal cost of a lower share price.

Agency conflicts: The costly selling effort required of the underwriter in book-built IPOs is reduced if the offer is underpriced. The bank will successfully bargain for a lower offer price when the issuer cannot observe its effort level or the investor interest, resulting in underpricing due to agency conflicts.

Litigation risk: The issuer, underwriter and auditor all bear litigation risk when investors incur losses caused by the failure to disclose materially relevant information. Underpricing is insurance against a possible lawsuit because it reduces the probability of investors suffering a loss and the recoverable losses.

Uncertainty: Uncertainty over the issuer value is measured by the variance of possible values. In the preceding theories greater uncertainty amplifies the necessary underpricing. But uncertainty without the initial market imperfection would not warrant underpricing. It is well documented empirically that initial returns increase with the proxies for uncertainty.

Risk aversion: Uncertainty over the initial aftermarket price can result in underpricing if the issuer and investors are risk-averse (Draho 2001a). Investors bear the risk over the market's initial price, and thus provide the issuer with insurance against an adverse market reception. The issuer underprices to pay for the insurance premium, which increases in the uncertainty over the firm value. Underpricing will decline as more private information is revealed in the primary market, increasing the precision of the forecast for the market price. Investors bear less residual pricing risk as this occurs.

Option to withdraw: An issuer can withdraw its IPO up until the time the offer is priced and shares allocated. The option to withdraw increases the bargaining power of the issuer vis-à-vis investors, which should translate into less underpricing (Busaba 2002). The bargaining power is contingent on the outside options. Issuers that can access the debt markets have more power. Busaba, Benveniste and Guo (2001) found that issuers that listed debt repayment as a use of the proceeds, indicating debt was an option, exhibited a higher probability of withdrawal and lower initial returns.

10.4.2 Issuer Objectives

An IPO is a major one-time event that impacts the issuer's performance and structure for the foreseeable future. As such, the issuer could have objectives it would like to achieve with the IPO that motivate additional underpricing. Some of the motives stem from a desire to help the firm specifically, while others only benefit the CEO and other executives.

Dynamic issuing strategy: Issuers that want to sell equity in stages could benefit from IPO underpricing. A large initial return designed to leave a good impression with investors might make it easier to complete a follow-on offering. Underpricing could also be used to signal the firm quality to investors, who cannot easily distinguish between good and bad issuers (Allen and Faulhaber 1989; Grinblatt and Hwang 1989; Welch 1989). High quality firms increase their underpricing to signal their value with the knowledge that they will be able to raise more proceeds at their true value in a follow-on offering. A similar argument suggests that issuers underprice to increase information production in the aftermarket (Chemmanur 1993). The initial return is compensation to investors who will incur a cost to learn the true quality. The benefit to the issuer is a more accurate share price for the follow-on.

All three arguments predict a positive relationship between the initial return and the probability of an SEO. The empirical evidence, however, offers little support for this prediction. Most studies have found either a negative or no relationship between the initial return and the likelihood of a follow-on.[26]

Control and monitoring: Two competing theories offer different predictions for the relationship between underpricing and the post-IPO ownership structure. The reduced monitoring hypothesis conjectures that managers want to avoid creating large outside blockholders. Underpricing attracts additional investors, giving the issuer more allocation discretion in a book-built IPO and greater rationing in a fixed-price offering (Brennan and Franks 1997). Either way, the shareholder base is dispersed. The large monitor hypothesis predicts the opposite. Managers want to create a large monitoring blockholder to improve the governace structure and raise the firm value. Greater underpricing is needed to compensate the blockholder for the monitoring service (Stoughton and Zechner 1998).

Only the reduced monitoring hypothesis has any empirical support. Brennan and Franks (1997) found that shareholder concentration decreased with the initial return in a sample of UK fixed-price IPOs.[27] Smart and Zutter (2003) compared dual- and single-class stock IPOs. Managers of dual-class issuers are entrenched and have less reason to worry about excess monitoring. The initial returns for dual-class IPOs were three percentage points lower than the single-class returns, controlling for offer characteristics. Single-class issuers also exhibited a negative correlation between underpricing and post-IPO institutional shareholdings. Field and Sheehan (2003) reported that among issuers without a blockholder prior to the IPO, those who underpriced more were less likely to acquire one after.

Wealth Sensitivity: A CEO's incentive to bargain hard with the underwriter for less underpricing is contingent on the sensitivity of his or her wealth to the offer price. A low sensitivity might mean that he or she is more tolerant of a low offer price. The sensitivity will be low if he or she sells few of his or her own shares in the IPO and if the number of primary shares floated is small relative to the number of pre-IPO shares outstanding. The latter condition keeps the dilution cost to the old shareholders from underpricing to a minimum.

Lower wealth sensitivities could account for the increased underpricing during the Internet bubble. Ljungqvist and Wilhelm (2003) documented that average initial returns increased from 17 to 56 percent from 1996 to 2000.

During this period the pre-IPO ownership stake of insiders, including the CEO, fell over 10 percent. Secondary sales, the percentage of IPOs with secondary sales and the secondary component of the offer also declined significantly. The percentage of secondary shares sold and the ratio of primary shares to shares outstanding were both negatively related to the underpricing. Loughran and Ritter (2002b) questioned the changing wealth sensitivity effect. While CEO percentage ownership decreased, the total number of shares owned increased. From a pure wealth perspective, underpricing should have decreased. Furthermore, pure primary offerings had smaller initial returns, opposite of the predicted relation.

Wealth sensitivities could dictate that some issuers try to minimize underpricing and pay a higher marketing cost – more prestigious underwriters and auditors – as a substitute. Habib and Ljungqvist (2001) found that underpricing decreased with the marketing expense and with insider selling, after controlling for the marketing cost. Issuers optimized at the margin; each dollar spent on marketing was estimated to reduce the wealth lost from underpricing by 98 cents.

Taxes: The tax treatment of compensation paid to employees seems to affect the desired underpricing. Rydqvist (1997) showed that a tax advantage to capital gains relative to ordinary wage income in Sweden gave companies the incentive to allocate their IPO shares to their employees. The share price appreciation for employees was taxed at the lower capital gains rate prior to 1990, when the average initial return was 41 percent. The government changed the tax laws in 1990 so that the price appreciation of shares allotted to employees would be taxed as ordinary income. The average initial return fell to 8 percent post-1990 and Rydqvist estimated that tax law change accounted for ten percentage points of the decline.

The tax treatment of stock options in the US provides another reason to underprice. Ordinary income tax must be paid on the difference between the option's strike price and the fair market value at exercise. Fair market value is considered to be the offer price prior to the IPO and the market price thereafter. Setting the strike price equal to the offer price and exercising before the IPO eliminates the immediate tax liability. The cost is a larger capital gain that will be taxed in the future when the shares are sold. The current tax savings increase with the initial return, which creates a tax incentive to underprice.

The explosive growth in option grants in the late 1990s created a major tax incentive to increase underpricing. Taranto (2003) reported that in his sample the average initial return rose from 16 to 75 percent from 1997 to 1999. The average ratio of options outstanding to the IPO offer size simultaneously increased from 37 to 71 percent. Taranto estimated that ten percentage points of the additional initial return in 1999 could be attributed to the increased use of options.

Analyst Coverage: Positive analyst coverage grew in importance during the 1990s. Whether recommending a stock on television or issuing strong earnings growth forecasts, star analysts could drive up an issuer's share price. Issuers interested in buying more coverage from their underwriter would implicitly pay for it through additional underpricing. The bank would then use this underpricing to generate more trading commissions and win new underwriting business.

Studies have documented a positive correlation between initial returns and subsequent analyst coverage (Rajan and Servaes 1997; Aggarwal, Krigman and Womack 2002). This could, of course, reflect analysts choosing to follow stocks that appear to be hot. Cliff and Denis (2003) demonstrated more convincingly that additional underpricing was designed to buy coverage. Among issuers in the lowest underpricing quintile, 74 percent had a buy recommendation from the lead underwriter and 16 percent had an *Institutional Investor* All-Star analyst from the lead follow their industry. The respective percentages for issuers in the top quintile were significantly higher at 84 and 35 percent. Issuers were far more likely to switch lead underwriters for their follow-on offering if the expected coverage did not materialize, even after controlling for underpricing.

Corruption: The CEOs of issuers should act in the interest of their shareholders and hire the underwriter that will maximize the IPO proceeds. The practice of spinning may have corrupted CEO behavior. Underwriters profited by allocating shares in heavily underpriced IPOs to the decision-makers at private companies. In return, the CEO would select the bank to be its lead underwriter. Spinning created a bias whereby issuers gravitated towards underwriters that underpriced the most. Loughran and Ritter (2002b) argued that the growing market share of prestigious underwriters who increased their underpricing in the late 1990s is evidence in support of the corruption hypothesis.

Houston, James and Karceski (2003) offered formal evidence that underwriters intentionally increased their underpricing during the bubble. Research analysts issued price targets for IPOs, based on the P/E or P/S multiples for comparable firms, almost immediately after the quiet period ended. Houston James and Karceski estimated that during the 1996–98 period IPO offer prices were overvalued by an average of 5 percent relative to the value imputed from the analyst-identified comps. However, offer prices were undervalued by about 20 percent for 1999–2000 using the same approach. The overall pattern suggests that offer prices were 'low-balled' during the bubble.

Marketing: The IPO has become a major branding event for issuers. Media coverage of a hot offering generates the kind of free instant publicity that would otherwise require a considerable expense. Underpricing could function as a substitute for conventional marketing techniques. Issuers likely to get the biggest 'bang for their underpricing buck' are those that target the mass consumer market. Chapter 4 presented the example of business-to-consumer Internet companies underpricing to attract traffic to their web site. Demers and Lewellan (2003) documented that the initial returns were a significant positive predictor of increased web traffic post-IPO.[28] The estimated average underpricing cost to attract a unique visitor was $562, similar to estimates for conventional marketing methods.

10.4.3 Behavioral Explanations

The initial return is a reasonable proxy for intentional underpricing when the issuer and investors behave rationally. Deviations from full rationality weaken the link between the two. Returns in excess of 200 percent for some Internet IPOs were unlikely a sole consequence of intentional underpricing. Behavioral explanations for the excessive initial returns can focus on either why the offer price was too low or why the first-day market price was too high.

Offer price: Unexpected wealth gains may be responsible for CEOs tolerating unnecessarily low offer prices. The CEO has an expectation for his or her post-IPO wealth based on the preliminary offer price and the number of shares he or she owns. Loughran and Ritter (2002a) argued that the CEO anchors on this expected wealth. Prospect theory – proposed by Kahneman and Tversky (1982) – suggests that individuals care more about their level of wealth relative to the anchored level than they do about the absolute amount. So when the IPO attracts strong investor interest and the offer price is partially revised upwards, the CEO focuses on the positive unexpected wealth increase and not the additional money left on the table. A rational CEO would, at least in theory, bargain hard for lower underpricing.[29]

Market price: The first-day stock price should be an unbiased estimate of the share's intrinsic value. Circumstances can arise, however, in which the price is optimistically biased. Investors have rational heterogeneous beliefs about the share value, especially in the case of highly uncertain IPOs.

247

Miller (1977) suggested that the combination of heterogeneous expectations and short sale constraints result in an upwardly biased price set by the most optimistic investors. Consistent with this prediction, Ofek and Richardson (2003) found a positive relation between the initial return for a sample of Internet IPOs and the tightness of short-sale constraints. In addition, Cook, Kieschnick and Van Ness (2003) documented a negative correlation between the initial return and the offer size. A small float makes it even more difficult to short IPO shares.

Irrational speculation could alternatively cause the biased market price. Barber and Odean (2002) concluded, after examining brokerage records, that retail investors are more likely to purchase 'attention-grabbing' stocks. It is well documented that, in the late 1990s, the number of media stories about an issuer prior to its IPO was positively related to the initial return and the early aftermarket retail trading volume.[30] Media coverage could be stimulated by investment bank promotion or simply reflect hype surrounding an IPO. Either way, retail investor sentiment towards these IPOs was unjustifiably positive. Market momentum could be a factor. Dorn (2003) showed that the first-day retail demand in German IPOs was positively correlated with the returns to similar stocks and the market in the preceding month. Initial returns increased in the retail demand, but the one-year returns were lowest for stocks attracting the strongest demand. This pattern suggests that retail investors bid up the initial market price above its proper value. Derrien (2002) added further evidence of retail investor speculation. The average initial return for French IPOs priced at the upper bound of the price range was 56.7 percent when retail demand was high, but only 14.9 percent when demand was low.

10.5 SUMMARY

The IPO selling mechanism governs how shares are priced and allocated. Theory argues that book-building is an optimal mechanism because of the discretion afforded the underwriter. The underwriter gathers information from regular institutional investors, who are compensated with large allocations in underpriced offerings. Neither fixed-price methods nor auctions allow the underwriter to discriminate between investors, reducing the amount of valuable information produced.

The empirical evidence is consistent with most of the predictions of the book-building theory, suggesting that it may be indeed be optimal. The offer price is set conditional on information provided by investors and is only partially adjusted in response to good information. Institutional investors receive a majority of the allotted shares. Larger allocations are given to regular investors and possibly to those who provide price information. Allocations during the Internet bubble, and perhaps before, were based on commissions generated, laddering and spinning. Fixed-price offerings are characterized by information cascades and herding, as well as the winner's curse for uninformed investors. Auctions, while little used anymore, appear to be inefficient at producing information.

Large initial returns are often the result of issuer-motivated objectives. There is some evidence that issuers underprice to achieve a dispersed ownership base. Financial incentives, including taxes, have changed to make CEOs more tolerant of underpricing. The CEOs were also willing to underpricing more if that bought better analyst coverage or allocations in other hot IPOs. The determination of the offer and first-day market prices appears to be influenced by behavioral factors. Issuers accept offer prices that are too low and retail investor speculation drives up the market price to irrational levels.

NOTES

1. The best-efforts contract is essentially a fixed-price mechanism. The offer price is set prior to the offer being open, the underwriter does not actively sell the issue and the underwriter has limited discretion in the share allocation.
2. Re-printed with permission from Ann Sherman.
3. The scenario is not 'correct' in a theoretical sense because the results are not derived from a fully worked out example. Nonetheless, it illustrates the basic intuition underlining the optimal mechanism.
4. The optimal mechanism would actually allow the underwriter to discriminate on price as well (Benveniste and Wilhelm 1990). However, US securities law forbids price discriminating among investors.
5. Reuter (2002) found that the level of participation of mutual fund families in IPOs was proportional to their brokerage commissions paid to the lead underwriter.
6. The mechanism assumes that retail investors are not willing to pay commissions in return for hot IPO allocations.
7. Spatt and Srivastava (1991) demonstrated that book-building is equivalent to an optimal second price auction.
8. Ausubel (2002) suggested reserving a portion of the offering for only large bids from institutional investors.
9. The book distinguishes among three types of bids: a 'strike bid' is an order for a specific number of shares or amount of money regardless of offer price; a 'limit bid' specifies the maximum price the bidder is willing to pay for the shares; a 'step bid' is a demand schedule as a series of limit bids.
10. Aussenegg, Pichler and Stomper (2003) found that book-building was the primary source of pricing information in German IPOs listed on the Neuer Markt, even when a gray market for the shares existed. Informative book-building took place before the price range was set, which marked the start of gray market trading.
11. Jenkinson, Morrison and Wilhelm (2003) reported that only 11 percent of European book-built IPOs were priced outside the preliminary range, which reflected the fact that information was gathered before the range was set.

12. Hanley and Wilhelm (1995) found no significant relationship between the initial return and the institutional allocation, which was around 70 percent. The robustness of their findings is questionable because their sample of 35 IPOs came from a single bank.

13. Asymmetric information among investors is not likely to be an issue when a gray market for the shares exists.

14. Two different European-based investment banks supplied the data for each study. The Cornelli and Goldreich data set included IPOs, SEOs and privatizations, whereas Jenkinson and Jones examined IPOs exclusively. One possibility for the Jenkinson and Jones (2003) sample is that investors provide the strongest pre-registration endorsement of IPOs that subsequently become hot, and thus do not have to provide price sensitive bids.

15. In Europe underwriters gather price information before the issue is even registered. The book-building phase may not be designed to reveal information, only to submit orders that are not price sensitive.

16. This fact was pointed out in Loughran and Ritter (2002b).

17. See Pulliam and Smith (2000; 2001). The example was taken from Loughran and Ritter (2002b).

18. This quote first appeared in Loughran and Ritter (2002b).

19. The test is hampered by the fact that the preliminary price range in Germany already reflected information gathered from investors. Thus, any constraints on price revision are less onerous than they appear.

20. This quote originally appeared in Chowdhry and Sherman (1996).

21. Re-printed from the *Journal of Financial Economics*, Vol. 68, Amihud, Y., S. Hauser and A. Kirsh, "Allocations, Adverse Selection and Cascades in IPOs: Evidence from the Tel Aviv Stock Exchange," pp. 137-58, Copyright (2003) with permission from Elsevier.

22. The auction specified a minimum and maximum price that could be bid. The maximum price was the offer price in over three-quarters of the IPOs, effectively making them fixed-price offerings.

23. This result is consistent with Chowdhry and Sherman (1996a), who argued that informed investors place larger orders even when they have the same wealth as the uninformed.

24. The lack of incentive to become informed stemmed from regulatory constraints. Investors could bid for no more than 5,000 shares in the auction, roughly equivalent to $100,000 based on the average offer price. The open offer component also restricted the maximum bid size to be 5,000 shares.

25. The seminal studies on initial returns are Ibbotson (1975), Ibbotson and Jaffe (1975), Stoll and Curley (1970), Reilly (1973) and Logue (1973).

26. Michaely and Shaw (1994) and Speiss and Pettway (1997) did not find any support for the prediction, although Jegadeesh, Weinstein and Welch (1993) found weak evidence in favor of it.

27. Amihud, Hauser and Kirsh (2003) found that the number of participating investors in pseudo-fixed-price Isreali IPOs increased with the underpricing. Issuers may have intentionally tried to attract a dispersed shareholder base or a herd may have emerged because of the underpricing.

28. The additional traffic does not necessarily translate into sales. Ducharme, Rajgopal and Sefcik (2001) found only weak evidence that underpricing led to an increase in revenue and Hand (2000) found almost no relationship.

29. The CFOs of recent IPOs surveyed by Ryan (2001) were not overly concerned about underpricing; only 35.8 percent considered it a problem. Yet most, 87.4 percent, looked at the IPO as a financing vehicle, designed to raise capital for long-term growth.

30. See Reese (1998), Ducharme, Rajgopal and Sefcik (2001) and Cook, Kieschnick and Van Ness (2003).

11 The IPO aftermarket

The final stage of the IPO process starts shortly after the shares are priced and allocated to investors. Secondary market trading commences and the issuer's life as a public company begins. An IPO is deemed a short-term success if all the shares are placed at the expected offer price and the price rises at the start of trading. Over longer horizons the decision to go public is justified by a stock price that continues to appreciate.

Short- and long-term returns are both influenced by actions taken by the underwriting syndicate. The underwriter is actively involved in the price discovery process and engages in price stabilization, if necessary. The support retards significant price declines in the short run by adding liquidity to the market. These market-making services help the issuer make a smooth transition to public ownership.

Long-term price performance is enhanced by research coverage provided by investment banks. Equity analysts that follow the stock produce timely information about the issuer, thereby increasing the stock's publicity and reducing asymmetric information amongst investors. The share value in the immediate aftermarket is also increased by the presence of a lockup agreement. Pre-IPO shareholders agree to lock up their shares and not sell for a fixed length of time without prior approval of the underwriter.

The timeline of events in the post-IPO period begins with the onset of aftermarket trading. Price stabilization can start immediately, but lasts for no more than a few weeks. The 'quiet period' ends 40 days after the offer date. The lead underwriter and other syndicate members cannot make public comments or recommendations prior to this date. Finally, the lockup agreement usually expires six months after the offer date.

11.1 AFTERMARKET TRADING AND PRICES

The start of aftermarket trading could be characterized as a controlled frenzy. The stock goes through a price discovery process as investors and market-makers learn the fair market value. The rush by investors to buy additional shares or flip their IPO allocations results in extraordinarily high initial trading volume. The market only begins to settle down after the first few days. At the center of all this activity is the lead underwriter. The lead has a responsibility to expedite the price discovery, provide liquidity when necessary and support the price when there is downward pressure. Understanding how the underwriter achieves these objectives and why is central to comprehending the workings of the aftermarket.

11.1.1 Market-Making Services

A *tatonnement* process in the pre-opening period and immediate aftermarket results in a rapid convergence to the equilibrium price and share allocation. Aftermarket trading reallocates the shares to the investors who want to own them at the market price. The market-clearing price is the outcome of a learning process that incorporates information not already reflected in the offer price. The formal mechanics of the process differ between the NASDAQ and the NYSE. The NASDAQ is a dealer market with multiple market-makers, including the underwriter, providing quotes for each stock. The NYSE is an exchange with orders flowing through the specialist. The underwriter is limited to floor broker transactions and submitting limit orders for NYSE-listed IPOs.

11.1.1.1 Pre-opening

The first objective of a market-maker is to arrive at a market-clearing price as quickly as possible to minimize the risk to his inventory position. A brief period prior to the start of trading allows investors to submit orders. The market-maker uses the order flow to set an opening price designed to clear the market. The pre-opening price discovery process is generally quite successful. The offer-to-opening price return accounts for over 90 percent of the offer-to-close initial return.[1] Only those investors lucky enough to receive an IPO allocation reap the gain from the first-day price pop.

NASDAQ: The pre-opening period for NASDAQ IPOs lasts for a maximum of five minutes. During the period all market-makers have the option to add, revise or cancel quotes – none of which are binding – before actual trading begins. The lead underwriter decides when trading will begin and first notifies NASDAQ officials as to the start time.[2] Aggarwal and Conroy (2000) examined the pre-opening for over 100 IPOs. The lead underwriter always entered the first quote and was one of 6.7 market-makers posting quotes. The co-managing underwriters, wholesalers or other market makers were also active in posting quotes. The opening quote already accounted for a large proportion of the offer-to-open return.

The primary purpose of the quotes is for the market-makers to learn the likely market-clearing price before trading starts. The lead underwriter essentially watched the quoting behavior of others after posting the initial quotes. Wholesalers were very active, entering about half of all quotes and were responsible for the majority of bid and ask quote improvements. The percentage change in the lead's bid quote was significantly responsive to bid quote revisions by the wholesalers, suggesting that the quotes were informative about investor demand. Overall, the offer-to-open return increased nearly one-to-one with the quote revisions.

NYSE: All stocks listed on the NYSE open each trading day with a call auction and the specialist is responsible for setting the market-clearing price. The same method is used to open trading on IPOs. Investors submit market and limit orders prior to the start of trading. The specialist attempts to set a price that will clear the market and balance the buy and sell orders. Corwin, Harris and Lipson (2001) estimated that the average IPO started trading 33 minutes after the opening bell largely because the volume of the opening trade is extremely heavy.

11.1.1.2 Volume and trading

The market-clearing price is essentially reached by the first aftermarket trade, but the reallocation of shares among investors takes a little longer. Aftermarket trading undoes some of the IPO allocation, which results in very high trading volume on the first day. The lead underwriter contributes some of this volume and for NASDAQ IPOs much of the volume flows through the lead.

NASDAQ: Ellis, Michaely and O'Hara (2000) documented that the lead-managing underwriter was typically the dominant market-maker in early aftermarket trading. The lead handled approximately 60 percent of the trading volume during the first few days. The percentage dropped to about 50 over the next few months and the lead was the dominant market-maker less frequently. Co-managing underwriters were not active liquidity providers. An average of ten market-makers posted quotes on the first trading day, dropping to seven after 20 days.

The lead underwriter accumulated a large inventory position on the first day due to the heavy trading volume. The average first-day volume as a percentage of shares issued was 62 percent in Ellis, Michaely and O'Hara and remained at an abnormally high 2 percent 60 days after the IPO. The average hides considerable variation in the volume. Some Internet IPOs had first-day volume of 180 percent (Aggarwal 2000). In Ellis, Michaely and

O'Hara the cumulative order imbalance – calculated as the difference between the volume due to sell- and buy-initiated trades – was about 10 percent of the issue size. The imbalance suggests liquidity providers like the lead underwriter were net buyers. The lead's inventory position reflected the imbalance, equaling 4 percent of the issued shares after the first day and 7.8 percent after 20 trading days. The large inventory position is indicative of price support activities.

NYSE: Corwin, Harris and Lipson (2001) reported that the average first-day volume for NYSE-listed IPOs equaled 55.5 percent of the issue size. The opening call auction involved 20 percent of the issued shares.[3] The volume and number of trades declined rapidly, reaching a stable level after ten days. The bid and ask depth on the first day for both hot and cold IPOs was ten times the normal level. Hot IPOs exhibited significant buy imbalances at the start of trading. Cold IPOs had a very large initial sell imbalance that continued on to the second day. The heavy volume created more liquidity, lowering trading costs. The average bid-ask spread, as a percentage of the offer price, on the first day was 3 and 8 percent for hot and cold IPOs, respectively. The spread costs increased to 14 and 22 percent by day 30.

11.1.2 Price Stabilization

The underwriting agreement usually includes a stipulation stating that the underwriter may engage in transactions that stabilize or maintain the share price at a level above that which might otherwise prevail in the open market. The direct outcome of stabilization is the provision of liquidity to absorb the excess supply and retard an unnecessary precipitous price decline. A commitment to stabilize has an indirect benefit on IPO pricing because it affects the willingness of investors to purchase shares at a particular offer price.

11.1.2.1 Motivation

Price stabilization activities should only occur if their provision increases the value of the IPO. The benefits of stabilization could arise after the offering by preventing an adverse outcome, or before by easing the initial selling effort. In either case, the benefit is derived from the implicit put option the underwriter provides to investors who receive an IPO allocation. A stabilizing bid at the offer price protects the investors against downside risk in the short run. Such price support could be economically efficient for a number of reasons.

Herding: An IPO that opens with a declining share price could suffer from a selling herd. An investor may sell his shares in the belief that other investors are selling their allocation. The information cascade that ensues causes a rush to sell, further exacerbating the price decline. The viability of an otherwise reasonable IPO quickly becomes an issue. Investors have the legal right to renege on confirmed buy orders for up to five business days after the offering becomes effective because the contract between broker and investor is not complete until the investor has had a chance to see the final prospectus. Price stabilization can prevent a selling herd and potentially a failed offering (Schultz and Zaman 1994). Additional underpricing would have the same effect, making price support and underpricing substitutes.

Litigation risk: The same threat of litigation that provided a motive for underpricing also justifies price stabilization (Schultz and Zaman 1994). Stabilization temporarily delays a price decline below the offer. In the interim, while stabilization occurs, market movements obscure the causes of any subsequent price decline. Therefore, stabilization makes it more difficult for investors to claim that the IPO was overpriced when other unanticipated information shocks could have caused the price drop.

Bonding mechanism: The optimal book-building mechanism relies on the underwriter's implicit commitment to set the offer price conditional on the information revealed by investors. The underwriter could falsely overstate the investor interest and try to set too high a price. Investors will not participate in the IPO without some assurance that the underwriter will not try to overprice. Price stabilization is an effective bonding mechanism to prevent overpricing (Benveniste, Busaba and Wilhelm 1996). The credibility of stabilization as a bonding device rests on the assumption that it is costly for the underwriter and is something to be avoided.

The bonding theory implies that underpricing and price stabilization are substitutes. Investors demand a certain amount of informational rent for revealing their interest. Various combinations of underpricing and put option value will satisfy this condition. For efficiency, the compensation must be targeted to informed institutional investors, which means that only these investors should directly benefit from price stabilization actions.

Winner's curse: Uninformed investors require underpricing before participating with informed investors in an IPO because of the winner's curse. Their participation can also be induced with a commitment to price stabilize (Chowdry and Nanda 1996). The promise of temporary stabilization eliminates the downside risk from buying shares in the IPO and is a substitute for underpricing. Price stabilization should be targeted towards uniformed retail investors to effectively combat the winner's curse, the opposite prediction of the bonding argument.

Risk reduction: The cost of the price stabilization put option to the underwriter increases in the uncertainty over the market value. The underwriter therefore has an incentive to engage in greater pre-IPO information production to minimize the uncertainty (Prabhala and Puri 1998). The underwriter might also conclude that the cost of price support is too great for highly uncertain IPOs and choose instead to increase underpricing. Evidence does suggest that stabilized IPOs were less risky than non-stabilized offers (Asquith, Jones and Keishnick 1998). Lewewllen (2003) found that the less risky IPOs were underwritten by reputable banks that might be trying to protect their reputation by stabilizing.

11.1.2.2 Methods and regulations

Stabilization is a deliberate attempt by the underwriter to manipulate the price in a manner that impedes the unfettered price discovery process. Manipulations of any sort run counter to the ideal of free and fair capital markets. Formal regulations have been adopted to limit what the underwriter can do to affect the aftermarket price. The Securities Exchange Act of 1934 specifically included sections prohibiting transactions that result in 'pegging, fixing, or stabilizing' the price of a security.

An exemption was made for price stabilization activities following an IPO, as long as the actions followed certain guidelines.[4] The possibility of price stabilization must be disclosed to investors, which is done by inserting a clause in the prospectus. Stabilization can only occur at or below the offer price, the intent being to retard price declines. Finally, underwriters are allowed to stabilize for only a reasonable period of time, which is generally interpreted to mean a couple of weeks after the IPO.

The SEC adopted Regulation M in 1996 – with Rule 104 governing stabilization and other syndication activities – which was very similar to the guidelines in the original Securities Act. A statement released by the SEC announcing the new rules defined price stabilization as 'transactions for the purpose of preventing or retarding a decline in the market price of a security to facilitate an offering'.[5] The SEC justified such practices by stating:

> Although stabilization is a price-influencing activity intended to induce others to purchase the offered security, when appropriately regulated it is an effective mechanism for fostering an orderly distribution of securities and promotes the interests of shareholders, underwriters and issuers. (SEC No. 34-38067 p. 81)

The underwriter has three stabilization methods at its disposal that are subject to varying degrees of regulation. Each method can be used at the discretion of the underwriter, who will decide whether or not to provide price support.

Stabilizing bids: The first method is 'pure' stabilization in that the underwriter posts a stabilizing bid to purchase shares at a price not to exceed the offer price. Rule 104 requires that an underwriter placing a stabilizing bid must 'disclose the purpose of such bids to the person to whom the bid is entered' (SEC No. 34-38067 p. 90). The underwriter must notify the NYSE and provide disclosures separately to the specialist. Stabilizing bids for NASDAQ-listed stocks are flagged with a symbol on the NASDAQ quotation display. Stabilizing bids are readily apparent to market makers and theoretically to investors as well. Stabilizing bids are only allowed while the syndicate is still intact, which lasts for only a very short time into the secondary market.

Penalty bids: Regulation M, Rule 100 defines a penalty bid as follows:

> An arrangement that permits the managing underwriter to reclaim a selling concession otherwise accruing to a syndicate member (or to a selected dealer or selling group member) in conjunction with an offering when the securities originally sold by the syndicate member are purchased in syndicate covering transactions. (SEC No. 34-38067 footnote 122)

Penalty bids are designed with the intent to deter syndicate members from allocating shares to investors who will immediately flip them. The deterrent is the loss of the selling concession for placing the shares. Penalty bids are a proactive form of stabilization because they seek to prevent downward pressure from ever arising. The lead underwriter is required to disclose the presence of penalty bids to the SEC and to maintain a record of their use. However, the underwriter does not have to publicly disclose the use of penalty bids. In addition, Regulation M does not cover the more subtle forms of punishment imposed on syndicate members, including the exclusion from future offerings.

Short covering: The underwriter can take an initial short position in the stock by overselling the IPO. Short covering in the open market creates additional demand that supports the price when there is selling pressure. The short position can alternatively be covered by exercising the overallotment option. An OAO is a standard feature of IPOs and it grants the underwriter the option to purchase additional shares from the issuer and resell them to investors at the offer price. The typical OAO is for 15 percent of the offer size and is exercisable for up to 30 calendar days after the offer date. The underwriter can completely hedge the upside price risk if the short position does not exceed the size of the OAO, yet still maintain buying power to support the price when there is a sell imbalance.

Share repurchases by the underwriter in the open market are referred to as syndicate covering transactions and are subject to the same Regulation M disclosure requirements as penalty bids. In practice, investors are not informed that a particular trade is a short-covering transaction. The underwriter only has to include a statement in the prospectus indicating that it may engage in stabilizing transactions in conjunction with the offering of securities.

11.1.2.3 Evidence

The empirical evidence produces two overwhelming conclusions. First, underwriters definitely engage in price stabilization activities. Under Regulation M underwriters are required to keep detailed records of stabilizing bids, penalty bids and short covering transactions. Analysis of the records confirms that stabilization takes place (Aggarwal 2000; Boehmer and Fishe 2002). Second, stabilization is largely affected through short positions and judicious exercising of the OAO. In fact, Aggarwal (2000) reported that pure stabilizing bids were never used, penalty bids were used sporadically and short positions and covering were always used.[6]

Aggarwal documented an average syndicate short position equal to 17.1 percent of the issue size.[7] The underwriter was more apt to cover the short position by repurchasing shares in the aftermarket when the price did not increase much. The average initial return for IPOs with positive aftermarket short covering was 9.3 percent, compared to 24.2 percent for IPOs with no short covering. The short position was covered entirely by exercising the OAO in the latter sub-sample.

The size of the initial short position adjusted to the level of investor interest in the primary market. Low interest IPOs are more likely to require stabilization, calling for a larger short position. Aggarwal reported that the average short position for IPOs priced below and above the initial filing range were 23 and 15.3 percent, respectively. The underwriter avoids an uncovered – greater than the OAO – short position when the price is expected to increase significantly. Aftermarket short covering accounted for 3.3 and 16 percent of the offer size following upward and downward revised offer prices, respectively.

The underwriter stabilized the price by supplying liquidity when there was strong selling pressure. Boehmer and Fishe (2002; 2004) found that the underwriter entered the buy-side when there were few other buyers, which typically happened after a decline in the price. The provision of liquidity occurred at various price levels, primarily near the offer price. The effect of short covering on the price was significant – Boehmer and Fishe (2004) reported that the negative price impact of selling was reduced by more than 70 percent for one particular IPO. Lewellen (2003) also reported that the support had a permanent effect on the price in her sample of IPOs.

The price support by the lead underwriter has a discernible impact on market-making behavior. The bid-ask spread was positively related to the difference between the share price and the stabilized offer price (Hanley, Arunkumar and Seguin 1993). As the price declines closer to the offer, the inventory risk to non-stabilizing market-makers is lowered because of the implicit floor price. The cost of market-making falls as a result and with it the bid-ask spread. Schultz and Zaman (1994) reported that the underwriter had the inside bid quote 86 percent of the time for IPOs trading at or below the offer price on the first day, compared to only 4.4 percent for the inside ask. The underwriter uses floor brokers and limit orders to provide stabilization on the NYSE. Corwin, Harris and Lipson (2001) showed that among IPOs trading below the offer price on the first day, the floor contributed 60 to 80 percent of the bid depth, but only 10 to 20 percent of the ask depth.[8]

The bonding theory argued that price stabilization is most effective if only institutional investors are targeted with the support. Penalty bids allow for targeted support because the investors who flip their allocation can be tracked. Nonetheless, Aggarwal (2000) found that only half of the observed underwriting contracts permitted the use of penalty bids, and in only half of those IPOs were penalty bids assessed. Penalty bids were utilized when first-day returns were low and the underwriter aggressively repurchased shares in the aftermarket to cover the short position.

Underwriters do appear to target their short covering trades to support institutional investors. Hanley, Lee and Seguin (1996) and Benveniste, Erdal and Wilhelm (1998) both used proxies for underwriter trades and concluded that price support benefits institutions. Boehmer and Fishe (2004) conducted a case study of a single NYSE-listed IPO and reported that one-third of the short covering trade volume was due to the 4.2 percent of all short trades negotiated in the upstairs market. The trades almost certainly involved institutional investors, who could sell large blocks directly to the underwriter at a stabilized price. Underwriter price support trades were about 13 times larger than trades in non-supported issues, according to Boehmer and Fishe (2002). The most likely counter-parties to these large trades are institutions. Aggarwal, Prabhala and Puri (2001) is the lone conflicting study. They compared IPOs with and without price support and found little evidence that stabilization trades were targeted to institutionally held shares.

The evidence also supports for the winner's curse stabilization motive. The permanent effect that stabilization has on the price means that retail investors directly benefit from these activities. More compelling, Lewellen (2003) documented that banks with a significant retail brokerage operation were more likely to stabilize. These banks repurchased 10 percent more of the offer size on the first day of cold IPOs than other top 20 banks. The finding implies that prestigious underwriters are most concerned about their reputation with retail investors and price stabilize to protect it. This contradicts the belief that stabilization is intended for institutional investors.

11.1.2.4 Costs and profits

Conventional wisdom assumes that price stabilization is costly for the underwriter and should be avoided. Not only is this belief wrong, but underwriters can and do make substantial profits from market-making activities. The initial short position becomes highly valuable when the price declines below the offer. Aggarwal (2000) estimated that underwriters earned an average profit equal to 1.25 percent of their spread fees from short covering trades in IPOs with an initial return of less than 5 percent. For IPOs with larger initial returns, the median loss from short covering was only 3.7 percent of the fees.

The profits from short covering trades are a lower bound for the profitability of aftermarket activities. The underwriter earns trading profits from market-making and bears an inventory cost from holding a large position in the stock. The inventory cost is minimized by optimally choosing the initial short position. Ellis, Michaely and O'Hara (2000) estimated that the lead underwriter accumulated inventory positions equal to 0.4 and 15.6 percent of the offer size on the first day when the price was above and below, respectively, the offer price. The inventory was countered by the initial 17 percent short position. The large inventory position arose exactly in the IPOs in which the OAO was only partially or not at all exercised. The cumulative profits generated from all aftermarket activities in the three months following the IPO averaged 23 percent of the spread fees and that increased in the initial return.

The case study by Boehmer and Fishe (2004) illustrates just how profitable price stabilization can be. The initial return for the IPO was 15 percent, but the price declined to 10 percent below the offer three weeks later. The underwriter had an initial short position of 15.01 percent, hedged almost perfectly with the OAO. The short covering transactions in the first 30 trading days resulted in a profit equal to 52 percent of the fees.

The assumption of costly price stabilization is based on the notion that the underwriter freely provides investors with a valuable put option. The commitment to stabilize is equivalent to a short position in the put option. In reality, the exact opposite holds. Fishe (2002) persuasively argued that the portfolio of an initial short position and the OAO is equivalent to a long put position. If the market price exceeds the offer price, the short position risk is hedged by the OAO. A market price below the offer makes the short position valuable and roughly equivalent to an American put option. The long put offers protection to the profits of the underwriter, not investors. Furthermore, the value of the long put increases with the offer price, actually giving the underwriter an incentive to overprice the IPO. It is not surprising then that underwriters profit from stabilization.

11.1.2.5 Initial returns

A close examination of IPO initial returns provides a good indication that underwriters price stabilize. The initial returns should be approximately normally distributed, with a positive mean due to underpricing, under the null hypothesis of no stabilization. Yet Ruud (1993) found that a quarter of IPOs in her sample had a first-day return of zero and the distribution was right-skewed. The clustering of initial returns at zero suggests that something other than a univariate normal distribution is appropriate. Asquith, Jones and Keischnick (1998) used a mixture distribution of two normal distributions to fit the data. Differentiating between stabilized and non-stabilized IPOs gave mean initial returns of 1.4 and 17.8 percent, respectively, for the two groups. They produced a histogram of initial returns, reprinted here as Figure 11.1, which reveals quite clearly the effect of price support on the initial return distribution.

The use of the initial return as a proxy for intentional underpricing must be modified to take into account the bias induced by price stabilization. The return distribution is truncated by the stabilization of overpriced offerings, leading to an overestimate of underpricing. After controlling for the truncation, Ruud (1993) concluded that the average initial return did not differ significantly from zero. Prabhala and Puri (1998) corrected a flaw in Ruud's methodology and reported mean unadjusted and stabilization-adjusted initial returns of 10.2 and 8.4 percent, respectively. Price stabilization is thus only a small part of the underpricing puzzle.

The research on initial returns has tried to determine which IPO characteristics best explain underpricing. Added to that list are aftermarket variables. Aggarwal and Conroy (2000) found that the initial return increased in the number of quotes in the pre-opening period and decreased with the time of day at which aftermarket trading began. Both variables

Figure 11.1 Distribution of IPO returns over the first month[9]

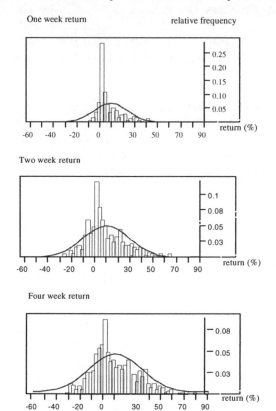

Source: Asquith, Kieschnick and Jones (1998).

proxy for investor interest. Aggarwal (2000) reported that the initial return decreased in the percentage of shares short covered in the aftermarket and increased in the percentage of the OAO exercised. The patterns are compatible with optimal stabilization by the underwriter.

11.1.2.6 Assessment

The analysis of price stabilization activities leads to two general conclusions. First, price stabilization services are not costly to the underwriter. To the contrary, it can be quite profitable. The underwriter's ability to credibly bond against overpricing is weakened when stabilization is not costly, although reputational concerns prevent a consistent pattern of overpricing. Nonetheless, the potential for aftermarket trading profits is a factor in the underwriter's decision-making process for the offer price.

The second conclusion is that there is a general lack of transparency in the stabilization process. Underwriters are only required to reveal pure stabilizing bids as such to investors, but this option is never used. Short covering transactions do not have to be disclosed. With the evidence indicating that short covering affects the market price, the distinction between price support and price manipulation becomes rather hazy. At a minimum, it is worthwhile to ask whether short covering transactions should be made explicitly clear to investors, especially in light of the substantial profits they generate. The apparent selective targeting of price support trades to institutional investors also raises questions of fairness in the application of stabilization. The anonymity of current stabilization activities has significant value to the underwriter and may be a sufficient cost to investors that it is ultimately harmful to the IPO process.

11.1.3 Flipping

The extraordinarily high first-day trading volume and the need for price stabilization are direct consequences of flipping. Investors who receive an IPO allocation are said to flip their shares if they sell them immediately in the aftermarket. Flipping could be motivated by the desire to lock in quick profits or to dump shares before price stabilization ends. Underwriters have traditionally viewed flipping with contempt because of the negative price impact that it creates and the excess volatility generated. Flipping is also at odds with the issuer's preference for a clientele of long-term investors.

Flipping does have its benefits and even the underwriters' scorn is somewhat contingent on the IPO performance. There would be no trading and liquidity on the first day without any flipping. Since investors generally avoid illiquid stocks, no flipping is worse than excessive flipping. More important from the underwriter's perspective is that trading profits increase in the amount of flipping, which can obviously change some attitudes.

The stated policy of most underwriters is to discourage flipping. They can try to enforce low flipping by assessing penalty bids to syndicate members whose clients flip their allocation and with the implicit threat of exclusion from future IPOs if an investor flips. Critics of the underwriter's selective allocation policy have no love loss for the perceived bias in the punishment of flippers. Retail investors usually face much more severe consequences if they flip as compared to institutional investors. The evidence of targeting price stabilization to institutions lends credence to this claim. Whether underwriters really do discourage flipping and who is actually flipping are questions that can only be answered empirically.

11.1.3.1 Flipping patterns

Three stylized facts regarding first-day flipping patterns are evident in the data.[10] First, the average trading volume measured as a percentage of the issue size has been in the range of 55 to 80 percent. The volume increased with the initial return, starting from a low of about 35 percent for negative initial return IPOs and going up to 189 percent for returns in excess of 60 percent. Second, flipped shares as a fraction of first-day trading volume averaged about 20 percent and the percentage decreased in the initial return. That is, flipping accounted for a larger fraction of total volume in cold IPOs. Third, approximately 20 percent of the issued shares were flipped. The percentage again increased in the initial return; about 10 percent for negative returns and over 30 percent when the return exceeded 20 percent.

The flipping evidence clarifies the factors contributing to first-day volume. The heavy volume is primarily a result of the same shares being traded repeatedly, not just excessive flipping. Greater flipping activity in hot IPOs contradicts the expectation that flipping is more pervasive in cold IPOs as investors dump overpriced shares.[11] Less flipping in cold IPOs suggests that the threat of penalty bids and exclusion from future IPOs are effective deterrents. The lucrative profits that underwriters make from the heavy volume in hot IPOs mollify any concerns about the damage caused by flipping.

11.1.3.2 Retail versus institutional

A widely-held perception seems to be that retail investors clamor for an IPO allocation so they can flip the shares and lock in the initial return profit. Investment bankers claim that institutions are preferred because they are more stable long-term investors who are less likely to flip. The flipping evidence tells a different story.

Institutional investors routinely flip a larger percentage of their allocation than retail investors and the percentage flipped for both groups increases with the initial return. Aggarwal (2003) reported that in her sample institutions flipped 47 and 20 percent of shares allotted to them in hot and cold IPOs, respectively, whereas retail investors flipped 28 and 11.5 percent. The average number of shares flipped per institutional trade was 37,097 and 3,083 in cold and hot IPOs. Retail flipping trades were much smaller; the median size was less than 400. Boehmer, Boehmer and Fishe (2002) similarly reported that institutional (retail) flipping increased from 21 (9) percent in cold IPOs to 31 (19) percent in hot offerings.

The increased institutional flipping in hot IPOs may be a consequence of oversubscribed offerings being rationed. Most institutions would find that holding a small stake in an IPO is not an efficient allocation of capital in a large portfolio. An institution could either buy additional shares in the aftermarket, which is expensive when the initial return is high, or flip the shares. The relatively small size of flipped trades for hot IPOs could reflect smaller allocations. But it might also be an attempt to split the order to minimize the price impact. Large trades in cold IPOs are facilitated by price stabilization.

11.1.3.3 Optimal flipping

The amount of flipping is not independent of the pricing and allocation decisions made by the underwriter. The positive relationship between underpricing and underwriter trading profits, linked together by flipping, implies that the optimal offer price from the underwriter's perspective involves a trade-off. The optimal price equates the marginal gain in trading profits from a lower price to the marginal loss from reduced spread fees.

The offer price advocated by the underwriter depends on the spread and the expected amount of flipping. A lower spread makes trading profits relatively more attractive and should result in additional underpricing (Boehmer and Fishe 2000). Part of the expected flipping is endogenously determined by the offer price. Another part is an exogenously fixed component; some investors plan to flip regardless of the price.[12] High expected exogenous flipping creates an incentive for the underwriter to overprice the IPO. The underwriter can ration the allocation to long-term investors, oversell the offering to the exogenous flippers and set the offer price too high with the knowledge that flipping will drive it down to the correct level (Fishe 2002). The high offer price increases the spread fees and generates larger short covering profits.

Boehmer and Fishe (2000) examined the relationships between the spread, underpricing, flipping and aftermarket profits. Flipping increased in the first-day return and the trading profits increased with flipping, both supportive of the predictions. They also found some evidence that IPOs with higher flipping ratios and trading profits were associated with lower spread fees, consistent with a trade-off between the two profit sources.

11.1.3.4 Forecasting

Trading patterns on the first day reflect whether the IPO was under- or over-priced. For example, a sell order imbalance is generally associated with a negative initial return. The share price should adjust immediately to the information embodied in the trading imbalance. If it does, the subsequent stock returns generated by IPOs will, on average, equal the expected rate of return. Consequently, the initial trading patterns should have no predictive ability for future returns.

The forecasting ability of early trading patterns for the long-run stock returns was examined in a number of studies. Boehmer, Boehmer and Fishe (2002) found no relation between either institutional or retail flipping and long-run returns. In contrast, Corwin, Harris and Lipson (2001) reported that NYSE IPOs with extreme sell imbalances in the pre-opening order flow underperformed IPOs with buy imbalances by an average of 18.3 percent in the first year. However, there was no relation between flipping and the one-year return. Krigman, Shaw and Womack (1999) documented a negative correlation between seller-initiated block trades – measured as a percentage of the first-day trading volume – and the one-year returns. Hogue et al. (2002) similarly showed that sell-signed block and non-block first-day trading volume relative to total volume was negatively related to the one and three-year returns. Overall, it appears that the market does not immediately discount the price sufficiently when there is heavy selling activity. The gradual downward drift results in poor long-run returns.

11.2 ANALYSTS AND RESEARCH

All newly public companies face the challenge of developing an effective communications program with their diverse group of new shareholders. The virtues of such an effort are many, as pointed out by a quote from a NASDAQ (2002) report.[13]

> An effective investor relations (IR) program can reinforce a company's strengths, strategy, and key executives – and it is vital to helping a company achieve its goal of maximizing shareholder value.

Company executives have many ways of communicating their beliefs and information to investors, including meetings with investment bank analysts, earnings forecasts, initiation of dividends or share repurchases. The methods chosen and emphasized by management depend on the specific needs and characteristics of the company.[14] However, the most important form of communication is analyst coverage. Continuing with the NASDAQ quote from above: 'The foundation of most IR programs is built on contact with sell-side analysts. They are the key link to the buy side, providing research, recommending stocks and overseeing transactions'.

Analyst coverage became the focus of considerable media attention during and after the Internet IPO bubble. Analysts such as Mary Meeker of Morgan Stanley and Henry Blodget of Merrill Lynch gained notoriety for their recommendations and price targets for recent Internet IPOs. Revelations in the bubble's aftermath made it clear that these recommendations were part of a disturbing pattern. Analysts were willing and, in many cases, forced to make and maintain positive recommendations on stocks that they privately knew were not warranted. Conflict of interests within the research departments of major investment banks were the cause of these biased recommendations. The intent of the bias was to win new investment banking business. The independence of research, fundamental to its long-term viability, was compromised to maximize short-term profits.

The attention garnered by the conflict of interest scandal only serves to highlight the importance of analyst coverage. Issuers' desire for positive coverage is at the root of the scandal, for without them selecting underwriters based on research, analysts would have freer reign to give unbiased recommendations. To appreciate why the scandal arose it is first necessary to understand the economic impact of analyst recommendations. The importance of analysts grew in the 1990s, but their future relevancy remains uncertain after the reforms to the investment banking industry. Consequently, conclusions drawn from the analysis of past analyst research may not be applicable in the future.

11.2.1 Coverage Initiation

The SEC strictly prohibits public comments about the issuer during the so-called 'quiet period' that lasts for 40 calendar days after the IPO. The regulation applies to the lead and co-managing underwriters, other syndicate members and the issuer. The regulations advise against issuing forecasts relating but not limited to revenues, income and earnings per share, and offering opinions about valuations in formal recommendations or research reports. Reiterating information contained in the prospectus is, however, permitted. Banks not connected to the IPO can publicly comment, although they generally refrain from doing so.

Analyst coverage initiation and intensity changed from the early 1980s to the late 1990s, which reflected the growing importance of analysts. Three patterns are clearly evident in the data.

Timeliness: Analysts have become much quicker to initiate coverage and make recommendations once the quiet period ends. In fact, it is now common practice for coverage to begin immediately. Bradley, Jordan and Ritter (2003) documented that 95 percent of IPOs received immediate coverage in 2000, compared to only 57 percent in 1996. Less than 20 percent of IPOs in the mid-1980s even had coverage initiated by any analyst within six months of the IPO (Das, Guo and Zhang 2002). By the mid-1990s the percentage was over 80.

Analysts affiliated with the lead or co-managing underwriters initiate coverage much sooner than non-affiliated analysts. Dunbar, Hwang and Shastri (1999), examining IPOs from 1992–93, reported that the lead analyst's coverage was initiated an average of 88 days after the IPO, compared to 178 days for non-affiliated underwriters. The difference in timeliness is no longer as great, but still present. The move towards immediate coverage, especially by affiliated analysts, underscores the implicit understanding that the underwriter is chosen in large part for the quality of subsequent analyst coverage.

Intensity: The intensity of coverage – measured by the number of analysts following a stock – increased in the 1990s and is positively correlated with the timeliness. The increased intensity is primarily due to a larger number of co-managing underwriters (see below) and the greater emphasis issuers' place on research coverage. The correlation between intensity and timeliness is likely caused by a third factor, issuer quality. Stocks that are more attractive to cover garner faster and greater coverage. For example, Das, Guo and Zhang (2002) found that when coverage was initiated within six months of the IPO versus one to three years later, an average of 2 and 1.2 analysts, respectively, covered the stock within its first three years.[15]

Coverage intensity in the past has varied with properties of the issuer and the IPO.[16] Intensity has been found to increase with the offer size, the initial trading volume, the market capitalization of the issuer and the number of firms in the industry. Issuers that had VC-backing, were underwritten by a prestigious bank and listed on the NASDAQ also had more coverage.

Buying coverage: Issuers are buying more coverage by increasing the number of co-managing underwriters. Each affiliated analyst has an incentive to cover the issuer because of the potential to win future investment banking business. Corwin and Schultz (2003) found that each additional co-manager resulted in 0.69 more analysts issuing reports within three months of the IPO. Chen and Ritter (2000) reported a similar result and they showed that the growth in intensity from the 1980s to the 1990s is, in large part, a consequence of more co-managers. The additional research coverage comes at no cost to the issuer because the spread fees are based on the gross proceeds. Cliff and Denis (2003) documented that issuers do pay for more coverage with greater underpricing. They found a positive relation between underpricing and the probability of a buy recommendation from the lead underwriter.

11.2.1 Benefit of Coverage

The desire to attract analyst coverage only makes sense if it has a positive impact on an issuer's value. Analysts produce three types of information: buy, sell or hold recommendations, forecasts for future earnings and growth, and price targets. Announcements of new recommendations have an immediate impact on the stock price, positive if it is a buy and negative for a sell. Earnings forecasts affect the overall price level. The price should equal the present value of future earnings, so small changes in forecasted growth rates can have a large affect on the price. Price targets for a stock have a horizon anywhere from six months to a few years. Analysts also produce general research reports that yield value-enhancing information, even if the price impact is not directly discernable.

Three hypotheses suggest why analyst coverage can have a beneficial impact on the stock price of the issuer. The size of the benefit is, however, conditional on the existing amount of coverage. The first analyst to initiate coverage of a stock will have the largest price impact because there was no prior research. The marginal benefit to each additional analyst declines as there is less new information produced. Thus, the benefits of coverage initiation for newly public companies should be particularly high.

Liquidity hypothesis: Increased analyst coverage helps traders become more informed and that ultimately results in a more informative stock price. Uninformed traders directly benefit because they face smaller expected losses from trading against informed investors and consequently will be more active (Brennan and Subrahmanyam 1995; Brennan and Tamarowski 2000). Greater trading volume improves liquidity and lowers the trading costs, which leads to a fall in the stock's expected return and a rise in the share price (Amihud and Mendelson 1986).

Monitoring hypothesis: Analysts are effective external monitors of company management (Moyer, Chatfield and Sisneros 1989). Published research reports and explicit recommendations may spur on improved operating performance. Jain and Kini (1999) reported a positive relationship between the stock price performance and the number of non-affiliated analysts following the stock. The casual link could be running the other way; analysts choose to follow stocks that are doing well.

Learning hypothesis: An analyst must expend considerable time and effort to learn about a company in order to cover its stock. Initiating coverage presumably demands greater effort than continuing existing coverage. Consequently, analysts' forecasts and recommendations may be more informative at coverage initiation than at any later time (Peterson 1987). McNichols and O'Brien (1997) reported that analysts' initiation earnings forecasts were more accurate than their continuation forecasts.

11.2.1.1 Valuation effects

The benefit of analyst recommendations can be measured directly by the abnormal stock price reaction following the announcement. Initial buy recommendations for all stocks have generated average CARs in the 3 to 7 percent range.[17] The CARs following sell recommendations are negative and tend to be even larger in absolute value. Sayrak and Dhiensiri (2003) found that the reputation of the analyst's bank was positively associated with the announcement return. The abnormal return for initiation buy recommendations is also larger than an existing buy that was reconfirmed by an analyst. Irvine (2002) estimated the incremental benefit of an initiation recommendation to be approximately 1 percent, demonstrating the importance of garnering coverage.

The price reaction to initial buy recommendations for IPOs is similar to initial buys for seasoned public companies. Estimates of the announcement CARs for initial buys have varied from a low of minus 0.19 percent to a high of 4.4 percent.[18] The measured variation is a result of different sample periods and sources of data, with the largest CARs occurring during the Internet bubble. Analyst coverage is usually initiated with a favorable rating and the announcement effect increases with the strength of the recommendation.[19] The abnormal returns were much larger when multiple analysts initiated coverage simultaneously, implying a confirming effect exists among recommendations (Bradley, Jordan and Ritter 2002).

11.2.2 Conflict of Interests

The stated objective of research is to provide valuable information to buy-side investors. In return, the investors direct their trading flow through the bank. The unspoken objective of analysts in the 1990s was to help win lucrative investment banking business. Since buy recommendations have a positive effect on the share price, issuers prefer banks that would provide favorable coverage. A conflict of interest arose when the unbiased recommendation for buy-side investors was at odds with the positive recommendation expected by the issuer. Investment banks have instituted 'Chinese walls' designed to create a clear separation between corporate finance and equity research, and minimize the potential for conflicts. The walls proved to be largely ineffective during the bull market of the late 1990s, resulting in potentially positively biased recommendations.

The anecdotal evidence that surfaced during the New York state Attorney General's office investigation into possible analyst conflicts was sufficient for many to conclude that intentional biases in the recommendations existed and that investors, in particular retail, were directly harmed. Stories of corruption aside, this does not constitute formal economic evidence that analysts are inherently biased and that investors are hurt as a result. It is difficult to argue against conflicted recommendations during the height of the Internet bubble, especially given the scarcity of anything but a strong buy. However, prior to this period of excess the potential for conflicts also existed. Examining IPOs from this earlier time offers a more nuanced treatment of possible biases, a valuable exercise as equity research evolves in the future.

11.2.3.1 Conflicted recommendations

Conflict of interests will be most severe for analysts affiliated with an investment bank that has a formal underwriting relationship – either lead or co-manager – with an issuer. Non-affiliated analysts have more freedom to issue unbiased recommendations. The possibility of conflicted analysts does not mean that biases arise or that investors are harmed. Only empirical evidence can confirm whether deleterious consequences of potential conflicts occur.

Without reading the mind of analysts, we can only rely on indirect evidence to deduce the existence of biases. A pattern of affiliated analysts issuing significantly more buy recommendations than non-affiliated analysts for the same stocks is suggestive of a bias. A conflicted affiliated analyst is more likely to issue a positive recommendation when the issuer has performed poorly to give the stock price a 'booster shot'. A bias should make affiliated analysts less discriminating in their buy recommendations than non-affiliated analysts, implying that their recommended stocks will produce worse long-run returns.

Michaely and Womack's (1999) analysis of IPOs from 1992 to 1993 strongly suggests that there is a conflict-induced bias. Affiliated analysts issued 50 percent more buy recommendations in the first month after the quiet period ended than non-affiliated analysts.[20] The stock price fell on average in the 30 days prior to an affiliated buy recommendation, but rose before a non-affiliated buy. The stock returns measured from the IPO date to the date of the buy recommendation were 7.9 and 23.9 percent for affiliated and non-affiliated analysts, respectively. Iskoz (2003), examining IPOs from the end of 1993 through to 2000, found that lead underwriter analysts were not significantly more likely to issue a positive recommendation than non-lead analysts. However, they were twice as likely to do so within the first two months after the IPO.

The long-run returns also support the bias hypothesis. Michaely and Womack showed that the average issuer who received only an affiliated buy recommendation generated raw stock returns over the first two post-IPO years that were 50 percent less than those for issuers with non-affiliated buys. The presence of a non-conflicted recommendation is a strong signal about the issuer's prospects. The poor predictive ability of affiliated analysts was not due to a lack of skill. Analysts issue buy recommendations for companies with and without a relationship to their bank. In 12 of the 14 brokerage firms studied, the unrelated companies produced higher average two-year stock returns than the banking clients. Since evaluation ability should be constant across firms, the difference could reflect a conflict bias.

Iskoz partitioned the IPOs into two subgroups depending on whether they had recommendations from either only the lead analyst or only non-lead analysts and then compared the one-year post-recommendation returns. When the recommendation was a strong buy, the lead-only IPOs significantly underperformed non-lead IPOs, but there was no difference between the two groups for IPOs with buy recommendations. Aggregating buy and strong buy IPOs together resulted in little difference between the performance of the lead and non-lead recommendated IPOs.

Biased recommendations do not automatically mean that investors are harmed. If they understand that a bias exists, they should discount the information content of affiliated recommendations. To test whether investors see through the bias, the announcement returns for affiliated and non-affiliated recommendations can be compared. Rational investors should respond less positively to affiliated buys than those made by non-affiliated analysts if they perceive a bias. The opposite price reaction could occur if the potential for bias is outweighed by an informational advantage. Affiliated analysts have superior information about the issuer value after the due diligence review, the road show and extensive time spent with senior management. A buy recommendation could send a strong signal about the firm's prospects.

The evidence weighs in favor of investors seeing through the bias. Estimates for the average announcement CAR for the initial affiliated buy ranged from -0.19 to 2.7 percent (Dunbar, Hwang and Shastri 1999; Michaely and Womack 1999). The corresponding CAR estimates for non-affiliated analysts were significantly larger, 1.36 to 4.4 percent. However, other studies have found no significant difference in the CARs (Lin and McNichols 1998; Bradley, Jordan and Ritter 2002). There is no evidence that investors' view affiliated recommendations as more informative.

11.2.3.2 Alternative explanations

The greater frequency of buy recommendations by affiliated analysts following the IPO could be the result of self-selection, not a conflict of interest. Issuers are more likely to select the underwriter who is most optimistic about the IPO's success and has the best expectation for the deal terms. The optimism will be reflected in the analysts' forecasts and recommendations. Self-selection is a factor in explaining the overwhelming majority of buy, relative to sell, recommendations for all stocks, as analysts cover the companies for which they have high expectations (McNichols and O'Brien 1997). Regarding IPOs, one analyst simply stated:

> It goes without saying that if you do a company's IPO, you are going to have a buy, because frankly if you don't you shouldn't be doing the deal ... for every deal Salomon has done in the last 12 months, I have personally turned down two deals. (Raghavan 1997, p. C1)

The possibility of a self-selection bias demands a reinterpretation of the recommendation CARs. The smaller reaction to an affiliated buy could reflect the fact that investors have already impounded into the price the underwriter's positive affirmation of the issuer's quality. The buy recommendation provides little new information. Dunbar, Hwang and Shastri (1999) measured the CARs following affiliated and non-affiliated initial buys to be -0.19 and 1.36 percent, respectively. However, the average CARs for non-initial affiliated buys was 2.55 percent, significantly larger than 1.36 percent. The large return for the non-initial buy suggests that investors recognize the superior information of the affiliated analysts and respond positively to the continued buy recommendation.

Additional evidence implying self-selection, not conflict of interests, is responsible for the recommendation patterns was offered by Iskoz (2003). One-year returns following lead analyst buys were much better than the returns after strong buys. A conflicted analyst would have switched the buys to strong buys because it would improve their performance record and please the issuers. Issuers with only lead analyst recommendations were much smaller than firms with only non-lead recommendations. Conflicted lead analysts would not waste their biased recommendations on small firms that are not a major source of underwriting profit. A plausible alternative explanation is that non-lead analysts did not share the lead analysts' optimism about the potential of these small, relatively unknown issuers. Self-selection led the lead analyst's bank to underwrite the IPO.

11.2.3.3 Institutional structure

Allegations of conflict of interests and biased research during the stock market bubble of the 1990s lead to a formal investigation into investment banking practices, headed by the New York state Attorney General's office, the SEC, the NYSE and NASDAQ. The investigation revealed compelling anecdotal evidence of a bias in recommendations. Internal emails sent by analysts at Merrill Lynch contained negative comments about companies on which they had public buy recommendations. The investigation culminated in a settlement between the regulators and a dozen major investment banks in April 2003 designed to eliminate future conflicts in research.

The conflict of interest scandal is the outcome of a gradual change in the investment banking industry that began in the 1970s. Deregulation led to a decline in the real value of trading commissions. Equity research is self-sufficient as long as the trading profits generated by the research covers the cost. By the late 1990s the research department at a top-tier bank was costing upwards of $1 billion a year. At the same time, underwriting and advisory work grew into a dominant source of revenue, subsidizing the cost of research. As the center of gravity within the banks shifted towards corporate finance, the focus of the research also evolved – from being exclusively geared towards buy-side investors to appeasing sell-side clients.

The evolution in research is captured by the role analysts played in the IPO process. Analysts frequently took part in the sales pitch to the issuer and the due diligence review. The banks benefited from a reduction in expertise overlap between departments and used the analysts' reputation to market the IPO to investors. Analysts' compensation was also based partly on their 'helpfulness' in winning banking business.[21] Considerable internal pressure was exerted on analysts to issue positive recommendations. A Morgan Stanley internal memo quoted in the *Wall Street Journal* in 1992, long before the conflict scandal, illustrates this point:

> Our objective ... is to adopt a policy, fully understood by the entire firm, including the Research Department, that we do not make negative or controversial comments about our clients as a matter of sound business practice. (Siconolfi 1992, p. C1)

The pressure on analysts to issue positive recommendations comes from the issuers as well. When the firm is not satisfied with the bias in the research coverage by its bank, it can threaten to take its substantial underwriting fees to a competitor.[22] The issuer can also punish analysts by cutting off access to the senior management. The analyst's ability to produce relevant and accurate research is constrained when he or she cannot speak to the CEO.

Buy-side investors, the people harmed by conflicted analysts, also dislike revisions to biased recommendations. An analyst who changes a buy to a hold or a sell has a negative impact on the share price, directly hurting buy-side clients who own shares in the company. One former analyst at CSFB stated: 'You got a lot of heat as an analyst. You got heat if you downgraded, you got heat from investors, companies would get angry or cut you off', (Smith 2002, p. 37).

The settlement reached by the banks and regulators is an attempt to resolve the conflict of interest problem. The settlement demanded a clear separation between research and banking. Analysts are no longer permitted to take part in the sales pitch to issuers to win new business. Contact with an investment banker must be chaperoned by internal legal counsel. Analyst compensation cannot be tied to investment banking deals and profitability.

Critics have argued that the settlement did not go far enough; only a complete separation of research from investment banking will prevent future conflicts. There is reason to believe that such a radical restructuring is unnecessary. Some recommendations during the bubble period were certainly conflicted and the patterns in the pre-bubble period are consistent with a conflict-induced bias. But one cannot discount the importance of the self-selection bias. Even independent analysts are likely to exhibit a positive bias in their research coverage. The real concern is whether investors are harmed by the potential for conflicts. The evidence that the value of affiliated recommendations is discounted suggests that investors were already aware of the potential bias and their skepticism should only be greater in the post-scandal world.

Concerns about future conflict scandals are also mitigated by the industry's incentive to self-police against such problems. Intermediaries like investment banks rely tremendously on their reputation with investors and issuers for being honest brokers. The temptation always exists for the banks to trade on their reputation and those of their analysts to issue unwarranted recommendations for companies in order to win their banking business and sell the offerings to investors. The cost to such deception is the inevitable damage to the reputations of both banks and analysts that diminishes their future earnings potential.

The factor that can sustain an equilibrium in which conflicts are held to a minimum is that positively biased recommendations do not necessarily help the banks win new business. According to Ljungqvist, Marston and Wilhelm (2003) the existence of a long-term relationship between a bank and a company and the reputation of both the bank and its analysts were far more important in winning that company's equity underwriting business (exclusive of IPOs). In fact, there was a negative correlation between the aggressiveness of the recommendations and the probability of winning the business after controlling for these other factors. Ljungqvist, Marston and Wilhelm interpreted this as evidence that the banks and analysts want to maintain good reputations for accuracy and honesty in their research. This equilibrium was upset during the bubble years because the enormous underwriting profits being made. Over the long term, reputation concerns should help to preserve research independence.

11.2.4 Earnings Forecasts

Research reports produced by analysts include forecasts for current and next year earnings, and forecasts for long-term growth in earnings. A bias in the earnings forecasts of affiliated analysts is possible, but less likely for two reasons. First, earnings forecasts are difficult to fudge and provide an objective test for analyst accuracy; evaluating the quality of recommendations is more subjective. An analyst concerned about his reputation has a strong incentive to issue unbiased forecasts. Second, recommendations are discrete in nature. Analysts are effectively limited to initiating coverage with a buy or a hold, giving an affiliated analyst little choice but to issue a buy. The finer partitioning of earnings forecasts reduces the upward bias unavoidable with recommendations.

The accuracy and bias of analyst forecasts for all stocks has been the focus of ongoing research. The overall evidence suggests that analysts underreact to negative information and overreact to positive information.[23] For example, analysts often do not lower earnings forecasts sufficiently when a company issues a warning, but extrapolate a recent positive earnings result into the future without accounting for mean-reversion. The combined effect is a systematic positive bias in the forecasts of earnings.

IPOs bring forth two additional concerns. The first is whether analysts are even more optimistic about IPOs than other firms. Rajan and Servaes (1997) reported forecast errors – the difference between forecasted and actual earnings – for current and next year earnings averaged 5 percent of the issuer's stock price. Much of the bias was a result of analysts being too optimistic about the industry prospects. After adjusting for size and industry forecast errors, the issuer error fell to 1.5 percent. Industry optimism is not surprising; firms go public when industry prospects are thought to be high.

The second concern is over the relative accuracy and bias of affiliated and non-affiliated analysts. The evidence weakly favors no bias in the forecasts. Dugar and Nathan (1995) and Lin and McNichols (1998) both found no difference in affiliated and non-affiliated earnings forecasts for IPOs. But Brav and Gompers (2003) reported a positive affiliated bias at the lockup expiration and Dechow, Hutton and Sloan (1999) documented a positive bias in affiliated forecasts following SEOs.

Analysts exhibit the greatest optimistic bias for the long-term growth prospects of issuers. Lin and McNichols (1998) found that forecast errors and the affiliated bias increased with the forecast duration. Analyst optimism also tended to increase in the level of expected growth.[24] For example, analysts' growth projections for companies like Yahoo and Amazon would exceed the actual growth by a greater percentage than the forecasts for manufacturers. The growth projections were most optimistic shortly after the IPO and gradually declined as analysts realized that the predicted growth would not be attained (Rajan and Servaes 1997).

The affiliated bias that is most prevalent in recommendations and long-term growth forecasts is due to three factors. First, affiliated analysts almost certainly initiate coverage with a buy, even if their current earnings forecasts are the same as non-affiliated analysts. Second, firm valuation is based on growth projections. The self-selection bias implies that the most optimistic investment bank will get the underwriting business. Third, the manipulation of a growth forecast or recommendation is more difficult to detect than short-term earnings forecasts and may be less costly to analysts.

11.3 LOCKUPS

Most IPOs feature a lockup provision as a formal part of the underwriting agreement. Pre-IPO shareholders agree to refrain from selling their shares on the open market for a fixed duration after the IPO without prior approval from the underwriter. The fraction of the insider shareholdings covered and the length of the lockup varies, although virtually all agreements now last for 180 days and cover about 95 percent of the unsold pre-IPO shares (Field and Hanka 2001).

11.3.1 Returns

The expiration of the lockup agreement is associated with a significant share price reaction. The average CAR surrounding the expiration date has been approximately -1.5 percent.[25] The average differs significantly between issuers with and without venture capital backing. The CAR for VC-backed companies is about -2.5 to -2.8 percent, whereas non-VC issuers experienced declines of only -0.5 percent. The price declines were permanent and not due to temporary downward price pressure. Trading volume also permanently increased after the lockup expiration, jumping 20 to 50 percent above the pre-expiration level.

The expiration price decline is a puzzle. Traders know with certainty the expiration date, whether the issuer was VC-backed, how many shares were locked up and who owns them. There is no reason for the price to consistently drop without any new information. Rational investors should arbitrage the abnormal return away.

A number of factors that could account for the abnormal return were considered by Ofek and Richardson (2000), three of which they rejected as possible explanations. First, a permanent increase in liquidity due to increased trading would not cause the price decline. In fact, increased liquidity raises the share value, which should produce a positive return. Second, a bid-ask bounce is not responsible for the decline. Unlocking shares leads to an imbalance of sell-initiated trades occurring at the lower bid price. After the surge in selling passes, trades will occur closer to the ask price. If this were true the price decline would be temporary, when in fact it is permanent. Third, information-motivated selling at the expiration cannot explain the decline. A normal level of selling is expected as insiders liquidate their holdings. Unexpected supply shocks that may be linked to inside information were not related to the CAR.

Ofek and Richardson also offered three reasons why the decline is not arbitraged away. First, investors who received an IPO allocation may not engage in arbitrage because of tax considerations. Any price appreciation since the IPO is taxed as ordinary income at the expiration date, but at the lower capital gains rate if the shares are held for six more months. Second, the bid-ask spread may be too wide for profitable arbitrage. Consistent with this possibility, the width of the spread and the absolute price drop were positively related. Third, arbitraging away the decline requires the ability to short sell, something that is not always easy to do with IPOs. This was the case; the more difficult it was to short sell, the larger was the decline.

The most plausible explanation for the decline is the existence of a downward sloping demand curve. The increased selling at the expiration shifts the supply curve further out, leading to a lower market price. The significantly larger price decline for VC-backed issuers may be attributable to the demand curve effect. The limited partners often sell the first chance they get, which is the lockup expiration, causing a surge in supply. Ofek and Richardson found some evidence that the price decline was greater when the demand curve appeared steeper.

11.3.2 Motivation

The lockup agreement is a relatively innocuous feature of the IPO process, yet still plays an important role in ensuring a successful offering. Locking up the shares reduces the need for price stabilization by limiting the selling pressure in the immediate aftermarket. Forcing the insiders to retain their large equity position, even if only temporarily, can mitigate some of the agency concerns investors may have.

The primary motivation for a lockup is the desire to overcome information asymmetries between firm insiders and investors. Insiders simply have access to information relevant for valuing the firm that is unavailable to investors. Consequently, high (low) quality firms tend to be undervalued (overvalued) by investors. Insiders who retain a large equity stake at the IPO can signal their belief that the firm quality is indeed high (Leland and Pyle 1977). The signaling value of a large stake is void if the insiders can sell their shares immediately after the IPO. Insiders of low quality firms could easily mimic their high quality counterparts by retaining a large equity stake for the IPO, but then dumping the shares as soon as possible in the aftermarket (Gale and Stiglitz 1989). Lockups raise the mimicking cost because the issuer quality could be revealed before the lockup expires.

The properties of lockup agreements are also a response to asymmetric information. Brav and Gompers (2003) proposed two competing theories. The commitment theory builds on the premise that high quality issuers are associated with less adverse selection risk. Investors know more about these firms and require a smaller bonding commitment from insiders before purchasing shares in the IPO. Thus, high quality and better known issuers have shorter lockup periods and lock up fewer shares. The alternative theory is a signaling argument. Informationally opaque, high quality start-ups want to reveal themselves as good firms. To effectively signal the quality insiders can lock up more shares for a longer period of time, making it prohibitively costly for low quality issuers to mimic.

Evidence reported in Brav and Gompers (2003) and Brau, Lambson and McQueen (2003) supports the commitment theory. Lockups were shorter for larger firms, those with VC-backing and for issuers affiliated with high quality underwriters and auditors. The percentage of shares locked-up decreased with lockup length, suggesting that a total amount of 'lockup commitment' is required, with the insiders choosing the preferred combination of length and number of shares. Lockup agreements for follow-on offerings typically last 90 days. Publicly traded firms are more transparent, which would explain the shorter lockup period.

11.3.3 Underpricing

According to the commitment theory, the lockup length is positively related to the severity of asymmetric information. Since underpricing also increases with information asymmetries, it should be positively correlated with the length of the lockup. Brav and Gompers (2003) did show that initial returns were positively related to the lockup length and interpreted this as additional support for the commitment theory.

The presence of a lockup agreement creates an incentive to increase underpricing. Insiders who cannot sell their shares until the lockup expires may care more about the stock price at the expiration date than the offer price. The optimal IPO pricing strategy for these insiders is the one that will maximize the share price six months hence. Aggarwal, Krigman and Womack (2002) argued that additional underpricing generates price momentum through research coverage, resulting in a higher share price at the expiration date. They found that underpricing was greater when managers retained more shares and options on shares. The larger first-day returns generated increased research coverage by non-affiliated analysts, which was positively correlated with the return up to the expiration date and that with the number of shares sold by management around the expiration.[26]

11.4 SUMMARY

The success of an IPO is contingent on its performance in the aftermarket. The lead underwriter actively makes a market for NASDAQ-listed IPOs and provides liquidity for NYSE-listed IPOs. The underwriter price stabilizes when necessary by taking an initial short position close to 15 percent of the offer size. If the price rises, the short position is covered by exercising the overallotment option; otherwise the position is covered through aftermarket buying. Short covering is difficult for investors to detect and can be quite profitable for the underwriter, raising questions about what should be allowed and disclosed. Price stabilization is often required because of flipping. Contrary to expectations, institutional, not retail, investors are more likely to flip their allocation and flipping is most prevalent in hot IPOs.

The second major aftermarket service provided by the underwriter is analyst research. Coverage by analysts has a positive impact on the share price because of the increased information production and buy recommendations. Conflicts of interest in analysts' recommendations were a major problem in the 1990s. Affiliated analysts are inclined to issue biased recommendations as a way to win and maintain banking business. Investors do partly see through the bias to discount the recommendation's value. There is some evidence that the biases are driven by self-selection optimism. Earnings forecasts exhibit a smaller affiliated bias. The future of analyst research and potential biases is uncertain in the wake of the industry reforms imposed by the regulatory authorities. The final IPO event, the lockup expiration, is characterized by price declines of 1 to 3 percent. The best explanation for the drop is downward sloping demand curves. The lockups serve the purpose of credibly signaling issuer quality.

NOTES

1. See Barry and Jennings (1993), Aggarwal and Conroy (2000) and Corwin, Harris and Lipson (2001).
2. The time when trading begins is not normally a surprise to regular market participants because certain underwriters are associated with opening at a specific time, which they try to stick to.
3. The 20 percent figure is a lower bound on the amount of flipping. Short sales would not account for much of the volume due to the difficulty of obtaining shares to short.
4. The exemption for price stabilization can be found in Section 10b-6 of the 1934 Act.
5. This and the subsequent quotes in this subsection are from SEC release No. 34-38067. The quotes originally appeared in Wilhelm (1999) and are reproduced here.
6. These conclusions were based on 114 IPOs from May to July 1997, right after Regulation M was adopted.
7. This is larger than the 15 percent OAO and the major reason why the lead underwriter accumulates a positive inventory position.
8. Corwin, Harris and Lipson (2001) also found an unusually large number of limit buy orders submitted at exactly the offer price for cold IPOs, consistent with a quote matching strategy in the presence of expected underwriter stabilization.
9. Re-printed from the *Journal of Finance*, Vol. 53, Asquith D., J. Jones and R. Kieschnick, "Evidence on Price Stabilization and Underpricing in Early IPO Returns," pp. 1759-73, Copyright (1998) with permission from Blackwell Publishing.
10. See Aggarwal (2003), Corwin, Harris and Lipman (2001) and Boehmer, Boehmer and Fishe (2002). Collectively they examined IPOs from 1997 to 2001.
11. Krigman, Shaw and Womack (1999) first argued that flipping was greater for cold IPOs. The conclusion was based on flipping relative to trading volume, not shares issued.
12. Forming this expectation is less difficult than it first appears because institutional investors often indicate during the road show whether they plan to flip their allocation.
13. This quote first appeared in Das, Guo and Zhang (2002).
14. Mohamran (2001) found that firms used earnings announcements when they had high return volatility, dividend initiations if stock return volatility was low and earnings were growing and share repurchases if the firm was undervalued. The reliance on analysts is ubiquitous and a feature of all IR programs.
15. The overall level of intensity for IPOs is still quite low; the average number of analysts following the largest public companies is 18 (Womack 1996).
16. See Rajan and Servaes (1997), Chen and Ritter (2000), Aggarwal, Krigman and Womack (2002), Das, Guo and Zhang (2002) and Bradley, Jordan and Ritter (2003).
17. See Womack (1996), Kim, Lin and Slovin (1997) and Branson, Guffey and Pagach (1998).
18. See Michaely and Womack (1999), Dunbar, Hwang and Shastri (1999) and Bradley, Jordan and Ritter (2002).
19. Irvine (2003) found that only 2 percent of initial recommendations were sell, 28 percent were hold and the rest buy or strong buy. The sample did not specifically look at IPOs, where the bias to buy recommendations may be even stronger.
20. More optimistic affiliated recommendations are also found surrounding SEOs, where the conflict of interest is likely to be as large (Lin and McNichols 1998).
21. In fact, at the largest investment banks the distinction between vice-president and managing director for analysts was very much related to the contributions to underwriting fees (Raghavan 1997).

22. The experience of NextCard Inc. provides a good example of this point (Smith 2002). The company had hired Morgan Stanley as its lead underwriter with the belief that it would have Mary Meeker, Morgan's star Internet analyst, covering the firm. NextCard eventually dropped Morgan, citing the lack of sufficient contact with Meeker in the primary market to satisfy NextCard's board.

23. See, among others, DeBondt and Thaler (1990), Dreman and Berry (1995), and Easterwood and Nutt (1999).

24. Dechow and Sloan (1997), Rajan and Servaes (1997), and Dechow et al. (1999) documented this pattern.

25. See Field and Hanka (2001), Bradley et al. (2001), Brav and Gompers (2003) and Ofek and Richardson (2000).

26. Determining the direction of influence for these observed patterns is difficult. Greater analyst coverage might be a consequence, not a cause, of the higher pre-expiration date stock returns. Likewise, managers might respond to the stock price appreciation by selling more shares than they had initially anticipated.

12 Post-IPO financing

An IPO, stripped of its restructuring implications, is a financing event that involves the sale of equity to a diverse group of new shareholders. Isolating the financing motive for going public is, however, difficult when there are other factors that influence the decision. Post-IPO financing patterns provide an additional opportunity to gain insight into the IPO decision. The timing and characteristics of public equity follow-on offerings can reveal the issuers' dynamic capital-raising strategy. Similarities between the SEO and IPO, in particular, would suggest that a company has gone public for financing reasons.

The control and governance structure that is a consequence of, and perhaps motive for, an IPO is affected by subsequent financing actions. A private placement of equity and the issuance of debt – public, private or bank – are the two main financing alternatives to public equity. Both options have specific consequences for dealing with agency conflicts, asymmetric information and the allocation of control within the firm. The options chosen and the reasons why offer indirect insight into how governance considerations affect the IPO decision.

12.1 CAPITAL STRUCTURE: THEORY AND EVIDENCE

Understanding the rationale for specific post-IPO financing decisions begins with an examination of the time series profile of debt and equity issuance. A firm's capital structure is the cumulative outcome of all past net equity and debt financing. Different theories offer conflicting predictions about the current capital structure composition and the factors that drive the financing choices. Testing the theories with post-IPO data provides guidance on the key issues influencing financial decisions, not to mention an assessment of the theories themselves.

12.1.1 The Trade-off Theory

The trade-off theory claims that the appropriate mix of debt and equity maximizes the total firm value to the claim-holders. The theory begins with the irrelevancy propositions of Miller and Modigliani (1958). In a world without imperfections, Miller and Modigliani showed that the value of a firm is independent of its capital structure, which is consequently indeterminate. Of course, the real world includes taxes, agency costs and the threat of bankruptcy. Incorporating these imperfections into the valuation model yields the trade-off theory. The tax advantage of debt favors an increase in leverage until the marginal tax saving equals the marginal cost of agency and bankruptcy costs associated with debt.

The trade-off theory's primary aim is to determine the optimal capital structure and less so with predicting financing decisions. Nevertheless, when the actual capital structure deviates too far from the optimal leverage ratio, the trade-off theory predicts that a firm will choose the financing action that gets it back to the target ratio. The complicating factor in testing the predictions made by the trade-off theory is that the optimal capital structure must first be derived, a difficult challenge by itself.

12.1.2 The Pecking-order Theory

Asymmetric information between firm insiders and investors over the value of the firm is another imperfection that influences the financing decision. Myers and Majluf (1984) demonstrated that when insiders have private information about the value of the existing assets there could be underinvestment in new projects if a public equity offering is the only financing option. The price investors are willing to pay for new equity is below fair value if they undervalue the assets in place. The sale of underpriced equity transfers wealth from old to new shareholders and will be avoided. Profitable investment is forgone if the gain to old shareholders is less than their wealth loss to new shareholders. Consequently, investors rationally interpret an equally offering as a signal that management believes the firm is overvalued.

Asymmetric information gives rise to what Myers (1984) called the pecking-order theory. The theory predicts that firms rank their financing options from most to least attractive. The first choice is internally generated funds because undervalued equity is not sold and the cost of issuing securities and the need to disclose information is avoided. After internal funds, the safest external assets take priority because they are the least affected by asymmetric information. The firm starts with riskless debt, moves on to risky debt, followed by hybrid securities like convertibles and, finally, equity. The theory does not predict a target leverage ratio. Instead, the capital structure is the cumulative outcome of past external financing.

12.1.3 The Market-timing Theory

Timing the market is a fruitless exercise in efficient capital markets. Security prices reflect all relevant information, prohibiting the creation of abnormal value through financial transactions. Consequently, a firm cannot opportunistically switch between mis-priced debt and equity in an attempt to reduce its cost of capital. The presence of asymmetric information does not violate the efficient markets hypothesis. As long as investors can infer the private information from the financing decision, issued securities are properly priced.

Deviations from efficient markets, possibly caused by irrational investors, present firms with temporary 'windows of opportunity' during which they can issue mis-priced, meaning cheap, securities. Debt is unlikely to be mis-priced significantly, but the share price can fluctuate widely from the intrinsic value. Management can use its superior information to issue overpriced equity or repurchase underpriced shares without fear that the action will impact the inefficient market price.[1]

The market-timing theory, advocated by Baker and Wurgler (2002) and others, predicts that equity will be issued after an abnormally positive stock price increase, benefiting old shareholders at the expense of new investors. The theory also predicts that the current capital structure is the cumulative effect of past financing decisions, as does the pecking-order theory. The major difference is that market-timing involves the issuance or repurchase of mis-priced securities, while the pecking-order theory imposes a preference ordering on the financing choices. If firms due try to revert to a target leverage ratio, market timing will have only a temporary affect on capital structure.

12.1.4 Post-IPO Financing

The limited available data provides a glimpse into the post-IPO financing strategies of issuers. Ideally, cross-sectional time series data would allow for the tracking of individual firm's financing actions. Unfortunately, few studies have constructed the dynamic panel data set necessary to examine companies over time. From the few that have some general conclusions about the financing patterns can be drawn, along with assessments of the theories.

1. Leverage ratios declined immediately at the IPO because of the equity infusion. The ratio of the book value of debt to the book value of assets fell approximately 25 percentage points from the pre-IPO year to the end of the IPO year (Baker and Wurgler 2002; Alti 2003). Firms

gradually increased their leverage ratios in the ten years after going public, but by only about 5 percentage points.

2. Hot and cold market IPOs differed significantly in the amount of equity raised in the IPO and the resulting leverage ratio. Alti (2003) reported that hot IPO proceeds relative to the end of year book value of assets was 12 percentage points higher than the proceeds for cold market IPOs. This led to an additional five-percentage point decline in the IPO year leverage ratio, after controlling for firm characteristics.

3. Firms accessed the public capital markets infrequently after the first few post-IPO years. Helwege and Liang (1996) found private debt to be the most common source of external finance, with close to 40 percent of firms using this option in the year after the IPO. The annual net debt and equity issues in years three through ten after the IPO were below 4 percent of the book value of assets (Baker and Wurgler 2002; Alti 2003).

4. Post-IPO financing did not follow the pecking-order theory. Helwege and Liang (1996) found that firms failed to exhaust their supply of internal capital before tapping the external markets, although firms with greater cash surpluses did tend to avoid raising external finance. Firms that issued equity could have obtained banks loans and greater information asymmetry did not lead to a higher probability of debt issuance.

5. Market timing considerations affected when and how much equity was raised, but the long-term effect on the capital structure is ambiguous. Alti (2000) documented that hot market issuers actively increased their book leverage in the first two post-IPO years, converging to the leverage ratio of cold market issuers and reversing the initial impact of IPO market timing. Baker and Wurgler (2000) measured the effect of market timing by calculaing an average of the prior yearly market-to-book ratios, where each year's ratio was weighted by the year's net external financing. A high average occurred if firms issued equity when the market-to-book ratio was high. This average was the most economically and statistically significant variable in explaining the cross-section of leverage ratios and its importance persisted and increased with the time from the IPO.

6. The annual net change in both debt and equity were affected by variables likely to determine the optimal capital structure. Baker and

Wurgler (2002) and Alti (2003) both found that the year-over-year change in leverage increased in the firm's tangible assets and size, but decreased in profitability.[2] Increased asset tangibility means there are more collateralizable assets to support additional leverage and a greater size increases debt capacity. High profitability increases the retained earnings, lowering the need for external financing and debt. Alti interpreted this as evidence in support of the trade-off theory, whereas Baker and Wurgler argued that market timing was still driving the capital structure.

A few main results jump out from the panel data evidence and point to the issues that deserve further inquiry. First, market timing does influence when equity is issued, although the long-term affect on capital structure is ambiguous. By examining follow-on offerings we can probe into the timing question more thoroughly. In addition, the aggregate data does not distinguish between public and private equity, which ignores their contrasting implications for control and monitoring structures. Second, firms increase their use of debt significantly in the first few years after the IPO. The motivation to issue debt and the choice of debt instrument are unanswered by the aggregate data. Finally, firms do not tap external capital sources frequently, especially once they start to generate sufficient internal cash flow to fund their operations and investment.

12.2 PUBLIC EQUITY

Follow-on equity offerings, also called seasoned equity offerings, are quite common and often part of a deliberate dynamic strategy for issuing equity in stages, starting with the IPO. A dynamic strategy could be motivated by a number of considerations. Asymmetric information and agency costs stemming from excess free cash could cause investors to discount the share value at the IPO. Breaking up one large IPO into a sequence of small offerings reduces these costs. Selling equity in stages allows both the issuer and investors to experiment and learn about each other, without too much cost or risk. Finally, a follow-on offering can be used to liquidate the secondary shares that the insiders were advised not to sell in the IPO.

12.2.1 Follow-on Data

The data on follow-on offerings exhibit four consistent patterns.[3] First, approximately one-third of all issuers complete a follow-on within three years of their IPO and about a third of those firms completed the follow-on within a year. The probability of a follow-on starts to drop after three years because by then the firm can rely on cheaper sources of capital, either internally generated funds or debt. Second, the average follow-on offer size was approximately the same as the issuer's IPO, although sizes varied from slightly smaller to three times larger.

Third, follow-ons occurred after abnormally good returns in the issuer's stock price. Loughran and Ritter (1995) measured an average return of 72 percent in the year prior to the SEO, about half of which was due to the market and half to the issuer. The average returns over the period commencing the day after the IPO to the follow-on date exhibited the same pattern. Speiss and Pettway (1997) reported an average issuer return of 63.8 percent versus the NASDAQ return of 12.8 percent over the same period.

Fourth, secondary sales comprised a much larger fraction of the follow-on than the IPO. Spiess and Pettway found that 16 percent of the initial follow-ons consisted entirely of secondary sales. The median percentage of the proceeds received by insiders as a result of secondary sales was 22 percent in follow-ons, but only 1 percent for IPOs.

The issue size and pre-issue return characteristics of follow-on offerings are very similar to those of IPOs. For the one-third of issuers that complete a follow-on within a few years of the IPO, the equity sold at both stages appears to be part of a strategic plan to raise capital. Thus, the decision to go public for these issuers was likely driven by financial concerns, especially those with limited secondary sales. The remaining firms that did not complete a follow-on perhaps placed greater emphasis on non-financial factors in their IPO decision.

12.2.2 Asymmetric Information

Poor public information about an issuer prior to the IPO can lead to severe mis-pricing. This is a boon to the overvalued firms that might try to exploit the mis-pricing with a large offering. Undervalued firms are in the opposite situation and may even delay their IPO. A dynamic issuing strategy can overcome some of the asymmetric information cost. Investors only learn a firm's true value if it is public. A small IPO satisfies this necessary condition, enabling the issuer to complete a larger follow-on offering after its quality has been revealed.

A two-stage process minimizes, but does not eliminate, the asymmetry cost. Overvalued firms will mimic this strategy, otherwise they would be exposed immediately and lose out on both IPO and SEO proceeds. Undervalued firms could try to signal their mis-pricing before issuing equity. One signaling option is to underprice the IPO (Allen and Faulhaber 1989; Grinblatt and Hwang 1989; Welch 1989).[4] Overvalued firms no longer mimic because the intentional underpricing eliminates the mis-pricing advantage. This theory predicts a positive relationship between underpricing and the probability of a follow-on offering. Another signaling option is to wait longer before completing the SEO, assuming that the probability of the true value being revealed increases. Welch (1996) predicted that high-quality issuers optimally underprice more and expect to wait longer for their SEO.

A less formal, albeit similar, argument made by many practitioners is that issuers intentionally underprice the IPO to 'leave a good taste in the mouths of investors' because they would like to tap the capital markets again in a follow-on offering. The conjecture also predicts that the probability of a SEO increases in the first-day return. However, no differentiation is made between under and overvalued issuers.

12.2.2.1 Evidence

The evidence for staging as a response to asymmetric information is mixed and some predictions are flat-out rejected. The probability of a follow-on offering did not increase with the initial return.[5] Other tests have tried to measure the efficacy of a two-stage issuing strategy with IPO underpricing. Slovin, Sushka and Bendeck (1994) found that larger IPO initial returns were associated with smaller negative SEO announcement returns. The relationship is consistent with good firms underpricing more to signal their true quality before the SEO. However, the small gain at the SEO was swamped by the loss in proceeds at the IPO. Speiss and Pettway (1997) similarly reported that the combined IPO and SEO net proceeds were negatively related to the IPO initial return.

The stock returns between the IPO and SEO do a better job of predicting a follow-on offering, with the returns and probability positively related (Jegadeesh, Weinstein and Welch 1993; Schultz and Zaman 2001). The direction of causation between the two is indeterminate. The positive return could be due to the market correcting the undervaluation as it learns the true value, allowing the firm to complete a properly priced SEO. Alternatively, exogenously good returns could result in overvaluation, giving the firm a reason to complete a follow-on.

Firms that underpriced more did wait longer before the SEO, confirming Welch's (1996) prediction. The finding is at odds with the conjecture that firms underprice to leave a good impression with investors when a quick SEO is planned. Intentionally underpricing the IPO to entice investors into buying future offerings may actually be costly. Investors are likely to have forgotten about the initial return by the time of the SEO and care far more about the recent performance.

12.2.3 Market Experimentation

It is commonly assumed that managers possess superior information relative to investors about their firm's investment opportunities. A more accurate statement is that managers are better informed compared to each individual investor. The pooled information of investors could, however, dominate that of the managers. Consider a company that sells a consumer product to the national market. Investors will have experience using the product and collectively have a good assessment whether a new feature of the product can succeed. The share price of a public company reflects the aggregate investor information about the firm's investment opportunities. Managers then use the share price as a guide for their investment decisions.[6]

Issuing equity in stages to take advantage of market feedback may be an optimal strategy. A small IPO can be thought of as an experiment to learn what investors think about the firm's prospects. The experiment analogy arises from the challenge of introducing a new product into the market. When a firm is uncertain about how consumers will perceive their product quality, it is best to start with a small initial supply. This way the firm can learn from consumers while minimizing the product introduction cost. Supply is increased if demand is favorable. Likewise, a firm can complete a follow-on offering conditional on the feedback it gets from investors after the IPO. To ensure sufficient information feedback, van Bommel (2002) suggested that issuers increase underpricing to generate greater information production.

Firms do appear to listen to market feedback when making capital expenditure decisions, which may stimulate follow-on offerings if the news is positive. Van Bommel and Vermaelen (2003) found a positive relation between the IPO initial return and subsequent capital expenditures. The initial return does not affect the total proceeds received from the offering and therefore cannot directly affect the capital available for investment. An unexpectedly positive investor reception to the offering signals to management that the firm's growth options are more valuable then previously thought, leading to additional investment.

12.2.4 Unit Offerings

A firm can pre-commit to a two-stage equity offering by including warrants in the IPO, in which case it is now called a unit offering. Investors receive warrants with each share they purchase. Warrants give their owner the right, but not the obligation, to purchase new shares from the firm at a pre-set strike price. The warrants usually cannot be exercised within a year of the IPO and have a life span that lasts no more than a few years. Warrants can also be stripped from the shares and sold in a secondary market after the IPO. Including warrants does not guarantee that the firm will have a second equity offering because they will not be exercised when the share price falls below the strike price.

Warrants are costly to the issuer because they are only exercised when the share price exceeds the strike price, diluting the value of existing shares. The cost of warrants does not appear to be a major deterrent to their use. Schultz (1993) found that warrants were included in over 20 percent of US IPOs in the early 1980s, although their current use is much lower.[7] Practitioners suggest that warrants are 'sweeteners', used when the interest in the IPO is low. This conjecture cannot explain why the issuer does not just lower the offer price instead of including warrants. A rational explanation for warrants is that they minimize the total cost of issuing equity over stages, making their inclusion efficient. Two theories justifying the use of warrants have been proposed.

Agency costs: A manager can use the capital supplied by an IPO to undertake an investment project. Suppose the project should be continued only if the first step is a success. A manager may continue to invest to save his job, even after the project has been revealed as unprofitable, if all the necessary capital was supplied in the IPO. Schultz (1993) argued that warrants could minimize potential agency costs. The warrants will only be exercised if a successful first stage raises the share price, ensuring that inefficient investment does not continue. Warrants are more likely to be included when there is greater *ex ante* uncertainty about the value of the investment projects and when post-IPO managerial ownership is low. The greater uncertainty demands additional underpricing for unit IPOs. This theory cannot explain why warrants are included in only a minority of offerings, yet agency costs of this sort could apply to most IPOs.

Asymmetric information: Insiders possess private information about the riskiness and quality of the firm. Risk-averse managers can choose the fraction of retained equity, the degree of underpricing and whether to include warrants in an attempt to signal the private information. Chemmanur and Fulghieri (1997) argued that including warrants maximizes managerial utility when the issuer is of high risk and high quality because both share retention and underpricing can be minimized. The dilution cost to the managers is low because the warrants are only exercised when the share price is high. The theory predicts that risky issuers use warrants, managerial share retention is low among unit IPOs, underpricing does not differ between unit and non-unit IPOs, and the proportion of firm value sold as warrants increases in the degree of firm risk.

291

The evidence on warrant use provides some support for both theories. Schultz (1993) found that unit offerings in the US tend to involve younger, smaller and riskier firms relative to non-unit issuers and to be more underpriced, all consistent with the agency explanation. In contrast, Australian unit IPOs were no more underpriced than non-unit offers, insiders retained a smaller portion of the equity and the proportion of firm value sold as warrants increased in firm riskiness, after controlling for retained equity (How and Howe 2001; Lee, Lee and Taylor 2000). These findings support the hypothesis that asymmetric information forces high-risk, high-quality firms to issue warrants to maximize managerial utility.

12.3 DEBT FINANCING

Increasing leverage in the years immediately following the IPO indicates that issuers either resume or initiate a reliance on debt financing. More debt can be supported as the issuers grow their revenues and increase the tangible asset base. The benefit is a lower cost of capital and the preservation of the insiders' control. Treating the objective of increasing debt as a given, the next priority is optimizing the portfolio of credit liabilities. The three principal securities are bank lending, private bonds and public bonds. The asymmetric information and agency concerns that determine the maturity structure and portfolio of debt provide indirect insight into the issuer's IPO decision.

12.3.1 Optimal Debt Portfolio

Debt contracts differ in their characteristics and hence optimality from the perspective of borrowers. The number of lenders can vary from one, in the case of a bank loan, to many public bondholders. Debt maturity can be short or long term. Covenants could severely restrict managerial actions or impose relatively little burden. The three types of debt differ along these dimensions. The characteristics of the borrower's economic environment – asymmetric information over assets-in-place, potential growth options and the need for external monitoring – determine which debt contract is ultimately chosen.

12.3.1.1 Debt maturity

The fixed maturity of a debt instrument can range from a few months to as long as 30 years. Three factors influence the maturity structure and they generally imply that new public firms are biased towards shorter maturities.

Mis-priced debt: Asymmetric information between managers and investors will result in more extreme pricing errors for long-term debt than short-term instruments because small errors compound over time. Managers with positive private information about the risk and payoff to the firm's assets therefore pay unnecessarily expensive rates. Kale and Noe (1990) argued that such firms would choose shorter maturities to combat this problem. Overvalued issuers want to take advantage of the mis-pricing by issuing long-term debt.

Growth options: New public firms often have numerous growth options, each potentially quite valuable. The options are exercised as positive information about the payoff is revealed. Myers (1977) argued that such firms would avoid long-term debt so that shareholders would not have to split the benefits of those options with debtholders. Fear of a debt overhang problem pushes recent IPO firms toward shorter maturities.

Monitoring: Debtholders monitor management just like equityholders. The unavoidable agency costs caused by imperfect monitoring, such as excessive risk-taking induced by the leverage, lowers the firm value and increases the price of debt. High quality firms can reduce their agency costs by using shorter maturities that require frequent monitoring and evaluations by the capital market (Easterbrook 1984).

12.3.1.2 Private versus public

Debt issuers can choose among public bonds, private bonds or bank loans. A public bond issue must be registered with and approved by the SEC before the sale occurs. Private bonds can be issued under SEC Rule 144A, which allows firms to market directly to institutional investors without registration. Private bonds are tightly held and illiquid, have low flotation costs and have more customed designed covenants relative to public bonds (Kwan and Carleton 1995). Bank debt is usually a revolving credit agreement. The theoretical literature has espoused the advantages of bank loans over bonds for small risky borrowers (see Chapter 3). Some additional considerations affect the instrument chosen for the debt portfolio.

Agency costs: Banks and concentrated private lenders exert greater influence over a manager than dispersed public bondholders, helping to minimize agency costs. Managers with large equity stakes are more likely to choose private sources because they internalize the agency costs. Firms with numerous growth options will also avoid public debt because the inferior monitoring increases the cost of underinvestment and asset substitution towards risky investments (Berlin and Loyes 1988; Krishnaswami, Spindt and Subramaniam 1999). The switch from private to public debt, as occurs with a bond IPO, thus has a negative connotation because it signals lower growth options.

Information asymmetry: Firms characterized by a high (low) degree of information asymmetry are more apt to borrow privately (publicly). Private lenders are better informed through their monitoring and screening efforts, resulting in private debt that is usually senior (Welch 1997) and collateralized (Rajan and Winton 1995), and therefore safer and cheaper than public debt. High quality firms have the most to lose from issuing mis-priced bonds, biasing them towards private debt.

Issuer quality: Diamond (1991) predicted that the riskiest firms, with low project quality and a high probability of bankruptcy, are the most likely candidates for private non-bank debt. Poor quality issuers may find the cost of bank monitoring outweighs the benefits, whereas private debtholders do not have the day-to-day influence of a bank. At the same time, the high ownership concentration of private bonds allows for greater re-negotiation flexibility when in default as compared to dispersed public bondholders.

12.3.2 Debt Patterns

The very limited data on post-IPO debt financing offers reasonable support for the theories of debt selection and maturity. The analysis focuses on the choice between debt instruments, not on the total amount of debt. Unfortunately, there are no studies that explicitly track the specific debt choices made by issuers for the first few public years. Indirect inferences based on debt financing patterns form the basis of most of the conclusions.

12.3.2.1 Bond IPOs

A gradual evolution in the debt porfolio occurs after firms go public. The primary change is that firms begin to tap the public bond market. The average length of time from the equity IPO to the bond IPO was approximately 3.3 years (Datta, Iskander-Datta and Patel 2000). Public bonds went from an average of 0 to 41 percent of the total outstanding debt because of the IPO. The new reliance on public debt markets comes at the expense of bank debt. Bottazzi and Da Rin (2002) reported that the percentage of total debt owed to banks declined from 25 percent prior to going public to 17 percent post-IPO for firms in Germany, France and Italy.

The theoretical models predicted that higher quality firms and those with more growth options would rely on private debt, banks in particular, with a shorter maturity before accessing the public bond market. The implication is that a bond IPO is a negative signal about the issuer quality and growth potential. The preliminary evidence from the data is roughly consistent with the predictions.

1. The announcement CAR of a bond IPO was a significant -1 percent, which contracts with the negligible price reaction to seasoned debt issues (Datta, Iskander-Datta and Patel 2000). The long-run stock returns were no better. The median firm underperformed its expected return by 56 percent over five years, which is about three times larger than the underperformance following seasoned issues (Spiess and Affleck-Graves 1999; Datta, Iskander-Datta and Patel 2000).

2. There was a significant decline in the issuer's growth options following the bond IPO. Patel (2000) reported that capital expenditures fell after the offering and remained lower than the pre-IPO level for five years, although they were still high on an absolute level. The market-to-book equity ratio, another proxy for growth options, declined after the bond IPO and remained low.

3. Bank lending was associated with higher asset efficiency and profitability, which could reflect the increased monitoring (Patel 2000). Firms with more expected growth options benefited from the bank monitoring, measured by the fact they did not generate poor long-run stock returns (Datta, Iskander-Datta and Patel 2000). These effects could be capturing banks' ability to screen out low-quality firms, not their superior monitoring.

4. The maturity structure had a non-monotonic evolution after firms went public. Bottazzi and Da Rin (2002) found that the fraction of total debt with a short maturity increased from 71 percent immediately prior to the IPO to 87 percent post-IPO for a sample of European issuers. However, once the firm conducts a bond IPO the average maturity lengthens. Datta, Iskander-Datta and Patel (2000) reported that the median maturity for US bond IPOs was ten years, with a range of five to 24 years. The typical bank revolving credit agreement has a maturity of five to six years. The lengthening of the maturity structure reflects the decline in the growth options and firm quality, proxied by the long-run stock returns.

12.3.2.2 Credit quality

Public firms follow a credit pecking-order when raising new debt financing, consistent with the predictions of Diamond (1991). Denis and Mihov (2003) showed that the primary determinant in the debt instrument choice is the credit quality of the issuer. Public bond issuers were large firms, had a large proportion of fixed assets to total assets, a high credit rating and were more profitable than bank and non-bank private borrowers. Firms that borrowed from non-bank private lenders tended to be the poorest performers, had the lowest credit rating and the highest *ex ante* probability of default. Medium quality firms borrowed from banks. This pattern was not driven by small risky issuers who lacked access to the public market, although recent equity IPOs will be overrepresented in the medium and low quality groups. In addition, there was no evidence that public debt was chosen because there would be reduced monitoring of entrenched managers.

12.3.2.3 Flexibility

Public bonds place fewer restrictions on the borrower compared to bank loans. Gilson and Warner (2000) equate fewer restrictions with more financial flexibility, which they define as a capital structure's ability to support activities at low transaction and opportunity cost. Since flexibility promotes faster firm growth, the debt instrument should be chosen to maximize firm performance.

Gilson and Warner examined a sample of junk bond issues in which the firms immediately used the proceeds to pay down bank credit revolvers.[8] The junk bonds placed far fewer contractual restrictions on borrowers, had longer maturities (10.2 vs 4.1 years) and were less secured (13.9 vs 50.0 percent). The junk bond issues occurred just after declines in operating earnings. The issuers were not distressed, but the decline put them closer to the constraints in their bank loan agreements, potentially limiting the borrower's ability to pursue value-increasing opportunities. The market reacted negatively to the announcement of a junk issue, partly because it signaled negative information about the firm's current prospects. The preference for junk bonds did not appear motivated by a managerial desire to reduce external monitoring, as most firms re-borrowed from banks.

12.4 PRIVATE EQUITY

Private equity remains a feasible and attractive financing option for companies even after going public. Private placements are targeted to only one or a few sophisticated investors, not the entire market, which makes them distinct from public offerings in two important respects. First, the asymmetric information problem that afflicts public offerings is less of a concern in a private placement. Second, ownership concentration actually increases following a placement. Control and monitoring structures more reminiscent of a private firm follow, undoing some of the consequences of the IPO.

12.4.1 Definition and Regulations

The fundamental legal difference between a public offering and a private placement is that the latter does not have to be registered with the SEC. Most private placements consist of unregistered shares, although the shares have registration rights if the SEC finds effective a registration statement allowing for the resale of the securities. The rules governing the sale and subsequent resale of privately placed equity are Regulations D and S, which cover sales within and outside the US, respectively.[9] The regulations dictate that a private placement is exempt from SEC registration if the issuer does not engage in the solicitation of public investors. Two additional restrictions affect who is allowed to purchase the equity and when it can be resold.

Participation restrictions: An unlimited number of accredited investors, but no more than 35 non-accredited investors, can participate in a Regulation D private placement. An investor is deemed accredited if he or she satisfies certain criteria, which essentially require that the investor be sophisticated and have a high net worth. The concept of accreditation is based on an assessment of whether or not the investor needs the protection of registration. The private placement market provides few or no Securities Act investor protections and is exempt from SEC-mandated disclosure requirements. Each non-accredited investor must be capable of evaluating the risks of the private placement without requiring the information that would be forthcoming in a registered offering.

Resale restrictions: The regulations limit the resale of privately placed unregistered shares. Under SEC Rule 144, investors can publicly resell shares with no limits after a two-year holding period. A limited number of shares can be publicly sold after one year. Rule 144A was adopted in 1990 by the SEC to allow for the resale of restricted securities to other qualified institutional buyers, regardless of the seller's holding period.

Wu (2001) describes a process of placing equity privately that is similar to a registered public offering. A booklet covering the offering terms, use of

297

proceeds and other material information is published to solicit potential investors. The company executives and its advisors then actively market the placement to investors. Informal communication between the investment bank placing the issue and prospective buyers helps to determine the offer price and share allocation. This is followed by formal negotiations between interested investors and the firm to set the placement terms.

12.4.2 Pricing Effects

Private placements are associated with two pricing effects that make them unique among financing options and raise questions about their motivation and implications.[10]

Discounts: Private equity is sold at a steep discount compared to the current share price. The discount – measured as a percentage of the market price – has averaged 15 to 20 percent. The discount does vary considerably, with some placements sold at a premium. Discounts for unregistered placements, approximately 30 percent, are large compared to the 15 percent for registered placements. The private placement discount is much larger than the 2 to 3 percent discount typical for SEOs and comparable to the 18 percent average underpricing for IPOs.

Announcement returns: Private placement announcements generate significant positive abnormal returns. The average announcement CAR has been estimated to be in the 1.7 to 4.5 percent range. The positive return contrasts with the widely documented -2 to -3 percent SEO announcement CAR. The announcement CARs actually understate the positive reception by investors to the placement. The discount results in a significant transfer of wealth from old to new shareholders. After adjusting for the discount, the announcement CAR indicates that old investors believe that the placement will increase firm value by 6 to 9 percent. However, over half of the value gain is paid to the new shareholders through the discount.

12.4.3 Motivation

The positive response to private placements indicates that investors believe that some aspect of the financing reveals or produces additional firm value. The diametrically opposite responses to placement and SEO announcements highlight the divergent information and control implications for the two financings. The motivation for the placement should play to its comparative strengths with regard to both factors. In addition, any theory for placements must simultaneously explain the value-creation and the large discount.

There are non-strategic reasons for choosing a private placement. A public offering involves higher direct expenses and fees, which small issuers may find prohibitive. Registered offerings take time because the issuer has to wait for SEC approval. A firm in need of capital immediately may turn instead to the private market. Companies that have not performed well in the past and are financially distressed could be closed off from the public market. In this case, investors may demand more control over the operations than a public offering can provide.

12.4.3.1 Monitoring

The increased ownership concentration that results from placing a block of equity with a few shareholders could directly affect the firm value through greater monitoring. The new blockholders have an incentive to actively monitor management to ensure a reasonable return on their investment. If increased monitoring motivates better managerial performance, thereby raising firm value, then the positive announcement return is warranted. Wruck (1989) suggested that managers voluntarily issue the new block to reap the monitoring gains. The large discount is compensation to the blockholders for the cost of active monitoring.

The contrasting price reactions to the announcement of private placements and SEOs might be due to the expected differences in the level of post-issue monitoring. Dispersed public offerings lower ownership concentration, reducing the aggregate monitoring. The privately placed shares are also illiquid. Investors who cannot easily sell their shares have a stronger incentive to monitor.

The empirical evidence offers little support for the monitoring explanation of the price effects. The average size of the private placement block was 15 to 20 percent of the post-issue outstanding equity (Wruck 1989; Wu 2001). Ownership concentration increased, but probably not sufficiently to generate additional value-enhancing monitoring. Wruck (1989) estimated that the average concentration of the managers, directors and shareholders with an initial 5 percent or greater stake increased from 31 to 37 percent. However, both Hertzel and Smith (1993) and Wu (2001) found only a small insignificant increase in ownership concentration.

The evidence on the relationship between firm value and concentration is no better. Wu (2001) found a weak correlation, while Wruck (1989) documented a non-linear relation. Firm value increased with the managerial concentration if the initial stake was below 5 percent or greater than 25 percent, but decreased in the intermediate range. Perhaps most telling, a placement that gave the investors a controlling interest in the firm, or put them on the board of directors, had a negative effect on firm value.

The illiquidity motive for monitoring had little support. The adoption of Rule 144 in July 1995 reduced the holding period from three to two years before an investor could sell unregistered shares. The illiquidity of the placement shares declined with the new rule, yet Wu (2001) found no significant change in either the discount or the announcement return from before to after the new rule.

12.4.3.2 Information

A poor information environment surrounding a firm can lead to severe undervaluation, greatly increasing the dilution cost of an equity issue. Small companies that operate in new industries and have most of their value derived from growth options are prime candidates to suffer from such information costs. Potential issuers can minimize this cost if investors become well informed prior to the offering. Hertzel and Smith (1993) argued that a private placement has an advantage over a public offering because the issuer can target a few sophisticated informed investors.

Hertzel and Smith extended their reasoning to develop an information-based theory for the placement pricing patterns. The discount is implicit compensation paid to investors for the cost of gathering and evaluating information. The discount increases with the cost and difficulty of obtaining information and decreases if the investors are *ex ante* informed. The willingness of private placement investors to commit funds to the firm signals undervaluation to the market, producing a positive announcement return.

Overall, the data are consistent with the information theory. Krishnamurthy et al. (2003) reported that private issuers were smaller, had higher levels of information asymmetry and had more growth options than their public issuer counterparts. Wu (2001) found that private issuers went public at an earlier stage in their life, were less likely to have had VC-backing, were followed by fewer analysts and had fewer institutional investors, all factors that would lead to greater information asymmetries.[11]

Private issuers were more inclined to target informed investors to compensate for the asymmetry. Wu defined informed investors as officers and directors of the company, VCs who backed the firm, key suppliers and customers, existing shareholders with 5 or more percent of the shares and institutional investors. Wu then found that unregistered placements involved informed buyers 65 percent of the time, compared to 42 percent for registered offerings.

The participation of informed investors in a placement resulted in smaller discounts, consistent with lower information costs. The average informed discounts ranged from 7.5 to 13.2 percent versus uninformed discounts of 11.5 to 21.3 percent (Krishnamurthy et al. 2003; Wu 2001). Hertzel and Smith further found that the discount increased when the firm was difficult to value and there was a high degree of uncertainty. Informed investor participation also resulted in larger announcement returns, indicative of a confirming effect. The informed and uninformed CARs were 3.7 and 1.4 percent, respectively, in Krishnamurthy et al. and 8 and 1.9 percent, discount adjusted, in Wu.

12.4.3.3 Managerial entrenchment

Self-interested managers are concerned with entrenching their position in the firm, not with adding external monitors that could constrain their actions. Barclay, Holderness and Sheehan (2001) argued that a private placement to a group of manager-friendly investors is motivated by the executives' desire to consolidate their control over the company. The discount is compenstion to the investors for allowing managers to consume private control benefits without fear of reprisal from shareholders. This theory does not offer a rationale for the positive announcement return.

Strong evidence supports the entrenching motive for the placement. Wu (2001) reported average pre-placement managerial ownership stake of 5.3 and 32.6 percent when managers did and did not, respectively, participate in the offering. Managers with small shareholdings may buy to strengthen their control.[12] Hertzel and Smith (1993) found that the average discount increased to 44.3 percent when managers participated, up from 18.7 percent when they did not, clearly violating the assumption that informed investors require smaller discounts. A better explanation is self-dealing favoritism on the part of management. Barclay, Holderness and Sheehan went on to show that firms that placed some of the shares with managers produced positive returns over the subsequent six months, suggesting that managers knowingly bought undervalued equity.

Another important piece of evidence supporting the entrenchment theory is the block-pricing puzzle. The sale of shares through a block trade is usually done at a premium, averaging between 10 and 20 percent, over the current market price (Barclay and Holderness 1989). The premium is at odds with the discount for private placements. Both transactions create a new blockholder who can monitor management. Yet if monitoring is costly and must be compensated, then block trades should be discounted as well. Alternatively, the block trade premium could pay for future private control benefits. But then private placements should also occur at a premium. The different premiums are not due to information effects. The seller in the block trade is usually an insider and is always an insider for a placement. Buyers are sophisticated in either transaction.

301

Barclay, Holderness and Sheehan proposed and tested an explanation for the different premiums that was based on the new blockholder's subsequent involvement in management. Investors who acquired their block through a trade became active in firm management about 85 percent of the time, compared to only 12 percent for private placement investors. The average premium paid by all active blockholders was 7.7 percent – 11 percent for block trades and -1.7 percent for private placements. After controlling for transaction characteristics, active placements were priced similar to block trades. Passive blockholders bought their shares at a 21 percent discount. The announcement CARs for all active and passive transactions were 6.0 and 1.4 percent, respectively. The initial positive response to passive placements was not warranted, as the subsequent six-month abnormal return was -12.8 percent. There was no negative drift in the stock price when buyers became active.

The entrenchment theory does a better job at explaining the use of private placements than either the monitoring or information theories. Investors who become active in firm management pay a premium in anticipation of the private control benefits. Passive investors help to entrench management and the discount compensates for the subsequent poor stock returns. Furthermore, most placement investors did not become active or contradict management actions, which is inconsistent with increased monitoring.

12.4.4 Long-run Performance

The positive announcement CARs for private placements imply that investors believe the issuer will improve its performance in the future. Managerial entrenchment suggests that, if anything, performance will decline. Analysis of the long-run operating performance and stock returns before and after the placement resolves the conflicting predictions. The entrenchment theory again has the better support, as evidenced by the following results.

1. Private placements occurred after abnormally positive stock price run-ups. Hertzel et al. (2002) found that in the year prior to announcement the average return for the issuers was 52.8 percent, significantly above comparable firms.

2. Private placements tended to follow periods of relatively poor operating performance. Hertzel et al. (2002) showed that the median firm had a negative return on assets in the year prior to and the year of the placement. The performance improved marginally, at best, after the

issue. Many firms were financially distressed at the time of the placement because of the poor operating returns.

3. Firms generated significantly negative long-run abnormal stock returns following a private placement. Hertzel et al. (2002) documented a three-year average abnormal return of -23.8 percent when issuers were compared to size and book-to-market benchmark firms. Similar returns were found by Krishnamurthy et al. (2003). The long-run returns earned by investors who bought shares in the placement were not abnormally poor because of the discount.

4. Long-run underperformance was confined to firms who placed shares only with investors unaffiliated with the company (Krishnamurthy et al. 2003).[13] There was no underperformance when affiliated investors bought shares. The investors in both placements did not experience the poor returns because of the discount. Affiliated investors should be better informed and know to avoid buying shares in an overvalued firm, even at a discount.

5. Long-run underperformance was contingent on the firm's financial health at the time of the placement. Krishnamurthy et al. (2003) showed that issuers in financial distress generated normal returns, whereas firms that were not distressed and that sold to unaffiliated investors produced negative abnormal returns. Companies that sell shares to outsiders when they are not financially constrained presumably could have chosen a public offering. The fact that they did not and that the firm underperformed suggests that the placement was intended to entrench management. The announcement CARs were positive for firms in financial distress, but negative for the underperforming group. Investors correctly anticipated, but not sufficiently, future underperformance.

12.5 SUMMARY

An examination of the post-IPO financing patterns fills out the picture on the initial motives for going public. Public equity financing is strongly influenced by market timing. However, the long-run effect of market timing on capital structure is ambiguous. Firms often follow a dynamic strategy for issuing equity as a way to overcome asymmetric information or get feedback from the market. About a third of all issuers completed a follow-on offering within a few years of the IPO. The IPO decision for these issuers appears to be motivated by financing considerations. Leverage increases in the years after the IPO. Firms begin to tap the public debt market when they have fewer growth options, lengthening the maturity structure of the debt portfolio.

Public firms sometimes return to the private equity market. The placement is typically sold at a 20 discount and the announcement is met with a favorably reaction by investors. The firms that do make a private placement suffer from information problems because of their smaller size, fewer institutional investors and less analyst coverage. The placement allows the issuer to target informed investors. The primary motive for a placement, however, seems to be a managerial desire to entrench their position by placing a block of equity with friendly investors. The long-run underperformance following private placements, especially those that appear to be entrenching, adds credibility to this claim.

NOTES

1. Graham and Harvey (2001) surveyed CEOs and CFOs, who admitted 'the amount by which our stock is undervalued or overvalued was an important or very important consideration' in issuing equity (p. 216).
2. Asset tangibility was defined as net plant, property and equipment divided by assets, profitability was measured by EBITDA and firm size was measured as log of net sales.
3. See Welch (1989), Michaely and Shaw (1994), Spiess and Pettway (1997) and Schultz and Zaman (2001).
4. In fact, a low quality firm may prefer a smaller issue size because it reduces the number of investors who will produce information about the firm, which lowers the probability that its true value is revealed before the SEO.
5. See Carter (1992), Michaely and Shaw (1994), Garfinkel (1993) and Jegadeesh, Weinstein and Welch (1993).
6. Boot and Thakor (1997) argue that the information flow from financial markets to the firm's capital budgeting decision is the main *raison d'etre* of the stock market. Subrahmanham and Titman (1999) suggested that market prices contain serendipitous information about the firm value that can only be known if the firm goes public.
7. Unit IPOs are even more popular in Australia, appearing in an estimated 17 to 34 percent of IPOs (How and Howe 2000; Lee, Lee and Taylor 2000).
8. Private firms constituted 40 percent of the sample, suggesting flexibility is an important factor for all high growth firms. These issuers were not the typical high tech/high growth firms. The median market-to-book was only 1.08, versus 3.58 for IPO firms (Brav and Gompers 1997).
9. Regulation S imposes far fewer restrictions on issuers in terms of the number and sophistication of potential investors, and allows greater freedom to advertise an offering outside the US.
10. See Wruck (1989), Hertzel and Smith (1993), Krishnamurthy et al. (2003), Wu (2001) and Hertzel et al. (2002) for the details.
11. Within the private placement subsample, registered sales are associated with more public information than restricted offerings and Regulation S offerings have even less information.

12. DeAngelo and Dunn (1988) found that many private placements were used as a defense mechanism by management because they were announced after a hostile tender offer.
13. An affiliate is defined as one of the following: officers or directors of the firm, relatives of officers and directors, consultants or attorneys to the firm, current large block shareholders, institutions affiliated with the firm and companies with product market agreements with the firm.

13 Long-run performance

The success of an IPO is best judged by how well the firm performs in the long run. The investor criterion for success is straightforward, the return on the initial IPO investment. Add to that the firm's operating performance as yardsticks used by issuer management and pre-IPO shareholders. A true assessment of the IPO decision may depend less on absolute performance measures than on the realized performance relative to the hypothetical alternative had the firm remained private. Since the counter-factual performance is unknowable, evaluating the IPO decision involves a certain degree of subjectivity.

Basing the evaluation solely on long-run stock returns could lead one to conclude that going public is a bad choice. IPOs, together with SEOs, comprise the 'new issues puzzle'. Researchers have documented that issuer stock returns following an equity offering are poor in absolute terms and may underperform relative to appropriate benchmarks. Consistent underperformance is a violation of the efficient markets hypothesis. The puzzle is why investors repeatedly buy overpriced equity and do not try to correct the mis-pricing.

Proclaiming that IPOs underperform and the market is inefficient is rather bold and demands further analysis of the existence and causes of abnormally poor returns. Examining the statistical and econometric methodologies used to detect abnormal returns is a necessary first step to determine the robustness of the underperformance conclusion. Conditional on the existence of underperformance, the next step is to look for potential causes. Factors pertaining specifically to the issuer are one possibility. Another is that investors fail to correct the mis-pricing because of bad or misleading information. Lastly, investor behavioral biases could result in the consistent pricing errors necessary for underperformance.

13.1 THE UNDERPERFORMANCE ANOMALY

Ritter (1991) produced the first academic evidence documenting poor abnormal returns following an IPO.[1] Investors who bought shares at the end of the first trading day would have earned three-year raw cumulative returns

306

far less than that of comparable stocks. Subsequent research using larger and longer sample periods confirmed the initial results of Ritter. The finding sparked an ongoing and as yet unresolved debate about the legitimacy of the conclusions. After presenting the early underperformance evidence, the robustness of the anomaly is documented.

13.1.1 Abnormal Returns

The calculation of abnormal performance requires two inputs: the raw stock return over the specified time horizon and a measure of the expected return. The simplest and most intuitive measure for raw returns is the buy-and-hold return (BHR). The BHR is the total return an investor would earn if he or she bought shares in an IPO at the closing price on the first trading day and sold at the end of the time horizon. The abnormal return is the difference between the realized and expected BHRs.

Loughran and Ritter (1995) expanded upon the initial study by Ritter (1991). Their sample consisted of 4,753 operating company IPOs from 1970 to 1990. The results strongly implied that IPOs generated abnormally poor returns, although no formal statistical tests were conducted. Each issuer was matched to a comparable public company that would provide a benchmark for the return performance. The selected match had the closest market capitalization not less than that of the issuer on the day before the IPO. Their major findings are listed below. Figure 13.1, reprinted from their paper, graphically illustrates just how much IPOs underperformed.

1. The average five-year BHRs for the issuers and non-issuers were 15.7 and 66.4 percent, respectively.[2] The corresponding geometric average annual returns were 5 and 12 percent.

2. The average five-year BHRs for the issuers and non-issuers for each calendar year cohort were calculated. The wealth relative for each year is the ratio of the average BHR for the issuers to the average for non-issuers. The average five-year wealth relative was 0.7. An investor would have had to invest 44 percent more capital in the IPOs at the start of the five years to finish with the same absolute level of wealth if he or she instead purchased the matching firms.

3. The average IPO did not underperform in the first six months, but severely underperformed in the next 18 months. Underperformance was most severe in years with heavy IPO volume. Volume in the mid- to late 1970s and the late 1980s was relatively light. The five-year

307

Figure 13.1 Five-year annual return for IPOs and non-issuers[3]

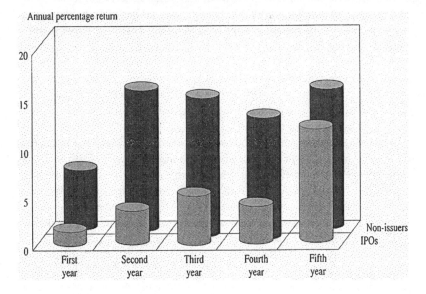

Source: Loughran and Ritter (1995).

wealth relatives in those years were almost always above 0.85 and exceeded 1.0 in a number of years. The early 1970s and early to mid-1980s had heavier volume and the wealth relatives were consistently below 0.7, dropping to 0.34 for 1980.

4. The average BHR and wealth relatives reported thus far were based on equal weight for each IPO. Value-weighting the returns based on market capitalization better captures actual investor experience. The average value-weighted wealth relative was 0.8, implying that underperformance was concentrated among smaller issuers.

The study by Loughran and Ritter (1995) was replicated by other researchers examining IPO long-run returns in a diverse group of countries covering Europe, Asia and South America. By and large, most of these early studies, summarized in Ritter (1998), found that IPOs generated abnormally poor stock returns in these other countries. Thus, it appeared that IPO underperformance was a global phenomenon. The variety of countries afflicted by underperformance, representing a broad range of regulatory and investing environments, suggests that the anomaly is not due to certain peculiarities of the US market, but rather is an IPO phenomenon.

13.1.2 Seasoned Offerings

The stock returns following seasoned equity offerings also exhibit underperformance (Loughran and Ritter 1995; Speiss and Affleck-Graves 1995). The average five-year BHR for SEO issuers and matched firms were 33.4 and 92.8 percent, respectively, in Loughran and Ritter. The corresponding geometric average annual returns were 7 and 15 percent and the average wealth relative was 0.7. An investor would again have to invest 44 percent more wealth in the seasoned issuers than the matches to finish with the same level of terminal wealth.

The temporal patterns for SEO returns were the same as those for IPOs. Underperformance began after six months and was most severe for the next 18 months. The calender time underperformance was greatest in years of heavy issuing volume. The value-weighted wealth relative rose to 0.76. Value-weighting had a smaller effect on SEO under-performance, indicating that it is more evenly spread across firms of different size.

The similarity of SEO and IPO performance is not surprising. Many seasoned issuers are relatively small and risky, and completed their IPO within the preceding few years. The timing of SEOs and IPOs have strong contemporaneous correlation and both occur after positive industry and firm stock returns. Therefore, underperformance is a new issues phenomenon.

13.2 METHODOLOGICAL PROBLEMS

The early analysis of IPO returns suffered from a number of methodological problems that weaken the claim of underperformance. For starters, a comparison between issuer and matched firm BHRs and wealth relatives do not constitute formal statistical tests. Drawing valid statistical inferences requires the use of well-defined test statistics. A second major problem is the determination of the correct expected return. Statistical issues are inconsequential if the economic model for the returns is not properly specified. After reviewing the economic and statistical problems, the findings from studies that use the updated methodologies are presented.

13.2.1 Model Specification

Measuring abnormal returns begins by specifying the baseline expected returns. Three methods are commonly used. The first is a reference portfolio, which could be the S&P 500, the NASDAQ or the CRSP value-weighted index. Reference portfolios are quick-and-dirty, but somewhat unsatisfying because they do not control for issuer-specific risk characteristics. The second method matches issuers with comparable public firms. The final approach estimates expected returns using an asset pricing model.

13.2.1.1 Comparable firms

The purpose of matching issuers with comparable firms is to control for risk and cash flow characteristics that are related to expected returns. The power of the control firm method is a function of the criteria used to select the matches. Loughran and Ritter (1995), for one, matched on size alone. Restricting matches to be from the issuer's industry is sometimes done because the issuer and match share common risk factors. However, there are two drawbacks to industry matching. First, there may be an insufficient number of possible matches of an appropriate size. Second, the industry as a whole can be incorrectly priced and post-event corrections in the valuation will obscure the IPO effect.

The most common matching criteria are size, measured by market capitalization, and book-to-market equity ratios. All NYSE-listed stocks are divided into size quintiles and within each quintile the firms are further subdivided into book-to-market quintiles, creating 25 different portfolios. NASDAQ and AMEX stocks are allotted to the appropriate size/book-to-market portfolio. Each issuer is assigned a portfolio based on its own size and book-to-market ratio and a matching firm is then randomly chosen from the portfolio.

13.2.1.2 Asset pricing models

Asset pricing models have the virtue of specifying and pricing the risk factors that determine the expected return for a stock. The theoretical foundation for pricing risk in the models contrasts with the somewhat *ad hoc* approach of the comparable firm method. Asset pricing models are also more amenable to formal statistical tests for abnormal returns. The three main asset-pricing models are CAPM, the Fama-French three-factor model and the arbitrage pricing theory (APT).

CAPM: According to CAPM the only relevant risk factor for a stock's expected return is the market return. The covariance of the stock's return with the market, measured by the stock's beta, prices the risk. The CAPM pricing equation is

$$E(r_i) = r_f + b_i(E(r_m) - r_f), \tag{13.1}$$

which states that the expected return for stock *i* equals the risk-free interest rate plus the stock's beta times the market risk premium.

The difference between the post-IPO realized return, net of the risk-free rate, and the net expected return is the stock's alpha, which is the 'unexplained' portion of the return. The alphas for individual stocks will be normally distributed around zero if CAPM is the correct pricing model. A formal test for abnormal returns regresses the net realized return on the market risk premium. The intercept term in the time series regression estimates the abnormal return. A significantly negative intercept implies abnormally poor returns.

The outcome of any test using an asset pricing model is only suggestive of underperformance because the model can always be mis-specified. Extensive testing of CAPM has generally produced evidence against the model's ability to explain the cross-section of stock returns. For this reason, CAPM is rarely used to detect underperformance.

Three-factor models: The most commonly used asset pricing model is the Fama-French three-factor model and its variants (Fama and French 1993). The model resembles CAPM with two additional pricing factors. Unlike CAPM, though, the model is not an equilibrium relationship. The two additional pricing factors are a size variable (SMB) – the difference between the return on small and large capitalization stocks – and a book-to-market equity variable (HML) – the difference between the return on high and low book-to-market ratio stocks. The Fama-French pricing equation is

$$E(r_i) = r_f + b_{i1}(r_m - r_f) + b_{i2} \, SMB + b_{i3} \, HML. \tag{13.2}$$

Testing for abnormal IPO returns proceeds as follows. For each month in the sample period a portfolio is formed that includes all stocks that had an IPO within the preceding three or five years, depending on the desired horizon. The monthly returns for the IPO portfolio and the three factors are calculated. The portfolio return, net of the risk free rate, is then regressed on the three factors. The intercept is measured in basis points, with an estimate of -0.25 equal to underperformance of 0.25 percent per month, or approximately 3 percent a year. The Fama-French regressions measure abnormal returns in calender time, as opposed to IPO event time for the comparable firm approach.

APT: The APT expected return for a stock equals the risk free rate plus the factor loadings on the realized factor values. There is no limit to the number of factors used nor are there constraints on the type of factors. The basic ATP pricing equation with *k* factors is

$$E(r_i) = r_f + b_{i1}F_1 + b_{i2}F_2 + \dots + b_{ik}F_k. \qquad (13.3)$$

The APT model has at least one advantage over the Fama-French model. Eckbo and Norli (2000) pointed out that both the size and book-to-market variables are calculated using market prices, thereby limiting their ability to detect abnormal returns. The market prices are not exogenous to the issuer or its private information and directly influence the decision to issue equity. A macro-factor APT model avoids this problem because the factors are arguably exogenous to the firm (Eckbo and Norli 2000; Eckbo, Masulis and Norli 2000). Examples of macro-factors include the change in aggregate per capita consumption, unexpected inflation and interest rate term structure premiums.

13.2.1.3 Model pros and cons

Each method has its own strengths and weaknesses that can lead to different conclusions about the existence of underperformance. The comparable firm method offers two advantages compared to the asset pricing models.

Sample-specific anomalies: The matching approach can control for cross-sectional variation in average returns due to chance sample-specific patterns (Fama 1998). The parameters of asset pricing models are estimated using pre-IPO returns. The validity of the estimated parameters over the post-IPO sample period is questionable, given the real possibility of sample-specific changes to the return-generating process. Using control firms that are also affected by the same chance patterns to measure abnormal IPO returns mitigates this problem.

Model mis-specification: The matching procedure avoids the problem of imposing an asset pricing model. No model can perfectly explain the cross-section of expected returns. Estimates of abnormal returns could easily be a consequence of a mis-specified model. The bad model problem becomes more severe as the measured horizon for IPO returns is extended because of the compounding of pricing errors (Brav, Geczy and Gompers 2000).

The comparables method does, as Eckbo and Norli (2000) pointed out, suffer from sample selection bias because it ignores the effect of private information on returns. The timing of a voluntary event like an IPO should reflect the private information possessed by managers. Matching firms are restricted to those that have not issued equity in the preceding few years. Thus, the pool of potential matches is constrained to the firms which, based on private information, decided not to issue equity. Both the issuers and matched-firms self-select into their respective samples. The assumption that the samples have similar cash flow and risk characteristics, and consequently expected returns, is questionable.

The Fama-French model has its own pros and cons. The main advantage over the comparable method is that simple statistics can be constructed to test the hypothesis of abnormal returns. A t-test can be applied to the null hypothesis of a zero intercept because of the multivariate normality assumption for the residuals. Formal asset pricing models constrain the cross-section of expected returns, enabling them to identify anomalies in the cross-section (Fama 1998). The comparable method generates firm-specific expected return estimates and thus cannot say anything about the cross-section.

The Fama-French model does suffer from two correctable statistical problems, but also a more fundamental issue that cannot be avoided.

Time-variant factor loadings: The firms in the IPO portfolio continually change through time. Consequently, the correct factor loadings – the betas in the regression – are also time-variant. Failure to correct for this problem can lead to false conclusions about underperformance. Mitchell and Stafford (2000) reported that the intercept for their sample of SEOs dropped from -0.38 to -0.24 as the factor loadings went from constant to time varying.

Residual variance: The number of firms in the IPO portfolio changes through time, creating residual heteroskedasticity that can affect the inferences about the intercept (Fama 1998). Weighting each month by issuing volume can correct this problem.

Poor explanatory power: A particular property of the Fama-French model weakens its ability to detect IPO underperformance. Fama-French regressions tend to have negative intercepts for portfolios of small growth (low book-to-market) stocks, whether or not IPOs are included in the portfolio (Brav and Gompers 1997). The model is biased towards finding IPO underperformance since a large fraction of IPOs fall into this category.

13.2.2 Calculating and Testing Abnormal Returns

Detecting abnormal performance involves more than just finding the difference between realized and expected returns. The time horizon over which the difference in returns is calculated must be specified. There is subjectivity in the choice of portfolio weighting and composition. These and other purely statistical issues will alter the measured abnormal returns, further complicating the efforts to detect IPO underperformance.

13.2.2.1 Measuring abnormal returns

Two methods are used to calculate abnormal stock returns: buy-and-hold abnormal returns (BHAR) and cumulative abnormal returns (CAR). These abnormal return measures are only applicable for the comparable firm and reference portfolio approaches. The BHAR is the difference between the IPO and comparable firm BHRs, both of which involve monthly compounding over the relevant time horizon. The CAR is calculated by first subtracting the comparable firm monthly return from the IPO return. The CAR is the sum of the monthly excess returns over the time horizon.

The consequences of compounding, both good and bad, lead to the fundamental difference between the two performance measures. The BHAR incorporates the effect of compounding and therefore closely resembles the actual investor experience. A simple example taken from Barber and Lyon (1997) illustrates how BHAR and CAR can give different impressions of abnormal performance. Suppose that an issuer and a matched firm had consecutive monthly returns of (0 percent, 44 percent) and (20 percent, 20 percent), respectively. The BHAR is zero, while the CAR is 4 percent. The example demonstrates the general phenomenon that CARs are biased estimators of BHARs.

The downside to compounding is that a small abnormal return in an early period will produce a non-zero BHAR, even if there are no abnormal returns in subsequent periods (Mitchell and Stafford 2000). Consequently, BHARs often exhibit extreme skewness and inflate the true abnormal return. The skewed distribution means that standard test statistics are not well defined, making inference difficult. The BHAR measure further amplifies the model mis-specification problem because it compounds the spurious abnormal returns. The same problem can afflict CARs, but to a lessor degree.

The statistical problems of BHAR have led some researchers to prefer CAR to detect abnormal returns (Fama 1998; Mitchell and Stafford 2000). The CARs have distributional properties and test statistics that are better understood. Fama (1998) also argued that measuring abnormal returns on a month-to-month basis offers three advantages. First, asset pricing models commonly assume normally distributed returns. Normality is better approximated over a month than a five-year period. Second, empirical tests of asset pricing models typically use monthly returns, never five-year returns. Third, share prices may adjust quickly after an abnormal return. The BHAR tends to overstate the time needed to correct the mis-pricing.

13.2.2.2 Equal- versus value-weighting

The measured abnormal performance is directly affected by the choice of weighting returns equally or based on market capitalization. In Loughran and Ritter (1995) the average wealth relative increased from 0.7 to 0.8 after switching from equal- to value-weighting. A legitimate case can be made that both weighting schemes are the proper way to estimate abnormal performance.

The preferred method comes down to the point of interest and the power of certain test statistics (Brav, Gezcy and Gompers 2000). Returns should be value-weighted if the objective is to quantify investors' average wealth change subsequent to the IPO. Equal-weighting is the superior option when the primary concern is to examine the effect of potential stock market mis-pricing on the IPO timing decision. IPO volume is greater when firms are overvalued. Small risky issuers are probably more mis-priced than large issuers and more apt to be 'market-timers'. Tests that equal-weight the returns have greater power to detect managerial timing.

The choice between equal- and value-weight is also applicable to time periods. Heavy volume periods are generally associated with greater underperformance than low volume periods. Tests to detect IPO market timing as a response to mis-pricing are weakened with the equal-weighting of time periods. Loughran and Ritter (2000) showed that the value-weighted Fama-French model underestimated by half the equal-weighted abnormal returns among small firms in high-volume periods. The Fama-French model is stacked against finding underperformance because it weights each period equally and thus underweights the time periods with a high volume of small, overvalued issuers.[4]

13.2.2.3 Purging reference portfolios

The inclusion of recent issuers in the benchmark return for current IPOs distorts the estimate of abnormal returns. The selection of a recent IPO as a comparable firm biases the test towards not finding underperformance, assuming that IPOs do generate abnormally poor returns. Loughran and Ritter (2000) demonstrated the effect of not purging recent equity issuers from the factor portfolios in the Fama-French regressions. IPOs tend to be small growth stocks with low book-to-market ratios. The small-firm portfolio would have more IPOs than a large-firm portfolio, especially after a period of heavy volume. The SMB factor return is biased down if IPOs underperform. A portfolio of value stocks – high book-to-market – would have fewer IPOs than a growth portfolio. The HML factor return would be biased higher after heavy volume. Failure to purge the portfolios produces 'factor contamination' that biases the intercept towards zero. Of course, purging the portfolios biases the test towards finding underperformance.

There is conflicting evidence on the quantitative effect of purging factor portfolios. Loughran and Ritter (2000) estimated that factor contamination reduced the measured underperformance by 18 basis points per month, or just over 2 percent per year, during the 1973–96 period.[5] Purging the factors in high volume periods led to much worse abnormal performance measures because it was during those times that mis-valuations were the greatest. Low volume periods were associated with little if any underperformance. Contrasting these findings is Brav, Geczy and Gompers (2000), who reported that purging recent issuers did not effect the measured performance.

13.2.2.4 Contemporaneous correlation

The power of test statistics to reject the null hypothesis of no IPO underperformance increases with the sample size and the number of independent observations. The actual number of truly independent observations is probably far less than the number of IPOs. Firms in the same industry are motivated to go public by the same factors, including possible mis-pricing. For example, the Internet IPO bubble in the late 1990s should not be interpreted as hundreds of independent return observations. When IPOs are not independent events there will be residual correlation in their returns not explained by the expected return model. A single unobservable factor can drive the returns of all recent IPOs in the same direction.

The effect of contemporaneous correlation in IPO returns is most severe for long-term BHARs. Many firms have an IPO event within a five-year window. A shock that negatively affects returns in year t will adversely affect the BHAR of all issuers with an IPO within t-5 years. Brav and Gompers (1997) calculated for each cohort year 1979–82 the ratio of one plus the compound return on the portfolio that invests in each IPO that went public in a given year to one plus the compound return on the NASDAQ composite index. The ratio was calculated for five years, starting from January of the cohort year. They plotted these ratios for VC-backed IPOs, which is reprinted here in Figure 13.2. The cohort year ratios moved in a parallel fashion, reflecting the strong cross-correlation and lack of independence in returns.

The cross-correlation problem is best dealt with using the Fama-French model. Mitchell and Stafford (2000) argued that comparable firms and BHAR cannot adequately deal with the problem. The decision to issue

Figure 13.2 Contemporaneous correlation of IPO returns[6]

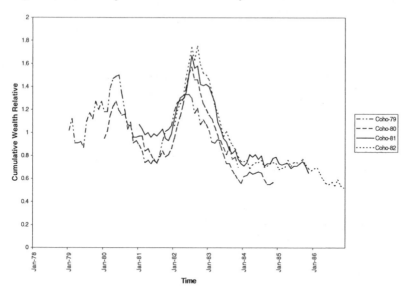

Source: Brav and Gompers (1997).

equity is not random and therefore randomly selecting a matching firm will lead to biased estimates. The calender-time portfolios can incorporate the efforts of cross-correlation and provide a more accurate assessment of underperformance.

13.2.2.5 Power of test statistics

The ability to detect IPO underperformance depends on the power of the test. The power is the probability of rejecting the null hypothesis of no underperformance when the hypothesis is false. Power is a function of the statistical properties of the test and the relevance of the test for the specific hypothesis. Loughran and Ritter (2000) argued that the Fama-French model has low power to identify abnormal returns for IPOs that are a result of market timing, especially when value-weighting. Tests that equal-weight IPOs should find greater abnormal returns than value-weighted tests if percentage mis-valuations are greater among small rather than large firms.

An ideal test statistic is one that has high power, but does not incorrectly reject the null hypothesis. A properly specified test statistic should produce empirical rejection rates equivalent to the theoretical rate. The following description illustrates how the bias is measured. Random samples can be drawn from a population of one-year stock returns with a known population mean. The null hypothesis is that the sample mean return will equal the population mean. In theory, the null hypothesis should only be rejected 5 percent of the time, if the confidence level is 95 percent. The test is unbiased if, after a large number of samples, the null has been rejected 5 percent of the time. Empirical rejection rates in excess or less than 5 percent correspond to positively and negatively biased test statistics.

Actual simulations of test statistics using the basic method described above were conducted by Kothari and Warner (1997) and Barber and Lyon (1997) for the entire pool of public stocks.[7] Kothari and Warner reported simulated rejection rates in excess of 25 percent for both CAR and BHAR measures. Thus, even a random sample of public firms would be found to generate abnormal returns far too often. The detection of IPO underperformance could very well be due to the mis-specification of the BHAR and CAR test statistics.[8] Between the two, Barber and Lyon concluded that BHAR was the better measure and that selecting matches based on size and book-to-market yielded well-specified test statistics.[9]

13.2.2.6 Rejecting the null hypothesis

The best efforts to confront the statistical and econometric problems inherent in tests for long-run IPO underperformance cannot overcome one final hurdle. All tests are for the joint null hypothesis that the market is efficient and that the model for expected returns is correct. But the true underlying process generating expected returns can never be known with certainty. Therefore, any evidence of abnormal returns is consistent with both inefficient markets and an incorrectly specified model, and we cannot be sure which part of the null hypothesis to reject.

Fama (1998) pointed out an additional problem in trying to reject the null hypothesis of efficient markets. An efficient market does not proclude the possibility that a random sample of stocks underperform some of the time. The only requirement is that the deviations do not follow a systematic pattern. Every sample period produces systematic deviations from the model's expected returns; that is, sample-specific patterns in average returns that are due to chance. A spurious anomaly can be detected even with the 'true' asset pricing model.

There is little disagreement that the Fama-French three-factor model is an incomplete description of stock returns. The perspective taken by Loughran and Ritter (2000) is that tests for abnormal returns are not tests of market efficiency. Rather, they are just tests of whether a given pattern in returns is independent of other previously documented return patterns. The lack of a consistent conclusion reached by the different methods of measuring abnormal performance should likewise not be viewed as evidence in favor of market efficiency. The different methodologies should lead to predictable differences in abnormal return estimates.

13.2.3 Updated Tests

Researchers' understanding of the statistical and econometric challenges in testing for abnormal returns has improved greatly since Loughran and Ritter (1995). Applying the updated techniques to the same data has changed the initial conclusion of underperformance, although the debate is still not satisfactorily resolved. The current stylized facts are summarized below.

Improved matching: IPO underperformance was largely eliminated when issuers were matched with comparable firms based on size and book-to-market.[10] The results in Brav, Geczy and Gompers (2000) demonstrate the importance of good matching. The average five-year equal-weighted BHAR relative to reference portfolios was -30 to -45 percent and the wealth relatives ranged from 0.75 to 0.82. The BHAR increased to 6.6 percent and the wealth relative was above 1.0 when IPOs were matched with size and book-to-market comparable firms.

Factor model: Brav, Geczy and Gompers (2000) demonstrated that when using the Fama-French model only the smallest third of IPOs and the equal-weighted returns showed any sign of underperformance. The inclusion of a fourth factor, momentum, resulted in intercepts insignificantly different from zero, even in these two cases. The Fama-French model successfully priced the IPOs, eliminating the abnormal returns.

Issuing volume: Loughran and Ritter (2000) showed, using the Fama-French model, that IPOs in high volume periods exhibited significant underperformance on both an equal- (-11.3 percent per year) and value-weighted (-6 percent per year) basis. Low volume periods produced no abnormal returns.

Event time: Measured underperformance is much more severe in event time compared to calender time returns. In Brav and Gompers (1997) the average annual geometric return for non-VC-backed IPOs was 4.14 percent over their first five years. These same IPOs generated an annual return of 15.5 percent over 1976–92 when calculated on a calendar-time basis. IPOs are weighted equally in event time but not in calendar time, which is why weighting each time period equally masks the underperformance in high volume periods.

319

Time-varying returns: The measured underperformance has varied over time. Ritter and Welch (2002) showed that IPOs during 1990–94, matched on size and book-to-market, averaged three-year BHARs of -12.7 percent, but IPOs over 1995–98 had average BHARs of 11.6 percent. Similarly, the Fama-French intercept for the 1973–89 period was an insignificant -0.15, but it was a significant -0.48 during 1990–2000.

Small growth firm puzzle: The smallest growth stocks have had particularly poor returns in the post-1963 period (Fama and French 1993). Benchmarking poor absolute IPO returns against this group leaves them with normal risk-adjusted performance. Explaining IPO underperformance reduces to explaining why small growth stocks in general have had poor returns.

Seasoned offerings: The measured underperformance of SEOs was still present for equal-weighted portfolios, and small and medium-sized issuers in the Fama-French model (Brav, Geczy and Gompers 2000). The abnormal returns did not shrink after improving the comparable firm matches. The continued underperformance of SEOs emphasizes their differences with IPOs. Over half of all IPOs fell in the portfolio of the smallest size and lowest book-to-market public firms. The SEO firms were more diversified and did not benefit as much from the small growth firm puzzle.

13.2.4 Economic Mis-specification

A correctly specified asset pricing model includes all relevant risk factors that have power to explain the cross section of returns. Among the three factors of Fama-French, only the market return has a sound theoretical justification. Two additional variables, leverage and liquidity, have been shown theoretically to affect expected returns and should be included. Other factors that are economically intuitive, but less formally rigorous, contribute to the understanding of IPO underperformance.

Leverage: A basic principal of asset pricing theory is that the expected return on equity increases in a firm's leverage (Miller and Modigliani 1958). Eckbo and Norli (2000) reported that the leverage ratios of issuers immediately following the IPO were significantly lower than the ratios of size-matched firms. They used a macro-factor APT model to test whether lower leverage reduced the expected return. The issuers exhibited less exposure to leverage-related risk factors such as unanticipated inflation and return spreads at both the long and short end of the term structure. Controlling for leverage eliminated the measured underperformance.

Liquidity: Amihud and Mendelsohn (1986) demonstrated that expected returns are negatively related to the liquidity of a stock. Eckbo and Norli (2000) tested for the effect of liquidity on the returns to IPOs. Issuers were significantly more liquid than size-matched firms for at least the first five years after the IPO. Expected returns were calculated using a Fama-French model with a liquidity risk factor computed as the return differential between low- and high-liquidity stocks. The liquidity factor was significant and lowered the expected return for issuers in absolute terms and relative to size-matched firms. The null hypothesis of no underperformance could not be rejected after controlling for liquidity.

Venture capital: Reputational concerns force venture capitalists to take public only high quality firms. The quality differential between issuers with and without VC-backing could manifest in divergent long-run returns. This would require that investors fail to fully impound the information VC-backing conveys at the IPO. Brav and Gompers (1997) compared the post-IPO returns of VC-backed and non-VC-backed issuers. In both the comparable firm approach and the Fama-French regressions the VC-backed issuers outperformed non-VC IPOs based on equal-weighted returns. The advantage was smaller with value-weighting.

Underwriter: Banks are also concerned with their reputation, which affects the type of firms they underwrite. Prestigious banks try to avoid lower quality IPOs that are more likely to produce poor long-run returns. Return differentials across bank quality tiers again require that investors fail to initially price the differences. Carter, Dark and Singh (1998) found that underperformance was less severe for IPOs underwritten by prestigious banks.

Ownership: Companies with solid corporate governance structures should produce better long-run value. Rigorous external monitoring of management is one source of the value gain. Field (1996) found that the size of the institutional holdings, a proxy for the amount of informed monitoring, at the end of the first quarter following the IPO was positively related to the long-run returns. Dor (2003b) found a similar relation, although it was limited to hot market issuers. Institutional investors purchased shares in firms with high growth expectations and that had experienced a strong price run-up. Dor interpreted this as evidence that institutional investors are better informed and that they profit from momentum trading during periods when retail investor sentiment is high.

321

13.2.5 Assessment

After reviewing the methodological problems inherent in testing for underperformance and the updated empirical evidence, what is one to conclude? IPO underperformance was not as significant as the initial studies suggested. Most, if not all, of the abnormally poor returns were an artifact of badly mis-specified models that did not include all relevant risk-pricing factors. This re-assessment of the initial underperformance conclusion has also held globally, as researchers have applied the update methodologies to other countries. Nonetheless, the inferior performance of hot market IPOs, the low returns measured in event time and the more consistent underperformance of SEO issuers prevent any unconditional declarations that the new issues puzzle has been resolved. The subsequent sections explore various factors that help to explain why underperformance would exist.

The lesson to be learned from the review is that extreme caution must be exercised when wading into the underperformance debate. The earlier discussion on testing the null hypothesis pointed out that sample specific anomalies could produce spurious conclusions about long-run returns. Inferences about IPO performance based on specific empirical techniques may be mistakenly covering for chance outcomes. Without knowledge of the correct asset pricing model, it is impossible to be certain about IPO abnormal returns.

13.3 ISSUER EXPLOITATION

Explanations for IPO underperformance must begin by tackling the first day closing price. Abnormally poor returns start with a market price that is too high and too slow to adjust to new information. Fully informed rational investors would arbitrage the initial price downward, reducing the potential for poor long-run returns. A violation of one or more of these assumptions is necessary for underperformance. This section considers whether issuers exploit their informational advantage, partly resulting from deliberate manipulation, by issuing overpriced equity.

13.3.1 Operating Performance

The long-run stock returns for an issuer are ultimately determined by its operating performance. High returns on investment and faster earnings growth should lead to better stock performance. A decline in the post-IPO operating performance would contribute to the anomalous stock returns.

Structural changes in the firm around the offer date could account for some of the decline. Another possibility is that the issuer times the IPO after a period of unsustainable good performance, unbeknownst to investors.

13.3.1.1 Measured performance

Studies have shown that the accounting performance of issuers declines significantly from the pre- to post-IPO period.[11] The measures of operating performance examined were the operating return on assets, profit margin and operating cash flows. Declines were observed in the raw operating performance and industry-adjusted measures, the latter of which are most important for drawing a link between operating performance and stock returns.[12] A decline in the raw operating performance could correspond with an overall slowdown in the entire industry. Unless the issuer shows a significant adjusted decline, it is unlikely that the operating returns would be responsible for the underperformance anomaly.

A few statistics demonstrate the level of performance decline. In Jain and Kini (1994) the raw and industry-adjusted ROA declined by 8 and 6.5 percentage points, respectively, from the year prior to the IPO to the first post-issue year. The operating ROA of issuers exceeded the performance of comparable non-issuers prior to going public, but then fell below the comparable performance after the IPO. However, issuers had higher sales and capital expenditure growth rates post-IPO relative to their matches. Mikkelson, Partch and Shah (1997) similarly found that industry-adjusted median operating income declined from nine to two cents per dollar of assets from pre- to post-IPO.

13.3.1.2 Explanations

The decline in post-IPO operating performance could be caused by a number of factors. It is well established that larger firms grow slower than smaller ones and younger firms grow faster than older ones.[13] Since issuers grow rapidly prior to the IPO, some of the decline might be an inevitable slow down. Other explanations more specific to the IPO event have been proposed.

Market timing: Managers may try to time the IPO when the performance peaks, knowing that investors incorrectly extrapolate past performance into the future. Two challenges exist for this explanation. First, managers continue to invest heavily after the IPO, suggesting they are just as naively optimistic as investors about the company's growth potential. Second, operating performance is not strongly correlated with post-IPO abnormal returns. Helwege and Liang (2004) found that the pre- and post-IPO operating performance of hot and cold market issuers were roughly comparable, yet only hot market IPOs underperformed.

Agency conflicts: The ownership stake of senior management begins a gradual decline with the IPO. The median stake of officers and directors in Mikkelson, Partch and Shah (1997) decreased from 67.9 percent prior to the IPO to 43.7 percent immediately afterward, and down to 28.6 (17.9) percent five (ten) years later. Managerial interests become less aligned with the remaining shareholders as the stake falls. Consequently, maximizing the operating performance and firm value could diminish in importance for managers. A positive relationship between managerial ownership and operating performance in non-IPO settings has been documented.[14] However, Mikkelson, Partch and Shah showed that the industry-adjusted absolute level of operating performance and the change in performance were unrelated to the change in managerial ownership.

Technological shocks: Technology-intensive firms experience discrete jumps in their productivity as new discoveries are made. A firm may go public to raise capital after a technological break through to finance the next stage of development. Clementi (2002) suggested that pre-IPO productivity gains, without a commensurate increase in the scale of operations, would mechanically lead to an increase in the ROA. The capital supplied by the IPO increases output, but decreasing returns to scale would cause the ROA to fall.

13.3.1.3 Seasoned offerings

The operating performance surrounding SEOs was examined by Loughran and Ritter (1997). They found that the operating performance peaked at approximately the time of the offering. The median ROA fell from 6.3 percent in the year of issue to 3.2 percent four years later. The median operating income to assets ratio similarly fell from 15.8 to 12.1 percent. The declines were much larger economically and statistically than those for matched non-issuers.

The decline in operating performance following the SEO was strongly correlated with the stock returns. The average raw stock return in the year prior to the SEO was 93 percent. The average annual return for issuers over the first five post-issue years was 9 percent, considerably lower than the 16.4 percent for matched non-issuers. The decline in returns and performance cannot be attributed to a reversion-to-mean effect. Issuers generated much lower post-SEO stock returns than did non-issuers who had the same pre-SEO operating growth rates. This result implies that issuers timed the offering after unsustainable growth.

13.3.2 Earnings Management

The decline in accounting measured operating performance may be less real than apparent. Management has considerable discretion over accounting choices, particularly the current accruals, which directly affects the level of reported earnings. The temptation to window-dress earnings prior to the IPO is obvious. Investors get a misleadingly positive impression of the firm's current and future financial health. In return, the issuer gets a higher offer price.

13.3.2.1 Accounting performance

The accrual accounting system affords managers considerable discretion on when to book revenue and expenses on the income statement. The strategic recognition of both can increase current reported earnings. The flip side to managing current earnings higher is that future reported income must be lower. The firm cannot borrow from future revenue or delay current expenses indefinitely.

A time series profile of earnings and accruals consistent with issuers actively inflating pre-IPO performance, followed by a post-IPO decline in earnings and ROA, was documented in Teoh, Wong and Rao (1998) and Teoh, Welch and Wong (1998a). The findings from these studies were reported in Chapter 8, with the key points summarized here. Abnormal current accruals declined monotonically from a significantly positive 4 percent of assets in the IPO year to a level insignificantly different from zero three years later. Cash flows from operations were poor in the IPO year and gradually improved over the next few years. Despite the improvement in cash flows, the decline in accruals caused a post-IPO decline in earnings. The median net income was significantly positive in the IPO year, but close to zero four years later.

There is a legitimate reason to believe that earnings management cannot, by itself, account for the decline in operating performance. The drop in performance is greatest in the IPO year, which includes time before and after the offer date. Yet the pre-IPO manipulation of earnings is likely to persist for at least six months after the IPO. Immediate accounting reversals may render earnings management sufficiently transparent to trigger lawsuits against the firm.

13.3.2.2 Stock returns

IPO investors form an expectation for future earnings based on the reported level and growth rate of current earnings. Earnings management biases investor expectations higher, leading to initial overvaluation. The gradual decline in earnings causes investors to revise downward their valuation of the firm. The revisions result in abnormally poor long-run stock returns. The more aggressive the issuer is in managing pre-IPO earnings, the worse the long-run returns should be.

Studies by Rangan (1998) and Teoh, Welch and Wong (1998a) documented a strong negative correlation between IPO year abnormal current accruals and the subsequent long-run stock returns.[15] Teoh, Wong and Welch ranked issuers based on IPO year abnormal current accruals. The median level of accruals in the highest (lowest) quartile equaled 40 (-15) percent of total assets. IPOs allotted to the highest quartile had a three-year average CAR that ranged between 20 and 30 percent less than the average CAR for IPOs ranked in the lowest quartile.

13.3.3 Insider Selling

IPOs occurring near peaks in operating performance and industry valuations make it tempting to conclude that firm insiders exploit their private information to go public at the most opportune time. The problem with inferring too much from IPO timing is that it is a crude measure of managerial beliefs about the firm value. Managers reassess the firm's investment opportunities following the pre-IPO valuation run-up. The firm could be taken public to raise capital to finance the now profitable projects, not to exploit overvaluation.

A better proxy of insiders' beliefs about the firm valuation is the sale of insider shares. Insiders presumably will be net sellers if they believe the firm is overvalued. Documenting an increase in insider sales in and before an equity offering is not proof that the managers optimally timed the issue. Both insider sales and equity offerings tend to mechanically follow price increases. What is required is a link between insider sales and post-issue returns that persuasively demonstrates that the equity was overvalued. Pre-IPO insider sales are not observable and the insider component of the IPO is usually limited. Insider sales before and in an SEO provide a good substitute. Three situations all point to the informativeness of insider selling and the predictability of subsequent underperformance.

Secondary SEOs: Lee (1997) showed that SEOs consisting of at least a majority of secondary shares did not underperform over the first three years post-SEO, except when the offering was preceded by insider net selling in the open market. Breaking down the secondary sales between true insiders – the CEO, officers and directors, founders of the firm and the chairman of the board – and other non-inside investors – investment banks, VCs, insurance companies, corporations and trusts – leads to a more refined conclusion. True insiders are better informed and more likely to sell overvalued shares. Non-insider sales are apt to be liquidity-motivated and not predictive of future returns. Clarke, Dunbar and Kahle (2004) found that when the largest seller in a pure secondary SEO was an insider, the five-year BHAR was a significant -33.33 percent. The non-insider dominated SEOs did not underperform. The operating performance also declined significantly following insider SEOs, but not after non-insider offerings.

Primary SEOs: Lee (1997) reported that SEOs consisting of a majority of primary shares generated significant three-year BHARs of -20 percent. The underperformance occurred regardless of whether insiders where net buyers or sellers prior to the SEO. The different long-run performance following primary and secondary SEOs found by Lee could be related to the free cash flow problem arising after a primary issue.[16] Agency costs stemming from managerial access to excess cash can lower the firm value, which is not immediately reflected in the share price.

Insider sales and revaluation: The price decline that occurs at the SEO announcement could be sufficient to eliminate the overvaluation that motivated the offering. Clarke, Dunbar and Kahle (2001) estimated the announcement CARs for subsequently cancelled and completed SEOs to be -3.3 and -1.7 percent, respectively. The corresponding interim abnormal returns from the filing date to either the withdrawal or the offer dates were -12.7 and 0.6 percent. The three-year abnormal returns after the withdrawal and offer dates were an insignificant -3 percent and a significant -14.3 percent. With the mis-pricing corrected, the SEO is no longer attractive and can be withdrawn. Insider selling was high prior to the SEO announcement and remained high in the interim period for completed offerings, but declined when the offering was subsequently withdrawn. Once again, insiders knew when to sell overvalued shares.

13.4 INVESTOR INFORMATION

Efficient pricing in the secondary market demands that investors have complete and accurate information. The timing of IPOs and insider sales suggests that issuers take advantage of investors' inferior information.

Long-run underperformance requires an initial market price that is too high and investors that are slow in correcting the mis-pricing. The continued supply of inaccurate information in the aftermarket further retards investors' ability to learn the true value.

13.4.1 Initial Overpricing

The phenomenal first-day closing prices of many Internet IPOs defy any conventional asset valuation model. It is easy to see in retrospect, but the investors purchasing these shares at the start of trading were far too optimistic about the prospects of the issuers. Three pieces of evidence all suggest that excessive investor optimism about issuers at the IPO is a general phenomenon and the resulting initial overpricing is related to the long-run abnormally poor returns.

Incorrect extrapolation: Extrapolating past and current earnings into the future using growth rates that cannot be sustained will lead to overpricing. Purnanandam and Swaminathan (2004) computed a measure of initial overvaluation by comparing the offer price to an estimated firm value. The estimate was calculated by capitalizing an issuer's earnings in the year prior to the IPO using the valuation multiples of comparable firms. Based on these estimates, the median IPO was overpriced by about 50 percent.[17] The initial price was strongly correlated with the long-run returns. IPOs priced above their estimated value generated three-year BHARs that were 10 to 40 percent lower than undervalued offerings.

Failed IPOs: The percentage of firms that fail and are de-listed shortly after the IPO is higher than the failure rate for the typical public company. Issuer share prices will be optimistically biased if investors do not apply a 'failure discount' to IPOs. Foster-Johnson, Lewis and Seward (2000) concluded that much of the long-run underperformance could be attributed to investors not properly accounting for the potential losses associated with failed IPOs. Conditional on survival, IPOs were priced correctly on average. The fact that surviving IPOs did not earn excess positive returns is a further indication that IPO values were not properly discounted. The survivors would be expected to outperform their benchmarks to compensate for the loss suffered on the failed IPOs.

Optimism: Investor optimism about the growth prospects of issuers may feed directly into a higher share price. Cornett, Mehran and Tehranian (1998) studied the case of equity issuance by commercial banks. Regulations require that banks maintain a minimum capital ratio. When the ratio falls below the mandated level, a bank increases its capital with a non-voluntary equity issue. Banks that voluntarily issue equity can be much more strategic in the timing of their issue to take advantage of investor optimism. Cornett, Mehran and Tehranian found that voluntary issuers experienced a post-issue decline in operating performance and produced abnormally poor long-run stock returns. In contrast, involuntary issuers' operating performance improved or remained unchanged and post-issue stock returns were as expected.

Initial overpricing could be a consequence of either investors exhibiting behavioral biases, a topic taken up later, or rational investors posssessing heterogenous expectations about the firm value. In the latter possibility, the most optimistic investors set the initial market price (Miller 1977). The overpricing is an increasing function of the variance of investor valuations, which should be large when the quality of public information is poor. Over time, as the diversity of opinion decreases, the marginal investor's valuation converges toward the mean value, resulting in poor long-run returns. Houge et al. (2003) did find that IPOs with greater diversity of opinion about their value performed poorly in the long run. In addition, Dor (2003b) documented that the level of institutional ownership shortly after the IPO was positively related to the long-run returns. Retail investors have less information than institutions and are more likely to be influenced by hype. Consequently, the initial price could be too high when the optimistic retail investors have a large ownership stake.

A natural question to ask is why pessimistic investors do not arbitrage the price down right away. The simple answer is that doing so is actually quite difficult. Obtaining shares to short is a challenge because of the limited float and restrictions on the banks' ability to lend shares. Ofek and Richardson (2003) demonstrated the difficultly of shorting the shares of Internet IPOs, but also showed that the prices began to fall after the supply of shares available for shorting increased substantially when the lockup agreements expired. Interestingly, the typical lockup expiration six months after the offer date coincides exactly with the onset of underperformance documented earlier. This explanation for underperformance is incomplete because the abnormal returns persist for years, requiring investors to remain too optimistic even after the short sales constraints are removed.

13.4.2 Analyst Forecasts

A major source of information for investors in the aftermarket is research reports produced by analysts. Positively biased coverage could create and sustain excessive investor optimism. Chapter 11 discussed the reasons why analysts' coverage could be optimistically biased. To show that analyst-induced investor optimism is a factor in the underperformance anomaly, the bias has to be correlated with the long-run returns.

Biased coverage: The evidence points to a clear positive bias in the coverage of equity issuers. Ali (1996) showed that analysts' earnings forecasts had a larger optimistic bias for equity issuers than for non-issuers during the first five post-issue years. Teoh and Wong (2002) reported that analysts were insufficiently skeptical about the management of accruals in the issue year and thus were too optimistic. High discretionary accruals significantly predicted the extent of positive forecast errors over the next four years. Teoh and Wong found no difference in the predictive power of accruals for forecast errors made by affiliated and non-affiliated analysts. Dechow, Hutton and Sloan (2000) confirmed that analysts' long-term growth forecasts were systematically too optimistic around equity offerings and reported that affiliated analysts were the most optimistic. Coincidentally, they found a positive relation between the fees paid to the affiliated analysts' bank and the level of the analysts' forecasts.

Long-run returns: Equity issuers that received the most positive coverage had the worst long-run returns. Teoh and Wong (2002) showed that the predicted forecast errors from the accruals were significantly associated with the post-issue underperformance. Dechow, Hutton and Sloan (2000) reported that long-run underperformance was most pronounced for those issuers with the highest growth forecasts made by affiliated analysts. The underperformance disappeared after controlling for the overoptimism in earnings growth forecasts. Rajan and Servaes (1997) subdivided IPOs into quartiles according to analysts' long-term earnings growth projections. The five-year BHRs for the highest quartile underperformed the lowest quartile by more than 100 percent. The general conclusion from these studies is that investors were insufficiently skeptical of analysts and did not discount the optimistic bias in the forecasts and recommendations, further perpetuating the underperformance.

13.4.3 Earnings Expectations

Investor optimism should result in unrealistically high expectations for earnings. Since the typical issuer has a decline in operating performance, the realized earnings would be less than investors expected. A consistent negative reaction to the earnings announcements would indicate that investors are routinely too optimistic. Brous, Datal and Kini (2001) found no negative abnormal stock price reaction to earnings announcements following SEOs. Denis and Sarin (2001) reported a negative abnormal return to the earnings announcement only in the second year post-SEO and only for the smallest issuers. Investors were not routinely surprised by earnings that missed their expectations, challenging the belief of excessive optimism.

The interpretation of investor reactions to earnings announcements must be tempered by the fact that firms actively engage in expectations management. Managers try to guide investor expectations down throughout the quarter to avoid the adverse consequences of a negative earnings surprise. The practice has become so ubiquitous that earnings reports are ofteny within a penny per share of the consensus forecast.

In response to this critique, Bagchee (2003) examined the price reaction to revisions in analysts' recommendations for IPOs. The revisions are less easy for investors to predict and provide a cleaner measure of the change in expectations. Optimistic investors should react more strongly to a downgrade because they already expect the firm to do well. Bagchee calculated revision announcement CARs for issuers and matched non-issuers, and then found the difference between the two. The average differential CAR for analyst downgrades was -3.13 percent, larger than the average of -1.8 for all revisions, good and bad, demonstrating the stronger reaction to downgrades. The -1.8 percent revision CAR constituted 15.7 percent of the three-year abnormal return. Thus, a notable part of the abnormal returns is due to investors correcting their optimistic expectations when recommendations are revised.

13.5 BEHAVIORAL FINANCE

Explanations for IPO underperformance based on managerial manipulation and timing or analyst-induced optimism ultimately prove to be insufficient. Rational investors would quickly learn to see through accounting tricks and earnings forecasts if they were consistently associated with abnormally poor returns. IPO prices would be discounted accordingly. The persistence of the underperformance anomaly suggests otherwise; investors repeatedly make the same mistake of buying overpriced IPOs. The evidence on initial overpricing hinted that some sort of deviation from full rationality is necessary to explain this type of investor behavior.

The past decade has witnessed a growing acceptance within the academic community of the notion that asset prices are determined as much by investor psychology as they are by risk-return calculations. At the center of this idea is the acknowledgement that investors are not fully rational, but rather suffer from iimitations to mental processing capabilities and behavioral biases. The combined evidence of non-rationality from psychology experiments and numerous asset-pricing anomalies has led some researchers to incorporate behavioral assumptions into models of stock prices. An examination of this theory and evidence offers a different take on the IPO underperformance anomaly.

13.5.1 Pricing Anomalies

A large and growing body of empirical research has documented asset pricing anomalies in a wide range of settings. Critics charge that this represents little more than data mining and that, at best, the evidence only implies spurious and transient patterns. The findings are further questioned on methodological grounds. Fama (1998) charged that possible model mis-specification will confound any inferences to be drawn about pricing anomalies. Notwithstanding these challenges, the evidence provides a compelling case for the pricing impact of behavioral biases. Two categories of mis-pricing evidence bear directly on the existence of IPO underperformance and the role of behavior.

Corporate finance events: IPOs are part of a group of discrete corporate finance events that convey information to investors. The common feature of these events is that they are all associated with post-event abnormal stock returns, some positive, others negative. Table 13.2 provides a list of the events associated with anomalous stock returns.

The consistent pattern of abnormal returns implies investors underreact to the information revealed by the event about the firm value. The stock price drifts over time as it gradually incorporates the full extent of the information. This is true whether the information is good, as with a share repurchase, or bad, such as when a dividend is omitted. Firms can try to manipulate the pre-event stock price through the release of misleading information, as in the case of managed earnings. Firms could also time the event to take advantage of what insiders believe is mis-pricing. If the latter occurs, the stock price would reflect a pattern of over- and underreaction. Investors react too strongly to pre-event information, overshooting the intrinsic value, and then underreact to the event signal.

Momentum and reversals: Stocks returns tend to have positive short-lag (one to three months) autocorrelations and negative long-lag (three to five years) autocorrelations.[18] These return patterns are consistent with price momentum in the short-run – stocks increasing (decreasing) in price continue to do so for a few months – and long-term reversals. DeBondt and

Table 13.1 Corporate finance post-event abnormal returns

Event	Author	Abnormal Returns %	Horizon (years)
Seasoned offerings	Loughran and Ritter (1995)	-59.4	5
Dividend omissions	Michaely, Thaler and Womack (1995)	-19.6	3
Accounting write-offs	Bartov, Lindhal and Ricks (1998)	-21.0	2
Spin-off	Cusatis, Miles and Woolridge (1993)	18.1	3
Dividend initiation	Michaely, Thaler and Womack (1995)	12.1	3
Repurchase tender offer	Lakonishok and Vermaelen (1990)	36.2	2
Open market share repurchase	Ikenberry, Lakonishok and Vermaelen (1995)	12.1	4
Stock split	Ikenberry, Rankince and Stice (1996)	12.1	3

Thaler (1985; 1987) first reported evidence that stocks that had been winners in the past three to five-years tend be losers in the future and vice versa for past losers. The best explanation for this pattern is that the market overreacts to recent earnings growth, extrapolating past trends into the future without considering mean reversion effects. Lakonishok, Shleifer and Vishny (1994) showed that strong past performers, firms with low earnings-to-price ratios, had low future returns and poor past performers, low ratio firms, had high future returns.

13.5.2 Cognitive Biases

In the realm of decision-making, perfectly rational behavior requires individual agents to acquire, process and evaluate all information relevant to the problem. They can objectively assess the probability of and payoff to the possible outcomes and make a final selection that maximizes expected utility. The evidence from a vast number of experiments conducted by psychologists challenges the paradigm of fully rational decision-making. Individuals exhibit systematic biases in their behavior and decisions across an array of different circumstances. These biases are not inate to human behavior, but rather the consequence of cognitive limitations and constraints. Individuals have a limited ability to examine all available data, have biased perceptions of themselves and are influenced by their emotional state when making a decision.

Financial markets offer a particularly ripe environment to examine behavioral biases in action. The objective of investors is fairly simple: maximize returns and minimize risk, subject to personal preferences. The exclusive focus on monetary payoffs provides an unambiguous prediction of what would constitute rational decision-making. Systematic deviations from optimal behavior point to behavioral biases. Financial economists have mined the experimental psychology literature to find evidence of biases applicable to the financial market setting. Hirshliefer (2001) surveyed the relevant literature and argued that three categories can account for most of the decision biases.

Heuristics: Limitations to cognitive capabilities force individuals to adopt rules of thumb, or heuristics, when making decisions. Applying a rule of thumb outside the appropriate context exaggerates the already implicit bias. The representativeness heuristic involves agents assessing the probability that an outcome belongs to a category, based on the degree to which the outcome is typical of the category. For example, investors may categorize a stock as a 'high performer' based on recent data (good performance is representative of a 'high performing' stock). In doing so, too little consideration is given to the small sample size. Representativeness would lead an investor to assign high probability to the performance continuing, while discounting the reversion-to-mean effect. At the other extreme, if the data is insufficient to cause the investor to change his or her categorization, then he or she fails to incorporate the evidence and exhibits conservatism.

Self-deception: Individuals tend to have deluded self-impressions, thinking of themselves as better than they really are. A well-documented phenomenon is overconfidence. Individuals have too much confidence in their ability to perform certain tasks and believe their knowledge is more accurate than it is. Supporting overconfidence is biased self-attribution. Individuals give themselves too much credit when the outcome of their action is a success and accept too little blame when the outcome is failure. Self-attribution causes individuals to become overconfident, rather than them learning their true ability over time. Both factors are related to the confirmatory bias: individuals interpret mixed signals in a manner consistent with their prior beliefs.

Emotions and control: An individual's state of mind can alter how he or she perceives risks and his or her own abilities. People in good moods are more optimistic about their choices than those in bad moods. Individuals can incorrectly attribute their mood or feelings to the wrong source, leading to incorrect judgements.

The basis for all decisions is individual preferences. The standard expected utility framework is the dominant model for financial decision-making.

Individual preferences are assumed to satisfy diminishing marginal utility and, generally, risk aversion. The utility effect from changes in wealth is evaluated based on the individual's absolute level of wealth, and gains and losses are treated symmetrically.

Considerable experimental evidence has shown that many of the principal assumptions of expected utility theory are violated. Individuals tend to anchor on their current level of wealth and evaluate changes in wealth relative to this level. Investors and gamblers suffer from the house money effect – a greater willingness to risk money recently won. Individuals display strong loss aversion even to very small risks. These deviations from the standard assumptions are not necessarily caused by cognitive biases; they could just simply reflect different preferences.

Prospect theory proposed by Kahneman and Tversky (1979) argues that individuals try to maximize their value function, which is kinked at their reference point (anchored level of wealth) because of loss aversion. The function is concave to the right of the reference point, reflecting risk aversion for gambles only involving gains, and convex to the left due to risk-seeking when the gamble only involves losses. The prospect theory value function appears to better fit the data on choice under uncertainty than the expected utility model (Camerer 1998).

13.5.3 Behavioral Theories

A behavioral-based theory for the stock return patterns surrounding equity offerings must be able to explain why the shares are mis-priced at the event and why investors underreact to event information. The stock returns for SEOs and industry returns in the case of IPOs have negative long-lag autocorrelations from pre- to post-event.

Pure noise trader and positive feedback trading models discussed in Chapter 2 offer two similar explanations for the patterns. In the first model, noise traders drive the price above the intrinsic value and rational investors cannot arbitrage it down. Firms time the market and issue overvalued equity. Investor sentiment and noise trading eventually declines and along with it the share price, producing the negative autocorrelation in returns. The feedback model is similar except that rational investors exploit the noise traders by driving the price even higher before selling. These mechanistic models are insufficient from a behavioral perspective because there is no psychological foundation for the behavior of noise traders.

Two models built on cognitive biases both offer an explanation for the post-event drift in the stock price. Daniel, Hirshleifer and Subramanyam (1998) assume that investors do not know the precision of their private information. Instead, they learn about it over time by observing public information. The self-attribution bias means that investor confidence rises too much when confirming news is received and falls too little with disconfirming news. Overconfident investors with good private information cause the stock price to overshoot the intrinsic value. An equity offering is a public signal for overvaluation. The overconfident investors react slowly to the public information, gradually adjusting their beliefs and the price.

A model proposed by Barberis, Shleifer and Vishny (1998) is built on the representiveness heuristic and conservatism. Earnings follow a random walk, but investors mistakenly believe that the earnings process fluctuates between a mean-reverting regime and an expected growth regime. A sequence of growing earnings will be incorrectly extrapolated, consistent with representativeness, if investors now believe the firm is in the growing regime. This leads to overreaction. Issuers who go public following growing earnings will be overvalued. Conservatism causes investors to slowly adjust their beliefs as the post-IPO earnings deviate from the preceding growth path, causing underperformance.

13.6 SUMMARY

The initial finding that IPOs produce abnormally poor long-run returns stimulated a large and growing body of research into the subject. Underperformance was documented in many countries and following SEOs. Persistent underperformance is a direct challenge to the efficient markets hypothesis and was met with a strong rebuttal on statistical and econometric grounds. Poorly specified test statistics and models for the benchmark expected returns were responsible for most, if not all, of the measured abnormal returns. IPO underperformance is mostly confined to hot market issuers and is part of a larger puzzle, the underperformance of small firms. Inferences about abnormal returns must be viewed cautiously because they involve a joint assessment on market efficiency, the model for expected returns and sample specific anomalies.

Explanations for underperformance begin progressively with issuers' exploiting their informational advantage. IPOs are timed when the firm has reached a peak in operating performance. Insider selling around equity offerings suggests that issuers take advantage of overpricing at the time of the offering. Some of the overvaluation is due to earnings management by the issuer. Those issuers who are most aggressive produce the worst long-run returns. The exploitation of investors' inferior information is borne out by the initial overpricing of IPOs. Biased earnings forecasts by analysts perpetuate investor optimism, which retards the price correction that would eliminate subsequent underperformance. Investor underreaction to the negative information about the valuation conveyed by an equity offering is consistent with behavioral biases. Fully rational investors should see through earnings management and analysts' forecasts to correct consistent mis-pricing. The IPO underperformance anomaly, to the extent that is actually exists, seems best explained by investor cognitive limitations.

NOTES

1. A 1985 *Forbes* article presented informal analysis demonstrating the poor performance of IPOs (Stern and Bornstein 1985).
2. The median five-year BHRs were lower at -39 and 16 percent for issuers and non-issuers, respectively, reflecting the skewness induced by a few extremely good performers.
3. Re-printed from the *Journal of Finance*, Vol. 50, Loughran, T. and J. Ritter, "The New Issues Puzzle," pp. 23-51, Copyright (1995) with permission from Blackwell Publishing.
4. Brav, Geczy and Gompers (2000) did not find that weighting the calender months equally reduced the power to reject the null of no underperformance.
5. The underperformance for value-weighted portfolios of IPOs was 35 basis points, or 4 percent a year.
6. Re-printed from the *Journal of Finance*, Vol. 52, Brav, A. and P. Gompers, "Myth or Reality? The Long-Run Performance of Initial Public Offerings: Evidence from Venture and non-Venture Capital-Backed Companies," pp. 1791-1821, Copyright (1997) with permission from Blackwell Publishing.
7. Barber and Lyon (1996) conducted similar simulations of the test statistics designed to detect abnormal operating performance.
8. Barber and Lyon (1997) trace the mis-specification back to the new listing bias, the rebalancing bias and the skewness bias.
9. Lyon, Barber and Tsai (1999) proposed two well-specified test statistics to improve on the existing methods. The first relied on the calculation of BHAR using a carefully constructed reference portfolio. The second calculated calendar-time portfolio abnormal returns. Brav (2000) proposed a Bayesian approach to correct for cross-correlation in returns.
10. See Brav and Gompers (1997), Eckbo and Norli (2000) and Brav, Geczy and Gompers (2000).
11. See Jain and Kini (1994), Mikkelson, Partch and Shah (1997) and Helwege and Liang (2004).
12. Industry-adjusted performance is the difference between issuer measures and the median change in performance of all firms in the industry.
13. See studies by Hall (1987) and Dunne, Roberts and Samuelson (1989).
14. For existing public firms see Morck, Shleifer and Vishny (1988) and for leveraged buyouts see Holthausen and Larcker (1996), Kaplan (1989) and Muscarella and Vetsuypens (1990).
15. Teoh, Welch and Wong (1998b) found the same relationship following SEOs.
16. Jung, Kim and Stulz (1996) and McLaughlin, Safieddine and Vasudevan (1996) found evidence that the negative stock price reaction to SEO announcements was due to the free cash flow problem.
17. The accuracy of the overvaluation estimates is questionable because they are based on past accounting earnings. The valuation accuracy of the multiples approach is much greater when forecasts for future earnings are used.
18. See Fama and French (1988), Cutler, Poterba and Summers (1991), Jagadeesh and Titman (1993), Richards (1997) and Rouwenhurst (1998), among many others.

14 Final thoughts

The introduction began with the assertion that an IPO is one of the most significant events in the life of a company. The breadth of topics covered in the 12 intervening chapters pertaining in some way to either why or how companies go public attests to the accuracy of that conjecture. An IPO fundamentally alters a firm's financial and governance structures, and has strategic implications for its ability to compete in the marketplace. Prudent owners and managers of a private firm will carefully weigh the costs and benefits of a public offering by applying all the tools of corporate finance. The firm's shares need to be valued, which requires an estimate of the cost of equity. The control benefits of a dispersed versus concentrated ownership structure should be compared. Alternative types of restructuring, such as a takeover by a public firm, are options that must also be considered. On top of these factors, the issuer has to decide how to go public, including which advisors to hire, the type of IPO mechanism to use and how the shares should be priced and allocated.

Unlike the issuer's IPO decision, the purchase decision for individual investors is easy reversed. Nonetheless, considerable sums of money are at stake when investors buy IPO shares, which makes the decision non-trivial. The positive average initial return mitigates much of the short-term risk from investing in an IPO. The same cannot be said for the long term, over which IPOs generate poor returns. Determining whether an issuer offers an attractive investment opportunity is not always easy given the paucity of public information at the IPO and the potential for optimistic bias in analyst recommendations thereafter.

IPOs matter too more than just the individual issuers and participating investors because they have an effect on the entire economy. The causal link between stock market development and economic growth reveals the overall benefit from firms going public. The recycling of informed capital from successful ventures to new start-ups, facilitated by IPOs, encourages investment in new technologies and emerging industries. Consequently, policy makers take a keen interest in ensuring that the new issues market functions efficiently. This entails designing and enforcing rules for the IPO mechanism that stimulate more firms to go public, maximize the expected proceeds and price the IPO fairly. Simultaneously, investors must be

338

granted sufficient protection rights to guarantee their participation in the public equity market.

The preceding chapters examined in great detail theoretical arguments and empirical evidence in an attempt to answer why and how companies go public. A final summary of the principal findings concludes the book, which includes an assessment of the current and possible future market developments and the role for policy.

14.1 THE IPO DECISION

Scholars and practitioners alike offer multiple reasons why companies decide to go public. The first major test that any explanation must pass is that it be consistent with the phenomenon of IPO clustering across time. Clustering at both the aggregate market level and within specific industries is a consequence of a number of factors. Issuers attempt to time the market by going public during temporary windows of opportunity characterized by share valuation peaks. Within-industry clustering is partly a result of positive information spilling over from successful offerings, affecting the IPO decision of current issuers. These two arguments highlight the importance of informational externalities in the going-public decision and are consistent with IPOs occurring when public equity is relatively cheap. Industry clustering is also a repercussion of strategic interaction among competitors. Firms go public to raise the capital necessary to remain competitive with rivals that have already gone public.

The most frequently cited reason why firms go public is to gain access to a large pool of cheap capital. Whether this expected benefit actually materializes is debatable. Large firms with a significant public float should find public equity to be cheaper than private sources and enjoy the corollary benefits of better bank terms and expanded financing options. But smaller issuers may incur greater financing costs by being public. An IPO involves high fixed advisory and listing fees, plus the administrative costs of being public. The poor liquidity and marketability of stocks that are relatively anonymous mitigates much of the cost of capital benefits from publicly traded equity.

The cost trade-off between public and private equity could change in the future in a manner that increases the attractiveness of private ownership. The private equity market has grown rapidly since the early 1980s and should continue to do so into the future. The fact that so many firms go public to raise capital indicates that there is no shortage of demand in the private market. As the market matures it will operate more efficiently, reducing the search costs for new investors and the illiquidity from a thinly traded market. The development of Internet-based markets that can match up suppliers and demanders of capital will further enhance this process.

A firm's value is a direct function of the quality of its corporate governance. Entrenched managers with little oversight do engage in value-reducing activities. There is no clear-cut governance advantage to either public or private ownership; the relative benefits are contingent on the specific characteristics of the firm and the quality of the stock market. Leveraged buyout advocates point to the concentrated ownership and large managerial stake as value-maximizing virtues. More firms will go or remain private in the future partly to take advantage of these benefits, but also as a way to avoid the onerous burdens imposed by the Sarbanes-Oxley Act. It is also possible that more companies will switch between public and private ownership on a regular basis, depending on which structure is optimal at the time.

The benefits of active, thick stock markets to economic growth are well documented. Unfortunately for policy makers interested in stimulating market development, private companies cannot be forced to go public. The government can, however, implement policy measures that make a public listing more attractive. A privatization program directly improves the quality of the stock market and usually results in a commitment to respect property rights and removes any threat of expropriation of private assets. The implementation and enforcement of laws protecting external investors encourages the supply of greater capital and reduces the cost of public equity. Requiring public firms to adopt rigorous accounting standards, whether GAAP or IAS, further alleviates investor concerns. Bottazzi and Da Rin (2002) showed that much of the initial success of the German Neuer Markt relative to similar European stock markets was due to the requirement that issuers use one of these two accounting standards.

Venture capitalists play a major role in the creation of new public companies, presenting another area for policy intervention. Any policy that encourages more firms to go public should benefit the VC industry because the flow of capital into VC funds and portfolio companies is positively correlated with the IPO volume. Direct government intervention into the VC sector requires more care. Armour and Cumming (2003) found that government sponsored VC programs in some countries actually reduced the overall level of investment by crowding out the funds supplied by private firms. They did show that the amount of capital supplied by VC funds to entrepreneurial firms increased in the 'investor friendliness' of a country's laws. Even more significant was the severity of the country's personal bankruptcy laws. The shorter the duration that a bankrupt individual had to wait before obtaining a fresh start, the greater the demand for VC funding.

Thus, laws and taxes that make entrepreneurial investment more attractive promote the development of the VC industry.

Another policy option that may not be as successful as expected is the encouragement of banks to become active VCs. Banks are the dominant suppliers of capital in many European countries, so it seems natural to look to them to increase VC investment. Yet the analysis by Hellman, Lindsey and Puri (2003) of US banks' VC investments suggests that they may not be effective at funding the start-up and early stage firms developing the newest technologies. The banks' VC investments were aimed more at firms that were likely to become lending clients of the bank, creating a synergy between the two activities. Despite the banks' reputed skills at originating and screening potential deals, they do not necessarily possess the right talent for finding and investing in entrepreneurial firms.

14.2 THE IPO PROCESS

The core of an IPO is the sale of shares by the issuer to investors. How this sale should occur is a matter of some debate. Theoretical analysis of IPO mechanisms generally supports the conjecture that the US-style book-building method is the most efficient option. The superiority of book-building is derived from its ability to induce investors to produce and then reveal information about the issuer to the underwriter, which is then incorporated into the offer price. The optimal theoretical mechanism involves the underwriter using specific rules for allocating and pricing the shares. Examination of price and allocation patterns for actual IPOs shows them to be consistent with the predicted behavior, although this does not mean that underwriters are intentionally following such rules. The growing dominance of book-building around the world reflects the endorsement of market regulators and issuers that it is indeed the best mechanism available.

Book-building is not without its critics, especially in light of the excesses of the Internet bubble and the revelations of illegal allocation practices by investment banks. Underwriters profited handsomely from the exorbitant underpricing and allocation of shares to investors in return for higher commissions and future banking business. Underwriters abused their discretion to the detriment of issuers and investors, in particular retail. For this reason, some market participants and academics have argued that book-building should be replaced with an auction mechanism. An auction would reduce the role of the underwriter, treat all investors equally and let the market determine the offer price.

Auction proponents must too answer some pointed questions about auction efficiency. They would have to explain why auctions have lost ground to book-building around the world and why issuers, when given a choice between the two, almost uniformly select book-building. Presumably if auctions were superior, they should beat out book-building in the underwriting market.

The drawback to auctions is their inability to generate sufficient information production and have that information incorporated into the price. Institutional investors do not like IPO auctions because they are not guaranteed an allocation of a particular size. Consequently, they often choose not to participate. Even if they do, their willingness to evaluate the issuer is diminished because the underwriter cannot discriminate in their favor with an allocation. Issuers then have less incentive to convey their private information to potential investors. As a result, IPOs sold via an auction tend to have too little information production both at the IPO and in the aftermarket, resulting in poor pricing. Granting retail investors equal participation in the offering can exacerbate the mis-pricing problem. Retail investors are comparatively not well informed, especially in hot markets, and were largely responsible for the extreme pricing of many Internet IPOs. Thus, auctions might be equitable and remove the underwriter's discretion in the pricing process, but the offer and market prices need not be efficient.

The pricing and allocation discretion that is at the heart of the criticism of book-building is also its greatest virtue. If used properly, the discretion can induce investors to become informed and reveal their information to the underwriter. Pricing IPOs is as much art as it is science. By speaking with investors and promising allocations in return for their opinions, underwriters can adjust the offer price to reflect what the market is willing to pay. The selective participation by investors in IPO auctions cannot capture this pricing subtlety.

These conclusions on mechanism efficiency hinge critically on the assumption that underwriters actually use their discretion in book-built IPOs to maximize the expected proceeds and not to line their own pockets. Increased public scrutiny of how the banks conduct future IPOs should partially deter potential abuse of the discretion. The settlement reached in April 2003 between the market regulators and the major banks imposed a ban on spinning, further limiting the potential for abuse. Whether this is sufficient to ensure that investment banks use the book-building method efficiently is a question that only time will answer. If it proves inadequate, some type of auction may be inevitable.

The investment bank W.R. Hambrecht currently uses a uniform price auction for the IPOs it underwrites. Modifications to this standard auction should help it perform better and make it more attractive to issuers and investors. Reserving a tranche of the allocation for bids of a sufficiently large size will help to ensure that institutions receive the number of shares they desire. Rejecting bids with unreasonably high limit prices will reduce uninformative bidding, which should encourage more information production and lead to a better offer price. A dirty auction that involves modest intentional underpricing below the market-clearing level might also help to attract more informed investors. Ausubel (2002) advocated a dynamic auction in which the offer price is continually raised until the market is cleared and investors pay their limit bids. The SEC would have to change its current regulation that all investors pay the same offer price before such an auction could be used.

The aforementioned settlement also placed clear restrictions on the participation of research analysts in the IPO process. For some, however, only a complete separation of investment banking and research into two entities will prevent future conflicts of interest. Any possible separation does come with a price. Research is costly to undertake and investors have not yet shown a willingness to pay for the full cost of it. In the aftermath of the settlement there were already signs that investment banks were curtailing their research activities. Any decline in research adversely affects the informativeness of stock prices, hitting newly public companies particularly hard. It will be interesting to see if analysts can remain somewhat unbiased and in compliance with the new regulations when the next IPO hot market occurs and scrutiny of their actions is diminished.

IPOs are at a crossroad in the current lull that has followed the late 1990s bubble. The new costs imposed on issuers when they are public – stricter governance requirements and potentially less analyst coverage – will deter at least some firms from going public. The IPO volume during the glory days of the bubble may be a thing of the past. Alternatively, the market, as is often the case, may collectively develop selective amnesia about the pitfalls of IPOs when the 'next big thing' comes along. The effectiveness of the new regulations to curb any abuses in the IPO process will only be really tested when the market is hot again. It will become clearer at that point whether more fundamental reforms are required. IPOs have long been a fascinating topic because of the mystery of how the entire process works. While much is now known, the future developments should prove to be equally as interesting to observe and study.

References

Admati, A. and P. Pfleiderer (1994), "Robust Financial Contracting and the Role of Venture Capital," *Journal of Finance*, 49, 371-402.

Admati, A., P. Pfleiderer and J. Zechner (1994), "Large Shareholder Activism, Risk Sharing and Financial Market Equilibrium," *Journal of Political Economy*, 102, 1097-1130.

Aggarwal, R. (2000), "Stabilization Activities by Underwriters After Initial Public Offerings," *Journal of Finance*, 55, 1075-1103.

Aggarwal, R. (2003), "Allocation of Initial Public Offerings and Flipping Activity," · *Journal of Financial Economics*, 68, 111-35.

Aggarwal, R. and P. Conroy (2000), "Price Discovery in Initial Public Offerings and the Role of the Lead Underwriter," *Journal of Finance*, 55, 2093-2122.

Aggarwal, R. and P. Rivoli (1990), "Fads in the Initial Public Offering Market?", *Financial Management*, 22, 42-53.

Aggarwal, R., N. Prabhala and M. Puri (2001), "Allocation and Price Support in IPOs: Who Benefits?", Georgetown University working paper.

Aggarwal, R., N. Prabhala and M. Puri (2002), "Institutional Allocations in Initial Public Offerings: Empirical Evidence," *Journal of Finance*, 57, 1421-41.

Aggarwal, R., L. Krigman and K. Womack (2002), "Strategic IPO Underpricing, Information Momentum, and Lockup Expiration Selling," *Journal of Financial Economics*, 66, 105-37.

Aghion, P. and P. Bolton (1992), "An Incomplete Contracts Approach to Financial Contracting," *Review of Economic Studies*, 77, 378-401.

Ahn, S. and D. Denis (2004), "Internal Capital Markets and Investment Policy: Evidence From Corporate Spin-offs," *Journal of Financial Economics*, forthcoming.

Akerlof, G. (1970), "The Market for 'Lemons': Qualitative Uncertainty and the Market Mechanism," *Quarterly Journal of Economics*, 84, 488-500.

Akhigbe, A., S. Borde and M. Whyte (2003), "Does an Industry Effect Exist for Initial Public Offerings," *Financial Review*, 38, 531-51.

Alexander, G., G. Benson and J. Kampmeyer (1983), "Investigating the Valuation Effects of Announcements of Valuing Corporate Sell-offs," *Journal of Finance*, 39, 503-17.

Alexander, J. (1993), "The Lawsuit Avoidance Theory of Why Initial Public Offerings are Underpriced," *UCLA Law Review*, 41, 17-73.

Alford, A. (1992), "The Effect of the Set of Comparable Firms on the Accuracy of the Price-Earnings Valuation Method," *Journal of Accounting Research*, 30, 94-108.

Ali, A. (1996), "Bias in Analysts' Earnings Forecasts as an Explanation for the Long-Run Underperformance of Stocks Following Equity Offerings," University of Arizona working paper.

Allen, F. and G. Faulhaber (1989), "Signaling by Underpricing in the IPO Market," *Journal of Financial Economics*, 23, 303-23.

Allen, F. and D. Gale (1999), "Diversity of Opinion and Financing of New Technologies," *Journal of Financial Intermediation*, 8, 68-89.

Allen, F. and D. Gale (2000), *Comparing Financial Systems*, Cambridge, MA: MIT Press.

Allen, J. and J. McConnell (1998), "Equity Carve-Outs and Managerial Discretion," *Journal of Finance*, 53, 163-85.

Alti, A. (2003), "IPO Market Timing," University of Texas, Austin working paper.

Altinkilic, O. and R. Hansen (2000), "Are There Economies of Scale in Underwriting Fees? Evidence of Rising External Financing Costs," *Review of Financial Studies*, 13, 191-218.

Amihud, Y. and H. Mendelson (1986), "Asset Pricing and the Bid-Ask Spread," *Journal of Financial Economics*, 17, 223-49.

Amihud, Y., S. Hauser and A. Kirsh (2003), "Allocations, Adverse Selection and Cascades in IPOs: Evidence from the Tel Aviv Stock Exchange," *Jounal of Financial Economics*, 68, 137-58.

Amir, E. and B. Lev (1996), "Value-Relevance of Nonfinancial Information: The Case of Wireless Communication," *Journal of Accounting and Economics*, 22, 3-30.

Ang, J. and J. Brau (2003), "Firm Transparency and the Costs of Going Public,"*Journal of Financial Research*, forthcoming.

Armour, J. and D. Cumming (2003), "The Legal Road to Replicating Silicon Valley," University of Alberta working paper.

Asquith, D., J. Jones and R. Kieschnick (1998), "Evidence on Price Stabilization and Underpricing in Early IPO Returns," *Journal of Finance*, 53, 1759-73.

Asquith, P. and D. Mullins (1986), "Equity Issues and Offering Dilution," *Journal of Financial Economics*, 15, 61-89.

Attari, M. and S. Bannerjee (1999), "The Investment Decision and Dual Class Shares," University of Iowa working paper.

Aussenegg, W., P. Pichler and A. Stomper (2003), "IPO Pricing with Bookbuilding and a When-Issued Market," Boston College working paper.

Ausubel, L. (2002), "Implications of Auction Theory for New Issues Markets," *Brookings-Wharton Papers on Financial Services: 2002*, 5, 313-43.

Ausubel, L. and P. Crampton (1998), "Auctioning Securities," University of Maryland working paper.

Back, K. and J. Zender (1993), "Auctions of Divisible Goods: On the Rationale for the Treasury Experiment," *Review of Financial Studies*, 6, 733-64.

Bagchee, D. (2003), "Investor Response to Sell-Side Analyst Revisions in IPO Recommendations: Do They Correct Expectations," University of Washington working paper.

Bajaj, M., D. Denis, S. Ferris and A. Sarin (2003a), "Firm Value and Marketability Discounts," *Journal of Corporation Law*, forthcoming.

Bajaj, M., S. Mazumdar, A. Chen and A. Sarin (2003b), "Competition in IPO Underwriting: Time-Series Evidence," Santa Clara Univeristy working paper.

Baker, M. and P. Gompers (1999), "Executive Ownership and Control in Newly Public Firms: The Role of Venture Capitalists," Harvard University working paper.

Baker, M. and P. Gompers (2003), "The Determinants of Board Structure at the Initial Public Offering," *Journal of Law and Economics*, forthcoming.

Baker, M. and J. Wurgler (2000), "The Equity Share in New Issues and Aggregate Stock Returns," *Journal of Finance*, 55, 2219-57.

Baker, M. and J. Wurgler (2002), "Market Timing and Capital Structure," *Journal of Finance*, 57, 1-32.

Balvers, R., B. McDonald and R. Miller (1988), "Underpricing of New Issues and the Choice of Auditor as a Signal of Investment Bank Reputation," *The Accounting Review*, 63, 605-22.

Bancel, F. and U. Mittoo (2001), "European Managerial Perceptions of the Net Benefits of Foreign Stock Listings," *European Financial Management*, 7, 213-36.

Barber, B. and J. Lyon (1996), "Detecting Abnormal Operating Performance: The Empirical Power and Specification of Test Statistics," *Journal of Financial Economics*, 41, 359-99.

Barber, B. and J. Lyon (1997), "Detecting Long-Run Abnormal Stock Returns: The Empirical Power and Specification of Test Statistics," *Journal of Financial Economics*, 43, 341-72.

Barberis, N., A. Shleifer and R. Vishny (1998), "A Model of Investor Sentiment," *Journal of Financial Economics*, 49, 307-43.

Barclay, M. and C. Holderness (1989), "Private Benefits From Control of Public Corporations," *Journal of Financial Economics*, 25, 371-97.

Barclay, M. and C. Holderness (1991), "Negotiated Block Trades and Corporate Control," *Journal of Finance*, 46, 861-78.

Barclay, M., C. Holderness, and D. Sheehan (2001), "The Block Pricing Puzzle," Bradley Policy Research Center working paper no. FR 01-05.

Baron, D. (1979), "The Investment Problem and the Design of Investment Banking Contracts," *Journal of Banking and Finance*, 3, 157-75.

Baron, D. (1982), "A Model of the Demand for Investment Banking Advising and Distribution Services for New Issues," *Journal of Finance*, 37, 955-76.

Baron, D. and B. Holmstrom (1980), "The Investment Banking Contract for New Issues Under Asymmetric Information: Delegation and the Incentive Problem," *Journal of Finance*, 35, 1115-38.

Barondes, R., A. Butler and G. Sanger (2000), "IPO Spreads: You Get What You Pay For," Louisiana State University working paper.

Barondes, R. and G. Sanger (2000), "Lawyer Experience and IPO Pricing," Louisiana State University working paper.

Barry, C. and R. Jennings (1993), "The Opening Price Performance of Initial Public Offerings of Common Stock," *Financial Management*, 22, 54-63.

Barry, C., C. Muscarella and M. Vetsuypens (1991), "Underwriter Warrants, Underwriter Compensation, and the Costs of Going Public," *Journal of Financial Economics*, 29, 113-35.

Barry, C., C. Muscarella, J. Peavy and M. Vetsuypens (1990), "The Role of Venture Capital in the Creation of Public Companies," *Journal of Financial Economics*, 27, 447-71.

Bartov, E., F. Lindahl and W. Ricks (1998), "Stock Price Behavior around Announcements of Write-offs," *Review of Accounting Studies* 3, 327-46.

Bartov, E., P. Mohanram and C. Seethamraju (2002), "Valuation of Internet Stocks – An IPO Perspective," *Journal of Accounting Research*, 40, 321-46.

Bates, T. and C. Dunbar (2002), "Investment Bank Reputation, Market Power, and the Pricing and Performance of IPOs," University of Western Ontario working paper.

Bayless, M. and S. Chaplinsky (1996), "Is There a 'Window of Opportunity' for Seasoned Equity Issues?", *Journal of Finance*, 51, 253-78.

Baysinger, B. and H. Butler (1985), "Corporate Governance and the Board of Directors: Performance Effects of Changes in Board Composition," *Journal of Law, Economics, and Organization*, 1, 101-24.

Beatty, R. (1989), "Auditor Reputation and the Pricing of Initial Public Offerings," *The Accounting Review*, 64, 693-709.

Beatty, R. (1993), "The Economic Determinants of Auditor Compensation in the Initial Public Offering Market," *Journal of Accounting Research*, 31, 294-302.

Beatty, R. and J. Ritter (1986), "Investment Banking, Reputation, and the Underpricing of Initial Public Offerings," *Journal of Financial Economics*, 15, 213-32.

Beatty, R. and I. Welch (1996), "Issuer Expenses and Legal Liability in Initial Public Offerings," *Journal of Law and Economics*, 39, 545-602.

Beck, T. and R. Levine (2003), "Stock Markets, Banks, and Growth: Panel Evidence," *Journal of Finance and Banking*, forthcoming.

Beck, T., A. Demirguc-Kunt, and R. Levine (2001), "Law, Endowments, and Finance," *Journal of Financial Economics*, 70, 138-81.

Bencivenga, V., B. Smith and R. Starr (1995), "Transaction Cost, Technological Choice and Endogenous Growth," *Journal of Economic Theory*, 67, 53-117.

Benninga, S. and O. Sarig (1997), *Corporate Finance: A Valuation Approach*, New York, NY: McGraw-Hill.

Benninga, S., M. Helmantel and O. Sarig (2004), "The Timing of Initial Public Offerings," *Journal of Financial Economics*, forthcoming.

Benveniste, L. and P. Spindt (1989), "How Investment Bankers Determine the Offer Price and Allocation of New Issues," *Journal of Financial Economics*, 24, 343-61.

Benveniste, L. and W. Wilhelm Jr (1990), "A Comparative Analysis of IPO Proceeds Under Alternative Regulatory Environments," *Journal of Financial Economics*, 23, 178-208.

Benveniste, L. and W. Busaba (1997), "Bookbuilding vs Fixed Price: An Analysis of Competing Strategies for Marketing IPOs," *Journal of Financial and Quantitative Analysis*, 32, 383-403.

Benveniste, L., W. Busaba and W. Wilhelm Jr (1996), "Price Stabilization as a Bonding Mechanism in New Equity Issues," *Journal of Financial Economics*, 42, 223-56.

Benveniste, L., W. Busaba and W. Wilhelm Jr (2002), "Information Externalities in the Role of Underwriters in Primary Equity Markets," *Journal of Financial Intermediation* 11, 61-86.

Benveniste, L., S. Erdal and W. Wilhelm Jr (1998), "Who Benefits From Secondary Market Price Stabilization of IPOs?", *Journal of Banking and Finance*, 22, 741-67.

Benveniste, L., A. Ljungqvist, W. Wilhelm Jr and X. Yu (2003), "Evidence of Information Spillovers in the Production of Investment Banking Services," *Journal of Finance*, 58, 577-608.

Bergemann, D. and U. Hege (1998), "Dynamic Venture Capital Financing, Learning and Moral Hazard," *Journal of Banking and Finance*, 22, 703-35.

Berger, A. and G. Udell (1995), "Relationship Lending and Lines of Credit in Small Firm Finance," *Journal of Business*, 68, 351-82.

Berger, A. and G. Udell (1998), "The Economics of Small Business Finance: The Roles of Private Equity and Debt Markets in the Financial Growth Cycle," *Journal of Banking and Finance*, 22, 613-73.

Berger, P. and E. Ofek (1995), "Diversification's Effect on Firm Value," *Journal of Financial Economics*, 37, 39-65.

Berglof, E. (1994), "A Control Theory of Venture Capital Finance," *Journal of Law, Economics, and Organization*, 10, 247-67.

Berglof, E. and L. von Thadden (1999), "The Changing Corporate Governance Paradigm," in D. Pleskovic and J. Stiglitz (eds), *World Development Conference*, Washington: The World Bank.

Berkman, H., M. Bradbury and J. Ferguson (2000), "The Accuracy of Price-Earnings and Discounted Cash Flow Methods of IPO Equity Valuation," *Journal of International Financial Management and Accounting*, 11, 71-83.

Berle, A. and G. Means (1932), *The Modern Corporation and Private Property*, New York, NY: Macmillan.

Berlin, M. and J. Loyes (1988), "Bond Covenants and Delegated Monitoring," *Journal of Finance*, 43, 397-412.

Bhattacharya, S. and G. Chiesa (1995), "Financial Intermediation with Proprietary Information," *Journal of Financial Intermediation*, 4, 328-57.

Bhattacharya, S. and J. Ritter (1982), "Innovation and Communication Signalling with Partial Disclosure," *Review of Economic Studies*, 50, 331-46.

Bhide, A. (1993), "The Hidden Costs of Stock Market Liquidity," *Journal of Financial Economics*, 34, 31-51.

Biais, B. and A.M. Faugeron-Crouzet (2002), "IPO Auctions: English, Dutch, ... French, and Internet," *Journal of Financial Intermediation*, 11, 9-36.

Biais, B. and E. Perotti (2000), "Machiavellian Privatization," *American Economic Review* 92, 240-48.

Biais, B., P. Bossaerts and J.C. Rochet (2002), "An Optimal IPO Mechanism," *Review of Economic Studies*, 69, 117-46.

Binay, M. and C. Pirinsky (2003), "How Important is Relationship for Underwriters and Institutional Investors?", Texas A&M University working paper.

Black, B. and R. Gilson (1998), "Venture Capital and the Structure of Capital Markets: Banks versus Stock Markets," *Journal of Financial Economics*, 47, 243-77.

Boardman, A. and C. Laurin (2000), "Factors Affecting the Stock Price Performance of Share Issue Privatizations," *Applied Economics*, 32, 1451-64.

Boehmer, B., E. Boehmer and R. Fishe (2002), "Do Institutions Receive Favorable Allocations in IPOs with Better Long-Run Returns?", University of Miami working paper.

Boehmer, E. and R. Fishe (2000), "Do Underwriter's Encourage Stock Flipping? A New Explanation for the Underpricing of IPOs," University of Miami working paper.

Boehmer, E. and R. Fishe (2002), "Price Support by Underwriters in Initial and Seasoned Public Offerings," University of Miami working paper.

Boehmer, E. and R. Fishe (2004), "Underwriter Short Covering in the IPO Aftermarket: A Clinical Study," *Journal of Corporate Finance*, forthcoming.

Boehmer, E. and A. Ljungqvist (2001), "The Choice of Outside Equity: An Exploratory Analysis of Privately Held Firms," New York University working paper.

Boehmer, E., G. Sanger and S. Varshney (1995), "The Effect of Consolidated Control on Firm Performance: The Case of Dual-Class IPOs," in M. Levis (ed), *Advances in Finance, Investment, and Banking*, Amsterdam: Elsevier.

Bolton, P. and D. Scharfstein (1990), "A Theory of Predation Based on Agency Conflicts in Financial Contracting," *American Economic Review*, 80, 93-106.

Bolton, P. and E. von Thadden (1998), "Blocks, Liquidity, and Corporate Control," *Journal of Finance*, 53, 1-26.

Boot, A. and A. Thakor (1997), "Financial System Architecture," *Review of Financial Studies*, 10, 693-733.

Booth, J. and L. Chua (1996), "Ownership Dispersion, Costly Information, and IPO Underpricing," *Journal of Financial Economics*, 41, 291-310.

Booth, J. and R. Smith (1986), "Capital Raising, Underwriting, and the Certification Process," *Journal of Financial Economics*, 15, 261-81.

Bottazzi, L. and M. Da Rin (2002), "Europe's 'New' Stock Markets," CEPR working paper no. 218.

Bower, N. (1989), "Firm Value and the Choice of Offering Method in Initial Public Offerings," *Journal of Finance*, 44, 647-62.

Brada, J. (1996), "Privatization is Transition– Or Is It?", *Journal of Economic Perspectives*, 10, 67-86.

Bradley, D. and B. Jordan (2002), "Partial Adjustment to Public Information and IPO Underpricing," *Journal of Financial and Quantitative Analysis*, 37, 595-616.

Bradley, D., J. Cooney Jr, B. Jordan and A. Singh (2004), "Negotiation and the IPO Offer Price: A Comparison of Integer Versus Non-Integer IPOs," *Journal of Financial and Quantitative Analysis*, forthcoming.

Bradley, D., B. Jordan and J. Ritter (2003), "The Quiet Period Goes Out with a Bang," *Journal of Finance*, 58, 1-36.

Bradley, D., B. Jordan, I. Roten and H. Yi (2001), "Venture Capital and IPO Lock-up Expirations: An Empirical Investigation," *Journal of Financial Research*, 24, 465-92.

Brander, J. and T. Lewis (1986), "Oligopoly and Financial Structure," *American Economic Review*, 76, 956-70.

Branson, B., D. Guffey and D. Pagach, 1998, "Information Conveyed in Announcements of Analyst Coverage," *Contemporary Accounting Research*, 15, 119-43.

Brau, J., B. Francis and N. Kohers (2003), "The Choice of IPO Versus Takeover: Empirical Evidence," *Journal of Business*, 76, 583-612.

Brau, J., V. Lambson, and G. McQueen (2003), "Why Lockups?", *Journal of Financial and Quantitative Analysis* forthcoming.

Brav, A. (2000), "Inference in Long-Horizon Event Studies: A Bayesian Approach with Applications to Initial Public Offerings," *Journal of Finance*, 55, 1979-2016.

Brav, A. and P. Gompers (1997), "Myth or Reality? The Long-Run Performance of Initial Public Offerings: Evidence from Venture and non-Venture Capital-Backed Companies," *Journal of Finance*, 52, 1791-1821.

Brav, A. and P. Gompers (2003), "Insider Trading Subsequent to Initial Public Offerings: Evidence from Expiration of Lock-up Provisions," *Review of Financial Studies*, 16, 1-29.

Brav, A., C. Gezcy and P. Gompers (2000), "Is the Abnormal Return Following Equity Issuance Anomalous?", *Journal of Financial Economics*, 56, 209-49.

Brennan, M. and J. Franks (1997), "Underpricing, Ownership, and Control in Initial Public Offerings of Equity Securities in the U.K.," *Journal of Financial Economics*, 45, 391-413.

Brennan, M. and A. Subrahmanyam (1995), "Investment Analysis and Price Formation in Securities Markets," *Journal of Financial Economics*, 38, 361-81.

Brennan, M. and C. Tamarowski (2000), "Investors Relations, Liquidity and Stock Prices," *Journal of Applied Corporate Finance*, 12, 26-37.

Brous, P., V. Datal and O. Kini (2001), "Is the Market Optimistic about the Future Earnings of Seasoned Equity Offering Firms?", *Journal of Financial and Quantitative Analysis*, 36, 141-68.

Brown, E. (1997), "The Best Software Business Bill Gates Does Not Own," *Fortune*, December, 242-50.

Bunsis, H. and P. Drake (1995), "The Decline of Auditors and Defendents in Initial Public Offering Lawsuits: An Empirical Analysis," Southern Methodist University working paper.

Burch, J. and B. Foerster (2002), *Securities Industry Association Capital Markets Handbook*, New York: Aspen Law and Business.

Burkart, M., D. Gromb and F. Panunzi (1997), "Large Shareholders, Monitoring, and the Value of the Firm," *Quarterly Journal of Economics*, 112, 694-728.

Busaba, W. (2002), "Bookbuilding, the Option to Withdraw, and the Timing of IPOs," University of Arizona working paper.

Busaba, W., L. Benveniste and R. Guo (2001), "The Option to Withdraw IPOs in the Pre-Market: Empirical Analysis," *Journal of Financial Economics*, 60, 73-102.

Camerer, C. (1998), "Bounded Rationality in Individual Decision Making," *Experimental Economics* 1, 163-83.

Campa, J. and S. Kedia (2001), "Explaining the Diversification Discount," *Journal of Finance* 57, 1731-62.

Campbell, J. and R. Shiller (1988), "Stock Prices, Earnings, and Expected Dividends," *Journal of Finance*, 43, 661-76.

Carlin, W. and C. Mayer (2003), "Finance, Investment and Growth," *Journal of Financial Economics*, 69, 191-226.

Carter, R. (1992), "Underwriter Reputation and Repetitive Public Offerings," *Journal of Financial Research*, 15, 341-54.

Carter, R. and S. Manaster (1990), "Initial Public Offerings and Underwriter Reputation," *Journal of Finance*, 45, 1045-65.

Carter, R., F. Dark and A. Singh (1998), "Underwriter Reputation, Initial Returns, and the Long-Run Performance of IPO Stocks," *Journal of Finance*, 53, 285-311.

Carter, R., R. Stover and K. Howe (1997), "Bank Loan Certification and Non-Bank Debt: Evidence From IPOs," University of Iowa working paper.

Chadha, S. (2003), "Do Insiders Knowingly Issue Overvalued Equity? Evidence from IPOs that get Delisted," University of Alabama working paper.

Chan, L., N. Jagadeesh, and J. Lakonishok (1996), "Momentum Strategies," *Journal of Finance* 51, 1681-1714.

Chemmanur, T. (1993), "The Pricing of Initial Public Offerings: A Dynamic Model with Information Production," *Journal of Finance*, 48, 285-304.

Chemmanur, T. and P. Fulghieri (1994a), "Investment Bank Reputation, Information Production, and Financial Intermediation," *Journal of Finance*, 49, 57-79.

Chemmanur, T. and P. Fulghieri (1994b), "Reputation, Renegotiation, and the Choice Between Bank Loans and Publicly Traded Debt," *Review of Financial Studies*, 7, 475-506.

Chemmanur, T. and P. Fulghieri (1997), "Why Include Warrants in New Equity Issues? A Theory of Unit IPOs," *Journal of Financial and Quantitative Analysis*, 32, 1-24.

Chemmanur, T. and P. Fulghieri (1999), "A Theory of the Going-Public Decision," *Review of Financial Studies*, 12, 249-80.

Chemmanur, T. and H. Liu (2001), "How Should a Firm Go Public? A Dynamic Model of the Choice Between Fixed Price Offerings and Auctions in IPOs and Privatizations," Boston College working paper.

Chen, H. (1998), "Competition and Collusion in the IPO Market," University of Florida working paper.

Chen, H. and J. Ritter (2000), "The Seven Percent Solution," *Journal of Finance*, 55, 1105-31.

Chevalier, J. (1995a), "Capital Structure and Product Market Competition: Empirical Evidence From the Supermarket Industry," *American Economics Review*, 85, 415-35.

Chevalier, J. (1995b), "Do LBO Supermarkets Charge More? An Empirical Analysis of the Effects of LBOs on Supermarket Pricing," *Journal of Finance*, 50, 1095-1112.

Chevalier, J. (2000), "What Do We Know About Cross-Subsidizing? Evidence From Investment Policies of Merging Firms," University of Chicago working paper.

Chiang, K. and T. Harikumar (2002), "Information Production and IPO Offering Price Clusters: Further Evidence Explaining Underpricing and Long-run Underperformance," University of Alaska Fairbanks working paper.

Choe, H., R. Masulis and V. Nanda (1993), "On the Timing of New Equity Issues: Theory and Evidence," *Journal of Empirical Finance*, 1, 3-31

Chowdry, B. and V. Nanda (1996), "Stabilization, Syndication, and the Pricing of IPOs," *Journal of Financial and Quantitative Analysis*, 31, 25-42.

Chowdhry, B. and A. Sherman (1996a), "The Winner's Curse and International Methods of Allocating Initial Public Offerings," *Pacific-Basin Finance Journal*, 4, 15-30.

Chowdhry, B. and A. Sherman (1996b), "International Differences in Oversubscription and Underpricing of IPOs," *Journal of Corporate Finance*, 2, 359-81.

Christie, W. and P. Schultz (1994), "Why Do Nasdaq Market Makers Avoid Odd-Eighth Quotes?", *Journal of Finance*, 49, 1813-40.

Christie, W., J. Harris, and P. Schultz (1994), "Why Did Nasdaq Market Makers Stop Avoiding Odd-Eighth Quotes?", *Journal of Finance*, 49, 1841-60.

Chua, L. (1995), "A Reexamination of the Costs of Firm Commitment and Best Efforts IPOs," *The Financial Review*, 30, 337-65.

Claessons, S., S. Djankov and L. Lang (2000), "The Separation of Ownership and Control in East Asian Corporations," *Journal of Financial Economics*, 58, 81-112.

Clarke, J., C. Dunbar, and K. Kahle (2001), "Long Run Performance and Insider Trading in Companies and Cancelled Seasoned Equity Offerings," *Journal of Financial and Quantitative Analysis*, 36, 415-30.

Clarke, J., C. Dunbar, and K. Kahle (2004), "The Long-Run Performance of Secondary Equity Issues: A Test of the Window of Opportunity Hypothesis," *Journal of Business*, forthcoming.

351

Clarke, J., C. Dunbar, and K. Kahle (2002), "All-Star Analyst Turnover, Investment Bank Market Share, and the Performance of Initial Public Offerings," University of Western Ontario working paper.

Clarkson, P. and D. Simunic (1994), "The Association Between Audit Quality, Retained Ownership, and Firm-Specific Risk in U.S. vs. Canadian IPO Markets," *Journal of Accounting and Economics*, 17, 207-28.

Clementi, G. (2002), "IPOs and The Growth of Firms," Carnegie Mellon working paper.

Cliff, M. and D. Denis (2003), "Do IPO Firms Purchase Analyst Coverage with Underpricing?", Purdue University working paper.

Coates, J. (2000), "Explaining Variation in Takeover Defenses: Failure in the Corporate Law Department," Harvard John M. Olin Discussion Paper Series No. 297, Cambridge MA.

Cochrane, J. (2001), "The Risk and Return of Venture Capital," Graduate School of Business University of Chicago working paper.

Coffee, J. (1991), "Liquidity Versus Control: The Institutional Investor as Corporate Monitor," *Columbia Law Review*, 91, 1277-1368.

Collins, M., H. Black and J. Wansely (1993), "The Effect of Antitakeover Legislation on Banking Firms: Evidence from Pennsylvania Act 36," *International Review of Financial Analysis*, 2, 191-8.

Comment, R. and W. Schwert (1995), "Poison or Placebo? Evidence on the Deterrence and Wealth Effects of Modern Antitakeover Measures," *Journal of Financial Economics*, 39, 3-43.

Cook, D., R. Kieschnick and R. Van Ness (2003), "On the Marketing of IPOs," University of Mississippi working paper.

Cooney, J., A. Singh, R. Carter and F. Dark (2001), "IPO Initial Returns and Underwriter Reputation: Has the Inverse Relationship Flipped in the 1990s?", University of Kentucky working paper.

Copeland, Tom and Vladimir Antikarov (2001), *Real Options*, New York, NY: Texere.

Copley, P. and E. Douthett (2002), "The Association Between Auditor Choice, Earnings Disclosure, and Ownership Retained by Firms Making Initial Public Offerings," *Contemporary Accounting Research*, 19, 49-76.

Cornelli, F. and D. Goldreich (2001), "Bookbuilding and Strategic Allocation," *Journal of Finance*, 56, 2337-69.

Cornelli, F. and D. Goldreich (2003), "Bookbuilding: How Informative is the Order Book?" *Journal of Finance*, 58, 1415-44

Cornelli, F. and O. Yosha (2003), "Stage Financing and the Role of Convertible Securities," *Review of Economic Studies*, 70, 1-32.

Cornett, M., H. Mehran and H. Tehranian (1998), "Are Financial Markets Overly Optimistic about the Prospects of Firms That Issue Equity? Evidence from Voluntary versus Involuntary Equity Issuances by Banks," *Journal of Finance*, 53, 2139-59.

Corwin, S. and J. Harris (1998), "The Initial Listing Decisions of Firms that Go Public," University of Georgia working paper.

Corwin, S. and P. Schultz (2003), "The Role of IPO Underwriting Syndicates: Underpricing, Certification, and Information Production," University of Notre Dame working paper.

Corwin, S., J. Harris and M. Lipson (2001), "The Development of Secondary Market Liquidity for NYSE-Listed IPOs," University of Georgia working paper.

Cumming, D. (2002), "Contracts and Exits in Venture Capital Finance," University of Alberta working paper.

Cumming, D. and G. Fleming (2002), "A Law and Finance Analysis of Venture Capital Exits in Emerging Markets," University of Alberta working paper.

Cumming, D. and J. MacIntosh (2003), "A Cross-Country Comparison of Full and Partial Venture Capital Exit Strategies," *Journal of Banking and Finance* 27, 511-48.

Cusatis, P., J. Miles and R. Woolridge (1993), "Restructuring Through Spin-offs: The Stock Market Evidence," *Journal of Financial Economics*, 33, 293-311.

Daines, R. (2001), "Does Delaware Law Improve Firm Value?", *Journal of Financial Economics*, 62, 525-58.

Daines, R. and M. Klausner (2001), "Do IPO Charters Maximize Firm Value? Antitakeover Protection in IPOs," *Journal of Law, Economics and Organization*, 17, 83-120.

Daley, L., V. Mehrotra and R. Sivakumar (1997), "Corporate Focus and Value Creation: Evidence from Spin-offs," *Journal of Financial Economics*, 45, 257-81.

Damadaran, A. (2002), *Investment Valuation: Tools and Techniques for Determining the Value of any Asset*, 2nd Ed, New York, NY: John Wiley & Sons.

Daniel, K., D. Hirshleifer and A. Subrahmanyam (1998), "Investor Psychology and Security Market Under- and Over-reactions," *Journal of Finance*, 53, 1839-86.

Das, S., M. Jagannathan and A. Sarin (2002), "The Private Equity Discount: An Empirical Examiniation of the Exit of Venture Backed Companies," Santa Clara University working paper.

Das, S., R. Guo and H. Zhang (2002), "Initiation of Analyst Coverage and Long-Term Performance of Initial Public Offerings," University of Illinios, Chicago working paper.

Datar, F., F. Feltham and J. Hughes (1991), "The Role of Audits and Audit Quality in the Valuing New Issues," *Journal of Accounting and Economics*, 14, 3-49.

Datta, S., M. Iskander-Datta and A. Patel (1997), "The Pricing of Initial Public Offerings of Corporate Straight Debt," *Journal of Finance*, 52, 379-96.

Datta, S., M. Iskander-Datta and A. Patel (2000), "Some Evidence on the Uniqueness of Initial Public Debt Offerings," *Journal of Finance*, 55, 715-43.

D'Souza, J., W. Megginson, and R. Nash (2001), "Determinants of Performance Improvements in Privatized Firms: The Role of Restructuring and Corporate Governance," University of Oklahoma working paper.

De Long, J., A. Shleifer, L. Summers and R. Waldmann (1990), "Positive Feedback Investment Strategies and Destabilizing Rational Speculation," *Journal of Finance*, 45, 379-95.

DeAngelo, H. and L. DeAngelo (1985), "Managerial Ownership of Voting Rights: A Study of Public Corporation with Dual Classes of Common Stock," *Journal of Financial Economics*, 14, 33-69.

DeAngelo, H. and E. Rice (1983), "Antitakeover Charter Amendments and Shareholder Wealth," *Journal of Financial Economics*, 11, 329-60.

DeAngelo, H., L. DeAngelo and E. Rice (1984), "Going Private: Minority Freezeouts and Stockholder Wealth," *Journal of Law and Economics*, 27, 367-401.

DeBondt, W. and R. Thaler (1985), "Does the Stock Market Overreact?", *Journal of Finance*, 40, 793-805.

DeBondt, W. and R. Thaler (1987), "Further Evidence on Investor Overreaction and Stock Market Seasonality," *Journal of Finance*, 42, 557-81.

DeBondt, W. and R. Thaler (1990), "Do Security Analysts Overreact?", *American Economic Review*, 80, 52-7.

DeBondt, W. and R. Thaler (1995), "Financial Decision-Making in Markets and Firms: A Behavioral Perspective," in R. Jarrow, V. Maksimovic and W. Ziemba (eds), *Finance, Handbooks in Operations Research and Management Science*, Amsterdam: North Holland.

Dechow, P., A. Hutton and R. Sloan (2000), "The Relation between Affiliated Analysts' Long-Term Earnings Forecasts and Stock Price Performance Following Equity Offerings," *Contemporary Accounting Research*, 17, 1-32.

Dechow, P. and R. Sloan (1997), "Returns to Contrarian Investment Strategies: Tests of Naive Expectations Hypotheses," *Journal of Financial Economics*, 41, 3-27.

Decker, W. (1994), "The Attractions of the U.S. Securities Markets to Foreign Issuers and the Alternative Methods of Accessing the U.S. Markets: From the Issuer's Perspective," *Fordham International Law Journal*, 17, S10-S24.

Deloof, M., W. De Maeseneire and K. Inghelbrecht (2002), "The Valuation of IPOs by Investment Banks and the Stock Market: Empirical Evidence," University of Antwerp working paper.

Demers, E. and B. Lev (2001), "A Rude Awakening: Internet Shakeout in 2000," *Review of Accounting Studies*, 6, 331-59.

Demers, E. and K. Lewellen (2003), "The Marketing Role of IPOs: Evidence from Internet Stocks," *Journal of Financial Economics*, 68, 413-37.

Demirguc-Kunt, A. and V. Maksimovic (1998), "Law, Finance, and Firm Growth," *Journal of Finance*, 53, 2107-39.

Denis, D. and D. Denis (1994), "Majority Owner-Majority Managers and Organizational Efficiency," *Journal of Corporate Finance*, 1, 91-118.

Denis, D. and V. Mihov (2003), "The Choice Between Bank Debt, Non-Bank Private Debt and Public Debt: Evidence From New Corporate Borrowings," *Journal of Financial Economics*, 70, 3-28.

Denis, D. and A. Sarin (2001), "Is the Market Surprised by Poor Earnings Realizations Following Seasoned Equity Offerings," *Journal of Financial and Quantitative Analysis* 36, 169-93.

Denis, D., D. Denis and A. Sarin (1997), "Agency Problems, Equity Ownership and Corporate Diversification," *Journal of Finance*, 52, 135-60.

Derrien, F. (2002), "Issuers, Underwriters, and Institutional Investors: Why They All Like the Book-Building Procedure," University of Toronto working paper.

Derrien, F. and K. Womack (2003), "Auctions vs. Bookbuilding and the Control of Underpricing in Hot IPO Market," *Review of Financial Studies*, 61, 31-61.

Desai, H. and P. Jain (1999), "Firm Performance and Focus: Long-Run Stock Market Performance Following Spinoffs," *Journal of Financial Economics*, 54, 75-101.

Dewenter, K. and P. Malatesta (1997), "Public Offerings of State-Owned and Privately-Owned Enterprises: An International Comparison," *Journal of Finance*, 52, 1659-79.

Dhiensiri, N. and A. Sayrak (2003), "The Value Effects of Analysts Coverage Initiations," University of Pittsburgh working paper.

Diamond, D. (1984), "Financial Intermediation and Delegated Monitoring," *Review of Economic Studies*, 51, 393-414.

Diamond, D. (1991), "Monitoring and Reputation: The Choice Between Bank Loans and Directly Placed Debt," *Journal of Political Economy*, 99, 689-721.

Djankov, S. and P. Murrell (2002), "Enterprise Restructuring in Transition: A Quantitative Survey," *Journal of Economic Literature*, 40, 739-92.

Dor, A. (2003a), "The Determinants of Insider's Selling at Initial Public Offerings: An Empirical Analysis," Northwestern University working paper.

Dor, A. (2003b), "The Performance of Initial Public Offerings and the Cross Section of Institutional Ownership," Northwestern University working paper.

Dorn, D. (2003), "Does Sentiment Drive the Retail Demand for IPOs," Drexel University working paper.

Draho, J. (2000), "The Timing of Initial Public Offerings: A Real Option Approach," Yale University working paper.

Draho, J. (2001a), "The Effect of Uncertainty on the Underpricing of IPOs," Yale University working paper.

Draho, J. (2001b), "The Coordinating Role of Public Information in Hot Market IPOs," Yale University working paper.

Drake, P. and M. Vetsuypens (1993), "IPO Underpricing and Insurance Against Legal Liability," *Financial Management*, 22, 64-73.

Dreman, D. and M. Berry (1995), "Analyst Forecasting Errors and their Implications for Security Analysts," *Financial Analysts Journal* 51, 30-40.

DuCharme, L., S. Rajgopal and S. Sefcik (2001), "Lowballing for 'Pop': The Case of Internet IPO Underpricing," University of Washington working paper.

Dugar, A. and S. Nathan (1995), "The Effect of Investment Banking Relationships on Financial Analysts' Earnings Forecasts and Investment Recommendations," *Contemporary Accounting Research*, 12, 131-60.

Dunbar, C. (1995), "The Use of Warrants as Underwriter Compensation in Initial Public Offerings," *Journal of Financial Economics*, 38, 59-78.

Dunbar, C. (1998), "The Choice of Between Firm-Commitment and Best-Efforts Offering Methods in IPOs: The Effect of Unsuccessful Offers," *Journal of Financial Intermediation*, 7, 60-90.

Dunbar, C. (2000), "Factors Affecting Investment Bank Initial Public Offering Market Share," *Journal of Financial Economics*, 55, 3-41.

Dunbar, C., C. Hwang and K. Shastri (1999), "Underwriter Analyst Recommendation: Conflict of Interest or Rush to Judgement?" University of Western Ontario working paper.

Dunne, T., M. Roberts, and L. Samuelson (1989), "The Growth and Failure of U.S. Manufacturing Plants," *Quarterly Journal of Economics*, 104, 671-98.

Easterbrook, F. (1984), "Two Agency-Cost Explanations for Dividends," *American Economic Review*, 74, 650-60.

Easterbrook, F. and D. Fischel (1991), *The Economic Structure of Corporate Law*, Cambridge, MA: Harvard University Press.

Easterwood, J. and S. Nutt (1999), "Inefficiency in Analysts' Earnings Forecasts: Systematic Reaction or Systematic Optimism?", *Journal of Finance*, 54, 1777-97.

Eckbo, E., R. Masulis and O. Norli (2000), "Seasoned Public Offerings: Resolution of the 'New Issues Puzzle'," *Journal of Financial Economics*, 56, 251-91.

Eckbo, E. and O. Norli (2000), "Risk and Long-Run IPO Returns," University of Toronto working paper.

Elkind, P (2001), "Where Mary Meeker Went Wrong," *Fortune*, May 14, 68-92.

Elkind, P. and M. Gimein (2001), "The Trouble with Frank," *Fortune*, September 3, 112-126.

Ellingsen, T. and K. Rydqvist (1997), "The Stock Market as a Screening Device and the Decision to Go Public," Stockholm School of Economics working paper.

Ellis, K., R. Michaely and M. O'Hara (2000), "When the Underwriter is the Market Maker: An Examination in the IPO Aftermarket," *Journal of Finance*, 55, 1039-74.

Emory, J. (1985), "The Value of Marketability as Illustrated in Initial Public Offerings of Common Stock: January 1980 Through June 1981," *Business Valuation Review*, September, 21-4.

Engel, E., E. Gordon and R. Hayes (2002), "The Rules of Performance Measures and Monitoring in Annual Governance Decision in Entreprenurial Firms," *Journal of Accounting Research*, 40, 485-518.

Erb, C., C. Harvey, and T. Viskanta (1996), "Expected Returns and Volatility in 135 Countries," *Journal of Portfolio Management*, 32-48.

Fama, E. (1980), "Agency Problems and the Theory of the Firm," *Journal of Political Economy*, 88, 288-307.

Fama, E. (1985), "What's Different about Banks?", *Journal of Monetary Economics*, 15, 29-39.

Fama, E. (1998), "Market Efficiency, Long-Term Returns, and Behavorial Finance," *Journal of Financial Economics*, 49, 283-306.

Fama, E. and K. French (1988), "Permanent and Temporary Components of Stock Prices," *Journal of Political Economy*, 96, 246-73.

Fama, E. and K. French (1993), "Common Risk Factors in the Returns on Bonds and Stocks," *Journal of Financial Economics*, 33, 3-56.

Fazzari, S., R.G. Hubbard and B. Petersen (1988), "Financing Constraints and Corporate Investment," *Brookings Papers on Economic Activity: Microeconomics* 1:141-205.

Fazzari, S., R.G. Hubbard and B. Petersen (2000), "Investment-Cash Flow Sensitivities are Useful: A Comment on Kaplan and Zingales," *Quarterly Journal of Economics*, 115, 695-705.

Feltham, F., J. Hughes and D. Simunic (1991), "Empirical Assessment of the Impact of Auditor Quality on the Valuation of New Issues," *Journal of Accounting and Economics*, 14, 375-399.

Field, L. (1996), "Is Institutional Investment in Initial Public Offerings Related to the Long-Run Performance of those Firms?", Penn State University working paper.

Field, L. (1999), "Control Considerations of Newly Public Firms: The Implementation of Antitakeover Provisions and Dual Class Shares Before the IPO," Penn State University working paper.

Field, L. and G. Hanka (2001), "The Expiration of IPO Share Lock-ups," *Journal of Finance*, 56, 471-500.

Field, L. and J. Karpoff (2002), "Takeover Defenses at IPO Firms," *Journal of Finance*, 57, 1857-89.

Field, L. and D. Sheehan (2003), "IPO Underpricing and Outside Blockholders," *Journal of Corporate Finance* forthcoming.

Fischel, D. (1987), "Organized Exchanges and the Regulation of Dual Class Common Stock," *Chicago Law Review*, 54, 119-52.

Fishe, R. (2002), "How Stock Flippers Affect IPO Pricing and Stabilization," *Journal of Financial and Quantitative Analysis*, 37, 319-40.

Foster-Johnson, L., C. Lewis and J. Seward (2000), "Busted IPOs and Windows of Misopportunity," Dartmouth College working paper.

Fulghieri, P. and M. Spiegel (1993), "A Theory of the Distribution of Underpriced Initial Public Offers by Investment Banks," *Journal of Economics and Management Strategy*, 2, 509-33.

Gale, D. and M. Hellwig (1985), "Incentive-Compatible Debt Contracts: The One-Period Problem," *Review of Economic Studies*, 52, 647-63.

Gale, D. and J. Stiglitz (1989), "The Informational Content of Initial Public Offerings," *Journal of Finance*, 44, 469-77.

Garfinkel, J. (1993), "IPO Underpricing, Insider Selling, and Subsequent Equity Offerings: Is Underpricing a Signal of Quality?", *Financial Management*, 22, 74-83.

Gertner, R. and D. Scharfstein (1991), "A Theory of Workouts and the Effects of Reorganization Law," *Journal of Finance*, 46, 1189-1222.

Gertner, R., R. Gibbons and D. Scharfstein (1988), "Simultaneous Signaling to the Capital and Product Markets," *Rand Journal of Economics*, 19, 173-90.

Gertner, R., E. Powers and D. Scharfstein (2002), "Learning About Internal Capital Markets From Corporate Spin-offs," *Journal of Finance*, 57, 2479-2506.

Gibbon, H. (1997), "A Seller's Manual: Guidelines for Selling State-Owned Enterprises," *Privatisation Yearbook*, London: Privatisation International, 16-26.

Gibbon, H. (2000), "Editor's Letter," *Privatisation Yearbook*, London: Thomson Financial, p. 1.

Gilson, R. and D. Schizer (2002), "Understanding Venture Capital Structure: A Tax Explanation for Convertible Preferred Stock," Columbia Law School working paper no. 230.

Gilson, S. and J. Warner (2000), "Private versus Public Debt: Evidence from Firms that Replace Bank Loans with Junk Bonds," Harvard Business School working paper.

Gilson, S., P. Healy, C. Noe and K. Palepu (2001), "Analyst Specialization and Conglomerate Stock Breakup," *Journal of Accounting Research*, 39, 565-82.

Gilson, S., E. Hotchkiss and R. Ruback (2000), "Valuation of Bankrupt Firms," *Review of Financial Studies*, 13, 43-74.

Gilson, S., K. John and L. Lang (1990), "Troubled Debt Restructurings: An Empirical Study of Private Reorganizations of Firms in Default," *Journal of Financial Economics*, 27, 315-54.

Giudici, G. and P. Roosenboom (2003), "Pricing Initial Public Offerings in 'New' European Stock Markets," Tilburg University working paper.

Gompers, P. (1995), "Optimal Investment, Monitoring, and the Staging of Venture Capital," *Journal of Finance*, 50, 1461-89.

Gompers, P. (1996), "Grandstanding in the Venture Capital Industry," *Journal of Financial Economics*, 42, 133-56.

Gompers, P. and J. Lerner (1997), "Risk and Reward in Private Equity Investments: The Challenge of Performance Assessment," *Journal of Private Equity*, Winter, 5-12.

Gompers, P. and J. Lerner (1998), "Venture Capital Disbursements: Short-run and Long-run Reactions," *Journal of Finance*, 53, 2161-83.

Gompers, P. and J. Lerner (1999), "Conflict of Interest in the Issuance of Public Securities: Evidence From Venture Capital," *Journal of Law and Economics*, 42, 1-28.

Gompers, P. and J. Lerner (2000), "Money Chasing Deals? The Impact of Fund Inflows on Private Equity Valuations," *Journal of Financial Economics*, 55, 281-325.

Graham, J. and C. Harvey (2001), "The Theory and Practice of Corporate Finance: Evidence From the Field," *Journal of Financial Economics*, 60, 187-243.

Graham, J., M. Lemmon and J. Wolf (2002), "Does Corporate Diversification Destroy Firm Value?", *Journal of Finance*, 57, 695-720.

Grinblatt, M. and C. Hwang (1989), "Signaling and the Pricing of New Issues," *Journal of Finance*, 44, 393-420.

Grossman, S. and O. Hart (1980), "Takeover Bids, the Free-Rider Problem, and the Theory of the Corporation," *Bell Journal of Economics*, 11, 42-64.

Grossman, S. and O. Hart (1986), "The Costs and Benefits of Ownership: A Theory of Vertical and Lateral Integration," *Journal of Political Economy*, 94, 691-719.

Grossman, S. and O. Hart (1988), "One Share-One Vote and the Market for Corporate Control," *Journal of Financial Economics*, 20, 175-202.

Guiso, L. (1998), "High-Tech Firms and Credit Rationing," *Journal of Economic Behavior and Organization*, 35, 39-59.

Habib, M. and A. Ljungqvist (2001), "Underpricing and Entrepreneurial Wealth Losses in IPOs: Theory and Evidence," *Review of Financial Studies*, 14, 433-58.

Hall, B. (1987), "The Relationship Firm Size and Firm Growth in the U.S. Manufacturing Sector," *Journal of Industrial Economics*, 35, 583-606.

Hand, J. (2000), "The Role of Accounting Fundamentals, Web Traffic, and Supply and Demand in the Pricing of U.S. Internet Stocks," University of North Carolina, Chapel Hill, working paper.

Hand, J. (2003a), "Profits, Losses and the Non-Linear Pricing of Internet Stocks," in Hand, J. and B. Lev (Eds.), *Intangible Assets: Values, Measures, and Risks*, Oxford: Oxford University Press.

Hand, J. (2003b), "The Market Valuation of Biotechnology Firms and Biotechnology R&D," in McCahery, J. and L. Renneboog (Eds.), *Venture Capital Contracting and the Valuation of High-Technology Firms*, Oxford: Oxford Univeristy Press.

Hand, J. and T. Skantz (1999), "The Market-Timing Characteristics of Equity Carve-outs," University of North Carolina, Chapel Hill working paper.

Hanley, K. (1993), "The Underpricing of Initial Public Offerings and the Partial Adjustment Phenomenon," *Journal of Financial Economics*, 34, 231-50.

Hanley, K. and W. Wilhelm (1995), "Evidence on the Strategic Allocation of Initial Public Offerings," *Journal of Financial Economics*, 37, 239-57.

Hanley, K., B. Arunkumar and P. Seguin (1993), "Price Stabilization in the Market for New Issues," *Journal of Financial Economics*, 34, 177-98.

Hanley, K., C. Lee and P. Seguin (1996), "The Marketing of Close-end Funds IPOs: Evidence From Transaction Data," *Journal of Financial Intermediation*, 5, 127-59.

Hannes, S. (2001), "The Missing Link in the Corporate Takeover Literature," Harvard University Law School working paper.

Hanouna, P., A. Sarin and A. Shapiro (2001), "Value of Corporate Control: Some International Evidence," University of Southern California Finance and Business Economics Working Paper No. 01-4.

Hansen, R. (2001), "Do Investment Banks Compete in IPOs?: The Advent of the '7% Plus Contract'," *Journal of Financial Economics*, 59, 313-46.

Hansen, R. and P. Torregrosa (1992), "Underwriter Compensation and Corporate Monitoring," *Journal of Finance*, 47, 1537-55.

Harrison, M. (1994), *Asia-Pacific Securities Markets*, Hong Kong: Longman Publishers.

Hart, O. and J. Moore (1994), "A Theory of Debt Based on the Inalienability of Human Capital," *Quarterly Journal of Economics*, 109, 841-79.

Hellmann, T. (1998), "The Allocation of Control Rights in Venture Capital Contracts," *Rand Journal of Economics*, 29, 57-76.

Hellmann, T. (2002), "IPOs, Acquisitions and the Use of Convertible Securities in Venture Capital," Stanford University working paper.

Hellmann, T. and M. Puri (2002), "Venture Capital and the Professionalization of Start-up Firms: Empirical Evidence," *Journal of Finance*, 57, 169-97.

Hellman, T., L. Lindsey and M. Puri (2003), "Building Relationships Early: Banks in Venture Capital," Stanford University working paper.

Helwege, J. and N. Liang (1996), "Is There a Pecking Order? Evidence From a Panel of IPO Firms," *Journal of Financial Economics*, 40, 429-58.

Helwege, J. and N. Liang (2004), "Initial Public Offerings in Hot and Cold Markets," *Journal of Financial and Quantitative Analysis*, forthcoming.

Helwege, J. and F. Packer (2001), "The Decision to Go Public: Evidence From Corporate Bond Issuers," Ohio State University Dice Center Working Paper No. 2001-12.

Hertzel, M., M. Lemmon, J. Linck and L. Rees (2002), "Long-Run Performance Following Private Placements of Equity," *Journal of Finance*, 57, 2595-2617.

Hertzel, M. and R. Smith (1993), "Market Discounts and Shareholder Gains For Placing Equity Privately," *Journal of Finance*, 48, 459-85.

Hirshleifer, D. (2001), "Investor Psychology and Asset Pricing," *Journal of Finance*, 56, 1533-97.

Hite, G. and J. Owers (1983), "Security Price Reactions around Corporate Spinoff Announcements," *Journal of Financial Economics*, 12, 409-36.

Hite, G., J. Owers and R. Rogers (1987), "The Market for Inter-firm Asset Sales: Partial Sell-offs and Total Liquidations," *Journal of Financial Economics*, 18, 229-52.

Hochberg, Y. (2003), "Venture Capital and Corporate Governance in the Newly Public Firm," Cornell University working paper.

Hoffmann-Burchardi, U. (2001), "Clustering of Initial Public Offerings, Information Revelation, and Underpricing," *European Economic Review*, 45, 353-83.

Hogan, C. (1997), "Costs and Benefits of Audit Quality in the IPO Market: A Self-Selection Analysis," *The Accounting Review*, 77, 67-86.

Holmen, M. and P. Hogfeldt (2001), "A Law and Finance Analysis of Initial Public Offerings," Stockholm University working paper.

Holmstrom, B. (1979), "Moral Hazard and Observability," *Bell Journal of Economics*, 10, 74-91.

Holmstrom, B. and J. Tirole (1993), "Market Liquidity and Performance Monitoring," *Journal of Political Economy*, 101, 678-709.

Holthausen, R. and D. Larcker (1996), "The Financial Performance of Reverse Leverage Buyouts," *Journal of Financial Economics*, 42, 293-332.

Horner, M. (1988), "The Value of the Corporate Voting Right: Evidence from Switzerland," *Journal of Banking and Finance*, 12, 69-83.

Houge, T., T. Loughran, G. Suchanek and X. Yan (2002), "Divergence of Opinion, Uncertainty, and the Underpricing of Initial Public Offerings," *Financial Management*, 30, 5-23.

Houston, J. and C. James (1996), "Bank Information Monopolies and the Mix of Private and Public Debt Choices," *Journal of Finance*, 51, 1863-89.

Houston, J., C. James and J. Karceski (2003), "What a Difference a Month Makes: Stock Analyst Valuations Following Initial Public Offerings," University of Florida working paper.

How, J. and J. Howe (2001), "Warrants in Initial Public Offerings: Empirical Evidence," *Journal of Business*, 74, 433-58.

Hsu, D. (2003), "What Do Entrepreneur's Pay for Venture Capital Affiliation?", *Journal of Finance* forthcoming.

Huang, Q. and R. Levich (1998), "Underpricing of New Equity Offerings By Privatized Firms: An International Test," *mimeo*, New York University.

Hughes, P. (1986), "Signaling by Direct Disclosure Under Asymmetric Information," *Journal of Accounting and Economics*, 8, 119-42.

Huyghebaert, N. and C. Van Hulle (2001), "Structuring the IPO: Empirical Evidence on Primary, Secondary, and Combined Offerings," Katholieke Universiteit Leuven working paper.

Ibbotson, R. (1975), "Price Performance of Common Stock New Issues," *Journal of Financial Economics*, 2, 235-72.

Ibbotson, R. and J. Jaffe (1975), "'Hot Issue' Markets," *Journal of Finance*, 30, 1027-42.

Ibbotson, R., J. Sindelar and J. Ritter (1994), "The Market's Problems With the Pricing of Initial Public Offerings," *Journal of Applied Corporate Finance*, 7, 66-74.

Ikenberry, D., J. Lakonishok and T. Vermaelen (1995), "Market Underreaction to Open Market Share Repurchases," *Journal of Financial Economics* 39, 181-208.

Ikenberry, D., G. Rankine and E. Stice (1996), "What Do Stock Splits Really Signal?", *Journal of Financial and Quantitative Analysis* 31, 257-75.

Irvine, P. (2003), "The Incremental Impact of Analyst Initiation of Coverage," *Journal of Corporate Finance*, 9, 431-51.

Iskoz, S. (2003), "Bias in Underwriter Analyst Recommendations: Does it Matter?", MIT working paper.

Jain, B. and O. Kini (1994), "The Post-Issue Operating Performance of IPO Firms," *Journal of Finance*, 49, 1699-1726.

Jain, B. and O. Kini (1999), "On Investment Bank Monitoring in the New Issues Market," *Journal of Banking and Finance*, 23, 49-84.

James, C. (1987), "Some Evidence on the Uniqueness of Bank Loans," *Journal of Financial Economics*, 19, 217-35.

James, C. (1992), "Relationship-Specific Assets and the Pricing of Underwriting Services," *Journal of Finance*, 47, 1865-83.

James, K. (2001), "Do Large Underwriters Form Investors Coalitions?: Evidence From 13F Data," *Journal of Finance*, forthcoming.

Jegadeesh, N. and S. Titman (1993), "Returns to Buying Winners and Selling Losers: Implications for Stock Market Efficiency," *Journal of Finance*, 48, 65-91.

Jegadeesh, N., M. Weinstein and I. Welch (1993), "An Empirical Investigation of IPO Returns and Subsequent Equity Offerings," *Journal of Financial Economics*, 34, 153-75.

Jeng, L. and P. Wells (2000), "The Determinants of Venture Capital Fundraising: Evidence Across Countries," *Journal of Corporate Finance*, 6, 241-89.

Jenkinson, T. and H. Jones (2003), "Bids and Allocation in European IPO Bookbuilding," *Journal of Finance* forthcoming.

Jenkinson, T. and A. Ljungqvist (2001), *Going Public: The Theory and Evidence on how Companies Raise Equity Finance*, 2nd ed, Oxford: Oxford University Press.

Jenkinson, T., A. Morrison and W. Wilhelm Jr (2003), "Why are European IPOs so Rarely Priced Outside the Indicative Price Range," University of Oxford working paper.

Jensen, M. (1986), "Agency Costs of Free Cash Flow, Corporate Finance, and Takeovers," *American Economic Review*, 76, 323-39.

Jensen, M. (1989), "Eclipse of the Public Corporation" *Harvard Business Review*, 67, 60-70.

Jensen, M. and W. Meckling (1976), "Theory of the Firm: Managerial Behavior, Agency Costs and Ownership Structure," *Journal of Financial Economics*, 3, 305-60.

Jensen, M. and K. Murphy (1990), "Performance Pay and Top-Management Incentives," *Journal of Political Economy*, 98, 225-64.

Jensen, M. and R. Ruback (1983), "The Market for Corporate Control: The Scientific Evidence," *Journal of Financial Economics*, 11, 5-50.

Jindra, J. (2000), "Seasoned Equity Offerings, Overvaluation, and Timing," Ohio State University working paper.

Johnson, J. and R. Miller (1988), "Investment Banker Prestige and the Underpricing of Initial Public Offerings," *Financial Management*, Summer, 19-29.

Johnson, S., P. Boone, A. Breach and E. Friedman (2000), "Corporate Governance in the Asian Financial Crisis," *Journal of Financial Economics*, 58, 141-86.

Jones, C. and M. Rhodes-Kropf (2003), "The Price of Diversifiable Risk in Venture Capital and Private Equity," Columbia University working paper.

Jones, J. (1991), "Earnings Management During Import Relief Investigations," *Journal of Accounting Research*, 29, 193-228.

Jones, S., W. Megginson, R. Nash and J. Netter (1999), "Share Issue Privatizations as Financial Means to Political Ends," *Journal of Financial Economics*, 53, 227-53.

Jung, K., Y. Kim and R. Stulz (1996), "Timing, Investment Opportunities, Managerial Discretion, and the Security Issue Decision," *Journal of Financial Economics*, 42, 159-85.

Kahn, C. and A. Winton (1998), "Ownership Structure, Speculation, and Shareholder Intervention," *Journal of Finance*, 53, 99-129.

Kahneman, D. and A. Tversky (1979), "Prospect Theory: An Analysis of Decision Under Risk," *Econometric*, 47, 263-91.

Kale, J. and T. Noe (1990), "Risky Debt Maturity Choice in a Sequential Equilibrium," *Journal of Financial Research*, 13, 155-65.

Kandel, S., O Sarig and A. Wohl (1999), "The Demand for Stocks: An Analysis of IPO Auctions," *Review of Financial Studies*, 12, 227-48.

Kaplan, S. (1989), "The Effect of Management Buyouts on Operating Performance and Value," *Journal of Financial Economics*, 24, 217-54.

Kaplan, S. (1991), "The Staying Power of Leveraged Buyouts," *Journal of Financial Economics*, 29, 287-313.

Kaplan, S. and R. Ruback (1995), "The Valuation of Cash Flow Forecasts: An Empirical Analysis," *Journal of Finance*, 50, 1059-93.

Kaplan, S. and A. Schoar (2003), "Private Equity Performance: Return, Persistence and Capital Flows," University of Chicago working paper.

Kaplan, S. and J. Stein (1993), "The Evolution of Buyout Pricing and Financial Structure in the 1980s," *Quarterly Journal of Economics*, 108, 313-57.

Kaplan, S. and P. Stromberg (2003a), "Financial Contracting Theory Meets the Real World: Evidence from Venture Capital Contracts," *Review of Economic Studies*, 70, 281-315.

Kaplan, S. and P. Stromberg (2003b), "Characteristics, Contracts, and Actions: Evidence From Venture Capital Analyses," University of Chicago working paper.

Kaplan, S. and L. Zingales (1997), "Do Financing Constraints Explain Why Investment is Correlated with Cash Flow?", *Quarterly Journal of Economics*, 112, 169-215

Keloharju, M. (1993), "The Winner's Curse, Legal Liability, and the Long-Run Price Performance of Initial Public Offerings in Finland," *Journal of Financial Economics*, 34, 251-77.

Keloharju, M. and S. Torstila (2002), "The Distribution of Information among Institutional and Retail Investors in IPOs," *European Financial Management Journal*, 8, 373-85.

Kim, M. and J. Ritter (1999), "Valuing IPOs," *Journal of Financial Economics*, 53, 409-37.

Kim, S., J. Lin and M. Slovin (1997), "Market Structure, Informed Trading, and Analysts' Recommendations," *Journal of Financial and Quantitative Analysis*, 32, 507-24.

Klein, A. (1996), "Can Investors Use the Prospectus to Price Initial Public Offerings?", *Journal of Financial Statement Analysis*, 2, 23-39.

Klein, A., J. Rosenfeld and W. Beranek (1991), "The Two Stages of an Equity Carve-out and the Price Response of Parent and Subsidiary Stock," *Managerial and Decision Economics*, 12, 449-60.

Koeplin, J., A. Sarin and A. Shapiro (2000), "The Private Company Discount," *Journal of Applied Corporate Finance*, 12, 94-101.

Koh, F. and T. Walter (1989), "A Direct Test of Rock's Model of the Pricing in Unseasoned Issues," *Journal of Financial Economics*, 23, 251-72.

Korajczyk, R., D. Lucas and R. McDonald (1991), "The Effect of Information Releases on the Timing and Pricing of Security Issues," *Review of Financial Studies*, 4, 685-708.

Kothari, S. and J. Warner (1997), "Measuring Long-Horizon Security Price Performance," *Journal of Financial Economics*, 43, 301-39.

Kovenock, D. and G. Phillips (1997), "Capital Structure and Product Market Behavior: An Examination of Plant Exit and Investment Decisions," *Review of Financial Studies*, 10, 767-803.

Krigman, L., W. Shaw and K. Womack (1999), "The Persistence of IPO Mispricing and the Predictive Power of Flipping," *Journal of Finance*, 54, 1015-44.

Krigman, L., W. Shaw and K. Womack (2001), "Why Do Firms Switch Underwriters?", *Journal of Financial Economics*, 60, 245-84.

Krishnamurthy, S., P. Spindt, V. Subramaniam and T. Woidtke (2003), "Does Investor Identity Matter in Equity Issues? Evidence from Private Placements," *Journal of Financial Intermediation*, forthcoming.

Krishnaswami, S. and V. Subramaniam (1999), "Information Asymmetry, Valuation, and the Corporate Spin-off Decision," *Journal of Financial Economics*, 53, 73-112.

Krishnaswami, S., P. Spindt and V. Subramaniam (1999), "Information Asymmetry, Monitoring and the Placement Structure of Corporate Debt," *Journal of Financial Economics*, 51, 407-34.

Kutsuna, K. and R. Smith (2003), "Issue Cost and Method of IPO Underpricing: Japan's Change from Auction Method Pricing to Book-Building," Claremont Graduate University working paper.

Laine, M. and S. Torstila (2003), "The Exit Rates of Liquidated Venture Capital Funds," Helsinki School of Economics working paper.

Lakonishok, J. and T. Vermaelen (1990), "Anomalous Price Behavior around Repurchase Tender Offers," *Journal of Finance*, 45, 455-77.

Lakonishok, J., A. Shleifer, R. Thaler and R. Vishny (1991), "Window-Dressing by Pension Fund Managers," *American Economic Review Papers and Proceedings*, 81, 227-31.

Lakonishok, J., A. Shleifer, and R. Vishny (1994), "Contrarian Investment, Extrapolation and Risk," *Journal of Finance*, 49, 1541-78.

Lamont, O. (1997), "Cash Flow and Investment: Evidence from Internal Capital Markets," *Journal of Finance*, 52, 83-109.

Lamont, O. and C. Polk (2001), "The Diversification Discount: Cash Flows versus Returns," *Journal of Finance*, 56, 1693-1721.

Landier, A. (2002), "Start-up Financing: From Banks to Venture Capital," University of Chicago working paper.

Lang, L. and R. Stulz (1994), "Tobin's q, Corporate Diversification, and Firm Performance," *Journal of Political Economy*, 102, 1248-80.

Lang, L., A. Poulsen and R. Stulz (1995), "Asset Sales, Firm Performance, and the Agency Costs of Managerial Discretion," *Journal of Financial Economics*, 37, 3-37.

La Porta, R., F. Lopez-de-Silanes and A. Shleifer (1999), "Corporate Ownership Around the World," *Journal of Finance*, 54, 471-517.

La Porta, R., F. Lopez-de-Silanes, A. Shleifer and R. Vishny (1997), "Legal Determinants of External Finance," *Journal of Finance*, 52, 1131-50.

La Porta, R., F. Lopez-de-Silanes, A. Shleifer and R. Vishny (1998), "Law and Finance," *Journal of Political Economy*, 106, 1113-55.

La Porta, R., F. Lopez-de-Silanes, A. Shleifer and R. Vishny (2000a), "Agency Problems and Dividend Policies Around the World," *Journal of Finance*, 55, 1-33.

La Porta, R., F. Lopez-de-Silanes, A. Shleifer and R. Vishny (2000b), "Investor Protection and Corporate Governance," *Journal of Financial Economics*, 58, 3-27.

La Porta, R., F. Lopez-de-Silanes, A. Shleifer and R. Vishny (2002), "Investor Protection and Corporate Valuation," *Journal of Finance*, 57, 1147-70.

Lee, C., A. Shleifer and R. Thaler (1991), "Investor Sentiment and the Closed-End Puzzle," *Journal of Finance*, 46, 75-109.

Lee, I. (1997), "Do Firms Knowingly Sell Overvalued Equity?", *Journal of Finance*, 52, 1439-66.

Lee, I., S. Lochhead, J. Ritter and Q. Zhao (1996), "The Costs of Going Public," *Journal of Financial Research*, 19, 59-74.

Lee, M., P. Lee and S. Taylor (2003), "Unit Initial Public Offerings: Staged Equity or Signaling Mechanism," *Accounting and Finance*, 43 63-85.

Lee, P., S. Taylor and S. Taylor (2002), "Auditor Conservatism and Audit Quality: Evidence from IPO Earnings Forecasts," University of Technology, Sydney, working paper.

Lee, P., S. Taylor and T. Walter (1996), "Australian IPO Underpricing in the Short and Long-Run," *Journal of Banking and Finance*, 20, 1189-1210.

Lee, P., S. Taylor and T. Walter (1999), "IPO Underpricing Explanations: Implications from Investor Application and Allocation Schedules," *Journal of Financial and Quantitative Analysis*, 34, 425-44.

Lee, P., D. Stokes, S. Taylor and T. Walter (2003), "The Association Between Auditor Quality, Accounting Disclosures and Firm-Specific Risk: Evidence From the Australian IPO Market," *Journal of Accounting and Public Policy*, forthcoming.

Lehn, K. and A. Poulsen (1988), "Leveraged Buyouts: Wealth Created or Wealth Redistributed?", in M. Weidenbaum and K. Chilton (eds), *Public Policy Towards Corporate Takeovers*, New Brunswick, NJ: Transaction.

Leland, H. and D. Pyle (1977), "Information Asymmetries, Financial Structure, and Financial Intermediation," *Journal of Finance*, 32, 371-87.

Leone, A., S. Rock aand M. Willenberg (2003), "Disclosure of Intended Use of Proceeds and Underpricing in Initial Public Offerings," University of Connecticut working paper.

Lerner, J. (1994), "Venture Capitalists and the Decision to go Public," *Journal of Financial Economics*, 35, 293-316.

Lerner, J., H. Shane and A. Tsai (2003), "Do Equity Financing Cycles Matter? Evidence from Biotechnology Alliances," *Journal of Financial Economics*, 67, 411-46.

Levine, R. (1991), "Stock Markets, Growth, and Tax Policy," *Journal of Finance*, 46, 1445-65.

Levine, R. (1999), "Law, Finance and Economic Growth," *Journal of Financial Intermediation*, 8, 36-67.

Levine, R. (2002), "Bank-Based or Market-Based Financial Systems: Which is Better?", *Journal of Financial Intermediation*, 11, 398-428.

Levine, R. and S. Zervos (1998), "Stock Markets, Banks, and Economic Growth," *American Economic Review*, 88, 537-58.

Levine, R., N. Loayza and T. Beck (2000), "Financial Intermediation and Growth: Causality and Causes," *Journal of Monetary Economics*, 46, 31-77.

Levis, M. (1990), "The Winner's Curse Problem, Interest Costs, and the Underpricing of Initial Public Offerings," *The Economic Journal*, 100, 76-89.

Levis, M. (1993), "The Long-Run Performance of Initial Public Offerings: The U.K. Experience 1980-88," *Financial Management*, 22, 28-41.

Levy, H. (1983), "Economic Valuation of Voting Power of Common Stock," *Journal of Finance*, 38, 79-93,

Lewellen, K. (2003), "Risk, Reputation and the Price Support of IPOs," MIT working paper.

Li, X. and R. Masulis (2003), "Venture Capital Investments by IPO Underwriters: Certification or Conflict of Interest?" University of Miami working paper.

Liaw, G., Y. Liu and K.C. Wei (2001), "On the Demand Elasticity of Initial Public Offerings: An Analysis of Discriminatory Auctions," *International Review of Finance*, 2, 151-78.

Lin, H. and M. McNichols (1998), "Underwriting Reputations, Analysts' Earnings Forecasts and Investment Recommendations," *Journal of Accounting and Economics*, 25, 101-27.

Lin, J., Y. Lee and Y. Liu (2003), "Why Have Auctions Been Losing Market Share to Bookbuilding in IPO Markets?" Louisiana State University working paper.

Lin, T. and R. Smith (1998), "Insider Reputation and Selling Decisions: The Unwinding of Venture Capital Investments During Equity IPOs," *Journal of Corporate Finance*, 4, 241-63.

Liu, J., D. Nissim and J. Thomas (2002), "Equity Valuation Using Multiples," Columbia University working paper.

Ljungqvist, A. (2003), "Conflicts of Interest and Efficient Contracting in IPOs," NYU Center for Law and Business working paper CLB 03-03.

Ljungqvist, A., F. Marston and W. Wilhelm, Jr. (2003), "Competing for Securities Underwriting Mandates: Banking Relationships and Analyst Recommendations," New York University working paper.

Ljungqvist, A., V. Nanda, and R. Singh (2001), "Hot Markets, Investor Sentiment, and IPO Pricing," New York University working paper.

Ljungqvist, A., T. Jenkinson and W. Wilhelm (2003), "Global Integration of Primary Equity Markets: The Role of U.S. Banks and U.S. Investors," *Review of Financial Studies*, 16, 63-99.

Ljungqvist, A. and M. Richardson (2003), "The Cash Flow, Return, and Risk Characteristics of Private Equity," NBER working paper no. 9454.

Ljungqvist, A. and W. Wilhelm (2002), "IPO Allocations: Discriminatory or Discretionary?", *Journal of Financial Economics*, 65, 167-201.

Ljungqvist, A. and W. Wilhelm (2003), "IPO Pricing in the Dot-Com Bubble: Complacency or Incentives?", *Journal of Finance*, 58, 723-52.

Logue, D. (1973), "On the Pricing of Unseasoned Equity Issues: 1965-1969," *Journal of Financial and Quantitative Analysis*, 8, 91-103.

Logue, D., R. Rogalski, J. Seward and L. Foster-Johnson (2001), "What's Special about the Role of Underwriter Reputation and Market Activities in IPOs?", *Journal of Business*, 75, 213-43.

Loughran, T. and J. Ritter (1995), "The New Issues Puzzle," *Journal of Finance*, 50, 23-51.

Loughran, T. and J. Ritter (1997), "The Operating Performance of Firms Conducting Seasoned Equity Offerings," *Journal of Finance*, 52, 1823-50.

Loughran, T. and J. Ritter (2000), "Uniformly Least Powerful Tests of Market Efficiency," *Journal of Financial Economics*, 55, 361-89.

Loughran, T. and J. Ritter (2002a), "Why Don't Issuers Get Upset About Leaving Money on the Table in IPOs?", *Review of Financial Studies*, 15, 413-43.

Loughran, T. and J. Ritter (2002b), "Why has IPO Underpricing Changed Over Time?" University of Florida working paper.

Loughran, T., J. Ritter and K. Rydqvist (1994), "Initial Public Offerings: International Insights," *Pacific-Basin Finance Journal*, 2, 165-99.

Lowenstein, L. (1985), "Management Buyouts," *Columbia Law Review*, 85, 730-84.

Lowry, M. (2003), "Why Does IPO Volume Fluctuate?", *Journal of Financial Economics*, 67, 3-40.

Lowry, M. and W. Schwert (2002), "IPO Market Cycles: Bubbles or Sequential Learning?", *Journal of Finance*, 57, 1171-1200.

Lowry, M. and W. Schwert (2004), "Biases in the IPO Pricing Process," *Journal of Financial Economics*, forthcoming.

Lowry, M. and S. Shu (2002), "Litigation Risk and IPO Underpricing," *Journal of Financial Economics*, 65, 309-35.

Lucas, D. and R. McDonald (1990), "Equity Issues and Stock Price Dynamics," *Journal of Finance*, 45, 1019-43.

Lyon, J., B. Barber and C. Tsai (1999), "Improved Methods for Tests of Long-Run Abnormal Stock Returns," *Journal of Finance*, 54, 165-201.

Maksimovic, V. (1988), "Capital Structure in Repeated Oligoplies," *RAND Journal of Economics*, 19, 389-407.

Maksimovic, V. and P. Pichler (1999), "Private Versus Public Offerings: Optimal Selling Mechanisms with Adverse Selection," University of Maryland working paper.

Maksimovic, V. and P. Pichler (2001), "Technological Innovation and Initial Public Offerings," *Review of Financial Studies*, 14, 459-94.

Maksimovic, V. and S. Titman (1991), "Financial Policy and Reputation for Product Quality," *Review of Financial Studies*, 4, 175-200.

Mandelker, G. and A. Raviv (1977), "Investment Banking: An Economics Analysis of Optimal Underwriting Contracts," *Journal of Finance*, 32, 683-94.

Mansi, S. and D. Reeb (2002), "Corporate Diversification: What Gets Discounted?", *Journal of Finance*, 57, 2167-83.

Marchisio, G. and D. Ravasi (2001), "Family Firms and the Decision to Go Public: A Study of Italian IPOs," Bocconi University School of Management working paper.

Masulis, R. and A. Korwar (1986), "Seasoned Equity Offerings: An Empirical Investigation," *Journal of Financial Economics*, 15, 91-118

Mauer, D. and L. Senbet (1992), "The Effect of the Secondary Market on the Pricing of Initial Public Offerings: Theory and Evidence," *Journal of Financial and Quantitative Analysis*, 27, 55-79.

Maug, E. (1996), "Corporate Control and the Market for Managerial Labor: On the Decision to Go Public," *European Economic Review*, 40, 1082-9.

Maug, E. (1998), "Large Shareholders as Monitors: Is There a Trade-off Between Liquidity and Control?", *Journal of Finance*, 53, 65-98.

Mayhew, B. and M. Wilkens (2002), "Audit Firm Industry Specialization as a Differentiation Strategy: Evidence from Fees Charged to Firms Going Public," University of Chicago working paper.

Maynard, T. (2002), "Spinning in a Hot IPO: A Matter of Business Ethics," Loyola Law School Research Paper No. 2002-22.

McGuinness, P. (1992), "An Examination of the Underpricing of Initial Public Offerings in Hong Kong: 1980-1990," *Journal of Business Finance Accounting*, 19, 165-86.

McLaughlin, R., A. Safieddine and G. Vasudevan (1996), "The Operating Performance of Seasoned Equity Issuers: Free Cash Flow and Post-Issue Performance," *Financial Management*, 25, 41-53.

McNichols, M. and P. O'Brien (1997), "Self-Selection and Analyst Coverage," *Journal of Accounting Research*, 35(suppl), 167-99.

McWilliams, V. (1990), "Managerial Share Ownership and the Stock Price Effects of Antitakeover Amendment Proposals," *Journal of Finance*, 45, 1627-40.

Megginson, W. and J. Netter (2001), "From State to Market: A Survey of Empirical Studies on Privatization," *Journal of Economic Literature*, 39, 321-89.

Megginson, W. and K. Weiss (1991), "Venture Capitalists Certification in Initial Public Offerings," *Journal of Finance*, 46, 879-903.

Megginson, W., R. Nash, J. Netter and A. Schwartz (2000), "The Long-Run Return to Investors in Share Issue Privatizations," *Financial Management*, 29, 67-77.

Megginson, W., R. Nash, J. Netter and A. Poulsen (2002), "The Choice of Private versus Public Capital Markets: Evidence from Privatizations," University of Oklahoma working paper.

Mello, A. and J. Parsons (1998), "Going Public and the Ownership Structure of the Firm," *Journal of Financial Economics*, 49, 79-109.

Merton, R. (1987), "A Simple Model of Capital Market Equilibrium with Incomplete Information," *Journal of Finance*, 42, 483-510.

Meulbroek, L., M. Mitchell, J. Mulherin, J. Netter and A. Poulsen (1990), "Shark Repellents and Managerial Myopia: An Empirical Test," *Journal of Political Economy*, 98, 1108-17.

Michaely, R. and W. Shaw (1994), "The Pricing of Initial Public Offerings: Tests of Adverse Selection and Signaling Theories," *Review of Financial Studies*, 7, 279-319.

Michaely, R. and K. Womack (1999), "Conflict of Interest and the Credibility of Underwriter Analyst Recommendations," *Review of Financial Studies*, 12, 653-86.

Michaely, R., R. Thaler and K. Womack (1995), "Price Reactions to Dividend Initiations and Omissions: Overreaction or Drift?", *Journal of Finance* 50, 573-608.

Mikkelson, W. and M. Partch (1986), "Valuation Effects of Security Offerings and the Issuance Process," *Journal of Financial Economics*, 15, 31-60.

Mikkelson, W., M. Partch and K. Shah (1997), "Ownership and Operating Performance of Companies that Go Public," *Journal of Financial Economics*, 44, 281-307.

Miller, E. (1977), "Risk, Uncertainty, and Divergence of Opinion," *Journal of Finance*, 32, 1151-68.

Miller, M. and F. Modigliani (1958), "The Cost of Capital, Corporation Finance and the Theory of Investment," *American Economic Review*, 48, 261-97.

Mitchell, M. and E. Stafford (2000), "Managerial Decisions and Long-term Stock Price Performance," *Journal of Business*, 73, 287-329.

Mohanram, P. (2001), "How Do Young Firms Choose among Different Modes of Investor Communication?", New York University working paper.

Morck, R. and M. Nakamura (1999), "Banks and Corporate Control in Japan," *Journal of Finance*, 54, 319-40.

Morck, R., A. Shleifer and R. Vishny (1988), "Management Ownership and Market Valuation: An Empirical Analysis," *Journal of Financial Economics*, 20, 293-316.

Morsfield, S. and C. Tan (2003), "Do Venture Capitalists Constrain or Encourage Earnings Management in Initial Public Offerings," University of Michigan working paper.

Moskowitz, T. and A. Vissing-Jorgenssen (2002), "The Returns to Entrepreneurial Investment: A Private Equity Premium Puzzle," *American Economic Review*, 92, 745-78.

Moyer, C., R Chatfield and P. Sisneros (1989), "Security Analyst Monitoring Activity: Agency Costs and Information Demand," *Journal of Financial and Quantitative Analysis*, 24, 503-12.

Muscarella, C. and M. Vetsuypens (1989), "A Simple Test of Baron's Model of Underpricing," *Journal of Financial Economics*, 24, 125-36.

Muscarella, C. and M. Vetsuypens (1990), "Efficiency and Organizational Structure: A Study of Reverse LBOs," *Journal of Finance*, 45, 1389-1413.

Myers, S. (1977), "Determinants of Corporate Borrowing," *Journal of Financial Economics*, 20, 293-315.

Myers, S. (1984), "The Capital Structure Puzzle," *Journal of Finance*, 39, 575-92.

Myers, S. and N. Majluf (1984), "Corporate Financing and Investment Decisions When Firms Have Information Investors Do Not Have," *Journal of Financial Economics*, 13, 187-221.

Nanda, V. (1991), "On the Good News in Equity Carve-outs," *Journal of Finance*, 46, 1717-37.

Nanda, V. and M. Narayanan (1999), "Disentangling Value: Misvaluation and the Scope of the Firm," *Journal of Financial Intermediation*, 8, 174-204.

Nanda, V. and V. Warther (1998), "The Price of Loyalty: An Empirical Analysis of Underwriter Relationships and Fees," University of Chicago working paper.

Nanda, V. and Y. Yun (1997), "Reputation and Financial Intermediation: An Empirical Investigation of the Impact of IPO Mispricing on Underwriter Market Value," *Journal of Financial Intermediation*, 6, 39-63.

Neill, J., S. Pourciau and T. Schaefer (1995), "Accounting Method Choice And IPO Valuation," *Accounting Horizons*, 9, 68-80.

Nelson, L. (2002), "Persistence and Reversal in Herd Behavior: Theory and Application to the Decision to Go Public," *Review of Financial Studies*, 15, 65-95

Nixon, T., R. Rosenfeldt and N. Sicherman (2000), "The Choice Between Spin-offs and Sell-offs," *Review of Quantitative Finance and Accounting*, 14, 277-88.

Ofek, E. and M. Richardson (2000), "The IPO Lock-up Period: Implications for Market Efficiency and Downward Sloping Demand Curves," New York University working paper.

Ofek, E. and M. Richardson (2003), "Dotcom Mania: The Rise and Fall of Internet Stocks," *Journal of Finance*, 58, 1113-37.

Ohlson, J. (1995), "Earnings, Equity Book Values, and Dividends in Equity Valuation," *Contemporary Accounting Research*, 11, 661-87.

Ohlson, J. (2001), "Earnings, Equity Book Values, and Dividends in Equity Valuation: An Empirical Perspective," *Contemporary Accounting Research*, 18, 107-10.

Opler, T. and S. Titman (1994), "Financial Distress and Corporate Performance," *Journal of Finance*, 49, 1015-40.

Pagano, M. (1989), "Trading Volume and Asset Liquidity," *Quarterly Journal of Economics*, 104, 255-74.

Pagano, M. (1993), "The Flotation of Companies on the Stock Market – A Coordination Failure Model," *European Economic Review*, 37, 1101-25.

Pagano, M. and A. Roell (1998), "The Choice of Stock Ownership Structure: Agency Costs, Monitoring, and the Decision to Go Public," *Quarterly Journal of Economics*, 85, 187-225.

Pagano, M., F. Panetta and L. Zingales (1998), "Why do Companies Go Public? An Empirical Analysis," *Journal of Finance*, 53, 27-64.

Pagano, M., A. Roell and J. Zechner (2002), "The Geography of Equity Listing: Why do European Companies List Abroad?", *Journal of Finance*, 57, 2651-94.

Parrino, R. (1997), "Spin-offs and Wealth Transfers: The Marriott Case," *Journal of Financial Economics*, 43, 241-73.

Partch, M. (1987), "Th Creation of a Class of Limited Voting Common Stock and Shareholder Wealth," *Journal of Financial Economics*, 18, 313-39.

Patel, A. (2000), "The Causes and Consequences of Initial Public Straight Debt Offers," Wake Forest University working paper.

Penman, S. (1999), "A Synthesis of Equity Valuation Techniques and the Terminal Value Calculation for the Dividend Discount Model," *Review of Accounting Studies*, 2, 303-3\23.

Penman, S. (2000), *Financial Statement Analysis and Security Valuation*, Boston, MA: McGraw-Hill.

Perotti, E. (1995), "Credible Privatization," *American Economic Review*, 85, 847-59.

Perotti, E. and F. Huibers (1999), "The Performance of Privatization Stocks in Emerging Markets: The Role of Political Risk," *Advances in Financial Economics*, 4, 1-27.

Perotti, E. and P. van Oijen (2001), "Privatization, Political Risk and Stock Market Development in Emerging Economies," *Journal of International Money an d Finance*, 20, 43-69.

Perotti, E. and E. von Thadden (2003), "Strategic Transparency and Liquidity: Will Capital Market Integration Force Convergence of Corporate Governance Forms?", *Journal of Financial and Quantitative Analysis*, 38, 61-85.

Peterson, D. (1987), "Security Price Reactions to Initial Reviews of Common Stock by the Value Line Investment Survey," *Journal of Financial and Quantitative Analysis*, 22, 483-94.

Petersen, M. and R. Rajan (1994), "The Benefits of Firm-Creditor Relationships: Evidence From Small Business Data," *Journal of Finance*, 49, 3-37.

Petersen, M. and R. Rajan (1995), The Effect of Credit Market Competition on Lending Relationships," *Quarterly Journal of Economics*, 110, 407-43.

Phillips, G. (1992), "Financial Slack, Refinancing Decisions and Firm Competition," Purdue University working paper.

Phillips, G. (1995), "Increased Debt and Industry Product Markets: An Empirical Analysis," *Journal of Financial Economics*, 37, 189-238.

Pickens, T. Boone Jr (1987), *Boone*, Boston, MA: Houghton Mifflin.

Pinto, B., M. Belka and S. Krajewski (1993), "Transforming State Enterprises in Poland: Evidence on Adjustment by Manufacturing Firms," *Brookings Papers on Economic Activity*, 213-61.

Povel, P. and M. Raith (2000), "Liquidity Constraints and Product Market Competition: Ex-ante vs. Ex-post Incentives," University of Minnesota working paper.

Powers, E. (2001), "Spin-offs, Selloffs and Equity Carve-outs: An Analysis of Divestiture Method Choice," University of South Carolina working paper.

Powers, E. (2003), "Decyphering the Motives for Equity Carve-outs," *Journal of Financial Research*, 26, 31-50.

Prabhala, N. and M. Puri (1998), "How Does Underwriter Price Support Affect IPOs: Empirical Evidence," Stanford University working paper.

Pratt, S. (1989), *Valuing A Business: The Analysis and Appraisal of Closely Held Companies*, 2nd Ed, Homewood, IL: Dow Jones.

Pugh, W., D. Page, and J. Jahera (1992), "Antitakeover Charter Amendments: Effects on Corporate Decisions," *Journal of Financial Research*, 15, 57-67.

Pullian, S. and R. Smith (2000), "Linus Deal is Focus of IPO-Commission Probe," *Wall Street Journal*, 12 December, C1.

Pullian, S. and R. Smith (2001) "CSFB Set Quota for Repayment of IPO Profits in Form of Commissions," *Wall Street Journal*, 10 August, C1.

Purnanandam, A. and B. Swaminathan (2004), "Are IPOs Underpriced?", *Review of Financial Studies* forthcoming.

Raghavan, A. (1997), "How One Top Analyst Vaults 'Chinese Wall' to do Deal for Firm," *Wall Street Journal*, 25 March, C1.

Rajan, R. (1992), "Insiders and Outsiders: The Choice Between Informed and Arm's Length Debt," *Journal of Finance*, 47, 1367-1400.

Rajan, R. and H. Servaes (1995), "The Effect of Market Conditions on Initial Public Offerings," University of Chicago working paper.

Rajan, R. and H. Servaes (1997), "Analyst Following of Initial Public Offerings," *Journal of Finance*, 52, 507-30.

Rajan, R. and A. Winton (1995), "Covenants and Collateral as Incentives to Monitor," *Journal of Finance*, 50, 1113-46.

Rajan, R. and L. Zingales (1998), "Financial Dependence and Growth," *American Economic Review*, 88, 559-86.

Rajan, R. and L. Zingales (2003), "The Great Reversals: The Politics of Financial Development in the 20th Century," *Journal of Financial Economics*, 69, 5-50.

Rajan, R., H. Servaes and L. Zingales (1999), "The Cost of Diversity: The Diversification Discount and Inefficient Investment," *Journal of Finance*, 55, 35-80.

Rajgopal, S., M. Venkatachalam and S. Kotha (2003), "The Relevance of Web Traffic to the Internet Stock Market Prices," *Journal of Accounting Research*, forthcoming.

Rangan, S. (1998), "Earnings before Seasoned Equity Offerings: Are They Overstated?", *Journal of Financial Economics*, 50, 101-22.

Ransley, R. (1984), "A Research Project Into the Operation and Development of the Unlisted Securities Market 1980-1984," London Business School, unpublished.

Rao, G. (1993), "The Relation Between Stock Returns and Earnings: A Study of Newly-Public Firms," Kidder Peabody and Co. working paper.

Reese, W. Jr. (1998), "IPO Underpricing, Trading Volume, and Investor Interest," Tulane University working paper.

Reilly, F. (1973), "Further Evidence on Short-Run Results for New Issues Investors," *Journal of Financial and Quantitative Analysis*, 8, 83-90.

Reuter, J. (2002), "Are IPO Allocations for Sale? Evidence from the Mutual Fund Industry," University of Oregon working paper.

Ritter, J. (1984), "The Hot Issue Market of 1980," *Journal of Business*, 32, 315-40.

Ritter, J. (1987), "The Costs of Going Public," *Journal of Financial Economics*, 19, 269-81.

Ritter, J. (1991), "The Long-Run Performance of Initial Public Offerings," *Journal of Finance*, 46, 3-27.

Ritter, J. (1998), "Initial Public Offerings," *Contemporary Finance Digest*, 2, 5-30.

Ritter, J. (2003), "Investment Banking and Securities Issuance," in G. Constantinides, M. Harris and R. Stulz (eds), *Handbook of the Economics of Finance*, Amsterdam: North Holland.

Ritter, J. and I. Welch (2002), "A Review of IPO Activity, Pricing and Allocations," *Journal of Finance* 57, 1795-1828.

Rock, K. (1986), "Why New Issues are Underpriced," *Journal of Finance*, 15, 187-212.

Roe, M. (1994), *Strong Managers, Weak Owners*, Princeton, NJ: Princeton Univeristy Press.

Roe, M. (2003), *Political Determinants of Corporate Governance*, Oxford: Oxford University Press.

Roell, A. (1996), "The Decision to Go Public: An Overview," *European Economic Review*, 40, 1071-81.

Rouwenhurst, G. (1999), "International Momentum Strategies," *Journal of Finance*, 53, 267-84.

Rupello, R. and J. Suarez (2002), "Venture Capital Finance: A Security Design Approach," CEMFI Discussion Paper No. 2097.

Ruud, J. (1993), "Underwriter Price Support and the IPO Underpricing Puzzle," *Journal of Financial Economics*, 34, 135-52.

Ryan, P. (2001), "Evidence from Chief Financial Officers Regarding the IPO Process," Colorado State University working paper.

Rydqvist, K. (1997), "IPO Underpricing as Tax-Efficient Compensation," *Journal of Banking and Finance*, 21, 295-313.

Rydqvist, K. and K. Hogholm (1995), "Going Public in the 1980s – Evidence From Sweden," *European Financial Management*, 1, 287-316.

Sachs, J., C. Zinnes and Y. Eilat (2000), "The Gains From Privatization in Transition Economies: Is Change of Ownership Enough?", CAER II Discussion Paper 63, Harvard Institute for International Development, Cambridge, MA.

Sah, R. and J. Stiglitz (1986), "The Architecture of Economic Systems: Hierarchies and Polyarchies," *American Economic Review*, 76, 716-27.

Sahlman, W. (1990), "The Structure and Governance of Venture Capital Organizations," *Journal of Financial Economics*, 27, 473-524.

Scharfstein, D. (1998), "The Dark Side of Internal Capital Markets II: Evidence From Diversified Conglomerates," NBER working paper no. 6352.

Scharfstein, D. and J. Stein (1990), "Herd Behavior and Investment," *American Economic Review*, 80, 465-79.

Scharfstein, D. and J. Stein (2000), "The Dark Side of Internal Capital Markets: Divisional Rent-Seeking and Inefficient Investment," *Journal of Finance*, 55, 2537-64.

Schargrodsky, Ernesto (2001), "Do Publicly Traded Firms Price Differently From Private Firms?", Universidad Torcuato Di Tella working paper.

Schipper, K. and A. Smith (1983), "Effects of Recontracting on Shareholder Wealth: The Case of Voluntary Spin-offs," *Journal of Financial Economics*, 12, 437-67.

Schipper, K. and A. Smith (1986), "A Comparison of Equity Carve-Outs and Seasoned Equity Offerings: Share Price Effects and Corporate Restructurings," *Journal of Financial Economics*, 15, 153-86.

Schrand, C. and R. Verrecchia (2002), "Disclosure Choice and the Cost of Capital: Evidence From Underpricing in Initial Public Offerings," University of Pennsylvania working paper.

Schultz, P. (1993), "Unit Initial Public Offerings: A Form of Staged Financing," *Journal of Financial Economics*, 34, 199-229.

Schultz, P. and M. Zaman (1994), "Aftermarket Support and Underpricing of Initial Public Offerings," *Journal of Financial Economics*, 35, 304-35.

Schultz, P. and M. Zaman (2001), "Do the Individuals Closest to Internet Firms Believe They are Overvalued?", *Journal of Financial Economics*, 59, 347-81.

Schwartz, E. and M. Moon (2000), "Rational Pricing of Internet Companies," *Financial Analysts Journal*, 56, 62-75.

Schwert, W. (1996), "Markup Pricing in Mergers and Aquisitions," *Journal of Financial Economics*, 41, 153-92.

Schwienbacher, A. (2002), "An Empirical Analysis of Venture Capital Exits in Europe and the United States," University of Namur working paper.

Seward, J. and J. Walsh (1996), "The Governance and Control of Voluntary Corporate Spin-offs," *Strategic Management Journal*, 17, 25-40.

Sharpe, S. (1990), "Asymmetric Information, Bank Lending, and Implicit Contracts: A Stylized Model of Customer Relationships," *Journal of Finance*, 45, 1069-87.

Sherman, A. (1992), "The Pricing of Best Efforts New Issues," *Journal of Finance*, 47, 781-90.

Sherman, A. (2000), "IPOs and Long-Term Relationships: An Advantage of Book-Building," *Review of Financial Studies*, 13, 697-714.

Sherman, A. (2001), "Global Trends in IPO Methods: Book-Building Versus Auctions," University of Notre Dame working paper.

Sherman, A. and S. Titman (2002), "Building the IPO Order Book: Underpricing and Participation Limits with Costly Information," *Journal of Financial Economics*, 65, 3-29.

Sheshinski, E. and L. Lopez-Calva (2003), "Privatization and its Benefits: Theory and Evidence," in K. Basu (ed) *Markets and Governance*, Oxford: Oxford University Press.

Shiller, R. (1990), "Speculative Prices and Popular Models," *Journal of Economic Perspectives*, 4, 55-65.

Shin, H. and R. Stulz (1998), "Are Internal Capital Markets Efficient?", *Quarterly Journal of Economics*, 113, 531-52.

Shirley, M. (1999), "Bureaucrats in Business: The Role of Privatization in State-Owned Enterprise Reform," *World Development*, 27, 115-36.

Shivakumar, L. (2000), "Do Firms Mislead Investors by Overstating Earnings before Seasoned Equity Offerings?", *Journal of Accounting and Economics* 29, 339-71.

Shleifer, A. and L. Summers (1990), "The Noise Trader Approach to Finance," *Journal of Economic Perspectives*, 4, 19-33.

Shleifer, A. and R. Vishny (1986), "Large Shareholders and Corporate Control," *Journal of Political Economy*, 94, 461-88.

Shleifer, A. and R. Vishny (1990), "Equilibrium Short Horizons of Investors and Firms," *American Economic Review Papers and Proceedings*, 80, 148-53.

Shleifer, A. and D. Wolfenzon (2002), "Investor Protection and Equity Markets," *Journal of Financial Economics*, 66, 3-27.

Siconolfi, M. (1992), "At Morgan Stanley, Analysts Were Urged to Soften Harsh Views," *Wall Street Journal*, 14 July, C1.

Silber, W. (1991), "Discounts on Restricted Stock: The Impact of Illiquidity on Stock Prices," *Financial Analysts Journal*, 47, 60-64.

Simmons, L. III (1997), "Pre-Offering Planning," in J. Riley and L. Simmons III (eds), *How to Prepare the Initial Public Offering*, New York, NY: Practicing Law Institute.

Simunic, D. and M. Stein (1987), "Product Differentiation in Auditing: Auditor Choice in the Market of Unseasoned New Issues," *Canadian Certified General Accountants' Research Foundation*, Vancouver, BC.

Sirri, E. and P. Tufano (1995), "The Pooling of Economics," in D. Crane, S. Mason and R. Merton (eds), *The Global Financial System*, Cambridge, MA: Harvard Business School Press.

Slovin, M., M. Sushka and Y. Bendeck (1991), "The Intra-Industry Effects of Going-Private Transactions," *Journal of Financial Economics*, 15, 3-29.

Slovin, M., M. Sushka and Y. Bendeck (1994), "Seasoned Common Stock Issuance Following an IPO," *Journal of Banking and Finance*, 18, 207-26.

Slovin, M., M. Sushka and S. Ferraro (1995), "A Comparison of the Information Conveyed by Equity Carveouts, Spinoffs, and asset Selloffs," *Journal of Financial Economics*, 37, 89-104.

Smart, S. and C. Zutter (2003), "Control as a Motivation for Underpricing: A Comparison of Dual- and Single-Class IPOs," *Journal of Financial Economics*, 69, 85-110.

Smith, D.G. (2001), "Control over Exit in Venture Capital Relationships," Northwestern School of Law of Lewis & Clark College working paper.

Smith, J. and R. Smith (2000), *Entrepreneurial Finance*, New York, NY: John Wiley.

Smith, R. (2003), "IPO 'Laddering' Case Expands," *Wall Street Journal*, 26 February, C1.

Smith, T. (2002), "The New Role for Analysts in the IPO Process," *Investment Dealers Digest*, December 12, 34-9.

Spatt, C. and S. Srivastava (1991), "Preplay Communication, Participation Restrictions, and Efficiency in Efficiency in Initial Public Offerings," *Review of Financial Studies*, 4, 709-26.

Speiss, D.K. and J. Affeck-Graves (1995), "Underperformance in Long-Run Stock Returns Following Seasoned Equity Offerings," *Journal of Financial Economics*, 38, 243-68.

Speiss, D.K. and J. Affeck-Graves (1999), "The Long-Run Performance of Stock Returns Following Debt Offers," *Journal of Financial Economics*, 54, 45-73.

Speiss, D.K. and R. Pettway (1997), "The IPO and the First Seasoned Equity Sale: Issue Proceeds, Owner/Manager's Wealth, and the Underpricing Signal," *Journal of Banking and Finance*, 21, 967-88.

Stein, J. (1989), "Efficient Capital Markets, Inefficient Firms: A Model of Myopic Corporate Behavior," *Quarterly Journal of Economics*, 104, 655-69.

Stein, J. (1997), "Internal Capital Markets and the Competition for Corporate Resources," *Journal of Finance*, 52, 111-33.

Stern, R. and P. Bornstein (1985), "Why New Issues are Lousy Investments," *Forbes*, 136, 152-90.

Stiglitz, J. (1985), "Credit Markets and the Control of Capital," *Journal of Money, Credit, and Banking*, 17, 133-52.

Stoll, H. and A. Curley (1970), "Small Business and the New Issues Market for Equities," *Journal of Financial and Quantitative Analysis*, 5, 309-22.

Stoughton, N. and J. Zechner (1998), "IPO-Mechanisms, Monitoring, and Ownership Structure," *Journal of Financial Economics*, 49, 45-77.

Stoughton, N., K. Wong and J. Zechner (2001), "IPOs and Product Quality," *Journal of Business*, 74, 375-408.

Stulz, R. (1988), "Managerial Control over Voting Rights: Financing Policies and the Market for Corporate Control," *Journal of Financial Economics*, 20, 25-54.

Subrahmanyam, A. and S. Titman (1999), "The Going-Public Decision and the Development of Financial Markets," *Journal of Finance*, 54, 1045-82.

Taranto, M. (2003), "Employee Stock Options and the Underpricing of Initial Public Offerings," University of Pennsylvania working paper.

Teoh, S.H. and T.J. Wong (2002), "Why New Issues and High-Accrual Firms Underperform: The Role of Analysts' Credulity," *Review of Financial Studies*, 15, 869-900.

Teoh, S.H., I. Welch and T.J. Wong (1998), "Earnings Management and the Long-Run Performance of Initial Public Offerings," *Journal of Finance*, 53, 1935-74.

Teoh, S.H., I. Welch and T.J. Wong (1998a), "Earnings Management and the Long-Run Performance of Seasoned Equity Offerings," *Journal of Financial Economics*, 50, 63-99.

Teoh, S.H., T.J. Wong and G.R. Rao (1998b), "Are Accruals During an Initial Public Offering Opportunistic?" *Review of Accounting Studies*, 3, 175-208.

Teslar, L. (1966), "Cutthroat Competition and the Long-Purse," *Journal of Law and Economics*, 9, 259-77.

Tinic, S. (1988), "Anatomy of Initial Public Offerings of Common Stock," *Journal of Finance*, 43, 789-822.

Titman, S. and B. Trueman (1986), "Information Quality and the Valuation of New Issues," *Journal of Accounting and Economics*, 8, 159-72.

Torstila, S. (2003), "The Clustering of IPO Gross Spreads: International Evidence," *Journal of Financial and Quantitative Analysis*, 38, 673-94.

Trueman, B., M. Wong and X. Zhang (2000), "The Eyeballs Have It: Searching for the Value of Internet Stocks," *Journal of Accounting Research*, 38, 137-62.

van Bommel, J. (2002), "Messages From Market to Management: The Case of IPOs," *Journal of Corporate Finance*, 8, 123-38.

van Bommel, J. and T. Vermaelen (2003), "Post-IPO Capital Expenditures and Market Feedback," *Journal of Banking and Finance*, 27, 275-305.

Vijh, A. (1999), "Long-Term Returns from Equity Carve-outs," *Journal of Financial Economics*, 51, 273-308.

Vijh, A. (2002), "The Positive Announcement Period Returns of Equity Carve-outs: Asymmetric Information or Divestiture Gains?", *Journal of Business*, 75, 153-90.

Villalonga, B. (2003), "Diversification Discount or Premium? New Evidence From BITS Establishment-Level Data," *Journal of Finance*, forthcoming.

Villalonga, B. (2004), "Does Diversification Cause the 'Diversification Discount'?", *Review of Financial Studies*, forthcoming.

Ward, S. (1997), "Going Public and Product Market Reactions," University of Vienna, working paper.

Weisman, S. (1999), "Valuation in Initial Public Offerings," in M. Hanan and R. Sheeler (eds), *Financial Valuation: Businesses and Business Interests, 1999 Update*, Boston, MA: Warren Gorham and Lamont.

Welch, I. (1989), "Seasoned Offerings, Imitation Costs, and the Underpricing of Initial Public Offerings," *Journal of Finance*, 44, 421-49.

Welch, I. (1991), "An Empirical Examination of Models of Contract Choice in Initial Public Offerings," *Journal of Financial and Quantitative Analysis*, 26, 497-517.

Welch, I. (1992), "Sequential Sales, Learning, and Cascades," *Journal of Finance*, 47, 695-732.

Welch, I. (1996), "Equity Offerings Following the IPO: Theory and Evidence," *Journal of Corporate Finance*, 2, 227-59.

Welch, I. (1997), "Why is Bank Debt Senior: A Theory of Asymmetry and Claim Priority Based on Influence Costs," *Review of Financial Studies*, 10, 1203-36.

Whited, T. (2001), "Is it Inefficient Investment that Causes the Diversification Discount?", *Journal of Finance*, 56, 1667-91.

Womack, K. (1996), "Do Brokerage Analysts' Recommendations Have Investment Value?", *Journal of Finance*, 51, 137-67.

Wruck, K. (1989), "Equity Ownership Concentration and Firm Value: Evidence From Private Equity Financings," *Journal of Financial Economics*, 23, 3-28.

Wu, Y. (2000), "The Choice Between Public and Private Equity Offerings," University of Chicago working paper.

Wurgler, J. (2000), "Financial Markets and the Allocation of Capital," *Journal of Financial Economics*, 58, 187-214.

Yetman, M. (2003), "Accounting-Based Value Metrics and the Informational Efficiency of IPO Early Market Prices," University of California, Davis working paper.

Yosha, O. (1995), "Information Disclosure Costs and the Choice of Financing Source," *Journal of Financial Intermediation*, 4, 3-20.

Zingales, L. (1994), "The Value of the Voting Right: A Study of the Milan Stock Exchange Experience," *Review of Financial Studies*, 7, 125-148.

Zingales, L. (1995a), "What Determines the Value of Corporate Votes?", *Quarterly Journal of Economics*, 110, 1047-1073.

Zingales, L. (1995b), "Insider Ownership and the Decision to Go Public," *Review of Economic Studies*, 62, 425-448.

Index

abnormal earnings 160, 176
  see also residual income model
abnormal returns, long run 307, 309,
  311
  measuring 314
absolute prediction errors 172-3
accredited investors 297
accruals
  abnormal 169-70, 325-6, 330
  definition 167-8
Accounting Principles Board 166
adverse selection risk 32, 202
affiliated investors 303
age of issuers 5
agency costs
  between owners and managers 44,
    81-2, 120, 123, 146, 149
  internal conflicts 146
  issuer-underwriter 199, 242
  warrants to deal with 291-2
alpha 311
Alex. Brown 188
allocations in book-built IPOs
  aggregate institutional 231-2
  benefit of discretion 223
  individual institutional 232-5
  in return for commissions 223-4,
    233-4
American Stock Exchange 189
analysts
  affiliated and unaffiliated 268,
    271-3, 276-7, 330
  amount of coverage 190, 268-9
  benefits of coverage 269-70
  biased coverage 269-70, 330
  conflict of interest 267, 270-76,
    343
  coverage initiation 267-8
  covering conglomerates, 140-41
  earnings forecasts 269-70, 276-7
  recommendations 269-70

relation to long-run returns 330
self-selection bias 273
underpricing to buy coverage 246,
  268-9
underwriter selection criterion
  191-2, 275
anti-dilution provision 93
anti-greenmail provision 105
anti-takeover provisions (ATP)
  adoption by issuers 104-6
  benefits and costs 102-3
  effect on share value 103, 109
  implications 85
  adoption puzzles 106
  types of 104-5
arbitrage pricing theory (APT) 43,
  311-12
arbitrage trading 34, 329
asset pricing models 310-12
asymmetric information
  between institutional and retail
    investors 32, 232, 238
  between issuers and investors
    affect on IPO timing 19-21
    cost of 19-20, 43
    financing implications 284
    two-stage sales 288-9
    warrant use 291-2
  divestiture motive 141, 150
  lockup motive 277
auctions for IPOs
  description of types 218
  dirty 218-19, 229, 343
  efficiency 227, 341-2
  information production 228-9, 342
  initial returns 239
  international use of 219-20
  Internet 219
  tacit collusion 227-8
  vs book-building 228-9, 239-41
auditor

compensation 37-8, 210
quality/risk trade-off 211
role in earnings management 169
role in IPO preparations 183-4
selection of 209-10

bank debt
advantages relative to bonds 56-7
growth of 116
monopoly power, cost of 57-8
versus stock markets 115
bargaining power 88-9, 100, 102
beauty contest 189
behavioral finance 331-6
behavioral models 335-6
best efforts contract 201-3
bid-ask
quotes 40, 253, 259
spread 254, 259, 277
Black-Scholes model 162
block trades
predictive ability of 266
premium 82-3
pricing puzzle 301-2
Blue sky laws 37-8
board of directors
classified 105
composition 100-102
role of 85, 92
venture capitalists on 94
bonding 74, 204, 255
bonds
IPOs 294-5
private 293-4
book-building
benefits of discretion and
flexibility 224-5, 342
description of process 216-17
efficient mechanism 221-3, 230,
235-6, 341-2
empirical pricing patterns 230-31
institutional allocations 231-5
international use of 219-20
versus auctions 228-9, 239-41
see also firm commitment contract
bookrunner 189-90
book value of assets 285-6
branding through an IPO 77
bundling IPOs for sale 30

buy-and-hold abnormal returns
(BHAR) 314, 316, 318
buy-and-hold returns (BHR) 307-9
buyout funds
LBOs 152
rates of return 52-3, 155
strategy 47
see venture capital funds

calendar time, measuring returns 311,
319
call option 55, 68, 71, 145, 162
capital allocation
economy wide 116, 121
internal to firm 146
capital asset pricing model (CAPM)
39, 159, 310-11
capital structure, optimal 284, 286
carried interest 46
carve-outs
announcement returns 139, 143,
150, 151
definition 137-8
information motive and affect
140-43
long-run returns 152
operating performance 149-50
timing 141-2, 150
cascades, information 29-30, 226
cash flows, post-IPO 169-70
cash flow rights 85, 91, 92, 93-4
cash flow-to-assets, operating (CFA)
148-9
Center for Research on Security
Prices (CRSP) 63, 309
CEO compensation 101-2
see also wealth sensitivity
certification
auditor 209
bank 57
underwriter 203-4
change of control 88-9
chief financial officer (CFO) 66, 119
civil law 118-19, 121-3
clean surplus accounting 176
clientele effect 139
closed-end fund discount 15
clustering of IPOs 12, 17, 23, 28-31,
42, 69
cognitive biases 333-5

collusive behavior
in competitive markets 66
underwriter–investor 225
underwriting spreads 194-5
commissions, for allocations 224-5, 233-4
common law 118-19, 121-2
comparable firms measure of under-performance 310, 314, 318-20
pros and cons 312-13
comparable multiples
accuracy 172-4
valuation method 160-62
confirmatory bias 334
conflict of interests,
divestiture motive 139
see also analysts
conglomeration, benefits of 144
conservatism 334, 336
control rights 81, 85, 98, 102
allocation in VC contracts 90-91, 94, 96
control share acquisition 105
convertible securities 91, 94
convertible preferred equity 92, 108
coordination failures 113
corporate finance event anomalies 332-3
corporate governance
external regulations 97, 117, 120
impact of stock market 115
issuer properties 97-107
relation to firm value 166
theoretical properties 80-88
with venture capitalists 90-5
corruption hypothesis 246
co-sale agreement 93
cost minimization
underwriter selection criterion 190-91
warrant use 196
cost of equity
assessment 45, 339
contracting costs 42-4
direct costs 37-8
market imperfections 39-41
cost of IPO 38-8, 191-2, 196, 201, 209
covenants 56
creditor rights 119, 121
Credit Suisse First Boston 188, 234

cross-correlation of returns 316-17
cross-listing on foreign markets 76
cross-subsidization 140-41, 146-7
cumulative abnormal returns (CAR)
for discrete events 20, 139, 141, 148, 150, 276, 270, 298
in the long run 314, 318

debt
banks vs bonds 296
benefits and costs of 54-5
maturity structure in IPOs 293, 295-6
overhang 54-5, 293
private versus public 293-4
debt/equity choice 54
defense mechanisms *see* anti-takeover provisions
de-listed IPOs 18, 328
demand curves 35, 277
demand registration rights 93
Department of Justice 138, 195
depreciation methods 167, 169
direct sale of SOEs 128-9
disclosure policy, optimal 68, 186
discount rates 49, 159-60
discounted free cash flow model 159, 162, 174
diversification discount 144-7, 157
diversity of opinion, affect on
contract choice 203
financing options 55
initial overpricing 329
divestiture of subsidiaries
announcement returns 139
managerial discretion 149-50
non-strategic motives 138-9
optimal method 150-51
refocusing and efficiency gains 143-9
two-stage sale 151
unlocking hidden value 140-43
dividends 120-21
dual-class stock 85, 99, 104, 123, 166, 244
due diligence 43, 74, 203
dynamic issuing strategy
asymmetric information 288-9
market experimentation 290
underpricing motive 244-5, 288

unit offerings 290-92

earnings, post-IPO 169-70
earnings expectations 330-31
earnings forecasts 269-70, 276-7
    for conglomerates 140
    errors 141, 275, 330
    relation to IPO volume 15-16
earnings management 167-71, 325-6
    non-opportunistic 171
    relation to long-run returns 326
EBITDA 180
economic growth 114, 116
efficient markets 285, 318
emotions and control 334-5
enterprise value 180-81
entrepreneurial pride 19
equal- vs value-weighting long-run
    returns 307-9, 315, 317, 319
event time, measuring returns 311,
    319
exit by venture capitalists
    duration 96
    options 89-90
    patterns 95
    stock market option 111
exit multiple 50, 179
expected returns 39-41, 49, 145, 309-
    11, 320-21
experimentation 290
exploitation hypothesis 18
expropriation of corporate resources
    84, 120
external capital, use of 120-21
externalites
    payoff 69
    stock market 112-13
    see also informational externalities

fair price provision 105
Fama-French model 159, 311
    pros and cons 313
    testing for abnormal returns 315,
      316, 319-20, 315
Federal Trade Commission 138
financial development 116-19, 122-3
financial services view 117
financial statements 166, 169
financial structure and competition
    70-71

financing
    constraints 59-60, 71
    options and terms 60-61
firm commitment contract 202-3
first-day return *see* initial return
first-mover problem 30
fixed price mechanism
    asymmetric information 238
    benefits 226
    description 217
    international use of 219-20
    subscription patterns 236-7
    winner's curse 237-8
flipping
    attitudes toward 263
    by institutional and retail investors
      264-5
    forecasting ability 266
    optimal amount 265
    volume 264
flow of capital into VC funds 52-3
follow-on offerings
    issuing patterns 112, 129, 287-8
    see also seasoned equity offerings
free cash flow problem 122-3, 146,
    153, 327
free-rider problem
    information production 228
    monitoring incentive 84

Genentech 23, 70
generally accepted accounting
    principles (GAAP) 109, 166-8,
    340
general partners (GPs)
    compensation 46
    definition 45
Goldman Sachs 188, 234-5
gray market 217
gross national product 120, 133
growth options 20, 23, 55, 293

herding 30, 226, 236-7, 255
heterogeneous expectations 237
heuristics 333
hold-up problem 90, 94
hostile takeovers 102-03
hot IPO markets 11, 12, 21, 25, 286
hybrid mechanisms 217-18

incentive contracts 148
industry
    competition 64-6, 71-2
    returns prior to equity offering 14,
      142
information
    cascades 29-30, 226, 246, 242
    disclosure
      optimal policy 68
      type of 66-7
    efficiency of stock prices 115
    production
      in auctions 228-9
      in book-building 223-4
      cost of 28-30, 32, 35, 42-3
      serendipitous 112
      specialization by underwriter 192-
        3, 206
      spillovers from IPOs 10, 30
    see asymmetric information
informational rent 222-3, 241-2
informational externalities
    endogenous 23-4, 26-8
    exogenous 23
initial overpricing 328-9
initial returns
    offer-to-open 252-3
    price stabilized 261-2
    retail sentiment driven 248
    time series profile 24-6
    see also underpricing
insider sales
    in the IPO 187
    post-IPO 18
    predicting long-run returns 326-7
insurance hypothesis 208-9
Institutional Investor All-Star analysts
    19, 206-7, 246
institutional investors 32, 34, 221,
    225, 228, 230, 231-5, 238, 240-41,
    259-60, 264-5, 329
internal capital markets 145-7
internal rate of return (IRR)
    definition 50
    measurement problems 51
International accounting standards
    (IAS) 109, 340
Internet IPOs 12, 18, 24, 28, 32-33,
    50, 69, 77, 177, 247, 267, 316
inventory cost methods 167, 169

investment banks
    see underwriters
Investment Dealers Digest 188
investment efficiency 112, 114, 121,
    147, 202
investor
    protection rights 118-20, 123, 128,
      133
    relations 266-7

Jones model 169

laddering 234-5
learning, affect on IPO timing 28-9
legal counsel
    cost of 37-8
    quality of advise 106
    role in IPO preparations 183-5,
      212
legal
    reforms 133
    traditions 117-19, 121, 122
legal liability of issuer and advisors
    207-8
Lehman Brothers 188
lemons problem 19, 186
leverage
    competitive effect of 71-2
    impact on expected returns 320
    ratios 35, 285-6, 320
    target ratio 284
leveraged buyouts (LBOs),
    characteristics 154-5
    competitive effects 70-72
    motives 153
    operating performance and returns
      155
    reverse LBOs 155-6
limit price 220
limited partners (LPs) 45, 90
line of credit 56, 63
    see revolving credit agreement
liquidation event 89
liquidation preference 92
liquidity
    affect on monitoring, 86-88
    benefit of 40, 113, 115, 269
    cost of 115
    definition 39
    illiquidity cost 40, 179

impact on expected returns 321
litigation risk 171, 181, 208-10, 242,
    255
lockups
    affect on underpricing 279-80
    expiration CARs 277-8
    motivations 278-79
long-run returns *see*
    underperformance anomaly
low-listing trap 113, 124, 132

management buyout (MBO) 152, 154
managerial
    discretion to control firm 149
    entrenchment 82, 103, 149, 301
    hubris 18
    incentives 84, 101, 115, 147-8,
        153
    labor market 77, 113
    myopia 103
    ownership 98-9, 154, 156, 300-301,
        324
    self-interest 106, 301
marketability 39
market feedback 112, 290
market-makers 252-3
market
    risk premium 311
    segmentation 40, 133
    timing 13-16, 286-7, 323
    timing theory 285
    visibility 73, 75
market-to-book ratio 14, 35, 120, 286
marketing benefit from IPO 75-6
Marvell Technologies 235
mechanism design problem 221, 225
Merrill Lynch 267
Miller-Modigliani irrelevancy
    propositions 283
minimum sales constraints 201-2
momentum and reversal of stock
    returns 333
money on the table 6, 33, 241
monitoring
    by blockholders 87-8, 299-300
    by debtholders 293-4
    by underwriter 193, 197-8, 269-70
    definition 83
    disincentive of liquidity 86-8
    in public and private markets 84-5

incentives 86, 101-2, 120
    underpricing motive 244
Montgomery Securities 198
Morgan Stanley 191-2, 234-5, 267,
    274

NASDAQ
    filing fee 38
    first-day trading 253-4
    listing requirements 185
    pre-opening 252-3
    selection of 184-5
National Association of Securities
    Dealers (NASD) 37-8, 196, 234-5
negative covenants 93
net present value (NPV) 21, 50, 162
Netscape 70
Neuer Markt 63, 109, 340
New York state Attorney General 271,
    274
new issues puzzle 306
noise traders 33, 335
non-compete clauses 95
Nouveau Marche 63
Nuovo Mercato 63
NYSE
    filing fee 38
    first-day trading 254
    listing requirements 185
    pre-opening 253
    selection of 184-5

offer price
    accuracy 173, 175
    range 24-5
    revision 24-8, 197, 206, 222
    selection in book-building 216,
        222, 230-31
Offre a Prix Minimum 218-19, 229
Ohlson model 176
operating performance
    post-IPO 21, 323-4
    pre- and post-divestiture 148-9
optimal contracts
    underwriting 199
    venture capital 90-91
Organization for Economic
    Cooperation and Development
    (OECD) 116, 129

overallotment option (OAO) 223,
257-8, 260-61
ownership structure 98-9, 121, 153
relation to long-run returns 321

partial adjustment phenomenon 231
participating convertible preferred
equity 92, 94
payoff externalities 69
P/E ratio 161
pecking-order theory 284, 286
penalty bids 257-9
Penny Stock Reform Act 216-17
Pickens, T. Boone 61
pioneer firms in a cluster 28-9
poison pills 104, 109
political culture and ideology 122-3
political risk
premium 130
affect of market development 133
portfolio diversification IPO motive 41
positive feedback trading 34, 335
post-IPO financing 285-7
power of test statistics 317-18
pre- and post-money valuation 50
predatory behavior 66, 71-2
preferred shares 91-2, 94
preliminary offer price 24, 28, 175, 222
preparations for going public 182-4
primary market 187
primary shares 137, 186, 327
price discovery process 252-3
price discrimination in IPO 89
price reaction to IPO announcement
78-9
price stabilization
affect on initial returns 261-2
assessment of 262-3
evidence of 258-60
methods and regulations 256-8
motivation 254-6
profits and costs 260-61
put option 254, 255, 256, 261
short position and covering 257-60
price target 269
pricing anomalies 332-3
private control benefits
affect on ATP use 106
examples and value of 82
private equity

market development 329-40
see also buyout funds; private
placements; venture capital
private firm discount, estimation of
acquisition method 180
IPO method 178-9
restricted stock method 179
private placements by public firms
announcement returns 298, 301-3
discounts 298, 301-2
information motive 300-301
long-run returns 302-3
managerial entrenchment 301-2
monitoring motive 299-300
regulations 297-8
privatizations
history of 124
initial returns 129
IPOs 125, 129-30
long-run returns 130
methods 127-8
motives for 125-6
program 128-9
total proceeds 124, 128-9, 131
proceeds revision 28, 35
product differentiation 65
property rights 118, 127, 129
prospect theory 247, 335
prospectus, IPO 29, 164-5, 184, 216
P/S ratio 161
public market equivalent (PME) 51
public policy options 110, 113-14,
119-20, 123, 340
purging reference portfolios 315-16

q-ratio 144, 146, 147
quiet period 267

real options
IPO timing decision 17
valuation model 162
redemption 'put' rights 93
red herring 216
rent-seeking by managers 146
registered shares 179, 397-8
registration period 27-8, 183-4
registration statement 183-4, 298
Regulation M 256-7
Regulations D and S 297
regulations divestiture motive 138

relationship lending 57
representativeness heuristic 334, 336
reputation
    development by issuer 73-4
    effect of going public 75
residual income model 160, 174, 176
retail investors 32, 34, 221, 223, 232,
    238, 248, 259-60, 264-5, 329
retained ownership 98
    signaling firm quality 43, 165, 186
return on assets (ROA) 148-9, 157,
    323
reverse LBOs 155-6
revolving credit agreements 56, 293,
    296
right of first refusal 93
risk
    affect on price support 256
    aversion, underpricing motive 243
    bearing by the underwriter 198
    divestiture motive 139
    factors 39-40, 133, 165, 310-12,
        320-21
    idiosyncratic 40-41
    sharing 39-40, 113-14
road show 216
Rule 144 297, 300
rule of law 118

Sarbanes-Oxley Act 97-8, 340
screening out bad issuers 32
seasoned equity offerings (SEOs)
    announcement CARs 20-21, 143,
        171, 289, 327
    long-run returns 309, 320, 327
    post-issue operating returns 324
    pre-issue returns 22
    timing 16, 20
secondary shares 16, 18, 137, 186-7,
    326-7
secondary sales 90, 288
Securities Acts of 1933 and 1934 207-
    8, 256
Securities and Exchange Commission
    (SEC) 6, 97, 133, 138, 216, 293
    disclosure requirements 185
    filing fee 38
    filing with 183-4
self-attribution bias 334, 336
self-deception 334

self-selection bias 273
selling concession 193, 257
selling memorandum 216
sell-off announcement returns 139, 150
sentiment, investor 13-17, 34, 174
settlement between regulators and
    banks 275
shareholder meeting requirements 105
shareholder rights 119-20
share-issue privatizations (SIP) 127-9,
    133
short covering 257-60
short-sales constraints 247-8, 329
signaling firm quality
    accounting choices 171
    auditor selection 211
    divestiture method 142
    IPO costs 74
    leverage 74
    lockups 278
    share retention 43, 165, 186
    underpricing 243-4, 288
    underwriter 43, 74, 165, 205
    venture capital 74, 165
small growth firm puzzle 313, 320
spanning 40
specialist 253
speculative trading 86-7, 248
spinning 189, 225, 234, 246
spin-offs
    announcement returns 139, 143,
        151
    definition 137
    information motive and effect
        140-43
    investment efficiency 147
    long-run returns 152
    operating performance 148-9, 150
    tax implications 137
spread, underwriting 37-8, 193-5
    affect on effort 197-8
    collusion at 7 percent 194-5
    components of 193
stabilizing bid 257-8
staging of venture capital 47-8, 92
stakeholder clause 105
Standard industrial classification
    (SIC) 148, 156
state-owned enterprises (SOEs) 124-32
    market capitalizations 131-2

operating performance 126
stock exchange, selection of 184-5
stock market
    development 114, 116, 128-9, 131
    effect on IPO decision 110
    pros and cons for economy 114-15
stock price
    aggregate information 61, 75, 88-9, 112, 114, 290
stock options 78, 101-2, 166
    tax treatment 245
strategic bidding in IPOs 32
strategic delay in IPOs 69-70
surplus extraction in sale of firm 88-9
syndicate structure 189-90
syndication of venture capital 92

takeover premium 82, 103, 106-7
takeovers, post-IPO 107
taxes
    implications for divestitures 137-8
    underpricing motive 245
term sheet 50, 92
timeline of IPO events 182-3
timing option 17
total surplus 88, 103
trade-off theory 283-4, 287
trading volume 253-4, 264
transfer agent/registrar 38
transparency, effect on IPO decision 68
turnover ratio 116, 134
two-stage sales
    divestitures 151
    motives for 88-9

uncertainty, affect on underpricing 242
underperformance anomaly 306-8, 319-20
    economic risk factors 320-21
    joint null hypothesis problem 318-9
    model specification 310-13, 319-20
    relation to initial overpricing 328-9
    relation to IPO volume 319
    statistical issues in measuring performance 314-18
    time-varying 17, 320
underpricing 24, 43
    affect of lockups 279

in auctions 227
auditor reputation 210
in book-buiding 222-4
due to agency conflicts 199
institutional reasons 242-3
insurance hypothesis 208-9
issuer and underwriter motives 224-5, 243-7
substitute for price support 255
syndicate structure 190
in two-stage offerings 288-9
underwriter reputation 204-5
underwriters
    compensation 37-8, 193-8
    contracts 198-203
    lead manager 189-90
    market-making activity 252-4
    market structure 188-9, 274
    objectives 224-5
    organizational structure 274-6
    rankings 188
    reputation
        affect on underpricing 205
        certification benefit 203-4
        development of 205-7
        impact on long-run returns 321
    selection criteria 190-93
    services 187, 196-8, 202-3
    specialization 192
    syndicate 189-90
    value-added 175
    warrants 195-6
underwriting agreement 200
unit offerings 290-92

VA Linux 234
valuation
    accuracy 163-4, 172-3, 246
    methods 159-63
    multiples 161, 328
    pre- and post-money 50
    private firms 178-80
    relation to investor rights 121
    using non-financial information 164-5, 175-7
value decomposition 176-7
venture capitalists 41, 77, 90
venture capital
    affect of stock markets 111
    contractual features 93-5

contractual provisions 92-3
discount rates 49
exit 89-90, 95-6
fund properties 45-6
impact on long-run returns 321
investments 47-8
policy options to stimulate 340-41
rates of returns 51-3
Venture Economics 51
VentureOne 51, 95
vesting provisions 95
vintage year 52
volume of IPOs
across countries 4
explanations for 12
relation to prices 26-8
time series profile in US 10-11, 25
voting rights
value of 83, 85, 98
of venture capitalists 99
voucher programs 127

warrants
underwriter compensation 195-6
unit offerings 290-92
wealth elasticities 101
wealth relatives 307-9
wealth sensitivity of CEOs
affect on underpricing 244-5
non-rational 247
wealth transfer motive for
restructuring 138
window of opportunity 10, 13, 285
winner's curse 224, 227, 237, 239,
242, 256
withdrawn offerings, affect on
clustering 27-8
contract choice 203
underpricing 243